GOD'S KINGDOM OF A THOUSAND YEARS *Has Approached*

An examination of much evidence in the Holy Bible and Twentieth-Century World History on whether God's Millennial Kingdom will begin its blessings within our own generation.

"And they lived and reigned with the Messiah for a thousand years. . . . They will be priests of God and the Messiah, and will reign with him a thousand years."—Revelation 20:4, 6, "The Authentic New Testament," by Hugh J. Schonfield, 1955 edition.

Dedicated

to the God whose time has approached
to introduce the thousand-year kingdom
of his Messiah for the eternal good
of distressed humanity

Abbreviations of Scripture translations quoted or cited in this book:

AV – *Authorized Version,* or *King James Version*
Dy – *Douay Version* (Roman Catholic) of the Holy Scriptures
INT – *The Kingdom Interlinear Translation of the Greek Scriptures*
Je – *The Jerusalem Bible* (Roman Catholic), English translation
Mo – *A New Translation of the Bible,* by James Moffatt
NA – *The New American Bible* (Roman Catholic)
NE – *The New English Bible*
NW – *Now World Translation of the Holy Scriptures*
Ro – *The Emphasised Bible* - A New Translation, by Joseph B. Rother-
       ham
RS – *The Holy Bible - Revised Standard Version*
We – *The New Testament in Modern Speech,* by R. F. Weymouth
Yg – *Young's Literal Translation of the Holy Bible,* by Robert Young

Any Bible quotation or citation not followed by any special abbreviation is made from the *New World Translation of the Holy Scriptures (NW)* in its revised edition of 1971.

DATING: In dating events the abbreviation B.C.E. means "Before Our Common Era," and the abbreviation C.E. means "Of Our Common Era," to distinguish the years before and after the year 1 C.E. The Publishers of this book do not use the abbreviation A.D. (Year of the Lord).

CONTENTS

CHAPTER 1

The "Thousand Years"
—Not a False Hope

TO ENDURE for a thousand years, a kingdom would really have to be good—strong. Such a royal government could not be planned, installed and maintained by a mere man or succession of men. No man-made kingdom in the hands of kings of a certain family line has ever lasted for even near a thousand years.

[2] What, then, about a kingdom in the hands of a single continuing monarch for ten centuries? An impossibility! No man has ever lived that long. According to the oldest genealogical records, the man Methuselah in southwestern Asia lived the longest of any human creature on earth. But even he came short of a millennium by thirty-one years.* In our own modern times the life expectancy of a man has been set far from that extraordinary age. In the most advanced lands of the day it has been brought to a life-span of less than seventy years by the aid of medical science. Woman has been given an edge of around six years over man. So royal rule for a thousand years by just one man or woman, no matter how good the subjects might think their ruler to be, is out of the question.

[3] Logically, then, we are not talking of a millennial kingdom from that human standpoint. We, as well as many millions of others yet alive, are able, as personal observers, to remember the most recent effort for a government a thousand years long. This "Thousand-

---

* See Genesis 5:25-27, in *The Holy Bible*.

1. What must be said on whether a man-made kingdom can endure for a thousand years?
2. Why is royal rule by a single human monarch out of the question?
3. What did the most recent "Thousand-Year Plan" envision for mankind?

7

Year Plan" was that of Adolf Hitler, Nazi dictator of Germany 1933-1945 C.E. Shortly after the United States was plunged into World War II, information on this Nazi plan was gleaned from seized Nazi documents and from German agents who had been taken into custody and from various other sources. This plan aimed at a Nazi world order that Hitler, if successful in World War II, would mercilessly enforce upon the world of mankind. It envisioned a virtual slave program, the workers for which would be recruited from non-German countries. This plan covered the thousand years to come.

[4] The Nazi leader Hitler, who came from the land of the Hapsburg family of kings, Austria, evidently had in mind the Germanic Holy Roman Empire, which lasted from the year 962 to 1806. In fact, we have the words of a Roman Catholic priest to that effect. Speaking on the night of February 16, 1940, to a capacity audience in the Memorial Continental Hall in Washington, D.C., Dr. Edmund A. Walsh, the regent of the Foreign Service School of Georgetown University, outlined the German war aims as a "re-establishment of the Holy Roman Empire." "Dr. Walsh said that he had heard Adolf Hitler say that the Holy Roman Empire, which was a Germanic empire, must be re-established."—New York *Times*, February 17, 1940.

[5] Boastfully the Nazi Fuehrer Hitler had said: "The National Socialist Reich [Empire] will endure a thousand years." But his police chief, Heinrich Himmler, was even more confident and responded: 'Ten thousand!' Once embarked on his egocentric plan, Hitler would be satisfied with nothing less than world rule or world ruin. In the book *The Last Days of Hitler*, the author, H. R. Trevor-Roper, says: 'It was always understood that Hitler would remain true to his original programme *Weltmacht oder Niedergang*,—world-

4. What earlier empire did Hitler evidently have in mind, and how did a priest testify thereto?
5. What did Hitler boast concerning the Nazi Reich, but how did his plan fare?

power or ruin. If world-power was unattainable, then (it was agreed by all who knew him) he would make the ruin as great as he could)' At this—and with good reason—some will be inclined to exclaim: 'How like the Devil!) At any rate, there was no reestablishment of the Holy Roman Empire, as many people of Hitler's religion had hoped—and the Nazi "Thousand-Year Plan" failed inside twelve years.

[6] The would-be world ruler Hitler may not have learned the lesson, but he ran smack up against the hard irremovable fact that a much earlier world ruler had to learn in the hard way. This was a non-German, non-Aryan man who ruled longer than Hitler, that is, for forty-three years (624-581 B.C.E.). He was the king of Babylon, and his name was a long one, Nebuchadnezzar. We may recognize him as the Semitic world conqueror who destroyed the Jewish city of Jerusalem in the year 607 B.C.E. and who deported whole populations just as Hitler did, dragging the surviving Jews, for the most part, into exile in distant Babylonian territories. Among the deported people was the Semitic prophet Daniel of the Jewish tribe of Judah. King Nebuchadnezzar had a strange dream, to which he attached great importance, and the slave, the prophet Daniel, was the only one able to interpret it. Daniel's interpretation came true.

[7] A year after the dream, Nebuchadnezzar as head of the Babylonian World Power began to brag, glorying over his capital city Babylon on the Euphrates River. Hardly had he finished his boast, when he heard a voice out of the invisible—out of heaven—saying words that he had heard in his dream. In Nebuchadnezzar's own account of this, which was preserved by the prophet Daniel, he writes: 'To you it is being said, O Nebuchadnezzar the king, 'The kingdom itself has gone away from you, and from mankind they are driving even you away, and with the

6. What earlier non-Germanic ruler learned a lesson that Hitler may not have, and who interpreted this ruler's dream correctly?
7. On what occasion did the dream begin to come true, and what lesson was the ruler to learn from his debasement?

beasts of the field your dwelling will be. Vegetation they will give even to you to eat just like bulls, and seven times themselves will pass over you, until you know that the Most High is Ruler in the kingdom of mankind, and that to the one whom he wants to he gives it.'"—Daniel 4:29-32.

8 What followed immediately? It is understandable why what now happened was not preserved for us in the Babylonian historical records, or why any record thereof by a Babylonian chronicler was removed or destroyed. But the honest, true-to-fact prophet Daniel, who was personally implicated in the matter, was inspired to make a record of it, for our consultation more than two and a half millenniums later. The proud King Nebuchadnezzar was instantly smitten with madness—and it was not his most revered god, Marduk (or, Merodach), who smote him. It was the Almighty God who foretold this madness that smote the boastful king, the king who had destroyed the sacred temple at Jerusalem in 607 B.C.E. And, just as predicted and ordained, "seven times" literally did pass over King Nebuchadnezzar while he was insanely chewing at

8. Who was the one that smote the boastful king, and who healed him?

grass like a bull out there in a nearby field. The mad king did not commit suicide, as Adolf Hitler did in 1945 just as his capital city Berlin was falling into the hands of the Red Communist armies of Russia. At the end of Nebuchadnezzar's seven years of madness, the Divine Smiter of him healed him and restored his sanity.

9 Did the king of Babylon learn his lesson? We can determine this from his own account, as preserved for us by the prophet Daniel. The account, given in the first person, reads:

10 "And at the end of the days I, Nebuchadnezzar, lifted up to the heavens my eyes, and my own understanding began to return to me; and I blessed the Most High himself, and the One living to time indefinite I praised and glorified, because his rulership is a rulership to time indefinite and his kingdom is for generation after generation. And all the inhabitants of the earth are being considered as merely nothing, and he is doing according to his own will among the army of the heavens and the inhabitants of the earth. And there exists no one that can check his hand or that can say to him, 'What have you been doing?' . . . Now I, Nebuchadnezzar, am praising and exalting and glorifying the King of the heavens, because all his works are truth and his ways are justice, and because those who are walking in pride he is able to humiliate." —Daniel 4:34-37.

11 Nebuchadnezzar himself tells us that he was restored to the throne of the Babylonian World Power, the Third World Power in a succession of seven world powers spoken of in the Holy Bible. (Daniel 4:36) Little did he know that that period of "seven times" in which he proved his unfitness to rule were prophetic of a greater period of "seven times" of larger duration, "the times of the Gentiles." Little did he know that during those larger "seven times" five world powers

would dominate the earth) the Babylonian, the Medo-
Persian, the Grecian, the Roman and the modern-time
British-American. Little did Nebuchadnezzar know
that (those "seven times," comprising all together
2,520 years, began in the year of his desolating of
Jerusalem and its temple and would end in the year
that would see the world of mankind embroiled in the
first world war—1914 C.E.) (Luke 21:24, *AV;* Daniel
4:16, 23, 25, 32) Yes, little did Nebuchadnezzar know
that at the end of those "seven times" of Gentile
domination in 1914 the "King of the heavens" would
give the "kingdom of mankind" to the one whom he
wanted to—His Messiah!—Daniel 9:25.

PREVIEW GIVEN BY DIVINE INSPIRATION

[12] The politicians of all the nations still think that
the "kingdom of mankind" is their proper concern and
is the proper field for their activity. Long ago King
Nebuchadnezzar of Babylon thought so. Quite recently
Adolf Hitler, with his dream of a thousand-years-long
political system, thought so. But the One concerning
whom Nebuchadnezzar was finally obliged to admit,
'His rulership is a rulership to time indefinite and his
kingdom is for generation after generation,' this One
still proves to be the (Ruler in the kingdom of mankind.) This kingdom over human affairs is still His
rightful field of interest and operation. The worldly
politicians, backed by the clergymen of Christendom,
have been unable to "check his hand," nor do they
have the authority to say to him: 'What have you
been doing?' (Daniel 4:34, 35) He did not consult
those politicians and their religious backers regarding
the one to whom He should give the "kingdom of
mankind" at the end of the "times of the Gentiles" in
1914 C.E. The politicians and their religious allies are
not of that importance as consultants, whereas He
is "the Most High himself, and the One living to time
indefinite."

---

12. What do worldly politicians still think regarding the "kingdom of
mankind," but whose hand have they been unable to check as to human
affairs?

[13] Reasonably, then, upon the basis of whose word can any prediction be made regarding a thousand years to come? Man cannot foretell even what will be tomorrow. "You do not know what your life will be tomorrow," said an observer of more than nineteen centuries ago. (James 4:14) But with the Most High himself, and the One living to time indefinite, this is different. What is time to Him?

[14] To this One it was well said by a man who lived for just one hundred and twenty years: "A thousand years are in your eyes but as yesterday when it is past, and as a watch [an ancient Jewish watch of four hours] during the night." (Psalm 90:4 and superscription) By a mere dream of the night and by the prophet Daniel's interpretation thereof to King Nebuchadnezzar, He was able to foretell what would happen in world history after a period of 2,520 years, ending in 1914 C.E. Could he not just as easily foretell with accuracy what will happen during a thousand years beginning with some point of time after 1914 C.E.? Most reasonably so! And what if He has already given us a description of such a thousand-year period? Then with that word as our basis, we can confidently speak of a thousand years to come.

[15] Those who use words drawn from the old Latin language would call that period of a thousand years a millennium, because the two roots of the word are the Latin mille, meaning "thousand," and annus, meaning "year." Over in Greece people would speak of it as a chiliastic period, because the Greek word chilia means "thousand." So the believers in this particular period of a thousand years would be called chiliasts, as well as millennialists or millenarians. People of Christendom use those terms in a reproachful way.

[16] Despite the reproach to which one exposes oneself

13, 14. Upon the basis of whose word can any prediction for a thousand years to come be made confidently? And why?
15. What are the thousand years called by users of Latin or Greek root words, and what are believers therein called?
16, 17. (a) What human experience with regard to 1000 C.E. shows we are not interested in the millennium because we are approaching 2000 C.E.? (b) Why is it well that man's seventh millennium of existence should begin many years before 2000 C.E.?

from those who do not understand, there should be real interest in this approaching period of a thousand years. Information concerning it is recorded in the written word of "the Most High himself, and the One living to time indefinite." Our own growing interest therein is not because we are approaching the year 2000 C.E., the end of the second millennium of our Common Era. That is not the significant thing. We remember what happened when mankind approached the year 1000 C.E., the end of the first millennium of our Common Era. Concerning this the *New Catholic Encyclopedia* says, under the subject "Millenarianism," page 853: "As the year 1000 neared, millenarianism became more prevalent because many eschatologists believed that the 7th day of creation was to be realized in human history in A.D. 1000 and that there would follow a glorious 10-century reign of the Christ." —Copyright 1967.

[17] For one thing, the end of six thousand years of human existence on earth and the beginning of mankind's seventh millennium of existence may come many years sooner than the year 2000 C.E. It is well that this is so. Today, with the world of mankind in such a deplorable condition and being threatened with destruction from so many angles, there are many students and investigators of these threats to human existence who express substantial doubts that mankind will be able to survive till the year 2000 C.E. They do not base their gloomy outlook for our future on any timetable in that most widespread sacred book, the Holy Bible. They base their outlook upon the hard facts of today and upon the now irreversible trend of things that involve all of us. These men who speak with authority give our human race far less than a thousand years to live on into the future. What reason have you, the reader, for not believing them?

[18] To the very contrary of these gloomy prophets who speak from the purely human standpoint, "the Most High himself, and the One living to time in-

18, 19. (a) Why is this information not confined to some secret eschatological society of initiates? (b) Over whose name is the Book of information written, and why?

definite," cheeringly speaks of a thousand years yet ahead of mankind and then some, the grandest years in all human history. This hope-inspiring information is not the private possession of some secret eschatological society of special initiated ones who are in the "know." The sources of this valuable information are openly accessible to hundreds of millions of people speaking 1,500 languages and dialects all around this globe. Wherever a person has a copy of the Holy Bible, this life-brightening information is available to him.

[19] Although the Bible was written by men, mere imperfect men, as secretaries or amanuenses, that sacred Book does not in its own pages claim to be the word of man. It is the work of divine inspiration, and so it is written over the name of "the Most High himself, and the One living to time indefinite." To this modern day of ours He takes the responsibility for what it says about the past and of the future before us. It is the Book of books!

[20] Where, then, in it do we find this information about those thousand years to come and the ages of eternity to follow? We find it in what is quite appropriately listed as the last book in the Holy Bible. It proves to be just what its name means, Revelation. Or, Unveiling, Apocalypse. O yes, it was written by a man, a man whom the Roman Empire branded as a criminal and put upon the penal island, Patmos, over there in the Aegean Sea and near the coast of Asia Minor, today Turkey. It is a real place, nothing mythical about it. As a young man this exiled prisoner had been a fisher at the Sea of Galilee in the then Roman Province of Galilee. He was John the son of Zebedee, and his fisherman brother was James. John tells us right at the start that he wrote Revelation, but under inspiration. But of what was it to be a revelation or an unveiling? As we read the answer, which should interest us of today, let us note to whom John assigns the responsibility for this book:

20. In what Bible book do we find this information on the millennium, and who wrote it?

→ ²¹ "This is the revelation given by God to Jesus Christ. It was given to him so that he might show his servants what must shortly happen. He made it known by sending his angel to his servant John, who, in telling all that he saw, has borne witness to the word of God and to the testimony of Jesus Christ. Happy is the man who reads, and happy those who listen to the words of this prophecy and heed what is written in it. For the hour of fulfillment is near."—Revelation 1:1-3, *New English Bible* (1970).

²² In those words, "For the hour of fulfillment is near," written almost nineteen centuries ago, is there a thrill for us today in this twentieth century C.E.? Certainly, measured in terms of time, "what must shortly happen" would by now, after nearly nineteen hundred years, not be too soon in happening, especially the beginning of the foretold "thousand years." We can fix better on the time when we read John's account of the thousand years and what immediately leads up to them. Let us read from Revelation 19:11 on:

²³ "Then I saw heaven wide open, and there before me was a white horse; and its rider's name was Faithful and True, for he is just in judgement and just in war. His eyes flamed like fire, and on his head were many diadems. Written upon him was a name known to none but himself, and he was robed in a garment drenched in blood. He was called the Word of God, and the armies of heaven followed him on white horses, clothed in fine linen, clean and shining. From his mouth there went a sharp sword with which to smite the nations; for he it is who shall rule them with an iron rod, and tread the winepress of the wrath and retribution of God the sovereign Lord. And on his robe and on his thigh there was written the name: 'King of kings and Lord of lords.'

---

21. To whom does John at the start assign the responsibility for the Revelation?
22. For us today, why is there a thrill in the words "For the hour of fulfillment is near"?
23. What features distinguish the rider of the white horse?

[24] "Then I saw an angel standing in the sun, and he cried aloud to all the birds flying in mid-heaven: 'Come and gather for God's great supper, to eat the flesh of kings and commanders and fighting men, the flesh of horses and their riders, the flesh of all men, slave and free, great and small!' Then I saw the beast and the kings of the earth and their armies mustered to do battle with the Rider and his army. The beast was taken prisoner, and so was the false prophet who had worked miracles in its presence and deluded those that had received the mark of the beast and worshipped its image. The two of them were thrown alive into the lake of fire with its sulphurous flames. The rest were killed by the sword which went out of the Rider's mouth; and all the birds gorged themselves on their flesh.

[25] "Then I saw an angel coming down from heaven with the key of the abyss and a great chain in his hands. He seized the dragon, that serpent of old, the Devil or Satan, and chained him up for a thousand years; he threw him into the abyss, shutting and sealing it over him, so that he might seduce the nations no more till the thousand years were over. After that he must be let loose for a short while.

[26] "Then I saw thrones, and upon them sat those to whom judgement was committed. I could see the souls of those who had been beheaded for the sake of God's word and their testimony to Jesus, those who had not worshipped the beast and its image or received its mark on forehead or hand. These came to life again and reigned with Christ for a thousand years, though the rest of the dead did not come to life until the thousand years were over. This is the first resurrection. Happy indeed, and one of God's own people, is the man who shares in this first resurrection! Upon such the second death has no claim; but they shall be priests of God and of Christ, and shall reign with him for the thousand years.

24. (a) What invitation was given to the birds flying in midheaven?
(b) What happened to those taking part in the battle?
25. What is then done to Satan the Devil, to last for how long?
26. Who sit upon the thrones seen in heaven, and what do they do?

[27] "When the thousand years are over, Satan will be let loose from his dungeon; and he will come out to seduce the nations in the four quarters of the earth and to muster them for battle, yes, the hosts of Gog and Magog, countless as the sands of the sea. So they marched over the breadth of the land and laid siege to the camp of God's people and the city that he loves. But fire came down on them from heaven and consumed them; and the Devil, their seducer, was flung into the lake of fire and sulphur, where the beast and the false prophet had been flung, there to be tormented day and night for ever."—Revelation 19:11 through 20:10, *New English Bible*.

[28] We notice the use of the expression "thousand years" six times in that account. We notice also that those thousand years begin after a battle between the "King of kings" and the "kings of the earth" along with the "beast" and the "false prophet," and then the chaining of Satan the Devil and flinging of him into the abyss. Those events are part of "what must shortly happen." Up till now the world has had nothing to compare with such events. Quite manifestly, then, those "thousand years" have yet to begin. They do not mean some indefinitely long time period, a period that we cannot accurately measure. They are a literal thousand years.

[29] Students who argue that those thousand years stand for an indefinite time length say that they began on the festival day of Pentecost of 33 C.E., when God poured out his holy spirit upon his newly formed Christian congregation at Jerusalem. But this argument leads into difficulties and to attempted explanations that are contrary to what actually happened to spirit-begotten Christians all during the more than one thousand nine hundred and forty years since that day of Pentecost when the Christian congregation came to

27. On earth, what followed the loosing of Satan, and what happened to him?
28. (a) So after what events do the thousand years begin? (b) Why, then, have those thousand years manifestly yet to begin?
29. What time length for those thousand years fits harmoniously with the proved timetable of God?

life spiritually until now. A *literal* millennium fits in harmoniously with the proved timetable of God.

[30] What those thousand years usher in upon our earth is something vitally necessary to the endless life and happiness of the world of mankind. How, then, can we reasonably hold back from at once examining closely the prophetic picture of the marvelous millennium that the apostle John so beautifully drew for us?

---

30. Why should we not be able to refrain from examining in detail the prophetic picture of those thousand years?

CHAPTER 2

War Between Heaven and Earth Precedes the Thousand Years

WE HAVE just read the description given us by the apostle John of the preview that he had of the thousand years. Such wonderful things are foretold for it that it is called The Millennium. Ah, but what did John describe as taking place immediately ahead of that glorious Millennium? It was a battle between heavenly forces and earthly human forces. Down till now such a fight has not taken place since the day of Pentecost of 33 C.E., the festival day when the Christian congregation came to life spiritually. by being begotten of God's life-giving spirit. True, Jesus Christ was in heaven and at God's right hand at that festival time, more than sixty years before John got the Revelation of "what must shortly happen." (Revelation 1:1, 2, *NE*) But even after John got the Revelation, no such battle occurred back there between the "King of kings" and the "kings of the earth." That battle is yet ahead of us, and we ought to be in-

---

1. (a) According to the Revelation, what conflict must precede the coming of The Millennium? (b) Why must that battle be evidently yet ahead of us, and what should be our attitude toward it?

terested in the advance account of it, because we are approaching it on a straight course.

[2] This approaching battle is not any dreaded third world war, in which the political superpowers, armed with an overload of nuclear and chemical weapons, will madly seek to annihilate one another. This is the coming battle in which all the "kings of the earth," no matter of what political ideologies, unite their forces against their common Opponent, a king and lord who is superior to them all and who is therefore called "King of kings and Lord of lords." He is not God, but, to quote Revelation 19:13, "the name he is called is The Word of God." This is the title that was given to the only-begotten Son of God in his prehuman existence in heaven with his heavenly Father, Jehovah God. —John 1:1-3, 18.

[3] During his human existence on earth as the man Jesus Christ, he did not lead any armies of fighting men on white horses, nor did he even choose to call twelve legions of heavenly angels to his aid. (Matthew 26:52-54) But now, since his glorification in heaven and since the end of the "times of the Gentiles" in 1914 C.E., he is authorized to act as the executional officer of the Supreme Judge, Jehovah God, and to do executional work upon earthly enemies just as that angel did, who, in the year 732 B.C.E., in one night killed off 185,000 soldiers of the Assyrian King Sennacherib, who had invaded the land of the people of Jehovah God, and this without the use of a nuclear bomb. (2 Kings 19:32-36; Isaiah 37:33-37) This explains why John was inspired to write concerning the heavenly Warrior Jesus Christ: "The one seated upon [the white horse] is called Faithful and True, and he judges and carries on war in righteousness."—Revelation 19:11.

[4] This is far more than a third world war between the nations of earth now armed with nuclear and

---

2, 3. (a) What kind of battle will that be as regards the participants therein? (b) How does the glorified Jesus Christ contrast with the earthly Jesus as to carrying on war?
4. What will it mean for the nations that out of the mouth of their common opponent a sharp long sword protrudes?

chemical weapons. This time the nations are fighting, not against blood and flesh, but against the one seated upon the symbolic white horse and against his heavenly angelic armies. And when he uses his tongue to speak and order an execution of his enemies, it is as if a long sword of an officer with authority were being applied. This is the meaning of the inspired words: "And out of his mouth there protrudes a sharp long sword, that he may strike the nations with it, and he will shepherd them with a rod of iron. He treads too the winepress of the anger of the wrath of God the Almighty. And upon his outer garment, even upon his thigh, he has a name written, King of kings and Lord of lords." —Revelation 19:15, 16.

[5] Instead of being a third world war between irreligious radical humans on one side and irreligious radical humans on the other side, this is "the war of the great day of God the Almighty." The nations, having by then disposed violently of the international religious "harlot," Babylon the Great, will then find themselves at that stage of world developments called Har–Magedon; just as it is written: "And they gathered them together to the place that is called in Hebrew Har–Magedon." (Revelation 16:14-16) It is at this world situation that the King of kings and the Lord of lords crushes the defiant nations, like grapes in a winepress, thus treading the "winepress of the anger of the wrath of God the Almighty." They will be like helpless sheep to him, upon whom he uses a "rod of iron" to break them to pieces like earthenware vessels of a potter. (Revelation 14:18-20; 2:26, 27; 12:5; Psalm 2:8, 9) There will be no dignified burial with military honors for those slain on earth in the "war of the great day of God the Almighty." That is why God's angel speaks of it as "the great evening meal of God" spread for the carrion birds:

[6] "Come here," cries out a sunlit angel to all the birds that fly in midheaven, "be gathered together to

5, 6. (a) At what location will the nations meet the King of kings in battle, and what crushing and breaking will take place? (b) What angelic invitation to the "great evening meal of God" shows whether the ones slain on earth will be buried with military honors?

the great evening meal of God, that you may eat the
fleshy parts of kings and the fleshy parts of military
commanders and the fleshy parts of strong men and
the fleshy parts of horses and of those seated upon
them, and the fleshy parts of all, of freemen as well as
of slaves and of small ones and great." And the account
of this "war of the great day of God the Almighty"
closes with the remark: "And all the birds were filled
from the fleshy parts of them." (Revelation 19:17, 18,
21) From this description of the ones whose corpses
the carrion birds are to devour, it appears that there
is a total mobilization and regimentation of the peoples of the nations for this War of all wars.

[7] Concerning the battle lineup at Har–Magedon the
apostle John writes: "And I saw the wild beast and
the kings of the earth and their armies gathered together to wage the war with the one seated on the
horse and with his army." (Revelation 19:19) Is this
"wild beast" a mere mascot, an animal supposed to
bring good luck, for the armies of these "kings of the
earth"? Of what value would a literal wild beast be
to the fighting forces at Har–Magedon? Of no value
at all! And a literal wild beast is not to be understood
here. It is a symbolic wild beast. It is really a world
figure of historical importance. How so? Because it
is the symbolic wild beast described in Revelation,
chapter thirteen, verses one to eight, concerning which
verse two says: "And the dragon gave to the beast
its power and its throne and great authority." It is the
worldwide political system that the "dragon," that is,
Satan the Devil, established long ago as his visible
instrument for governing all the people of the world.
It has carried on its beastly practices throughout the
earth for more than a thousand years, yes, for more
than four thousand one hundred years, since the
twenty-second century B.C.E.

[8] This symbolic wild beast began ravaging the
earth's inhabitants in the days of Nimrod, a hunter

---

7. What is the "wild beast" that is found in the battle lineup of the
kings of the earth at Har–Magedon?
8. When did that symbolic wild beast begin its activities, to spread its
authority to what extent?

of literal wild beasts. It was about the year 2189 B.C.E. that this Nimrod began engineering the building of the Tower of Babel in the land of Shinar, in the valley of Mesopotamia. Becoming world famous, he came to be called "Nimrod a mighty hunter in opposition to Jehovah." He established the old or original Babylonian empire, and about this Genesis 10:10-12 tells us: "The beginning of his kingdom came to be Babel and Erech and Accad and Calneh, in the land of Shinar. Out of that land he went forth into Assyria and set himself to building Nineveh and Rehoboth-Ir and Calah and Resen between Nineveh and Calah: this is the great city." (Genesis 10:8-12; 11:1-9) From that small beginning this symbolic wild beast continued extending its power and authority over more and more people until finally it has its political throne established over all the earth.

[9] Throughout the past millenniums this symbolic wild beast has had various members of its political system act as the dominant world power. That is why Revelation, chapter thirteen, pictures this symbolic wild beast as having seven heads, to represent seven world powers in succession, namely, (1) Egypt, (2) Assyria, (3) Neo-Babylonia, (4) Medo-Persia, (5) Greece, (6) Rome, and (7) the dual world power of Britain and America. With its symbolic "ten horns," this seven-headed wild beast has horned, gored and pushed around the worshipers of Jehovah God, including the genuine followers of the Son of God, Jesus Christ, since the days of the enslavement of the sons of Israel in Egypt until now. No wonder, then, that Revelation 19:19 pictures the "kings of the earth and their armies" as lined up with the "wild beast" in battle array against the heavenly angelic army of the "one seated on the horse," Jesus Christ!

[10] Revelation 19:20 mentions also as being with the "kings of the earth and their armies" what is called

9. (a) What do the seven heads of the symbolic wild beast picture? (b) Against whom has it used its "ten horns"?
10. (a) What is the "false prophet" in the battle lineup of the kings of the earth, and what does it prophesy? (b) What is the "image of the wild beast" the making of which it proposes?

"the false prophet that performed in front of [the wild beast] the signs with which he misled those who received the mark of the wild beast and those who render worship to its image." This is not a religious prophet belonging to religious Babylon the Great, but is a political prophet. It is the same political organization that is pictured in Revelation 13:11-17. There it appears as the two-horned wild beast that proposed the making of the image of the wild beast and then gave breath to that image so that it spoke authoritatively. That two-horned wild beast is the dual world power of Britain and America, or the Seventh World Power, and the political "image" of the seven-headed wild beast is today the organization for world peace and security, the United Nations. The whole world knows today that this Seventh World Power of Britain and the United States of America endeavors to dictate to the world of mankind and makes impressive prophecies concerning the future of mankind. But it is not the prophet of Jehovah God, inspired by Him. It is "false."

[11] The symbolic wild beast has reached its full state of development, having had its seventh head since the year 1763 C.E. By now we have also had more than a quarter of a century of the United Nations (not to speak of its predecessor, the League of Nations). Under the driving force of pursuing their own national goals and preserving their own national sovereignties in defiance of God's kingdom as rightful government for the earth, the "kings of the entire inhabited earth" are irresistibly being gathered to the "war of the great day of God the Almighty." The time for the unparalleled battle at Har–Magedon, which the apostle John saw in pictorial preview, should be quite near, nearer than the self-occupied people of the world think! With God the Almighty and his King of kings being the ones against whom the "kings of the earth and their armies" are drawn up in total warfare, the

---

11, 12. (a) What spirit moves the kings and their armies to the war at Har–Magedon? (b) Why must the tide of battle go only one way, and what outcome of it does John show in his preview?

tide of battle can go only one way, from its very start. We can have confidence, therefore, that the apostle John is correct in his prophetic description of the battle, as follows:

THE BATTLE AT HAR–MAGEDON

[12] "And I saw the wild beast and the kings of the earth and their armies gathered together to wage the war with the one seated on the horse and with his army. And the wild beast was caught, and along with it the false prophet that performed in front of it the signs with which he misled those who received the mark of the wild beast and those who render worship to its image. While still alive, they both were hurled into the fiery lake that burns with sulphur. But the rest were killed off with the long sword of the one seated on the horse, which sword proceeded out of his mouth. And all the birds were filled from the fleshy parts of them."—Revelation 19:19-21.

[13] This battle account makes it certain that God the Almighty takes on as his opponent the entire visible organization of the symbolic dragon, "the original serpent, the one called Devil and Satan." In support of that visible worldwide organization, symbolized by the seven-headed wild beast, go all its component parts, namely, the "kings of the earth and their armies," the military commanders, the strong men, the horse riders, the freemen and the slaves, the small ones and the great. The "false prophet" is also a part of that visible planetary system, for it is the dual world power of Britain and America, the dominant part of the whole visible organization of this world. The whole world system is not wily enough to elude the execution of divine judgment for all its ungodly deeds and the way it has preyed upon the people. The symbolic wild beast, along with its false prophet, is "caught," yes, caught while committing its last misdeeds against the faithful worshipers of Jehovah God.

13. (a) How much of the enemy organization does Almighty God take on as his battle opponent? (b) While doing what is the "wild beast" caught, and who runs it down?

The King of kings, Jesus Christ, is the one who runs down this ferocious wild beast. Like a *maneater,* it is destroyed.

[14] Never again will this beastly world system of political rule, along with its political "false prophet," victimize mankind. Not as dead, nonfunctioning political institutions, but, as Revelation 19:20 states, "while still alive, they both were hurled into the fiery lake that burns with sulphur." Never will they come out of this "fiery lake" alive, for their death in battle is not due to the death that the sinner Adam brought upon all his human offspring. The "fiery lake" symbolizes another kind of death, an endless death from which there is no resurrection. Revelation itself (20:14) explains it, saying: "This means the second death, the lake of fire." All human efforts in patriotically fighting to perpetuate this political system for running human affairs will fail!

[15] Will there, then, be a resurrection for the others, who as rulers or as ruled people fight for the symbolic wild beast and false prophet against God's kingdom in the hands of his King of kings? There is a total extermination of them. The tongue of the militant King of kings, which proceeds out of his mouth like a sharp long sword, orders the execution of them all, and the angelic armies of heaven carry out his royal orders. So those willful opposers of God's Messianic kingdom are all killed off. They are not counted as having suffered an honorable death, making the "supreme sacrifice" for country and government. They are not buried in memorial tombs, in nationally maintained military cemeteries to be visited annually on a Memorial Day or Decoration Day. As undeserving of a resurrection, they are pictured as having their corpses left lying exposed on the battlefield of Har–Magedon, their stinking bodies attracting all the birds that live on carrion flesh. It is foretold: "All the birds were filled from the fleshy parts of them." They gorge them-

14. What does the hurling of the "wild beast" and the "false prophet" signify for them?
15. What shows whether there will be a resurrection of the dead for the rulers and the ruled people slain at Har–Magedon?

selves to bursting on the "great evening meal of God."
—Revelation 19:17-21.

[16] It is to be noted that the account does not say
that the literal earth over which the "kings" have
reigned is burned up. No, but the earth survives the
"war of the great day of God the Almighty" at Har–
Magedon. Also, "all the birds that fly in midheaven"
survive, to feast upon the fleshy parts of the bodies
strewn over the earth. But there are also human
survivors on earth after the "war of the great day of
God the Almighty." This is not shown here directly
in this battle account. Yet this must be so! Why? Because not all the inhabitants of the earth at the time
of the battle will be misled by the "false prophet."
There will be exceptions, though comparatively few,
to "those who received the mark of the wild beast and
those who render worship to its image." (Revelation
19:20) What about the "great crowd," whom the
apostle John saw earlier in the vision and who were
seen standing before God's throne and before the
Lamb Jesus Christ? They are not among those fighting
against God's Messianic kingdom at Har–Magedon.

[17] Telling about these, John says: "They keep on
crying with a loud voice, saying: 'Salvation we owe
to our God, who is seated on the throne, and to the
Lamb.'" After making inquiry about these, one of the
twenty-four heavenly elders tells John: "These are
the ones that come out of the great tribulation, and
they have washed their robes and made them white
in the blood of the Lamb." (Revelation 7:9-14) This
"great crowd" that comes "out of all nations and
tribes and peoples and tongues" was definitely not
against the Messianic kingdom of God. It refused
to receive the "mark of the wild beast" and to "render
worship to its image."

[18] So the "great crowd" will not fall slain with

16. What must be said of survival of the war at Har–Magedon, as to
(a) the earth, (b) the birds, and (c) exceptions to the worshipers of
the wild beast?
17. What does Revelation, chapter seven, show regarding the attitude
of the "great crowd" toward God and his Messianic kingdom?
18. Why will the earth not be found empty of human life when Christ's
thousand-year reign begins?

people executed at Har–Magedon, but will "come out of the great tribulation," the grand climax of which will be the "war of the great day of God the Almighty." Surviving that "great tribulation" and hailing victorious Jehovah God and the Lamb Jesus Christ, the "great crowd" will, as with palm branches, look forward joyfully to the thousand years ahead. So the earth will not be found empty of human life as the glorious thousand years of Christ's reign begins.

CHAPTER 3

Enjoying the Visionary Preview of the Thousand Years

OUR earthly globe will not be reduced to ashes and smoke by being burned up in the "war of the great day of God the Almighty" at Har–Magedon. This is shown by what happens to Satan the Devil right after that war. How so? Because he and his demon angels are found still alive at the earth, to which they were cast down in defeat after a war broke out in heaven after the birth of God's Messianic kingdom in the heavens. Down Satan and his demons plunged to earth's vicinity, to be retained there for a "short period of time." (Revelation 12:7-13) Because they are restrained to the earth clear through the "war of the great day of God the Almighty," God's angel needs to come down to the earth to take further action against them. Respecting this we read in John's account of his vision:

² "And I saw an angel coming down out of heaven with the key of the abyss and a great chain in his hand. And he seized the dragon, the original serpent, who is the Devil and Satan, and bound him for a thou-

---

1, 2. (a) Will our earth be burned up in the war at Har–Magedon? (b) How is this shown by what is done to Satan and his demons thereafter?

sand years. And he hurled him into the abyss and shut it and sealed it over him, that he might not mislead the nations anymore until the thousand years were ended. After these things he must be let loose for a little while."—Revelation 20:1-3.

³ At the time that Satan the Devil was cast out of heaven, his demon angels were cast out with him and confined to the neighborhood of the earth. So what is done to their ruler applies also to them. They are seized, chained and abyssed with Satan the Devil for the thousand years. Not only does this put a stop to their further misleading the worldly nations, but it puts an end to their waging warfare against the remnant yet on earth of the Christian heirs of God's Messianic kingdom. Concerning this, Revelation 12:13, 17 tells us: "Now when the dragon saw that it was hurled down to the earth, it persecuted the woman that gave birth to the male child [symbolizing God's Messianic kingdom in the heavens]. And the dragon grew wrathful at the woman, and went off to wage war with the remaining ones of her seed, who observe the commandments of God and have the work of bearing witness to Jesus."

⁴ This devilish warfare fails to kill off all the remnant of Kingdom heirs who keep God's commandments and bear witness to His Son, Jesus Christ. It also fails to kill off the "great crowd" who accept this witness to the Messiah Jesus and who come from all nations of the earth and join the Kingdom remnant in worshiping Jehovah God at his spiritual temple. Testifying to their survival, Revelation 7:9-15 says concerning this "great crowd" out of all races, nations and tribes: "These are the ones that come out of the great tribulation, and they have washed their robes and made them white in the blood of the Lamb. That is why they are before the throne of God; and they are rendering him sacred service day and night in

---

3. Is Satan the Devil the only one abyssed, and to what warfare on his part does this put an end?
4, 5. (a) Does that warfare kill off all the Kingdom remnant and the "great crowd," and what testimony on this do we have? (b) Of whose presence, then, does Satan's abyssing relieve the earth?

his temple; and the One seated on the throne will spread his tent over them."

⁵ Thus the confining of Satan and his demon angels in the abyss does not leave the earth desolate of all human inhabitants. The abyssing relieves the earth, not of the presence of the Kingdom remnant and of the "great crowd," but, rather, of the presence of Satan the Devil and his demon angels. During their thousand years of imprisonment in the abyss they will be as if they 'were not.'—Compare Revelation 17:8.

EARTH'S RULERS FOR A THOUSAND YEARS

⁶ No longer will Satan the Devil be the ruler of the world of mankind or the "god" of the system of things. (John 12:31; 14:30; 16:11; 2 Corinthians 4:4) Who, then, will rule the inhabited earth during the thousand years that Satan the Devil is abyssed and "is not"?

⁷ In the vision the apostle John saw by whom the rulership of the earth was to be administered. He says: "And I saw thrones, and there were those who sat down on them, and power of judging was given them. Yes, I saw the souls of those executed with the ax for the witness they bore to Jesus and for speaking about God, and those who had worshiped neither the wild beast nor its image and who had not received the mark upon their forehead and upon their hand. And they came to life and ruled as kings with the Christ for a thousand years. (The rest of the dead did not come to life until the thousand years were ended.) This is the first resurrection. Happy and holy is anyone having part in the first resurrection; over these the second death has no authority, but they will be priests of God and of the Christ, and will rule as kings with him for the thousand years."—Revelation 20:4-6.

⁸ The thrones that John saw were up in heaven, not

---

6. Satan's abyssing raises what question as to the rulership of the earth?
7. What did John see in vision that answers this question?
8, 9. (a) Where were the thrones seen located, and how many of them actually were there? (b) So John was seeing the beginning of what "day," and how did Paul speak of it at Athens?

on earth, for these are the thrones of those who are to rule as kings with the Christ for a thousand years. The number of thrones was therefore not indefinite. The number was 144,000, to correspond with the 144,000 spiritual Israelites who are sealed with the "seal of the living God" and who follow the Lamb Jesus Christ "no matter where he goes." (Revelation 7:1-8; 14:1-5) During the past thousands of years that Satan the Devil has been the "ruler of this world" there has been such an absence of justice or miscarriage of justice that it will be an excellent thing when the power of judging mankind is committed to these 144,000 associate judges of the Lord Jesus Christ. So when the apostle John saw those 144,000 thrones and those who sat down on them, he was seeing the beginning of the glorious judicial day that was spoken of to the Court of Areopagus, Athens, nineteen centuries ago, in these words:

[9] "God . . . has fixed the day on which he will have the world judged, and justly judged, by a man of his choosing; of this he has given assurance to all by raising him from the dead."—Acts 17:22-31, *New English Bible*, of 1970.

[10] The apostle John further identifies the occupants of the judicial thrones as being the 144,000 Kingdom joint heirs of the Lord Jesus Christ by going on to say: "Yes, I saw the souls of those executed with the ax for the witness they bore to Jesus and for speaking about God, and those who had worshiped neither the wild beast nor its image and who had not received the mark upon their forehead and upon their hand." —Revelation 20:4.

[11] The apostle John did not see headless "souls." By using the descriptive word "souls" he was not talking like spiritistic mediums about "disembodied spirits." He was using the word "souls" in the way that the inspired Holy Scriptures use the word, and he meant live, conscious beings in bodies, through which bodies they expressed their personalities. Only, in order to

10, 11. What kind of "souls" were they that John saw, and for what work were they equipped?

occupy judicial thrones in the invisible heavens, their bodies would have to be spirit bodies. In the discussion of the resurrection of the dead, we are told in 1 Corinthians 15:44: "It is sown [in death] a physical body, it is raised up a spiritual body." Hence the apostle John saw live, conscious heavenly bodies, persons equipped with mental abilities for judgment work, and these John identified as being those "executed with the ax" for the witness of Jesus and God's Word.

"EXECUTED WITH THE AX"

[12] However, not all the 144,000 Kingdom joint heirs of Jesus Christ were executed with the ax or beheaded for the witness they bore to Jesus and for speaking about God. Not in a literal way! The apostle James, the natural brother of John, was killed by the sword, possibly beheaded, by King Herod Agrippa I. (Acts 12: 1, 2) According to tradition, the apostle Paul was beheaded at Rome, Italy. (2 Timothy 4:6-8) But not all the 144,000 suffer a martyr's death by having their heads chopped off. Certainly it is not God who does the executing of them with the ax, either literally or figuratively, inasmuch as it was for speaking about Him that they are all executed with the ax. It is the political state that executes them. In the case of the Roman Empire, of which the apostle John was a prisoner on the penal island of Patmos, this power of execution was symbolized by the ax wrapped within a bundle of rods with which criminals were scourged and beheaded. This symbol was called the *fasces,* and  Fasces was carried in procession by lictors before the highest Roman magistrate. Benito Mussolini the *Duce* of the Fascist Party popularized this symbol during his regime in Italy.

[13] In effect the political state of this world executes the 144,000 Kingdom heirs by judging them as un-

12. (a) Have all Kingdom joint heirs of Christ been executed with the ax literally? (b) Does God figuratively do the executing with the ax, or who does so, and for what?
13. According to Revelation 20:4, why does the political state world wide figuratively execute the 144,000 Kingdom heirs with the ax?

worthy to live under its authority. It sentences them to death, as it were. The reason for this is made plain by the apostle John. In what way? In that, as John says, they "had worshiped neither the wild beast nor its image" and "had not received the mark upon their forehead and upon their hand." In other words, these 144,000 Kingdom heirs had not worshiped the political state in any of its varied expressions throughout the earth. Neither had the remnant of these Kingdom heirs in this twentieth century worshiped that international organization for world peace and security now known as the United Nations, but known previously as the League of Nations. The symbolic "wild beast," the worldwide political state, is the one that is hurled into the destruction symbolized by the "fiery lake that burns with sulphur" in the "war of the great day of God the Almighty" at Har–Magedon.—Revelation 13: 1-17; 14:9-11; 19:19, 20; 20:4.

¹⁴ The 144,000 Kingdom heirs do not worship the symbolic "wild beast," meddling in its politics, running for political offices, sharing in its sanguinary warfare. Thus they do not receive a mark on their foreheads nor on their hands, to symbolize that they are slaves of the state and are lending it an active hand in carrying on its worldly activities, often beastly. Neither do the 144,000 worship the "image to the wild beast," ascribing salvation to a man-made international organization for world peace and security. They worship only the God about whom they speak and give their allegiance to Him as the Universal Sovereign. They do not magnify the earthly political state, but bear witness to Jesus, the Son of God, as being the Christ, the Messiah, whom the Most High God has appointed to rule the world of mankind for a thousand years. Little wonder that the "wild beast" executes the 144,000 as with the ax!

¹⁵ Whether finishing their earthly course by a violent martyr's death or not, all the 144,000 Kingdom heirs

---

14. In what way do the 144,000 Kingdom heirs not worship the wild beast or receive its mark on forehead or hand?
15. What do all the 144,000 experience finally on earth, and how is it that they can sit down on judicial thrones in heaven?

do at last die in a physical way. How is it, then, that they can enter into the kingdom of the heavens and sit down on those judicial thrones up there? It is not by any immortality of the human soul, but is by a resurrection from the dead. Says John concerning "those executed with the ax for the witness they bore to Jesus and for speaking about God": "And they came to life and ruled as kings with the Christ for a thousand years."—Revelation 20:4.

[16] They "came to life" again, not on earth as human creatures or human souls, but up in heaven as spiritual sons of God. It is as such that they are seen by the apostle John in vision. They have a span of life longer than that of mankind today. They can live longer than Methuselah did, who lived 969 years. (Genesis 5:25-27) They can live for the thousand years of their reigning with Christ and then on into endless eternity, for they are clothed upon with immortality at their resurrection from the dead. (1 Corinthians 15:50-57) At the instant of their being resurrected they are at the fullness of life, without weakness, without corruption, without any of the imperfection that had previously attached to their dying physical bodies that they had inherited from sinful Adam and Eve. They are perfectly alive, justified by Almighty God to everlasting life in the spirit.—1 Corinthians 15:42-55.

[17] In order to emphasize this difference between their instantaneous state at resurrection and the state of the rest of the world of mankind at the start of the thousand years, the apostle John proceeds to say: "These came to life again and reigned with Christ for a thousand years, though the rest of the dead did not come to life until the thousand years were over." (Revelation 20:4, 5, *New English Bible*) This proves that even the "great crowd" of worshipers at God's spiritual temple, who survive the "great tribulation," will not instantaneously be made perfect in their flesh

16. In their coming to life again, it is as what kind of creatures, and what now is the measure of their life?
17. (a) Will the "great crowd" of survivors of the "great tribulation" be made instantaneously perfect after the abyssing of Satan? (b) When will they be able to keep God's law flawlessly, and why?

and pronounced worthy of everlasting life on earth immediately after the binding and abyssing of Satan the Devil and his demons. By the uplifting aids and blessings of the thousand-year reign of Jesus Christ, they will progress gradually to human perfection and to ability to live sinlessly in the flesh and to keep God's laws flawlessly. But what about those billions of humans asleep in earthly memorial tombs and watery graves?

[18] As regards these, John's preview of the thousand years shows us what happens to them, saying: "And the sea gave up those dead in it, and death and Ha'des gave up those dead in them, and they were judged individually according to their deeds." (Revelation 20:13) Among those thus coming forth from Ha'des or the common grave of dead mankind will be that evildoer hung on an execution stake alongside Jesus, to whom Jesus said: "Verily I say unto thee this day: With me shalt thou be in Paradise." (Luke 23:43, Rotherham's translation; *New World Translation*) This evildoer will come forth from Ha'des into the earthly Paradise reestablished for mankind by the kingdom of Jesus Christ. In that Paradise the evildoer will share the opportunity along with all the other resurrected human dead to correct his life course and be cured of human imperfection and sinfulness. In this way, by the end of the thousand years of Christ's reign, he will be able to reach the goal of human perfection in God's image and likeness. All those attaining to human perfection and sinlessness on earth by the end of the thousand years must, however, undergo a final test of their loyalty to God's universal sovereign rule, in order to keep their perfect life.

[19] Those perfected humans on earth who maintain their integrity and prove faithful to God's rightful rule will be declared righteous by the Supreme Judge, Jehovah God. These innocent ones He will declare to

18. (a) Those coming forth from Ha'des during the millennium will include what human sympathizer of Jesus? (b) When will such resurrected human dead come to human perfection, and how?
19. (a) So, then, how is it that "the rest of the dead did not come to life until the thousand years were ended"? (b) What is done to those who do not pass the test of loyalty to God's sovereignty?

be worthy of eternal life, and He will assign to them
the right to endless life in happiness in the earthly
Paradise. Free of all condemnation, these obedient
ones now really live from God's perfect standpoint. In
this manner it is, then, that "the rest of the dead did
not come to life until the thousand years were ended."
(Revelation 20:5) Those perfected humans who do
not faithfully pass that test of godly loyalty after the
thousand years are ended will be everlastingly destroyed, just as John in his preview presents the matter, saying: "And death and Hades were hurled into
the lake of fire. This means the second death, the lake
of fire. Furthermore, whoever was not found written
in the book of life was hurled into the lake of fire."
(Revelation 20:14, 15) So these disloyal ones do not
attain to life eternal.

"THE FIRST RESURRECTION"

[20] After interjecting that statement about the "rest
of the dead," the apostle John refers back to the
coming to life again on the part of those who were
"executed with the ax for the witness they bore to
Jesus and for speaking about God" and proceeds to
say: "This is the first resurrection. Happy and holy
is anyone having part in the first resurrection; over
these the second death has no authority, but they will
be priests of God and of the Christ, and will rule as
kings with him for the thousand years."—Revelation 20:5, 6.

[21] Can it be that this "first resurrection" of these
144,000 Kingdom joint heirs of the Christ is what the
apostle Paul speaks of at Ephesians 2:1-6? There the
apostle writes to the first-century Christians in the
city of Ephesus, Asia Minor, and says: "And you were
dead, through the crimes and the sins in which you
used to live when you were following the way of this
world, obeying the ruler who governs the air, the
spirit who is at work in the rebellious. . . . But God

20-22. (a) When John returns to discussing "the first resurrection,"
why does a question come up regarding Ephesians 2:1-6? (b) Similarly
with regard to Colossians 2:11-13, where Paul discusses Christian circumcision?

loved us with so much love that he was generous
with his mercy: when we were dead through our sins,
he brought us to life with Christ—it is through grace
that you have been saved—and raised us up with him
and gave us a place with him in heaven, in Christ
Jesus."—*The Jerusalem Bible*, Roman Catholic, of
1966.

[22] Similarly, when discussing Christian circumcision
with Christians in Colossae, Asia Minor, the apostle
Paul wrote: "This is circumcision according to Christ.
You have been buried with him, when you were bap-
tised; and by baptism, too, you have been raised up
with him through your belief in the power of God
who raised him from the dead. You were dead, because you were sinners and had not been circumcised:
he has brought you to life with him, he has forgiven
us all our sins."—Colossians 2:11-13, *Je*.

[23] We do have to admit that this passing from death
to life in a figurative way, or in a spiritual sense, is
one of the "first" experiences in a Christian's course.
So, taking this experience to be the "first resurrection" mentioned in Revelation 20:5, 6, the *New Catholic Encyclopedia* (copyrighted 1967) goes on to say
under the title "Millenarianism":

> . . . The "first resurrection" symbolizes Baptism, . . .
> by which one shares in Christ's resurrection. . . . All the
> faithful, both those on earth and those in heaven, share
> in the 1,000 year reign of Jesus, a symbol for the entire
> life span of the Church considered in its glorious aspect
> from the Resurrection of Christ until the Last Judgment,
> . . . The chaining of Satan during this same period signi-
> fies that the influence of Satan has been notably reduced,
> not completely removed. The lessening of Satan's influence
> is the result of the effectiveness of Christ's Redemption.
> After a final struggle near the end of time . . . Satan
> will be completely conquered by Christ. . . .

[24] Does such an explanation of the "first resurrection" harmonize with what John writes in Revelation

23. (a) Because the foregoing scriptures refer to one of the "first"
experiences in a Christian's life, what does the *New Catholic Encyclopedia* say about the "first resurrection"? (b) Hence, about Satan's
binding for a thousand years?
24, 25. How long has been the Church's life-span since Pentecost of 33
C.E., and what does Paul say about ruling as kings in the Christian
congregation during his time?

20:1-6? Well, since the day of the Festival of Weeks in the year 33 C.E., when the Christian congregation at Jerusalem began to be baptized with God's holy spirit, until now, the "life span of the Church" has proved to be, not just one thousand years, but nearly double that. During all these nearly two millenniums has any member of the true Christian congregation "reigned," even in the midst of the congregation itself?

²⁵ Who of the apostles thus "reigned"? Not the apostle Paul! For he wrote to certain ambitious members of the congregation in Corinth: "You have begun ruling as kings WITHOUT us, have you? And I wish indeed that you had begun ruling as kings, that we also might rule with you as kings. For it seems to me that God has put us the apostles last on exhibition as men appointed to death, because we have become a theatrical spectacle to the world, and to angels, and to men." (1 Corinthians 4:8, 9) To his missionary companion Timothy, he presented the matter of reigning as coming after the Christian's physical death, saying: "Faithful is the saying: Certainly if we died together, we shall also live together; if we go on enduring, we shall also rule together as kings; if we deny, he also will deny us."—2 Timothy 2:11, 12.

²⁶ And what about the apostle John? While on the Roman penal isle of Patmos as an exile, he quoted the resurrected Lord Jesus Christ as saying to the Christians in Laodicea: "To the one that conquers I will grant to sit down with me on my throne, even as I conquered and sat down with my Father on his throne." (Revelation 3:21) All the reigning was future, after the physical death of the faithful disciples of Jesus Christ. There was to be no reigning on this earth, from the day of the Christian's baptism in water.

²⁷ By what kind of resurrection is it that "they

---

26. According to Jesus' words to the Laodiceans, what is shown as regards a Christian's reigning on earth from the day of his baptism? 27, 28. (a) Does Revelation 20:4 picture them as coming to life from a figurative death by a willing water baptism? (b) By what means is the death pictured as coming, and for what, and so from what kind of death must the "first resurrection" be?

came to life and ruled as kings with the Christ for a thousand years"? By a figurative resurrection or by a literal resurrection from actual death and the grave? Revelation 20:4 does not speak of their coming to life from the figurative death that they *willingly* experience when they are baptized in water as Jesus himself was. No, but it is the death that they experience when they are "executed with the ax for the witness they bore to Jesus and for speaking about God."

[28] This 'execution with the ax' comes upon them not by *their* will, but by the will of the enemies of God and of Christ, and it occurs *after* their baptism in water and because they bear witness to Jesus as the Christ and speak about God as the rightful Ruler of the universe (including our earth). This 'execution with the ax' results eventually in a real physical death. Consequently, their 'coming to life again' to rule as kings is from a literal, physical death, and not from a figurative one that takes place at water baptism. Likewise, the ruling as kings does not begin on earth after a spiritual resurrection that follows their baptism in water. The resurrection meant in Revelation 20:4-6 is the real, literal resurrection from the sleep of death in Sheol or the common grave of mankind.

[29] Another point in proof of this must not be overlooked: Revelation 20:6 says: "Happy and holy is anyone having part in the first resurrection; over these the second death has no authority." That second death is symbolized by the "fiery lake that burns with sulphur." (Revelation 19:20; 20:14) Is this true of those who have merely been baptized with water and who have spiritually been made alive from death in trespasses and sins and who have been raised up together spiritually and been "seated . . . in the heavenly places in union with Christ Jesus"? (Ephesians 2:1, 5, 6) No, it is still possible for these baptized

---

29, 30. (a) Is it true of those who have had merely a figurative resurrection that "over these the second death has no authority"? (b) What does Paul say on this in Hebrews 10:26-31?

ones to prove unfaithful while on earth under test and to come under the penalty of the "second death," total annihilation. That is why the apostle Paul warned the baptized, anointed Christians in Corinth, Greece: "Let him that thinks he is standing beware that he does not fall." (1 Corinthians 10:12) Also, Hebrews 10:26-31 warns the baptized, anointed Christians:

[30] "If we practice sin willfully after having received the accurate knowledge of the truth, there is no longer any sacrifice for sins left, but there is a certain fearful expectation of judgment and there is a fiery jealousy that is going to consume those in opposition. Any man that has disregarded the law of Moses dies without compassion, upon the testimony of two or three. Of how much more severe a punishment, do you think, will the man be counted worthy who has trampled upon the Son of God and who has esteemed as of ordinary value the blood of the covenant by which he was sanctified, and who has outraged the spirit of undeserved kindness with contempt? For we know him that said: 'Vengeance is mine; I will recompense'; and again: 'Jehovah will judge his people.' It is a fearful thing to fall into the hands of the living God."

[31] Also, in Hebrews 6:4-8 we read: "It is impossible as regards those who have once for all been enlightened, and who have tasted the heavenly free gift, and who have become partakers of holy spirit, and who have tasted the fine word of God and powers of the coming system of things, but who have fallen away, to revive them again to repentance, because they impale the Son of God afresh for themselves and expose him to public shame. For example, the ground that drinks in the rain which often comes upon it, and that then brings forth vegetation suitable to those for whom it is also cultivated, receives in return a blessing from God. But if it produces thorns and thistles, it is rejected and is near to being cursed; and it ends up with being burned."

31. What does Hebrews 6:4-8 say on this?

[32] In view of this, the "first resurrection" is not that figurative resurrection that follows baptism in water and that leaves the baptized one still exposed to the possibility of the "second death," liable to its "authority." It is the real, literal resurrection from Sheol to life as a spirit son of God in the invisible heavens to which Jesus Christ himself ascended. To these the promise of Jesus applies: "Prove yourself faithful even to death, and I will give you the crown of life. Let the one who has an ear hear what the spirit says to the congregations: He that conquers will by no means be harmed by the second death." (Revelation 2:10, 11) Those having part in the "first resurrection" cannot be harmed by the "second death" and are not subject to its "authority" because in this resurrection they have been clothed upon with immortality and incorruption.—1 Corinthians 15:53, 54.

[33] We can now appreciate the reason why this is called "the first resurrection." It is because it is the same kind of resurrection that Jesus Christ experienced on the third day of his death, a resurrection to instantaneous fullness of life, so that the resurrected Jesus Christ became "the firstborn from the dead." (Revelation 1:5; Colossians 1:18) It precedes in time the 'coming to life' of the "rest of the dead." It is not only first in time, but also "first" in being the best resurrection that the dead could experience. It is a resurrection to incorruptible, immortal life as a spirit son of God in God's own heavens.

[34] Indeed, then, it can be exclaimed: "Happy and holy is anyone having part in the first resurrection." (Revelation 20:6) They are truly "holy" in that no unfaithfulness on their part that would deserve "the second death" is possible for them. Also, by this resurrection it is made possible for them to be heavenly "priests of God and of the Christ" and to "rule as

---

32. Only those Christians who experience what kind of resurrection are not subject to the "authority" of the "second death" or harmed by it?
33. In what two ways can it be called "the first resurrection"?
34. How are those having part in the "first resurrection" holy?

kings with him for the thousand years." Satan the
Devil will not be the world's ruler then.

A REAL, DEFINITE "THOUSAND YEARS"

[35] So the chaining and abyssing of Satan the Devil
and his demon angels does not signify what the *New
Catholic Encyclopedia* says, namely, the notable reducing of Satan's influence during this present system of things, such a lessening of Satan's influence
resulting from the "effectiveness of Christ's Redemption." Certainly true Christians on earth have not
felt such a lessening of Satan's influence, any notable
reduction of it, since their baptism in water. Rather,
the apostle Peter found it necessary toward the end
of his earthly life to write this warning to the Christians: "Keep your senses, be watchful. Your adversary, the Devil, walks about like a roaring lion, seeking to devour someone." (1 Peter 5:8) For the same
reason the apostle Paul gave them this advice:

[36] "Put on the complete suit of armor from God
that you may be able to stand firm against the machi-
nations of the Devil; because we have a wrestling,
not against blood and flesh, but against the governments, against the authorities, against the world rulers of this darkness, against the wicked spirit forces
in the heavenly places. On this account take up the
complete suit of armor from God, that you may be
able to resist in the wicked day and, after you have
done all things thoroughly, to stand firm."—Ephesians 6:11-13.

[37] Furthermore, in Revelation 12:1-17, the apostle
John describes with symbols the birth of God's Messianic kingdom and the operations of the "great dragon," "the original serpent, the one called Devil and
Satan," after this one has been cast out of heaven
and down to our earth. Then, as a special warning to
true Christians in this twentieth century when these

35, 36. (a) Have Christians, since baptism, experienced a lessening of
Satan's influence due to the "effectiveness of Christ's Redemption"?
(b) What do the advices of Peter and Paul indicate would be the case?
37. What does Revelation 12:17 indicate as to whether Satan has been
figuratively chained since Christ's act of redemption?

things occur, John adds these words: (And the dragon grew wrathful at the woman, and went off to wage war with the remaining ones of her seed, who observe the commandments of God and have the work of bearing witness to Jesus.) (Revelation 12:17) Does all this sound like any notable reducing of the power and influence of Satan toward Christians after their baptism in water? Is this a chaining of Satan?

[38] However, according to what the apostle John actually says, why is it that Satan the Devil is seized, chained and hurled into the abyss? It is (that he might not mislead the nations anymore until the thousand years were ended.) (Revelation 20:1-3) By the word "nations" John means, not the baptized, anointed 144,000 Kingdom heirs, but people who are not true, genuine followers and imitators of the Lord Jesus Christ. At the time of the Devil's being cast out of heaven he is spoken of as ('Satan, who is misleading the entire inhabited earth') (Revelation 12:9) The faithful 144,000 Kingdom heirs are not part of those "nations" of the inhabited earth who are being misled. So, not the 144,000 partakers of the "first resurrection," but the "nations" are the ones whose further misleading is to be stopped by the binding and abyssing of Satan the Devil and his demon angels.

[39] Well, then, has the misleading of such nations by Satan the Devil been decreased, reduced, lessened, during these more than one thousand nine hundred years since the baptism of the Christian congregation with God's holy spirit on the day of the Festival of Weeks at Jerusalem in 33 C.E.? To this question, who is there so blind and so unacquainted with human history as to answer Yes? The opposite has been true. Today, in this age of the greatest enlightenment of mankind in a scientific way, the worldly "nations" are being misled to an extent never before known, and with more serious consequences. Why? Because this international deception by Satan and his demons means

---

38. Satan is bound and abyssed to keep from further misleading whom?
39. Has there been a reduction in Satan's misleading of the nations since Pentecost of 33 C.E., and what does Revelation 12:12 foretell?

the destruction of all these misled nations in the very near future. With good reason the "loud voice in heaven" said at the ousting of Satan the Devil: ("Woe for the earth and for the sea, because the Devil has come down to you, having great anger, knowing he has a short period of time)"—Revelation 12:10-12.

[40] So this argument by religionists of Christendom that the "thousand years" of the abyssing of Satan the Devil does not mean a literal thousand years but applies to the "entire life span of the Church" on earth (already more than 1,900 years long) is proved to be false!

[41] According to the Bible's timetable, the beginning of the seventh millennium of mankind's existence on earth is near at hand, within this generation. Now as at no time in the past the inhabitants of earth need the binding and abyssing of Satan the Devil in a real way. The world events immediately ahead of this are about to take place, and mankind's great adversary and oppressor will be sealed up in the abyss for ten centuries of time. The royal rule of Christ and his resurrected congregation for a thousand years of peace and blessing to the human family is before us with all its glorious possibilities! A "great crowd" of dedicated Bible believers who are now putting their hopes in the millennial reign of Christ have divine assurance of being preserved from death and being ushered into that brightest period of all human history. What a blessed prospect for them!

[42] Will not that "great crowd" get tired of having the same rulers over them for a thousand years? Will they not, long before the end of that time period, want a change of government and clamor for a popular election of a different set of rulers? Or will they not, rather, learn to love these heavenly priests and kings over them more and more and be thankful to have

40, 41. (a) What argument of religionists regarding the thousand years of Satan's binding is thus proved false? (b) What does mankind need to take place in a real way, and who now are putting their hopes in Christ's millennial reign?
42. What questions arise as to the attitude of the "great crowd" toward their millennial rulers, and so what is it timely for us to consider?

them remain in office for all of God's appointed time? These are serious questions, for under this millennial kingdom this "great crowd" will have the opportunity to live as long as that heavenly government endures— a thousand years, and thereafter to time without end. In now considering these interesting questions, it becomes timely for us to examine more fully what kind of kings and priests there will be and how precious their services will be to all mankind, the living survivors and the dead. (2 Timothy 4:1) This calls for us to look into their background of the past and what the Most High God has required of them in order to count them worthy to serve as millennial kings and priests.

CHAPTER 4

Kings for a Thousand Years
Without Successors

MAN-MADE kingdoms have not turned out to be satisfying to human needs. From at least the twenty-second century before our Common Era, or more than 4,150 years ago, the human family began to have man-made kingdoms. The name of the first human king on record is Nimrod, the great-grandson of the ark-builder Noah, and Nimrod appears to have been a self-made king, according to the record of Genesis 10:8-12.

[2] Noah, who outlived the beginning of Nimrod's kingdom, did not make him the king of Babel (or Babylon). Noah did not make even himself a king, but continued merely as the patriarchal head of the expanding human family. (Genesis 9:28, 29; 10:32 to 11:9) Today, for the most part, the peoples have tired

A

---

1. From whose time onward have man-made kingdoms proved unsatisfying?
2. (a) What was Noah's attitude toward kingdom? (b) For what type of government do the majority of people have a decided preference today?

of having kings with their hereditary successors in their natural families. There is a decided preference for people's governments, such as republics and democracies with popularly elected presidents. Under these democracies the people soon tire of one set of rulers provided mostly by one political party and seek for a change by electing to office candidates provided by another political party.

[3] Humans are not the only ones tired of man-made kingdoms with their hereditary successors. God is also. In fact, God is tired of all the man-made governments on earth today.* If the people have not yet had their fill of them, He has. In fact, it is on His property (the earth) that these man-made governments have carried on their misrule or unsatisfying rule, inadequate rule. That is why He had it declared in the place where the first man-made king came to power, in Babylon itself, that in His own chosen time he would destroy all these man-made governments to make way for the thousand-year reign of his Son, Jesus Christ. Through his prophet Daniel he said to Nebuchadnezzar, the king of Babylon: "In the days of those kings the God of heaven will set up a kingdom that will never be brought to ruin. And the kingdom itself will not be passed on to any other people. It will crush and put an end to all these kingdoms, and it itself will stand to times indefinite."—Daniel 2:44.

[4] According to this purpose of His, the Most High God of heaven does not love those kings and other political rulers on earth. They do not love Him either, even though many of them may be kings and political rulers of what is called Christendom. If they did love Him, they would be doing what Jesus Christ, the Son of God, said to his disciples: "Keep on, then, seeking first the kingdom and his righteousness," and they would not be holding political office in some man-made

---

* Compare Isaiah 1:14; 7:13; 43:24.

---

3. Who has had his fill of man-made kingdoms, and what did he have declared in the location of the first man-made kingdom?
4, 5. (a) Who are the rulers over mankind whom God loves? (b) According to the apostle John, the love of such rulers for God ensures their love also of whom else?

government today. (Matthew 6:33) It is very important for mankind to have as king over them a person whom the God of heaven loves. That holds true for the associates of such a king: for mankind's good they should be persons whom God loves. That is why he will keep them in office. That is why he puts them in office, in the first place. They are and will be lovers of the one living and true God. This means, necessarily, that they will be lovers of the people on earth also. On this very point the apostle John wrote:

⁵ "If anyone makes the statement: 'I love God,' and yet is hating his brother, he is a liar. For he who does not love his brother, whom he has seen, cannot be loving God, whom he has not seen. And this commandment we have from him, that the one who loves God should be loving his brother also.")—1 John 4:20, 21.

⁶ Human kings and other political rulers have been very jealous of their national or state boundaries, which act as dividers between nations and peoples. Each political ruler seeks to hold control within his own territory, and he expects the people therein to be loyal to him. Under this system of things, the earth has been cut up into many national and state territories in each of which national sovereignty is insisted upon, and this has not worked for the unifying of all mankind. National rivalries have developed. So now an intriguing question arises.

⁷ The divine purpose is not to have Jesus Christ rule as king alone for the thousand years. The beloved Son of God is not to stand up alone as King on the heavenly Mount Zion, the seat of government. But, as the apostle John tells us: "I saw, and, look! the Lamb standing upon the Mount Zion, and with him a hundred and forty-four thousand having his name and the name of his Father written on their foreheads. . . . And they are singing as if a new song before the throne and before the four living creatures and the elders; and no one was able to master that song but the hundred

---

6. How has the insistence of rulers on keeping their boundaries and sovereignties affected mankind?
7. What is God's purpose concerning heavenly rulership of the earth, and how does Revelation 14:1-5 indicate this?

and forty-four thousand, who have been bought from the earth. . . . These are the ones that keep following the Lamb no matter where he goes. These were bought from among mankind as firstfruits to God and to the Lamb, and no falsehood was found in their mouths; they are without blemish."—Revelation 14:1-5.

[8] Since there will thus be 144,001 royal rulers over the earth, does this mean that the earth will be divided up into 144,000 territories, with one of the 144,000 over each individual territory, and with the people therein being responsible to that particular one as king under Jesus Christ the Head King? Would not such a parceling out of the inhabitants of the earth result in boundaries, even though invisible, and would not this create some measure of difference between earth's inhabitants on different sides of the boundaries? Also, would a former Chinese-speaking Kingdom heir be appointed over an area inhabited by Chinese-speaking people, a Russian-speaking Kingdom heir over a Russian-speaking population, an English-speaking Kingdom heir over English-speaking, and so on according to the distinct language groups? Will divisive language barriers continue to exist, hindering mutual understanding?

[9] These are natural questions, proper questions. But in this regard it must be said that the Bible does not indicate what assignments of kingly responsibility will be given out through the Head King Jesus Christ to the individuals making up the 144,000 joint heirs of Christ. Over the past nineteen centuries since the founding of the Christian congregation in 33 C.E., these 144,000 joint heirs of Christ have been taken out from nations, peoples and tribes of many languages. Said the resurrected Jesus Christ to his disciples who were gathered together in Galilee some days before he ascended back to heaven: "Go therefore and make disciples of people of all the nations, baptizing them." (Matthew 28:19)

---

8. What questions arise as to the territorial assignments to members of the 144,000 Kingdom heirs, and also language considerations?
9. (a) From among whom have the 144,000 Kingdom heirs been taken out, in accord with what command of Jesus? (b) What question comes up as to their language differences?

Are we to imagine that up in heaven, in Kingdom glory, the 144,000 associate kings will be divided by language differences and need interpreters? The apostle Paul wrote about the "tongues of men and of angels." —1 Corinthians 13:1.

[10] Unquestionably, the resurrected glorified 144,000 will all speak but one heavenly language, the gift of this language being conferred upon them in their new spirit bodies at their resurrection from the dead. This does not mean that their former earthly language will be erased from their minds. No, for it will be by identifying themselves by their former human language that they will be able to recognize themselves as being the same persons. But at their heavenly resurrection they will speak the language of the Lord Jesus Christ, and he will speak the language of his heavenly Father, Jehovah God.

ONE RACE, ONE LANGUAGE

[11] Likewise, the present-day language barrier on earth will be removed from mankind under the thousand-year reign of Christ and his 144,000 associate kings. God's original purpose for the earth was that it should be comfortably filled with human creatures speaking one common language, the language of their first earthly father, the perfect man Adam. In the garden of Eden the human race started out with one language. After the planetary flood of Noah's day, God gave mankind a fresh righteous start with one language, the language of righteous Noah, the tenth man in line of descent from Adam. That one language continued on down till the attempt at building the Tower of Babel.

[12] Then Almighty God broke up the unity of the builders who were combining their efforts in a bad work. How? It was by confusing the language and thus causing them to scatter as language groups to separate

10. What will be the language of the 144,000 in heaven, and what becomes of their former earthly languages?
11. Under the millennial kingdom, what will be done about present-day language barriers on earth, and how, and why?
12. How will God undo the language effects from the action he took at the Tower of Babel?

parts of the earth. (Genesis 11:1-9) In harmony with His original purpose, God will bring mankind as a whole back to the one family language, the language with which He endowed mankind's first human father, only with a far larger vocabulary, possibly with embellishments from other languages that God invented at the Tower of Babel.

[13] For those who lived prior to the Flood, including the eight human survivors of that Noachian deluge, this will present no great problem at their resurrection from the dead to life on earth under God's Millennial kingdom. But for the vast majority of the rest of mankind, it will mean learning a new language, the language God purposes for all humankind. In view of good language instructors used by the Kingdom, there should be no great problem on this account. Even resurrected babies can be taught the new language from infancy. In this way they will all be able to communicate with one another directly, with full understanding of one another's language terms and expressions. What a unifying effect this will have on the human family! Think of their all being able to read the inspired Hebrew Scriptures,* each one for himself, and to observe how all its prophecies have come true and how it also contains an accurate historical account down to the days of the prophet Malachi! Then the honest-hearted ones will be able to say, as did the apostle Paul: "Let God be found true, though every man be found a liar."—Romans 3:4.

[14] As with the language barrier, so with the present-day barriers due to race, nation and tribe. For the 144,000 Kingdom heirs who share in the "first resur-

---

* This does not mean, however, that the one universal language of God's new order of things will be printed and written in the present-day square style Hebrew alphabetic letters. Even today there are extant Hebrew publications that are spelled out in the Latin style alphabetic letters used in the English language. For example, the textbook *Taryag Millim,* published in South Africa in 1949; the biography *Avi,* printed in Jerusalem in 1927; also parts of the newspaper *Deror,* which was published in Tel Aviv in 1933-1934.

---

13. For whom will a temporary language problem thus be produced, but what benefits will result?
14. How will present-day interracial, international and intertribal barriers be done away with for those who take part in the first resurrection?

rection," these latter barriers will all be in the past. Those barriers have all attached to the flesh. Their resurrection will not be with the fleshly body that they formerly had here on earth, for it is written: "This I [the apostle Paul] say, brothers, that flesh and blood cannot inherit God's kingdom, neither does corruption inherit incorruption." (1 Corinthians 15:50) "Even if we [Christians] have known Christ according to the flesh, certainly we now know him so no more." (2 Corinthians 5:16) In the "first resurrection" the 144,000 Kingdom heirs come into the "divine nature," not human nature with all its present-day interracial, international, intertribal barriers. (2 Peter 1:4) They will all be brothers in a special heavenly family, sons of God: "If, then, we are children, we are also heirs: heirs indeed of God, but joint heirs with Christ." (Romans 8:17) Thus there will be unity among them according to the "divine nature."

[15] However, even during the time of their being here in the flesh under test on the earth, these 144,000 Kingdom heirs have not allowed racial, national and tribal barriers of mankind in general to divide. According to the flesh they are "disciples of people of all the nations." (Matthew 28:19) But they are Christ's disciples *first*, and they consider themselves as being of this or that race, nation and tribe only second. Their being Christ's baptized disciples unifies them on earth and surmounts all fleshly, human obstacles. That is why they declare themselves and maintain themselves strictly neutral toward the interracial, international, intertribal conflicts of this world and do not take part in politics, local, national or international. They stick to what Jesus Christ requested in prayer to God concerning them:

[16] "I make request concerning them; I make request, not concerning the world, but concerning those you have given me; because they are yours . . . I have given your word to them, but the world has hated

15, 16. (a) How do the 144,000 Kingdom heirs surmount human, earthly obstacles in order to keep unity? (b) They stick to what request made by Jesus in prayer to God in their behalf?

them, because they are no part of the world, just as I
am no part of the world. . . . Also, I have given them
the glory that you have given me, in order that they
may be one just as we are one. I in union with them
and you in union with me, in order that they may be
perfected into one, that the world may have the knowledge that you sent me forth and that you loved them
just as you loved me.—John 17:9-23.

INTERNATIONAL PEACEFULNESS OBSERVED

[17] This is why, on earth, the 144,000 Kingdom heirs
have not imitated Roman Catholics in fighting with
carnal weapons against Roman Catholics, Orthodox
Churchmen against Orthodox Churchmen, Protestants
against Protestants and natural Jews against natural
Jews, because of living under national governments that
are engaged in deadly warfare. They have not gone
forth disciple-making with the Gospel message or the
Holy Bible in one hand and a sword or machine gun in
the other hand. Although from many distinct nations,
they have carried out the principle stated in the prophecy of Isaiah 2:4: ("They shall beat their swords into
plowshares, and their spears into pruninghooks: nation
shall not lift up sword against nation, neither shall they
learn war any more." (Authorized or King James
Bible Version) And if they have clung to this divine
rule when they themselves were on earth, they will
enforce it when they are kings over the earth, requiring their subjects on earth to abide by the same
peaceful rule.

[18] As a happy forerunner of this, there is a great
international crowd that is now associated with the
remnant of those Kingdom heirs and that is abiding
by that same peaceful rule of conduct. It is the remarkable group that was foretold as due to gather
together in this time in world history, just as the
apostle John describes it, saying: ("After these things

17. (a) How have the 144,000 not imitated the religionists of Christendom and Jewry as to warfare? (b) What Scriptural rule will
they as heavenly kings enforce on earth's people?
18. What other international group on earth is abiding by this
rule of conduct, as foreseen by the apostle John?

I saw, and, look! a great crowd, which no man was able to number, out of all nations and tribes and peoples and tongues, standing before the throne and before the Lamb, dressed in white robes; and there were palm branches in their hands. And they keep on crying with a loud voice, saying: 'Salvation we owe to our God, who is seated on the throne, and to the Lamb [Jesus Christ].' . . . 'These are the ones that come out of the great tribulation, and they have washed their robes and made them white in the blood of the Lamb. That is why they are before the throne of God; and they are rendering him sacred service day and night in his temple; and the One seated on the throne will spread his tent over them.'"—Revelation 7:9-15.

[19] Since Jehovah God spreads his tent of protection over this "great crowd" of today and brings them safely through the approaching "great tribulation," those who enter alive into God's new system of things over the earth will be a peaceful international crowd. The war-making nations will then be gone! Human society in God's new order will start off with a "great crowd" of tribulation survivors all of whom are at peace with one another already. In their love of everlasting life they will continue to act in harmony with the words quoted by the apostle Peter: "He that would love life and see good days, let him restrain his tongue from what is bad and his lips from speaking deception, but let him turn away from what is bad and do what is good; let him seek peace and pursue it."—1 Peter 3:10, 11; Psalm 34:12-14.

[20] After the storm of the "great tribulation," earth-wide peace like a rainbow will be radiant over the cleansed planet. Jehovah's millennial King, the Lamb Jesus Christ, will not permit that peace to be disturbed. Otherwise, he would not be living up to the prophecy long ago pronounced concerning him: "There has been a child born to us, there has been a son given to us;

19. God's new system will start off with people on earth already living in what relationship with one another, and what words of Peter to lovers of long life will they heed?
20. (a) In order to fulfill what Bible prophecy concerning him, will Christ not let that peace be disturbed? (b) How will Christ's reign be like that of Solomon?

and the princely rule will come to be upon his shoulder. And his name will be called Wonderful Counselor, Mighty God, Eternal Father, Prince of Peace. To the abundance of the princely rule and to peace there will be no end, upon the throne of David and upon his kingdom in order to establish it firmly and to sustain it by means of justice and by means of righteousness, from now on and to time indefinite. The very zeal of Jehovah of armies will do this." (Isaiah 9:6, 7) Let us remember that Jesus Christ is "something more than Solomon." (Matthew 12:42) The forty-year reign of King Solomon, the son of David, was marked by peace, in accordance with the very name Solomon, which means "Peaceable." Jesus Christ, though, will maintain a peace of a thousand years.

"UPON THE THRONE OF DAVID AND UPON HIS KINGDOM"

21 If we read Isaiah 9:6, 7 again, we notice that the "princely rule" of the Prince of Peace is to be "upon the throne of David and upon his kingdom." We cannot disconnect this promised endless peace from the throne and kingdom of David, who ruled as king in Jerusalem during the years 1070-1037 B.C.E. It is not made dependent upon any president of the United States of America or upon the United Nations as a man-made organization for world peace and security. Why is this so?

22 It is because of an unbreakable covenant or divine promise that "Jehovah of armies" made respecting King David at Jerusalem early in his reign there. On what basis? Well, David was no atheist, no agnostic. He was a very religious man, but not like the idol worshipers or polytheists of the non-Israelite nations of his time. Read for yourself the many psalms or lyrical poems composed by David and as contained in the Book of Psalms, and you will find that David was a wholehearted worshiper of Jehovah, the God of Abra-

---

21. From whose throne and kingdom can the princely rule of the Prince of Peace not be disconnected, neither its peace?
22. (a) On what basis would Jehovah's zeal fulfill that prophecy? (b) As regards religion, what kind of man was David?

ham and of Isaac and of Jacob. In one of his best-known psalms, Psalm 23, David said: "Jehovah is my Shepherd. I shall lack nothing. Surely goodness and loving-kindness themselves will pursue me all the days of my life; and I will dwell in the house of Jehovah to the length of days." (Psalm 23:1, 6) Also, in Psalm 40:8, 9 he said: "To do your will, O my God, I have delighted, and your law is within my inward parts. I have told the good news of righteousness in the big congregation. Look! My lips I do not restrain. O Jehovah, you yourself know that well."

23 Some months after King David had made Jerusalem his capital city, he had the sacred Ark of the Covenant, "the ark of the true God," brought up to Jerusalem and placed in a tent that was pitched near the royal palace. David felt keenly the difference between his palatial residence, "a house of cedars," and that of Jehovah's Ark of the Covenant. Finally he suggested to the prophet Nathan the building of a worthy temple for Jehovah's ark. (2 Samuel 7:1-3) But God sent to David this word:

24 "Blood in great quantity you have spilled, and great wars you have waged. You will not build a house to my name, for a great deal of blood you have spilled on the earth before me. Look! There is a son being born to you. He himself will prove to be a restful man, and I shall certainly give him rest from all his enemies all around; for Solomon is what his name will become, and peace and quietness I shall bestow upon Israel in his days. It is he that will build a house to my name." —1 Chronicles 22:8-10.

25 This did not mean that Jehovah did not appreciate David's loving desire to build a house of worship in honor of God's name. Jehovah did, and to show his appreciation he made a covenant or made a solemn promise to build a house for David, not a literal house of residence but a house of a line of kings in David's

---

23, 24. (a) After bringing the Ark of God's covenant to Jerusalem, what did David desire to do about its housing? (b) What did Jehovah tell David about building?
25. In appreciation, what house did Jehovah promise to build for David?

family. By the prophet Nathan this word was sent to King David: (Jehovah has told you that a house is what Jehovah will make for you. . . . And your house and your kingdom will certainly be steadfast to time indefinite before you; your very throne will become one firmly established to time indefinite.)—2 Samuel 7:11-16.

²⁶ In gratefully acknowledging this divine covenant, David said in prayer: "(And now, Jehovah God, the word that you have spoken concerning your servant and concerning his house carry out to time indefinite and do just as you have spoken. And let your own name become great to time indefinite, saying, 'Jehovah of armies is God over Israel,' and let the very house of your servant David become firmly established before you. For you, Jehovah of armies the God of Israel, have made a revelation to your servant's ear, saying, 'A house I shall build for you.' That is why your servant has taken heart to pray to you with this prayer. And now, O Sovereign Lord Jehovah, you are the true God; and as for your words, let them prove to be truth, since you promise to your servant this goodness. And now take it upon yourself and bless the house of your servant for it to continue to time indefinite before you; for you yourself, O Sovereign Lord Jehovah, have promised, and due to your blessing let the house of your servant be blessed to time indefinite.)—2 Samuel 7:25-29.

²⁷ The Sovereign Lord Jehovah answered that prayer of David. That is why, over three hundred years later, by his prophet Isaiah, he declared that the zeal of Jehovah of armies would firmly establish the princely rule of the Prince of Peace "upon the throne of David and upon his kingdom" and would sustain it "from now on and to time indefinite." (Isaiah 9:6, 7) More than a century afterward, when the kingdom of the descendants of David at Jerusalem was about to be

26. In grateful acknowledgment, what did David say in prayer concerning Jehovah's name and His purpose concerning the "house"?
27. To show that he was holding to the Kingdom covenant with David, what did Jehovah say through Isaiah, and later through Ezekiel, to King Zedekiah?

destroyed, Jehovah showed that he was holding to his Kingdom covenant with David by declaring that the right to the kingship would not depart from the house of David. Addressing himself to Zedekiah, the last king to sit upon David's throne at Jerusalem, Jehovah spoke by the prophet Ezekiel and said: 'Remove the turban, and lift off the crown. This will not be the same. Put on high even what is low, and bring low even the high one. A ruin, a ruin, a ruin I shall make it. As for this also, it will certainly become no one's until he comes who has the legal right, and I must give it to him.'—Ezekiel 21:25-27.

> ²⁸ The throne of David was overthrown at the destruction of Jerusalem in the year 607 B.C.E., and the surviving Jews were exiled to Babylon. Seventy years later a remnant of God-fearing Jews were released from Babylon to return to the land of Judah and to build another temple on the location of the first temple that had been built by King Solomon at Jerusalem. Zerubbabel the son of Shealtiel, a descendant of King David, was made the governor of Judah and Jerusalem. Jehovah raised up the prophets Haggai and Zechariah to encourage Governor Zerubbabel in the work of rebuilding the temple. Still showing loyalty to the Kingdom covenant with David, Jehovah inspired the prophet Zechariah to say: "In that day there will come to be a well opened to the house of David and to the inhabitants of Jerusalem for sin and for an abhorrent thing." —Zechariah 13:1.

²⁹ More than four hundred years passed by and the land of Palestine came under the control of the imperialistic Romans. Under appointment by the Roman Senate, a non-Jewish Edomite called Herod the Great came to be king of Jerusalem and the province of Judea. After all those centuries, had not Jehovah God forgotten all about that covenant with David for an everlasting kingdom, the peace of which was to have

---

28. (a) When was the kingdom of the house of David overthrown, and what office did Zerubbabel hold over Judah seventy years later? (b) What did Zechariah prophesy concerning cleansing David's house? 29. When did Jerusalem and Judah get an Edomite king, and what question might there have been about the Kingdom covenant with David?

no end. All together, more than a thousand years had gone by since God made that covenant, and by now had not the covenant become obsolete, out-of-date, no longer showing any signs of life because of seemingly being in a state of lapse? Faithless men might have thought so. But what about God?

BIRTH OF KING DAVID'S EVERLASTING HEIR

[30] The unforgetting God, the divine Maker of the Kingdom covenant, held himself bound to fulfill his covenant promise to David. He kept watching the male descendants of faithful King David for whom he had promised to build a royal house. He saw one of the lines of descent from David passing, not through King Solomon, but through another of David's sons, Nathan. This particular line runs on down through twenty others and brings forth Zerubbabel, who became governor of Jerusalem in the days of the prophet Zechariah. Zerubbabel had a son named Rhesa, after whom there was a further unbroken line of descent through sixteen others, after which Heli was born as the son of Matthat. (Luke 3:23-31) Then God took note, not of a male descendant, but of a daughter of Heli. She was born in the city of Bethlehem in the Roman province of Judea during the last half of the first century B.C.E. She was called Mary.

[31] In course of time Mary was taken northward to the city of Nazareth in the Roman province of Galilee. There she became of marriageable age, and she was brought into an engagement to marry a carpenter named Joseph the son of Jacob, a resident of Nazareth.

[32] This marriage engagement was very appropriate. Why so? For the reason that Joseph, although a lowly carpenter in the obscure town of Nazareth, was a descendant of King David, not through Nathan, but through David's first royal successor, Solomon. Thus Joseph had a legal claim to the throne of his royal

---

30, 31. (a) What line of descent from King David did Jehovah watch? (b) Whose daughter in the line of descent did Jehovah notice, and to whom did she get engaged to marry?
32. Why was that engagement to marry Joseph appropriate, and what question about David's heir arose?

ancestor David. Was Joseph now to become the direct, natural father of the long-promised everlasting heir of King David?

[33] Well, before the wedding took place and Joseph took Mary away from her home to the home he provided for her as his legally wedded wife, a most unusual thing happened, something that the Brain-Age men of this twentieth century refuse to believe. The time was now about the end of the year 3 B.C.E. It was a marked time for God, for which he had long waited. Suddenly the evidence came to light that God was with Mary the daughter of Heli, not only for the kind of Jewish girl that she was but because she was a descendant of the royal family of David of the tribe of Judah. So what took place was working toward the fulfillment of the inspired prophecy pronounced by the patriarch Jacob over his fourth son, Judah. This was away back in the year 1711 B.C.E., and the dying Jacob said over Judah:

[34] "A lion cub Judah is . . . like a lion, who dares rouse him? The scepter will not turn aside from Judah, neither the commander's staff from between his feet, until Shiloh [or, The One Whose It Is] comes; and to him the obedience of the peoples will belong."—Genesis 49:8-10.

[35] How did God show that he was with Mary the virgin girl of the tribe of Judah and of the royal family of David? God did something for Mary that was greater than what he had done for an aged relative of Mary named Elizabeth, the wife of the Levite priest Zechariah. God miraculously revived the reproductive powers of Zechariah and Elizabeth, so that she was now in the sixth month of her pregnancy and was soon to give birth to a son who would come to be called John the Baptist. But what did God do for the virgin Jewess Mary, whose time of betrothal to the carpenter Joseph was not yet full? The medical doctor Luke tells us:

33, 34. (a) Why did Jehovah give evidence of being with Mary? (b) What now took place worked for fulfillment of what prophecy of Jacob on his deathbed?
35, 36. (a) What miraculous thing had God done for Elizabeth the aged relative of Mary? (b) What did the angel Gabriel tell Mary of God's purpose toward David's throne?

[36] 'In her sixth month the angel Gabriel was sent forth from God to a city of Galilee named Nazareth, to a virgin promised in marriage to a man named Joseph of David's house; and the name of the virgin was Mary. And when he went in before her he said: 'Good day, highly favored one, Jehovah is with you.' But she was deeply disturbed at the saying and began to reason out what sort of greeting this might be. So the angel said to her: 'Have no fear, Mary, for you have found favor with God; and, look! you will conceive in your womb and give birth to a son, and you are to call his name Jesus. This one will be great and will be called Son of the Most High; and Jehovah God will give him the throne of David his father, and he will rule as king over the house of Jacob forever, and there will be no end of his kingdom.' —Luke 1:26-33.

[37] This meant that Mary's intended husband Joseph was not to be the direct natural father of Jesus! What? A birth of a son without a human father? To explain to her how this miraculous virgin birth would come to be, the angel Gabriel went on to say: 'Holy spirit will come upon you, and power of the Most High will overshadow you. For that reason also what is born will be called holy, God's Son. And, look! Elizabeth your relative has also herself conceived a son, in her old age, and this is the sixth month for her, the so-called barren woman; because with God no declaration will be an impossibility.'—Luke 1:34-37.

[38] Did Mary consent to become in this way the earthly mother of the one who was to be the everlasting and permanent heir of King David? Luke 1:38 tells us: 'Then Mary said: 'Look! Jehovah's slave girl! May it take place with me according to your declaration.' At that the angel departed from her.' Thereafter holy spirit did come upon Mary, and power of the Most High God did overshadow her. So she became pregnant miraculously, not by her intended husband Joseph. This meant that Jehovah God the

---

37. How did Gabriel explain Mary's bearing a son without a human father?
38. What now took place with Mary, and of whom was her child to be the Son?

Most High was the Father of the child Jesus now conceived in her. Other inspired scriptures explain that Jehovah God transferred the life of His beloved heavenly only-begotten Son to an egg cell in Mary and made her fruitful. (John 3:16; Philippians 2:5-11) There was nothing unholy about this. That is why "what is born will be called holy, God's Son." This all occurred at God's fixed time, just as it is written: 'When the full limit of the time arrived, God sent forth his Son, who came to be out of a woman and who came to be under law [the Mosaic law].'—Galatians 4:4.

THE PERMANENT HEIR OF THE KINGDOM COVENANT

[39] What the angel Gabriel told Mary made certain that her son Jesus was to be the Permanent Heir of King David: 'Jehovah God will give him the throne of David his father, and he will rule as king over the house of Jacob forever, and there will be no end of his kingdom.' (Luke 1:32, 33) Not the Jews of nineteen centuries ago nor the natural Jews of today were to give this Jesus the throne of his forefather David. The heavenly Father, Jehovah God, was to give him that throne of the Kingdom, which, in David's case, was only "over the house of Jacob," the patriarchal father of the twelve tribes of Israel. So by means of the virgin Jewess Mary her firstborn son was born into the royal family of David, and by her Jesus had a fleshly natural right to David's kingdom. In proof of this fact the apostle Paul was inspired to write about the good news from God: 'Concerning his Son, who sprang from the seed of David according to the flesh, but who with power was declared God's Son according to the spirit of holiness by means of resurrection from the dead—yes, Jesus Christ our Lord.'—Romans 1:1-4.

[40] After Mary's pregnancy was discovered, her intended husband was given an explanation and told to take Mary as his wife to his home for her. Joseph did

39. (a) Who was to make Mary's son Jesus king over the house of Jacob? (b) What kind of right did Jesus inherit through Mary? 40. (a) What did Joseph feel obligated toward God to do respecting Mary's son Jesus, thus conferring what upon Jesus? (b) Whose son does Luke call Joseph, and why?

so, there at Nazareth. He realized his obligation toward God to adopt God's Son by Mary as his own firstborn son and thereby give Jesus the legal right to David's throne, forasmuch as Joseph was a descendant of David through King Solomon.* (2 Samuel 7:13-16) This is what Joseph did by having Jesus circumcised on the eighth day of his birth and calling his name Jesus and also by presenting the babe Jesus on the fortieth day of his birth in purification rites for himself and Mary at the temple in Jerusalem. (Matthew 1:17-25; Luke 2:21-24) This is why he was called "the son of Joseph." (John 1:45; 6:42) This is why, too, in Doctor Luke's genealogy of Jesus Christ he says: "Furthermore, Jesus himself, when he commenced his work, was about thirty years old, being the son, as the opinion was, of Joseph, son of Heli." (Luke 3:23) Joseph, who was really the son of Jacob, was also called the "son of Heli" because he had married Heli's daughter Mary and so was Heli's son-in-law.

[41] Jesus Christ was later called "Jesus of Nazareth" and "Jesus, from Nazareth of Galilee." (John 19:19, AV; Matthew 21:11) Does this mean that Jesus was born in Nazareth? No, for before his birth his mother Mary and her husband Joseph, because of both of them being born in Bethlehem of Judah, were obliged to move down to Bethlehem in the year 2 B.C.E. for registration purposes under the decree of the Roman

---

* If Joseph of the royal lineage of King David had wanted to wait to bestow the "legal right" to the Davidic throne upon a direct natural son of his, such as James, Joseph (II), Simon or Judas, this legal claim would not have taken effect. (Ezekiel 21:27) Why not? Because Joseph was a descendant of King Solomon through Jeconiah (or Coniah, or Jehoiachin), concerning whom we read, in Jeremiah 22:24-30: "'As I am alive,' is the utterance of Jehovah, 'even if Coniah the son of Jehoiakim, the king of Judah, happened to be the seal ring on my right hand, from there I would pull you off!' . . . This is what Jehovah has said, 'Write down this man as childless [as regards heirship to David's throne], as an able-bodied man who will not have any success in his days; for from his offspring not a single one will have any success, sitting upon the throne of David and ruling anymore in Judah.'" (Matthew 1:11-16; 13:55) Consequently, Joseph's conferring the legal title upon his adopted son Jesus would not be in vain, inasmuch as Jesus the son of Mary the virgin became no natural descendant of Jeconiah (Coniah), but descended from King David through the line of his son Nathan the son of Bath-sheba. Hence, Jesus' genealogy as recorded in Luke 3:23-38 does not list the name of Jeconiah (Coniah, or Jehoiachin).

---

41. Where was the one called "Jesus of Nazareth" born in 2 B.C.E.?

emperor, Caesar Augustus. Jesus thus came to be born in Bethlehem, which was called "the city of David," because David the son of Jesse himself had been born there.—Luke 2:1-7, *AV*.

[42] We have more than the testimony of the angel Gabriel that this Jesus the son of Mary was to be the Messiah or Christ, the Anointed One who was to be the permanent inheritor of the throne and kingdom of David. We have the testimony of another heavenly angel on the night of Jesus' birth about the beginning of October, 2 B.C.E. This glorious angel appeared to shepherds who still had their flocks out in the fields near Bethlehem at that time of the year.

[43] To the frightened shepherds the angel said: 'Have no fear, for, look! I am declaring to you good news of a great joy that all the people will have, because there was born to you today a Savior, who is Christ the Lord, in David's city. And this is a sign for you: you will find an infant bound in cloth bands and lying in a manger.' That this was no ordinary birth was shown by what then happened: 'And suddenly there came to be with the angel a multitude of the heavenly army, praising God and saying: 'Glory in the heights above to God, and upon earth peace among men of goodwill.' '—Luke 2:8-14.

[44] Satan the Devil became aware of the birth of this Son of God who was to become "Christ the Lord." Jealous over his own rulership of this world, Satan the Devil tried to have the young child Jesus killed sometime after his being presented at the temple in Jerusalem, and this by the hand of suspicious King Herod the Great. So God's angel told Joseph to flee with the mother and child down to Egypt until further notice. After King Herod's death God's angel told Joseph to return to the land of his people. But, because King Herod's son Archelaus was ruling over the Roman province of Judea, including Bethlehem, Joseph bypassed Bethlehem and returned to Nazareth in the

42, 43. What angelic testimony besides that of Gabriel do we have to the effect that Mary's son was to be God's Messiah?
44. Why was the child Jesus taken down to Egypt, and how is it that he became a carpenter in Nazareth?

province of Galilee. There Jesus was brought up and came to be called a Nazarene. There this future King worked as a carpenter.—Matthew 2:1-23; 13:55; Mark 6:1-3.

[45] However, the word Christ or Messiah, meaning Anointed One, could not really apply to Jesus until he actually became anointed. His ancestor, the shepherd David of Bethlehem, had been anointed by God's prophet Samuel many years before he actually was enthroned as king in Israel. (1 Samuel 16:1-13; 2 Samuel 2:1-4; 5:1-3) It went similarly with Jesus. In his thirtieth year as a perfect human being, his relative, John the Baptist, began his baptismal work because he then started announcing God's kingdom, saying: "Repent, for the kingdom of the heavens has drawn near." (Matthew 3:1, 2) From this announcement Jesus knew that the time had come for him to apply himself exclusively to the interests of God's Messianic kingdom. As he neared the end of his thirtieth year of human life he left Nazareth and made his way to John, who was baptizing people in the Jordan River. Why? Not to be baptized as a symbol of repentance over sins, of which he had none, but to symbolize his presenting of himself completely to Jehovah God in order to do the divine will in connection with the "kingdom of the heavens," the kingdom of God. John did not understand this. Hence we read:

[46] "Then Jesus came from Galilee to the Jordan to John, in order to be baptized by him. But the latter tried to prevent him, saying: 'I am the one needing to be baptized by you, and are you coming to me?' In reply Jesus said to him: 'Let it be, this time, for in that way it is suitable for us to carry out all that is righteous.' Then he quit preventing him. After being baptized Jesus immediately came up from the water; and, look! the heavens were opened up, and he saw descending like a dove God's spirit coming upon him. Look!

45. To become really the Messiah or Christ, what did Jesus, like David, need to have? (b) When and why did Jesus go to the Jordan River to be baptized?
46. (a) How did Jesus there at his baptism become the Messiah or Christ? (b) Why did God there call the baptized Jesus his Son?

Also, there was a voice from the heavens that said: 'This is my Son, the beloved, whom I have approved.')' (Matthew 3:13-17) By that descent of God's spirit upon the baptized Jesus he was anointed, anointed not by John the Baptist, but by God. In this way he became the Messiah, the Christ, the Anointed One. This was in early autumn of the year 29 C.E. God also pronounced him then his Son, because now by His spirit he had begotten Jesus to be his spiritual Son. (John 1:32-34) He was now a spiritual Messiah or Christ, higher than a human Messiah.

>⁴⁷ Did Jesus Christ now try to make himself an earthly king "over the house of Jacob," at Jerusalem? No! In the wilderness of temptation, he refused an offer by Satan the Devil to make him the king, not merely over the house of Jacob, but over all the kingdoms of this world. (Matthew 4: 1-11; Luke 4:1-13) Later, after performing a marvelous miracle of feeding a multitude, he withdrew from an attempt by thousands of well-fed Jews to make him their earthly king. (John 6:1-15) He knew that his kingdom was to come from the One

47. What opportunities to become a mere human Messiah did Jesus refuse, and what work did he take up in accord with his anointing?

who had anointed him to be Messianic King, Jehovah God. Appreciating the preliminary work that his being anointed with God's spirit entailed upon him, Jesus Christ took up the peaceful work of teaching and preaching God's kingdom throughout the land of the "house of Jacob." Especially so after the imprisonment of John the Baptist in the year 30 C.E.

[48] In the synagogue at Nazareth he read to the Nazarenes the prophecy of Isaiah 61:1, 2, saying: "Jehovah's spirit is upon me, because he anointed me to declare good news to the poor, he sent me forth to preach a release to the captives and a recovery of sight to the blind, to send the crushed ones away with a release, to preach Jehovah's acceptable year." With that as the theme for his sermon, the baptized Jesus began by saying: "Today this scripture that you just heard is fulfilled." (Luke 4:16-21) By this he was giving his former townspeople to understand that he was Jehovah's Anointed One, the Messiah, the Christ. During all the rest of his earthly life he made it his endeavor to fulfill what his anointing with Jehovah's spirit authorized, commissioned him to do.

[49] Consequently, he did not meddle in the politics of this world or form an army like the Maccabees and drive out the Romans from the land and reestablish the kingdom of David at Jerusalem. Why not?

[50] The reason for not doing so He explained to the Roman governor, Pontius Pilate, to whom he had been handed over by his religious enemies to be executed as a seditionist against the Roman Empire. In answer to the governor's question, "Are you the king of the Jews?" Jesus finally said: "My kingdom is no part of this world. If my kingdom were part of this world, my attendants would have fought that I should not be delivered up to the Jews. But, as it is, my kingdom is not from this source." At this Pilate said: "Well, then, are you a king?" Bearing witness to the truth;

48. In the synagogue of Nazareth, what prophecy of Isaiah did he read to the Nazarenes, and what did he endeavor to do for the rest of his earthly life?
49, 50. (a) Did Jesus form an army to reestablish the kingdom of Israel? (b) What explanation did Jesus give to Pilate for being a king and yet not fighting for a kingdom?

Jesus answered: "You yourself are saying that I am a king." Yes, king of a kingdom that is no part of the world to which the Roman Empire was then the world power.—John 18:33-37.

[51] Jesus' words, "my attendants," meant whom? Why, his unarmed disciples, including his twelve apostles ("sent-forth ones"). These too he instructed to refrain from the politics of this world and its violent combats and to specialize on teaching and preaching peaceably the good news of the promised kingdom of God.

[52] When he sent forth the twelve apostles on one occasion, he did not tell them to organize an underground political movement and stir up insurrection among the Jews; but he said: "As you go, preach, saying, 'The kingdom of the heavens has drawn near.' Cure sick people, raise up dead persons, make lepers clean, expel demons. You received free, give free." (Matthew 10:1-8) When Jesus later sent out seventy other evangelizers he gave them similar instructions and told them what to preach, saying: "Also, wherever you enter into a city and they receive you, eat the things set before you, and cure the sick ones in it, and go on telling them, 'The kingdom of God has come near to you.'"—Luke 10:1-9.

[53] On Nisan 11 of the year 33 C.E., just before his death on Passover Day, Jesus gave his remarkable prophecy concerning his future presence and the conclusion of the system of things. In this prophecy he did not fail to foretell the outstanding work that his attendants, his disciples, should do, for he said: "This good news of the kingdom will be preached in all the inhabited earth for a witness to all the nations; and then the end will come." (Matthew 24:3-14) Before the complete end of this system of things this Kingdom-preaching world wide must be done by his disciples:

51, 52. (a) What did Jesus instruct his "attendants" to do? (b) Did Jesus tell the twelve apostles and then the seventy evangelizers to carry on political activities or evangelical work, and how?
53, 54. (a) In his prophecy on his presence and the conclusion of this system, what preaching did Jesus foretell? (b) Carrying on this preaching allows for no meddling in what, as they know that the government they preach is of what source?

"Also, in all the nations the good news has to be preached first." (Mark 13:10) Their doing this Kingdom-preaching peacefully among all nations did not allow for them to meddle in worldly politics and take sides in international conflicts.

[54] Like their Leader Jesus Christ, they were merely to preach the good news of God's Messianic kingdom. They were not authorized and empowered to set up that kingdom over the earth. It was not to be an earthly government; it was "not from this source." It was a heavenly government with superhuman power over all mankind. Naturally, then, only the Most High God of heaven could set up that Messianic government over all the inhabitants of the earth.

[55] Who, then, in heaven or on earth, can find fault with the earthly life of the Messiah, the Christ, the one anointed to rule as king over all mankind for a thousand years? Who can rightfully object to his becoming the Millennial King as if he were not worthy or qualified? No one can. Pointing to the faultless life of Jesus Christ on earth, the apostle Peter said to the Roman centurion Cornelius and his Gentile friends: "You know the subject that was talked about throughout the whole of Judea, starting from Galilee after the baptism that John preached, namely, Jesus who was from Nazareth, how God anointed him with holy spirit and power, and he went through the land doing good and healing all those oppressed by the Devil; because God was with him. And we are witnesses of all the things he did both in the country of the Jews and in Jerusalem." (Acts 10:37-39) All the testimony is to the effect that Jesus Christ on earth fulfilled all that he was commissioned by his anointing to do. He fulfilled all the Bible prophecies concerning him, even down to a martyr's death.

---

55. As far as concerns carrying out his anointing and fulfilling Bible prophecies, can objections be raised as to Jesus' being qualified to rule all mankind?

CHAPTER 5

How the Associate Kings Are Put in Office

WHAT king better than Jesus Christ the Son of God could all mankind have over itself? What human king loved his people so much as to leave all his glory and lay down his life innocently in his people's behalf? And even if he did unselfishly lay down his life for his people, of what lasting benefit would this be to them? But in the case of Jesus Christ the Son of God, he left his heavenly glory with his Father and became a mere man, perfect indeed and yet "a little less than godlike ones," "a little lower than angels." (Psalm 8:5; Hebrews 2:9) Then, according to God's will, he humbled himself still further to be violently killed even by humans after God anointed him to be the Messianic King. Not only was this an incomparable demonstration of love for mankind, but his death provided a perfect human sacrifice acceptable to God for the everlasting benefit of all humankind. Who better than this one could commend himself to mankind as suitable to be their king?

[2] Nineteen centuries ago men who believed in mere human political rulership did not desire him as their king; which was why they cried out to the Roman governor for the executing of him as if he were a false Christ, a false Messiah. Today the vast majority of mankind, even in Christendom, do not want him as a real King but do a lot of politicking for human rulership and belittle, oppose and persecute Christians who really imitate their Leader, Jesus. But what does it matter that the overwhelming majority of mankind

---

1. Why could there be no one more suitable to be king over mankind than Jesus Christ?
2. (a) How are people today like those of the first century as respects wanting Jesus Christ as king? (b) What is it that really counts as regards whom mankind will get as king?

today do not want Jesus Christ as their real heavenly King? Does that decide matters for mankind, the living and the dead? What counts is Almighty God's decision. He approved of his Son Jesus at the time that he was baptized by John the Baptist in the Jordan River. He approved of his Son Jesus at the time that this faithful Son was gloriously transfigured before three witnesses in a very high mountain in northern Palestine. (Matthew 3:17; 17:5) God approved of his sinless Son when, in his dying moments on the execution stake at Calvary, he called out with a loud voice: "Father, into your hands I entrust my spirit."—Luke 23:46.

[3] In an all-excelling expression of his approval of his martyred Son, the God who works what puny men call impossibilities raised Jesus Christ from the dead on the third day. On what level of existence? As a mere human of blood and flesh, "a little lower than angels"? No! but on a level far higher than that of angels, on a heavenly level of life higher than that which he emptied himself of when he submitted to having his life transferred to the womb of the virgin Jewess Mary. (Philippians 2:5-11) Said the apostle Peter, who was one of the first to see him in a materialized body after his resurrection: "That which corresponds to this is also now saving you . . . through the resurrection of Jesus Christ. He is at God's right hand, for he went his way to heaven; and angels and authorities and powers were made subject to him."—1 Peter 3:21, 22; Hebrews 1:1-4; Luke 24:34; 1 Corinthians 15:5.

[4] Thus the triumphant Son of God who had been made a "son of David" through a virgin birth in David's line of descent came to be far higher than King David. The apostle Peter pointed this out in his inspired speech to thousands of Jews on the day of the Festival of Weeks, the fiftieth day from the resur-

---

3. (a) What all-excelling expression of approval did God give of his martyred Son Jesus Christ? (b) To what level of life did God resurrect him?
4, 5. How did Jesus Christ the "son of David" become the "Lord" of David, and who was the first one to point this out?

rection of Jesus Christ. Peter, filled with holy spirit, said to them:

[5] "This Jesus God resurrected, of which fact we are all witnesses. Therefore because he was exalted to the right hand of God and received the promised holy spirit from the Father, he has poured out this which you see and hear. Actually David did not ascend to the heavens, but he himself says, 'Jehovah said to my Lord: "Sit at my right hand, until I place your enemies as a stool for your feet."' Therefore let all the house of Israel know for a certainty that God made him both Lord and Christ, this Jesus whom you impaled." —Acts 2:32-36.

[6] In his coming resurrection from the dead under the Messianic kingdom David will have to acknowledge the glorified Jesus Christ as his "Lord." David will then call him "my Lord." (Psalm 110:1) He will have to acknowledge the Lord Jesus Christ, exalted from earth to heaven, as the most vital one of his descendants, "the root and the offspring of David," "The Lion that is of the tribe of Judah, the root of David." (Revelation 22:16; 5:5) This is why the genealogy of David's descendants in two lines of descent ends with Jesus the son of Mary the virgin Jewess. In fact, the genealogy of Jesus Christ runs back, not just to King David, not just to the patriarch Abraham, but all the way back to the first Adam, who, in the day of his creation in the Garden of Eden, was called the "son of God." (Matthew 1:1-18; Luke 3:23-38) Jesus Christ is the only one whose ancestry all the way back to the first human "son of God" was preserved without a break or gap in the long line.

[7] King David reigned in Israel for only forty years. (1 Kings 2:10, 11; 1 Chronicles 29:26, 27) All together, through a line of twenty male successors to King David, his royal family reigned in Israel for 470 years, or from 1077 to 607 B.C.E. What other dynasty

6. (a) After his resurrection, what acknowledgment will David have to make regarding Jesus? (b) What kind of genealogical record does Jesus have as a man?
7. (a) How long did the royal dynasty in King David's family reign in Israel? (b) How long will Jesus Christ reign without any earthly rival, and how so?

of kings in one family can equal that in any other country? However, Jesus Christ, ~~as David's heavenly Lord, will reign without an earthly rival king for a thousand years over all mankind~~. This will be without successors on his heavenly throne, for he is immortal. He has the "~~power of an indestructible life~~"; and so, "~~because of continuing alive forever~~," he can have his kingdom "~~without any successors~~." (Hebrews 7:16, 24) As the angel Gabriel said to Mary at Nazareth, "~~there will be no end of his kingdom~~." (Luke 1:33) Consequently, he is King David's Permanent Heir.

> **ASSOCIATES, NOT SUCCESSORS**

[8] The 144,000 joint heirs of Jesus Christ are not his successors in the Kingdom. They are merely associate kings, over whom He is the divinely appointed Head. Accordingly, the way in which Revelation 20:4 states the matter is: "And they came to life and ruled as kings with the Christ [not, after the Christ] for a thousand years." It is just as Jesus Christ said to his faithful apostles on Passover night, after he had set up a new celebration that came to be called the Lord's Supper or Evening Meal: "You are the ones that have stuck with me in my trials; and I make a covenant with you, just as my Father has made a covenant with me, for a kingdom, that you may eat and drink at my table in my kingdom, and sit on thrones to judge the twelve tribes of Israel." (Luke 22:28-30) Hundreds of years before Christ, the prophet Daniel pointed forward to that same joint participation, saying:

[9] "But the holy ones of the Supreme One will receive the kingdom, and they will take possession of the kingdom for time indefinite, even for time indefinite upon times indefinite." "The Ancient of Days came and judgment itself was given in favor of the holy ones of the Supreme One, and the definite time arrived that the holy ones took possession of the kingdom itself. And the kingdom and the rulership and the grandeur

---

8, 9. (a) Are the 144,000 to be the successors of Jesus Christ, and how did he, after setting up the Lord's Supper, speak of their privileges in the Kingdom? (b) How did Daniel foretell that same joint participation?

of the kingdoms under all the heavens were given to the people who are the holy ones of the Supreme One. Their kingdom is an indefinitely lasting kingdom, and all the rulerships will serve and obey even them." —Daniel 7:18, 22, 27.

¹⁰ From this it follows that the 144,000 holy ones of the Most High God will be kings with Christ for a thousand years without successors. It is said of these: "These are the ones that keep following the Lamb no matter where he goes. These were bought from among mankind as firstfruits to God and to the Lamb." (Revelation 14:4) Being bought from among mankind, they were once ordinary men and women just like all the rest of mankind, but from this fact earth's inhabitants over whom these 144,000 will rule as kings have nothing to fear. They have become "holy ones," just as any "firstfruits to God and to the Lamb" would have to be strictly "holy." Is there anything to fear from the rulership of Jesus Christ? No! And likewise there is nothing to be uneasy about as to the rulership of the 144,000 "bought from among mankind." They have obeyed the apostle Paul's counsel: "Keep this mental attitude in you that was also in Christ Jesus." (Philippians 2:5) Also, the apostle Peter's counsel in 1 Peter 4:1:

¹¹ "Therefore since Christ suffered in the flesh, you too arm yourselves with the same mental disposition; because the person that has suffered in the flesh has desisted from sins."

¹² It is evident that the 144,000 need to have developed in them the mental, moral and spiritual image of their Leader and Teacher Jesus Christ. This is one of the requirements that Jehovah God foreordained about them. Although He did not foreordain the individual persons from among mankind who should make up those bearing in themselves this image of

---

10, 11. (a) What must be said as to whether the 144,000 have successors and as to their being "firstfruits to God and to the Lamb"? (b) Because of what mental attitude are the 144,000 not to be feared as kings?
12. (a) What did God foreordain with regard to the associate kings of Christ? (b) When and how did Jehovah God give first recognition to this governmental class?

Jesus Christ, God did foreordain how many there should be of them—144,000. He did foreordain how he would deal with them and to what glorious heavenly station he would bring them. Because, from the very time of man's rebellion in the Garden of Eden, Jehovah God was concerned about the government for a new system of things over mankind, he gave first recognition to this governmental class. This recognition He voiced in the divine decision he made known to Satan the Devil, "the original serpent," saying: "I shall put enmity between you and the woman and between your seed and her seed. He will bruise you in the head and you will bruise him in the heel."—Genesis 3:15.

[13] Jesus Christ is, of course, the principal one of that promised "seed" of God's woman. But it also includes those faithful disciples who are to be associated with Christ in the bruising of the Serpent's head. (Romans 16:20) So, addressing himself to a congregation of those who had been called and who were striving to make this calling of them sure and irrevocable, the apostle Paul wrote encouragingly, in Romans 8:28-32:

[14] "Now we know that God makes all his works cooperate together for the good of those who love God, those who are the ones called according to his purpose; because those whom he gave his first recognition he also foreordained to be patterned after the image of his Son, that he might be the firstborn among many brothers. Moreover, those whom he foreordained are the ones he also called; and those whom he called are the ones he also declared to be righteous. Finally those whom he declared righteous are the ones he also glorified. What, then, shall we say to these things? If God is for us, who will be against us? He who did not even spare his own Son but delivered him up for us all, why will he not also with him kindly give us all other things?"

[15] Note that those called are, regardless of whoever

13, 14. (a) What is Jesus Christ with reference to the promised "seed" of God's woman? (b) What did the apostle Paul encouragingly write to the Christians striving to make their calling secure?
15. (a) How, according to God's foreordination, will the government of His new order be harmonious in itself? (b) How, by God's action, will those in this government be "righteous"?

they might individually prove to be, "foreordained to be patterned after the image of his Son, that he might be the firstborn among many brothers." This requires and ensures that they will all be Christlike as sons of God. Thus God foreordained that the government of His coming new order should be a harmonious government, not divided in itself, not at disagreement within itself. Everyone in that government has to be "righteous." That is why God has to make special provision, yet just provision, in order to declare these called ones "righteous," and this He does through the blood of the Lamb Jesus Christ. When resurrecting them from the dead, He will make them righteous as perfect spirit creatures in harmony with their righteous personality. (Romans 5:1, 9; 8:1) Such ones whom God declares righteous now by reason of their faith in the blood of Jesus Christ, God dignifies, honors, glorifies with blessed privileges in His service now on earth. He sets before them future glory in the Kingdom.

[16] All mankind can be sure that those whom God approves and resurrects to Kingdom glory will not conduct themselves in office like the politicians of the present worldly governments. Jesus did not set the politicians of this world before his disciples as an example to imitate. There will be no political rivalry between his 144,000 associates in the heavenly kingdom. Not according to what we read in Luke 22:24-27: "There also arose a heated dispute among them over which one of them seemed to be greatest. But he said to them: 'The kings of the nations lord it over them, and those having authority over them are called Benefactors. You, though, are not to be that way. But let him that is the greatest among you become as the youngest, and the one acting as chief as the one ministering. For which one is greater, the one reclining at the table or the one ministering? Is it not the one reclining at the table? But I am in your midst as the one ministering.' "

16. How did Jesus show his disciples whether the politicians of this world are the ones for them to imitate?

[17] About two thousand years ago the Son of God was sent into this world, but not to become a politician campaigning for votes or fighting against political rivals, even in the nation of Israel. He came to do what no earthly politician can do, namely, to reconcile the people of all races, nations and tribes to God, with whom they were at enmity. He came in order to bring mankind back to peaceful, friendly relations with the great Life-Giver, Jehovah God. This meant self-sacrifice for the Son of God. He is rightly said to be the Ambassador from God, who was sent to a hostile race of people in order to plead with them to become reconciled to God and thereby escape being destroyed by Him.

[18] The Christian disciples were the ones who accepted that Ambassador from God and his ambassadorial work in their behalf. The apostle Paul wrote to such disciples in Rome and said: "God recommends his own love to us in that, while we were yet sinners, Christ died for us. Much more, therefore, since we have been declared righteous now by his blood, shall we be saved through him from wrath. For if, when we were enemies, we became reconciled to God through the death of his Son, much more, now that we have become reconciled, we shall be saved by his life. And not only that, but we are also exulting in God through our Lord Jesus Christ, through whom we have now received the reconciliation."—Romans 5:8-11.

"AMBASSADORS SUBSTITUTING FOR CHRIST"

[19] Since his ascension to heaven in the spring of the year 33 C.E., Jesus Christ has been no longer on earth to carry on personally this work of ambassadorship. Therefore his reconciled disciples must carry on the ambassadorial work as substitutes for him. The political rulers and governments of this world do not

---

17. Why, when sent to this world, was Jesus rightly God's Ambassador to mankind?
18. Those who became disciples of Christ reacted in what way to God's Ambassador? With what effects?
19. (a) Since Christ's ascension to heaven, how is the ambassadorial work carried on toward mankind? (b) How do the world's political rulers look upon the ambassadors from Christ, and why so?

recognize these disciples as ambassadors from the Highest Government of the universe. Neither do these Christian ambassadors treat or negotiate with the political ambassadors of the nations to bring about at one negotiation the reconciliation of a whole nation by one single treaty through those diplomatic ambassadors. The political rulers and governments look upon commissioned disciples according to the flesh, from the old standpoint, and do not send diplomatic representatives to them as they have done for centuries with the Vatican of the Roman Catholic Church. They view these untitled disciples, without diplomatic dress and credentials, as being just ordinary humans. They do not discern these to be new creatures spiritually, with something new to offer.

[20] Because the apostle Paul, who did not represent the Jewish government at Jerusalem, was not recognized as a Christian ambassador by the Roman Empire, did that make him any less a real ambassador from the Government of the Most High God? Yet, even while not being honorably recognized by the Roman government, Paul spoke of himself as such while under arrest in Rome, saying to the congregation in Ephesus, Asia Minor: "Keep awake with all constancy and with supplication in behalf of all the holy ones, also for me, that ability to speak may be given me with the opening of my mouth, with all freeness of speech to make known the sacred secret of the good news, for which I am acting as an ambassador in chains; that I may speak in connection with it with boldness as I ought to speak."—Ephesians 6:18-20.

[21] A commissioned Christian should not adopt the viewpoint of the political governments of this world that are at enmity with Jehovah God. The Christian has received his ambassadorship from God through Christ, and he must recognize the responsibilities that this new honor conferred upon him places upon him. Because he is not a worldly ambassador, he does not

20. Although he was not recognized by Rome as an ambassador, how did Paul speak of himself when writing to the Ephesians?
21. In discharging their responsibilities, to whom do the Christian ambassadors go?

go to the political governments in his new capacity. In this matter of reconciliation with God, the governments cannot act for the whole nation and alter the relationship of their subjects to God. It is an individual matter; each person must decide and act for himself. That is why the spiritual Christian ambassadors go *directly* to the people, not through their political governments. Discounting the old standing and giving full value to the new responsibility, the apostle Paul put the matter squarely, saying:

²² "Consequently if anyone is in union with Christ, he is a new creation [or, creature]; the old things passed away, look! new things have come into existence. But all things are from God, who reconciled us to himself through Christ and gave us the ministry of the reconciliation, namely, that God was by means of Christ reconciling a world to himself, not reckoning to them their trespasses, and he committed the word of the reconciliation to us. We are therefore ambassadors substituting for Christ, as though God were making entreaty through us. As substitutes for Christ we beg: 'Become reconciled to God.' The one who did not know sin he made to be sin for us, that we might become God's righteousness by means of him. Working together with him, we also entreat you not to accept the undeserved kindness of God and miss its purpose." —2 Corinthians 5:17 through 6:1, *margin*.

²³ Being "ambassadors substituting for Christ" places serious restrictions upon God's representatives who are new creatures in union with Christ. What restrictions? Those similar to the restrictions that rest upon ambassadors of the political nations. Not only today, but also in Bible times, ambassadors had no right to meddle in the politics of foreign nations to which they were sent. (Luke 19:12-15, 27) They might make an appeal to those foreign governments, or even a protest, but they must strictly keep out of the politics of such alien nations. They must be loyal to their own

22. What ministry do the Christian ambassadors fulfill, for whom do they substitute, and what do they entreat reconciled ones not to do?
23. Being "ambassadors substituting for Christ" places what serious restrictions upon God's representatives?

home government and jealously take care of its interests when they are dealing with foreign governments. If they do not do this, they can be refused recognition or their credentials be turned down and their presence in the land can be denied.

[24] The 144,000 who are joint heirs with Christ recognize that they are, while on earth, "ambassadors substituting for Christ." In the light of the Holy Scriptures they see clearly what their being such ambassadors really means with regard to their relationship to this world that is at enmity with God. (Romans 5:10) With the apostle Paul, they confess: "Our citizenship exists in the heavens, from which place also we are eagerly waiting for a savior, the Lord Jesus Christ." (Philippians 3:20) In this hostile world they must faithfully represent the heavenly kingdom that the Lord Jesus Christ commanded them to preach world wide. (Matthew 24:14) Their being spiritual ambassadors to an enemy world does not allow them to meddle and take an active part in the politics of any nation whatsoever of this world. They cannot engage in political electioneering or hold public office in a worldly government any more than a worldly ambassador can divide his loyalty and assume political office in a land foreign to his own. In this way they keep clean from any community responsibility for the misconduct and bloodshed committed by any nation on earth.

[25] In the face of this we can appreciate more what the apostle John says of the faithful 144,000 who become Kingdom associates of Christ: "I saw the souls of those executed with the ax for the witness they bore to Jesus and for speaking about God, and those who had worshiped neither the wild beast nor its image and who had not received the mark upon their forehead and upon their hand. And they came to life and ruled as kings with the Christ for a thousand years."

24. Where is the citizenship of these spiritual ambassadors, what government do they represent, and from what worldly activities do they refrain and thus keep clean?
25. How do the 144,000 Kingdom joint heirs keep from worshiping the "wild beast" and its "image" and from having its mark on forehead and hand?

(Revelation 20:4) Under the enlightening power of God's spirit they see the "wild beast," the number of which is 666, to be the Devil's worldwide political system by means of which he is the "ruler of this world." They see that, today, the "image" of that political wild beast is another political organization, namely, the United Nations, the man-made organization for the peace and security of this world that is at enmity with God. It is only by keeping clean and un-entangled from the politics and conflicts of this symbolic "wild beast" that they keep from having the mark of the wild beast on forehead or hand.

²⁶ The 144,000 are neither slaves nor worshipers of the "wild beast" and its political "image." They do not display themselves openly as by a mark on the un-covered forehead as being slaves of this "wild beast" of human rulership under Satan the Devil. They do not show its political "mark" on their hand as by slavishly and worshipfully giving the "wild beast" their active support and "right hand of fellowship." They do obey the apostle Paul's counsel in Romans 13:1-7 and conscientiously show "subjection to the superior authorities" of this world, paying taxes and such due things. But this subjection is not total; it is only rela-tive, for a serious reason. What? This: when the laws and rulings of these earthly superior authorities clash with the laws and rulings of the Most High God, then they must conscientiously follow the course set by Christ's apostles before the Supreme Court in Jeru-salem: "We must obey God as ruler rather than men." (Acts 5:29) Only by doing this can they keep free of the "mark" of the "wild beast" and prove themselves worthy to reign with Christ above.

²⁷ The 144,000 faithful ones will therefore carry none of the political uncleanness of this self-seeking world into the heavenly kingdom of the Christ. As for any identification being displayed upon their foreheads,

26. Although keeping free from the worship of the "wild beast" and its "mark," what do the 144,000 render to the "superior authorities" of the world, but to what extent?
27. According to Revelation 22:4, what identification do the 144,000 display on their foreheads?

Revelation 22:3-5 says concerning these loyal servants of God: "His slaves will render him sacred service; and they will see his face, and his name will be on their foreheads. . . . Jehovah God will shed light upon them, and they will rule as kings forever and ever."

BENEFIT OF BEING A THOUSAND YEARS IN OFFICE

[28] What a grand privilege and opportunity it will be for them to rule as kings with the Christ for the thousand years after the binding and abyssing of Satan the Devil and his demons! This will allow them ample time to carry out to completion and success the work that Jehovah God has assigned to be done during this first thousand years of His new order. Neither they nor Jesus Christ will have any successors, who might come along into office and try to reverse the things that they have accomplished or insist on carrying on things in another way. According to Revelation 20:7-10, Satan the Devil and his demons will, after being let loose at the end of the thousand years, try to reverse matters. They will try to undo everything that was accomplished by the millennial government for God's glory and man's blessing, but they will not succeed. Any humans that Satan then succeeds in misleading will then find their rebellion against divine rulership to be ineffective and short-lived. With Satan and his demons these earthly rebels will be obliterated from the realm of the living.

[29] The millennial reign of Jesus Christ and his 144,000 Kingdom joint heirs will not prove to be in vain. The restoration of mankind to human perfection in an earth-wide paradise will stand as an accomplished fact. Yes, Jesus Christ the Son of God will not have died in vain, and the purpose for which God lovingly

---

28. (a) For the 144,000, what will be the benefit of reigning for a thousand years without successors? (b) What will Satan and his demons do, when let loose, regarding divine rulership, and what will happen to the misled ones?
29. (a) How, at the end of the thousand years, will things show that not in vain did God send his Son or His Son die? (b) In what way will Christ and the 144,000 have reason to rejoice that they did not reign for a thousand years in vain?

sent him into this world will not have failed. In the faithful upholders of Jehovah's universal sovereignty who loyally pass the test at the loosing of Satan for a little while, it will be overwhelmingly demonstrated that Almighty God the Creator can put men and women on this earth who will unbreakably maintain their integrity to Him. They will for this deserve to be declared righteous by the Supreme Judge Jehovah God and to be favored with the inviolable right to serve Him in peace and happiness in the earthly Paradise forever. (Revelation 20:5) At this outcome of the divine judgment of mankind Jesus Christ and his 144,000 associate kings will rejoice and know that their reign of a thousand years brought successful results.

[30] However, the glorious vision seen by the apostle John reveals to us that the 144,000 Kingdom joint heirs do more than rule as kings with Christ for a thousand years. Revelation 20:6 says of these 144,000 partakers of the "first resurrection" that "they will be priests of God and of the Christ." Why must they also be "priests" for a thousand years? What will this bring about that mere kingship does not accomplish? We shall not be satisfied about the coming thousand years until we find out.

---

30. What other office besides that of kings must the 144,000 carry out with Christ for a thousand years, and what questions does this raise?

CHAPTER 6

Priests for Ten Centuries
>   with No Scheming Priestcraft

HUMAN history is full of the records of priests, from the earliest times. Why mankind has been so misled, deceived, exploited and oppressed by priests is that the vast majority of these have not been priests of the one living and true God. This very fact was called to the attention of a priest who served the supreme god of the pagan Greeks nineteen hundred years ago. In what way?

2 This occurred about 47-48 C.E., in the city of Lystra, in the Roman province of Lycaonia, Asia Minor. The inhabitants of this city worshiped the god whom the Romans called Jupiter but whom the Greeks called Zeus. A glaring contrast came to be shown between the deity Zeus or Jupiter and the one living and true God, when two men preaching the kingdom of God came to the city. One of these men was Paul, who years previously had belonged to the Jewish sect of the Pharisees, and the other was Barnabas, who had been a Levite attached to the temple at Jerusalem. What now happened we shall let the medical doctor Luke relate to us:

3 "Now in Lystra there was sitting a certain man disabled in his feet, lame from his mother's womb, and he had never walked at all. This man was listening to Paul speak, who, on looking at him intently and seeing he had faith to be made well, said with a loud voice: 'Stand up erect on your feet.' And he leaped up and began walking. And the crowds, seeing what Paul had done, raised their voices, saying in the Lycaonian tongue: 'The gods have become like humans and have

---

1, 2. (a) Why have the priests of historical record so mistreated the people? (b) When was a contrast shown at Lystra between the Grecian god Zeus and the living God of the Jews?
3. What miraculous cure at Lystra caused the priest of Zeus there to want to offer sacrifice?

come down to us!' And they went calling Barnabas Zeus, but Paul Hermes [Mercury], since he was the one taking the lead in speaking. And the priest of Zeus, whose temple was before the city, brought bulls and garlands to the gates and was desiring to offer sacrifices with the crowds.

[4] "However, when the apostles Barnabas and Paul heard of it, they ripped their outer garments and leaped out into the crowd, crying out and saying: 'Men, why are you doing these things? We also are humans having the same infirmities as you do, and are declaring the good news to you, for you to turn from these vain things to the living God, who made the heaven and the earth and the sea and all the things in them. In the past generations he permitted all the nations to go on in their ways, although, indeed, he did not leave himself without witness in that he did good, giving you rains from heaven and fruitful seasons, filling your hearts to the full with food and good cheer.' And yet by saying these things they scarcely restrained the crowds from sacrificing to them."—Acts 14:8-18, *margin*.

[5] Some of the people in Lystra became disciples of Jesus Christ and worshipers of the "living God," but not the crowds of people in general. How fickle and unstable the religiously excited crowds are was shown by the fact that sometime later they permitted Jewish enemies of Christianity to persuade them to the point of stoning the miracle-working Paul, leaving him lying, as if dead, outside the city. Evidently the city priest of Zeus did not object, and the crowds of Lystra continued on worshiping Zeus and letting this priest of Zeus go on misleading and exploiting them. And the Jewish persecutors of Christianity were pleased to have it that way in Lystra.—Acts 14:19-22.

[6] According to the record, even Jewish priests in

4. How did Barnabas and Paul prevent sacrificing from being made to them?
5. What later on showed how fickle religiously excited crowds are, and so what priestcraft continued on at Lystra?
6. How does the record concerning Jesus' trial and impalement prove that even priests of the living God can turn out bad?

the service of the "living God" have turned out bad. For example, on that notorious Passover Day of 33 C.E., when the crowds were clamoring for the impalement of Jesus Christ and the Roman governor tried to restrain them, asking, "Shall I impale your king?" who were the ones leading in rejecting Jesus Christ as king of the Jews? The record says: "Pilate said to them: 'Shall I impale your king?' The chief priests answered: 'We have no king but Caesar.' At that time, therefore, he handed him over to them to be impaled." (John 19:14-16) Later that day, when passersby were speaking abusively of Jesus while hanging nailed on the execution stake at Calvary, who were among those deriding him? The plain-speaking record tells us: "In like manner also the chief priests with the scribes and older men began making fun of him and saying: 'Others he saved; himself he cannot save! He is King of Israel; let him now come down off the torture stake and we will believe on him. He has put his trust in God; let Him now rescue him if He wants him, for he said, "I am God's Son." ' "—Matthew 27:39-43.

⁷ By the mention of "chief priests" is meant specifically Annas (who had been deposed from being high priest) and his son-in-law Caiaphas. (Luke 3:1, 2; John 18:13, 24; Acts 4:5, 6) When these chief priests and the rest of the Jerusalem Supreme Court (the Sanhedrin) commanded the Christian apostles Peter and John "nowhere to make any utterance or to teach upon the basis of the name of Jesus," Peter and John said to those chief priests: "Whether it is righteous in the sight of God to listen to you rather than to God, judge for yourselves. But as for us, we cannot stop speaking about the things we have seen and heard." (Acts 4:18-20) Sometime afterward all twelve apostles of Jesus Christ were before that same Jerusalem Supreme Court, and the high priest as the presiding officer heard these apostles say to him

---

7. When Peter and John and later the twelve apostles were before the Jewish Sanhedrin of Jerusalem, what became evident regarding the relationship of the chief priests to God?

and all the rest of the Court: "We must obey God as ruler rather than men." (Acts 5:29) It was evident that those Jewish chief priests had ceased to serve the "living God." They no longer represented Him.

[8] In the face of such a Biblical record, it is not without parallel that the men bearing the title of "priest" in the religious systems of Christendom have made such an odious, despicable record for themselves, as religious and secular histories show. It would make a person shudder and become fearful if he thought that earthly priests like that were to be included among those of whom Revelation 20:6 says: "They will be priests of God and of the Christ, and will rule as kings with him for the thousand years." We are glad that the inspired Holy Scriptures rule such men out of fitness for the millennial priesthood with Jesus Christ in the heavens.

[9] But, in all fairness, it must be said that not all the Jewish priests serving at the temple in Jerusalem turned out to be bad priests. The Bible record assures us of this after telling of how the then governing body of the Christian congregation straightened out a difficulty that had arisen in the Jerusalem congregation. Acts 6:7 goes on to say: "Consequently the word of God went on growing, and the number of the disciples kept multiplying in Jerusalem very much; and a great crowd of priests began to be obedient to the faith."

[10] Of course, after getting baptized in the name of the Lord Jesus as the Messiah and Son of God, those priests of the family line of Aaron the brother of the prophet Moses gave up their jobs as priests at the temple in Jerusalem. In the same way Joseph Barnabas of Cyprus gave up his job as a Levite at the

8. What men with a record that runs parallel with that of those Jewish chief priests will be ruled out of the millennial priesthood with Christ?
9. What does the Bible show as to whether all the Jewish priests were like those chief priests?
10. What happened to the temple job of the priests and Levites that believed in Jesus, and of what priesthood did they become members?

same temple. (Acts 4:36, 37) However, those ex-priests now became members of a grander priesthood. This was the "royal priesthood" of which the apostle Peter assured the Christians who had the heavenly hope, saying: "But you are 'a chosen race, a royal priesthood, a holy nation, a people for special posses-sion, that you should declare abroad the excellencies' of the one that called you out of darkness into his wonderful light."—1 Peter 2:9; 1:3, 4.

[11] Remarkably, though, no priesthood on earth fur-nished the High Priest of that "royal priesthood," that "kingdom of priests." (Exodus 19:6) Jesus Christ was indeed a Jew or Israelite according to the flesh, but he was not born in the family line of Aaron of the tribe of Levi, to which the Jewish priesthood was restricted. Being the "son of Mary," Jesus was born into the royal family of David and hence into the tribe of Judah. "For it is quite plain that our Lord has sprung up out of Judah, a tribe about which Moses spoke nothing concerning priests." (Hebrews 7:14) So it cannot be said that Jesus Christ's heavenly High Priesthood was based on his having been a human priest on earth. How he became a priest besides being a king we must examine here. However, his true priesthood was patterned after that of Jewish high priest Aaron.

THE VALUE OF A TRUE PRIEST OF THE "LIVING GOD"

[12] Of what value is a priest, anyhow? Well, he does something that a mere king cannot do. Speaking, not of a valueless priesthood of a pagan god, but of the priesthood of the family of Aaron the Levite, Hebrews 5:1-3 says: "For every high priest taken from among men is appointed in behalf of men over the things per-taining to God, that he may offer gifts and sacrifices for sins. He is able to deal moderately with the ig-norant and erring ones since he also [like High Priest

11. Why was Jesus Christ not a human Jewish priest on earth, but after whose high priesthood was his true priesthood patterned?
12. According to Hebrews 5:1-3, of what value is a priest, anyhow?

Aaron] is surrounded with his own weakness, and
on its account he is obliged to make offerings for
sins as much for himself as for the people."

[13] If there were no human sins against the "living
God," there would be no need of a priest, particularly
a high priest. The perfect man Adam in the Garden
of Eden needed no priest, for he was created sinless
by Jehovah God, who is not the source of sin. (Genesis
2:7, 8; Ecclesiastes 7:29) Jesus Christ, who is called
"the last Adam," was born into a race of sinners, but
he needed no priest, for he had a virgin birth through
Mary and his life was direct from God. He was born
sinless and grew up sinless and remained sinless down
to his sacrificial death. (1 Corinthians 15:45-47; Hebrews 7:26; 1 Peter 2:21-24) Because of his sinlessness, he could become a high priest and offer a perfect
sacrifice.

[14] Who made Jesus Christ a high priest, although
he was of the royal tribe of Judah? Did he decide to
make himself a high priest? No; he could not do that.
This is explained for us in Hebrews 5:4-6, in these
words: "Also, a man takes this honor, not of his own
accord, but only when he is called by God, just as
Aaron also was. So too the Christ did not glorify
himself by becoming a high priest, but was glorified
by him who spoke with reference to him: 'You are
my son; I, today, I have become your father.' Just
as he says also in another place: 'You are a priest
forever according to the manner of Melchizedek.' "

[15] By resurrecting Jesus Christ from the dead, Almighty God fulfilled those words quoted from Psalm
2:7 as written by David, and thus God became an
everlasting Father to the resurrected Jesus Christ,
and this one, being raised incorruptible, became the
everlasting Son of his heavenly Life-Giver, Jehovah
God. Being now an incorruptible Son, he could be

13. (a) When was there no need of a priest for mankind? (b) Why
was Jesus able to become a high priest and offer up a sacrifice?
14, 15. (a) How did Jesus become a high priest—by his own decision
to make himself such, or how? (b) By Jehovah's resurrecting Jesus,
how was Psalm 2:7 fulfilled, and how was Jesus then able to be a
priest like Melchizedek?

made a "priest forever" who needed no successor, and thus he would be a priest "according to the manner of Melchizedek!"—Acts 13:33-37; Psalm 110:4.

[16] That mysterious historic figure Melchizedek—who was he? He was not a Hebrew. He was not an Israelite. He was not a Levite. He was not a Jew. Suddenly, somewhere between the years 1943 and 1933 B.C.E., he appears on the scene in the neighborhood of where Jerusalem is today. "Abram the Hebrew" met him there while on his way back from warfare to near where Hebron is today. Here is all that the Hebrew Scriptures tell us about this encounter: "Then the king of Sodom went out to meet him after he returned from defeating Chedorlaomer and the kings that were with him, to the Low Plain of Shaveh, that is, the king's Low Plain. And Melchizedek king of Salem brought out bread and wine, and he was priest of the Most High God. Then he blessed him and said: 'Blessed be Abram of the Most High God, Producer of heaven and earth; and blessed be the Most High God, who has delivered your oppressors into your hand!' At that Abram gave him a tenth of everything."—Genesis 14:17-20.

[17] This does not say who the human father of Melchizedek was, so that we could say that Melchizedek inherited his priesthood from this father. Neither does it tell us when Melchizedek died, so that we can say that his priesthood ended then. So his priesthood extended to an indefinite time. In agreement with this, no successor is reported for Melchizedek. In these respects he could be used to foreshadow the High Priest Jesus Christ. Or, Jesus Christ could be said to be a "priest forever according to the manner of Melchizedek." Jesus Christ did not get his priesthood from Melchizedek; he was not a priestly successor of Melchizedek. He was only in "manner" like that king-priest of Salem.

16. Who was this Melchizedek, and, according to the book of Genesis, how did he come onto the scene of history?
17. In what respects did Melchizedek foreshadow Jesus Christ as High Priest, and was Jesus the successor of Melchizedek?

[18] Since the name Melchizedek means "King of Righteousness" and since Jesus Christ is in "manner" like him, this ensures that the High Priesthood of Jesus Christ for a thousand years will be a righteous priesthood without scheming, intriguing priestcraft. This is nicely explained for us in Hebrews 6:20 through 7:3, where we read: "Jesus who has become a high priest according to the manner of Melchizedek forever. For this Melchizedek, king of Salem, priest of the Most High God, who met Abraham returning from the slaughter of the kings and blessed him and to whom Abraham apportioned a tenth from all things, is first of all, by translation, 'King of Righteousness,' and is then also king of Salem, that is, 'King of Peace.' In being fatherless, motherless, without genealogy, having neither a beginning of days nor an end of life, but having been made like the Son of God, he remains a priest perpetually."

[19] How was Melchizedek "made like the Son of God" or used as an illustration of Jesus Christ the Son of God? In that Jehovah God used Melchizedek as a pattern when speaking about an oath that He was going to make in behalf of his Son Jesus Christ. God inspired King David to say, in Psalm 110:1-4: "The utterance of Jehovah to my Lord is: 'Sit at my right hand until I place your enemies as a stool for your feet.' . . . Jehovah has sworn (and he will feel no regret) : 'You are a priest to time indefinite according to the manner of Melchizedek!' " So, as in the case of Melchizedek, the priesthood of Jesus Christ was not made to rest upon human descent and inheritance. He did not need to get his priesthood either through Melchizedek or through the priestly family of Aaron of the tribe of Levi. Jesus'· priesthood rested upon the oath of Jehovah God and upon his being resurrected incorruptible from the dead to heavenly life at the right hand of God.

18. According to the name Melchizedek, what kind of priesthood will that of Jesus Christ be, and how does Hebrews 6:20 through 7:3 explain matters about Melchizedek?
19. How was Melchizedek "made like the Son of God" in the matter of priesthood, and so on what did Jesus' priesthood depend?

[20] The priesthood of the Levite family of Aaron was established by the Law that Jehovah God gave to the people of Israel through the mediator Moses at Mount Sinai, Arabia. But the family of Aaron, having inherited sin and imperfection from the transgressor Adam, did not and could not produce a perfect high priest; there was no priestly perfection produced by it. (Romans 5:12) So the situation of all mankind called for a change of priesthood from Jehovah God, a change from an imperfect, dying priesthood to a perfect, everlasting priesthood. So this called for a high priest like ancient Melchizedek. This is what is meant when Hebrews 7:11-14 says:

[21] "If, then, perfection were really through the Levitical priesthood, (for with it [the Levitical priesthood] as a feature the people were given the Law,) what further need would there be for another priest to arise according to the manner of Melchizedek and not said to be according to the manner of Aaron? For since the priesthood is being changed, there comes to be of necessity a change also of the law. For the man [Jesus Christ] respecting whom these things are said has been a member of another tribe, from which no one has officiated at the altar. For it is quite plain that our Lord has sprung up out of Judah, a tribe about which Moses spoke nothing concerning priests."

[22] The Jewish high priest Aaron and his successors in office were not made priests with an oath sworn by Jehovah God. But Jesus Christ, without any priestly connections on earth, was made a high priest by God's oath. His life was interrupted briefly by his dying as a perfect human sacrifice, but he was resurrected to heavenly life incorruptible to be a high priest forever like Melchizedek. The contrast between him and the Levitical priesthood of Aaron and his successors is set out in Hebrews 7:23-28, where we read:

[23] "Furthermore, many [sons of Aaron] had to be-

20, 21. (a) In behalf of dying mankind, why was there need of a change of priesthood, from that of Aaron to that like Melchizedek's? (b) How is this stated in Hebrews 7:11-14?
22, 23. (a) In contrast with the Levitical high priest, how was Jesus made a high priest? (b) According to Hebrews 7:23-28, how can Jesus as high priest save completely those approaching God through him?

come priests in succession because of being prevented by death from continuing as such, but he [the Greater Melchizedek] because of continuing alive forever has his priesthood without any successors. Consequently he is able also to save completely those who are approaching God through him, because he is always alive to plead for them. For such a high priest as this was suitable for us, loyal, guileless, undefiled, separated from the sinners, and become higher than the heavens. He does not need daily, as those high priests do, to offer up sacrifices, first for his own sins and then for those of the people: (for this he did once for all time when he offered himself up;) for the Law [of Moses] appoints men high priests having weakness, but the word of the sworn oath [of God] that came [more than four hundred years] after the Law appoints a Son, who is perfected forever."

²⁴ So what is the point being driven at here? This, as set out in the next two verses (Hebrews 8:1, 2), in this sum-up: "Now as to the things being discussed this is the main point: We have such a high priest as this, and he has sat down at the right hand of the throne of the Majesty in the heavens, a public servant of the holy place and of the true tent, which Jehovah put up, and not man." Should not mankind, therefore, be most thankful to God that they will have such a High Priest as this approaching God and pleading for them during the assigned thousand years during which Satan the Devil and his demons will be bound and in the abyss? Yes! Truly such a provision of God ensures the very best for mankind.

²⁵ Jesus Christ, when on earth as a perfect man, never served as a public servant at the temple in Jerusalem. He was not authorized by the Law of Moses to do so, for he was not a Levite or of the priestly family of Aaron. However, he served at a higher holy place, at a higher or more important temple, that was

24. Jesus Christ is high priest at what kind of "holy place," and for his priesthood during what period of time should mankind be thankful?
25. Why did Jesus not serve as high priest at the temple in Jerusalem, and of what was the Jerusalem temple a type?

not put up at Jerusalem by men such as King Herod the Great or Governor Zerubbabel or King Solomon. Those man-made temples, like the sacred tent of meeting that the prophet Moses set up, were merely typical, illustrative. (Exodus 40:1-33) There is no record that King Melchizedek built a temple in Salem and needed such a building to serve as "priest of the Most High God." So nothing like that in connection with Melchizedek can be used as a type. But the Greater Melchizedek, Jesus Christ, serves as High Priest at the antitypical holy place and temple, namely, "the holy place and the true tent, which Jehovah put up."

THE TRUE TEMPLE

26 The sacred tent put up by Moses at Mount Sinai and the temples at Jerusalem had two compartments, the first compartment being called The Holy and the second or innermost compartment being called The Most Holy or Holy of Holies, the Holiest of all.

27 In the first compartment, The Holy, the pieces of furniture were the golden table for the presentation of the loaves commonly called "the showbread" and the golden lampstand with seven branches topped by lamps, and the stationary golden incense altar. Here

26, 27. (a) Into what compartments were the sacred tent and the Jerusalem temple divided? (b) What were the pieces of furniture in the respective compartments of the tent and Solomon's temple?

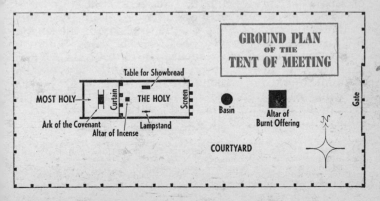

GROUND PLAN OF THE TENT OF MEETING

MOST HOLY

Curtain

THE HOLY

Screen

Table for Showbread

Ark of the Covenant

Altar of Incense

Lampstand

Basin

Altar of Burnt Offering

Gate

COURTYARD

N

in the light of the golden lampstand the high priest could arrange the loaves of presentation and offer fragrant incense at the altar. But in the innermost compartment or Most Holy there was, in the case of the tent pitched by Moses and the temple built by King Solomon, the sacred golden Ark of the Covenant, with its golden lid or cover surmounted by two golden cherubs facing each other with outstretched wings. The light in this innermost compartment or Most Holy was furnished by the miraculous light, called the Shekinah Light, that hovered above the propitiatory cover and between the two cherubs.

28 Before presenting the blood of the atonement sacrifices once each year on the Day of Atonement, the Aaronic high priest would take a portable incense burner or a hand censer and pass beyond the inner curtain that separated the first compartment from the innermost compartment (the Most Holy) and burn incense before the Ark of the Covenant in the illumination from the Shekinah Light. This would prepare matters for him to return later with the blood of the two atoning sacrifices and sprinkle this toward the propitiatory cover (the Mercy Seat) of the Ark of the Covenant. In this way he made atonement for the sins of himself and of his Levitical house or tribe and then for the sins of the people of Israel. This was the atonement procedure as outlined in the Law covenant of Moses.—Hebrews 9:1-10; Numbers 7:89.

29 The sacred tent of meeting was set up by Moses in the wilderness of Sinai on the first day of the spring month Nisan of the year 1512 B.C.E. King Solomon completed his temple at Jerusalem in 1027 B.C.E. and thereafter dedicated it on the fifteenth day of the autumn month of Tishri of the year 1026 B.C.E. (1 Kings 8:1, 2, 65, 66) But when did the antitypical tent or temple, the "true tent" with its "holy place," come into existence? It was while the typical temple

---

28. How did the Jewish high priest prepare matters for sprinkling the blood of the atonement sacrifices in the Most Holy, and for whose sins did he thus make atonement?
29. (a) When was the sacred "tent" pitched by Moses inaugurated, and when also Solomon's temple? (b) When was the true tent or temple brought into existence?

built by King Herod the Great was still standing in Jerusalem. It was in the early autumn of the year 29 of our Common Era. How was this so? What happened then to call for the true temple?

30 In that year 29 C.E. the antitypical High Priest came into existence, and, like the Levite high priest Aaron, he had to have a sacred tent or temple at which to officiate. This antitypical sacrificing High Priest is the Lord Jesus, anointed with God's holy spirit to be a spiritual high priest. This anointing with holy spirit came upon him after he was baptized in the Jordan River by John the Baptist. His thus becoming the Messiah or Anointed One at the age of thirty years occurred three and a half years before his sacrificial death for the sins of mankind. (Daniel 9:24, 25, 27; Luke 3:21-23) At this time the great antitypical Day of Atonement began, and Jesus Christ had something better than High Priest Aaron had on the typical atonement day back there in the year 1512 B.C.E., after the sacred tent or tabernacle had been set up. What was this? In Hebrews 8:3-6 and 9:11-14 we are told:

31 "Every high priest is appointed to offer both gifts and sacrifices; wherefore it was necessary for this one also to have something to offer. If, now, he were upon earth, he would not be a priest, there being men who offer the gifts according to the Law, but which men are rendering sacred service in a typical representation and a shadow of the heavenly things; just as Moses, when about to make the tent in completion, was given the divine command: For says he: 'See that you make all things after their pattern that was shown to you in the mountain.' But now Jesus has obtained a more excellent public service, so that he is also the mediator of a correspondingly better covenant, which has been legally established upon better promises.'

32 "However, when Christ came as a high priest

30, 31. (a) On what occasion and how did the antitypical High Priest come into existence? (b) What antitypical day for taking sins away then began, and how did what Jesus offered compare with what Aaron offered?
32. As typified in the case of Aaron, into what did Jesus Christ enter, and with what for cleansing our conscience from dead works?

of the good things that have come to pass, through the greater and more perfect tent not made with hands, that is, not of this creation, he entered, no, not with the blood of goats and of young bulls, but with his own blood, once for all time into the holy place [corresponding to the Most Holy of the tent] and obtained an everlasting deliverance for us. For if the blood of goats and of bulls and the ashes of a heifer sprinkled on those who have been defiled sanctifies to the extent of cleanness of the flesh, how much more will the blood of the Christ, who through an everlasting spirit offered himself without blemish to God, cleanse our consciences from dead works that we may render sacred service to the living God?"

[33] So, when the perfect man Jesus became God's anointed High Priest after his baptism in water, what was it that he had to offer to God in sacrifice? It was, not the body of some subhuman animal the blood of which could never wash human sins away, but his own perfect human body, which he had by reason of his birth by a virgin woman, Mary. He recognized that Almighty God had prepared and equipped him for this course of sacrifice. He recognized that at this marked time it was God's will for him to undertake this course of self-sacrifice. Accordingly, when he came to John the Baptist to be immersed in the Jordan River, he came presenting himself to God to do the divine will from now on. His baptism in water symbolized his presenting of himself to do God's will even to a sacrificial death. Concerning this, Hebrews 10:4-10 says:

[34] "It is not possible for the blood of bulls and of goats to take sins away. Hence when he comes into the world he says: 'Sacrifice and offering you did not want, but you prepared a body for me. You did not approve of whole burnt offerings and sin offering.' Then I said, 'Look! I am come (in the roll of the

33, 34. (a) By being immersed in the Jordan River, what did Jesus symbolize? (b) What had God prepared for the man Jesus, and why did he offer it, and how often?

book it is written about me) to do your will, O God.")'
After first saying: ("You did not want nor did you approve of sacrifices and offerings and whole burnt offerings and sin offering')—sacrifices that are offered according to the Law—then he actually says: ('Look! I am come to do your will.') He does away with what is first that he may establish what is second. By the said 'will' we have been sanctified through the offering of the body of Jesus Christ once for all time.")

[35] On the ancient typical atonement day the high priest Aaron applied some of the blood of the atonement victims to the altar and also burned the fat of the atonement victims upon this altar, which was in the middle of the courtyard in front of the sacred tent of meeting. (Leviticus 16:16-19, 25) What, then, was the antitypical "altar" upon which Jesus Christ as a spiritual high priest offered up the sacrifice of his perfect humanity? It was not a material altar like that copper altar in the courtyard of the tent of meeting. It was not the execution stake upon which he hung till dead at Calvary, for that stake was something accursed and was not sanctified by his precious blood. (Deuteronomy 21:22, 23; Galatians 3:13) Rather, it was something spiritual upon which Jesus Christ could offer up the value of his perfect human living body. It was the divine "will" or good pleasure. To do this "will" he came presenting himself. It was God's willingness to accept now a human sacrifice instead of animal victims. So, on the basis of this divine "will," Jesus offered the value of his human life.

[36] Thus the antitypical "altar" came into existence, concerning which Hebrews 13:10 says to the anointed Christians: ('We have an altar from which those who do sacred service at the tent have no authority to eat.') How materially minded and unscriptural it is, therefore, for certain priests of Christendom to erect a material "altar" in their church buildings or other

---

35. (a) On the typical Atonement Day, what was applied to the altar, and what was offered thereon? (b) What was the antitypical "altar" for Jesus' offering of himself?
36. Who are authorized to eat from this spiritual "altar," and with what result to themselves?

place of worship and claim to offer up the sacrifice of Christ again and again, as in their celebration of the "Mass"! Those who have the authority to eat from the true spiritual "altar" are "sanctified through the offering of the body of Jesus Christ once for all time."

[37] Just as the ancient copper altar stood in the middle of the courtyard before the sacred tent of meeting, so along with the antitypical spiritual "altar" there came into existence the antitypical "courtyard." This represents, not a locality or place, but a condition of a person on earth. Jesus Christ the anointed High Priest was in that antitypical courtyard because he was in the condition of a perfect human creature. His condition on earth was therefore literally just, righteous, faultless, unblemished. Like the sons of Korah the Levite, he found a resting place for himself at the grand altar of Jehovah's will in the courtyard of the true "grand tabernacle" of Jehovah God. (Psalm 84:1-3) He delighted in doing the divine will. —Psalm 40:8.

[38] Not only did the antitypical altar and courtyard then come into existence to accommodate the new spiritual High Priest, the anointed Jesus, but the antitypical tent or temple likewise came into existence. From then on the "true tent, which Jehovah put up," was at the disposal of the new spiritual High Priest.

[39] What is that "true tent" or temple? Is it a new special building that the Creator has made for himself up in the invisible heavens? No, for God does not need such a thing. The Most High God has always had a place of residence in heaven. He is not an all-pervasive spirit that is omnipresent, present everywhere at the same time. Being an intelligent Person, he has his location, his place of residence where he can be approached. Jesus Christ taught his disciples to pray:

---

37. (a) Along with the spiritual "altar," what came into existence as typified in connection with the ancient "tent"? (b) What did this courtyard typify in Jesus' case?
38, 39. (a) What else came into existence along with the antitypical courtyard and altar? (b) What question does this raise, and what words of Jesus show location for God?

'Our Father in the heavens, let your name be sanctified.' He warned us against despising any of the "little ones" who believe in him and explained why, saying: 'For I tell you that their angels in heaven always behold the face of my Father who is in heaven.' (Matthew 6:9; 18:10) That is, such heavenly angels have access to the divine Father.

⁴⁰ However, Almighty God can change the aspect of his exclusive place of residence. Thus at the time that he brought forth his spiritual High Priest by anointing Jesus Christ, just baptized, God could make his own heavenly residence take on a new aspect, having new appointments or features about it, with relation to mankind in their sin (not in relation to the sinless angels). The holiness of his heavenly residence was intensified in contrast with the exceeding sinfulness of mankind. His personal residence now presented itself as the holy place of a God who is just and yet who is merciful so as to accept a suitable perfect sacrifice in behalf of unholy mankind. But this sacrifice, or its value, must be presented by a High Priest who is sinless and holy and who can have personal acceptable access to God. So his heavenly throne becomes a propitiatory throne. In this way God made his heavenly residence take on the spiritual characteristics of the Most Holy or Holiest compartment of the typical tent or temple.

⁴¹ This is the Bible viewpoint. We remember that the high priest Aaron took the blood of the atonement day sacrifices into the Most Holy of the earthly tent of meeting, passing the inner curtain or veil in order to do so. (Leviticus 16:12-17; Hebrews 9:7) In order to fulfill the typical picture, High Priest Jesus Christ must enter the real Most Holy. Where does the Bible show it to be, and what is it?

⁴² Listen: 'Therefore it was necessary that the typ-

---

40. What could God do with reference to his heavenly residence to make it compare with the Most Holy of the sacred "tent"?
41, 42. (a) Into what was Aaron permitted to enter "once a year," and how? (b) What was the Most Holy into which Jesus Christ entered, at what time period, and how often?

ical representations of the things in the heavens should be cleansed by these means, but the heavenly things themselves with sacrifices that are better than such sacrifices. For Christ entered, not into a holy place made with hands, which [holy place] is a copy of the reality, but into heaven itself, now to appear before the person of God for us. Neither is it in order that he should offer himself often, as indeed the high priest enters into the holy place from year to year with blood not his own. Otherwise, he [Jesus] would have to suffer often from the founding of the world. But now he has manifested himself once for all time at the conclusion of the [typical] systems of things to put away sin through the sacrifice of himself." —Hebrews 9:23-26.

[43] Instead of climaxing the antitypical Day of Atonement by entering into a typical "holy place" inside the typical tent or temple, High Priest Jesus Christ entered "into heaven itself" where the "person of God" is. This heavenly residence of the very person of God is the true Most Holy, the Holy of Holies, the Holiest of all.

[44] In the typical tent or temple on earth the Most Holy was screened off by a curtain or veil, and so the Most Holy was said to be within the curtain. So that curtain represented the human fleshly barrier that has to be passed for one to pass from human life on earth into the invisible heavens. Jesus Christ by death and resurrection passed this barrier in order to enter into the heavenly Most Holy. This is what is meant in Hebrews 6:19, 20, where, after the heavenly hope of the 144,000 faithful disciples is spoken of, it says: "This hope we have as an anchor for the soul, both sure and firm, and it enters in within the curtain, where a forerunner has entered in our behalf, Jesus who has become a high priest according to the manner of Melchizedek forever." Hope anchored "within the curtain" is heavenly.

43, 44. (a) What, then, is God's holy residence as regards his temple? (b) What separated the Holy from the Most Holy, and how did Jesus Christ pass this in the antitype?

THE "HOLY" OF GOD'S SPIRITUAL TEMPLE

45 Let us not overlook the fact that the Most Holy was not all that there was to the earthly tent or temple. Besides its innermost compartment, the Most Holy, the tent or temple had another compartment in front of the dividing curtain. This compartment was called The Holy. (Hebrews 9:1-3) Since the Most Holy typified "heaven itself" where the "person of God" is, what did the Holy in front of the curtain or screen represent? Whereas the Most Holy could be entered by the high priest only "once a year" on the atonement day, the Holy could be entered regularly, not only by the high priest, but also by all the under-priests. The priests entered into this first compartment, The Holy, directly from the courtyard where the altar was; but they had to pass a screen or hanging that separated the Holy from the courtyard.

46 So the Holy represented a condition of greater sacredness than the courtyard did. As the Holy was screened off and its contents were thus hidden from the eyes of those in the courtyard, the Holy typified a spiritual condition superior to what is pictured by the courtyard, which pictured a human condition with a righteous standing before God. Jesus Christ entered the condition pictured by the Holy compartment when he was begotten by God's holy spirit after his water baptism and thus became a spiritual Son of God. (Matthew 3:13-17) By being anointed also with the spirit of God, Jesus as a spiritual Son of God was clothed with priestly office; he became God's High Priest, as pictured by High Priest Aaron.

47 From this standpoint it can be seen that the Holy compartment represented the spirit-begotten condition of those who are inducted into this spiritual priesthood. In that condition these spiritual priests on earth enjoy spiritual light as by a golden lampstand, eat spiritual food as from a golden table of loaves of

45. (a) What else was there to the "tent" besides the Most Holy?
(b) Who entered into the Holy, how often, and how?
46, 47. (a) When and how did Jesus enter into the antitypical Holy?
(b) So what does the Holy represent, and what privileges do the antitypical priests enjoy therein?

presentation, and offer up the incense of prayer and service to God as though standing at a golden incense altar.—Exodus 40:4, 5, 22-28.

[48] By measuring from the day of his baptism and anointing with holy spirit down to the day of his death (from 29 to 33 C.E.), Jesus Christ was in that spirit-begotten priestly condition pictured by the Holy compartment for three and a half years. His services in this condition could not be properly discerned and appreciated by mere natural men, even by his faithful disciples, because they looked at matters from a natural human standpoint. The day of the Festival of Pentecost of the year 33 C.E., with its pouring out of holy spirit, had not yet arrived. (John 7:39) Their discernment was blocked as by the "screen of the entrance of the tabernacle," which hid the things inside the Holy compartment.—Exodus 40:28, 29.

[49] Inside the Holy condition, the spirit-begotten priestly condition, the High Priest Jesus Christ on earth was blocked from direct approach to the heavenly presence of God because of still being in the flesh as a perfect human creature. There was that symbolic "curtain" between him and the heavenly Most Holy, just as when Moses "put the curtain of the screen in place and shut off approach to the ark of the testimony."—Exodus 40:21.

[50] Jesus Christ as High Priest passed that symbolic curtain of the "true tent" on Nisan 16 of the year 33 C.E., by being resurrected from the dead, no longer just spirit-begotten and in the flesh, but now fully brought forth as a spirit Son of God in the invisible heavens. The apostle Peter states it correctly when he writes: "Even Christ died once for all time concerning sins, a righteous person for unrighteous ones, that he might lead you to God, he being put to death in the flesh, but being made alive in the spirit."

48. How long was Jesus in the condition pictured by the Holy, and why did his disciples not have clear discernment about him?
49. How was Jesus in the antitypical Holy blocked from direct approach to the heavenly Most Holy?
50. (a) When did Jesus Christ pass the inner "curtain," and how? (b) What oath concerning priesthood then went into effect toward Jesus Christ, and why?

(1 Peter 3:18) On that eventful day God's sworn oath concerning an everlasting priesthood "according to the manner of Melchizedek" went into effect toward Jesus Christ, now that he was rewarded with the "power of an indestructible life." (Hebrews 7:16, 24; Acts 13:33-37; Romans 1:1-4) After making appearances to his faithful disciples by special manifestation during the following forty days, he ascended to heaven and presented to God himself in the true Most Holy the value of his perfect human sacrifice.—Acts 1:1-11; Hebrews 9:24.

[51] With that presentation of the merit of Christ's sacrifice in the heavenly Most Holy, the great antitypical Day of Atonement ended. In the case of High Priest Aaron of the tribe of Levi, the national atonement day was only one literal twenty-four-hour day long. But in the case of High Priest Jesus Christ, the antitypical Day of Atonement proved to be a period of almost three years and eight months. Ten days after Jesus' ascension to heaven the evidence was given to his faithful disciples on earth that the merit of his perfect human sacrifice as presented to God in the heavenly Most Holy had been accepted. How? By the pouring out of holy spirit upon them at Jerusalem on Sunday, Sivan 6, the day of the Festival of Weeks or the day of Pentecost, of the year 33 C.E. (Acts 2:1-36) This marked something new with respect to the "true tent, which Jehovah put up." This we shall now see.

SPIRITUAL UNDERPRIESTS

[52] There is no record that King-Priest Melchizedek of ancient Salem had any underpriests. But the Son of God, who has become a "high priest according to the manner of Melchizedek" has underpriests. (Hebrews 5:8-10) This was foreshadowed by the priestly family of Aaron the Levite. Jehovah God called Aaron

51. (a) When did the antitypical Day of Atonement end, and how long had it lasted? (b) How was the evidence given that the merit of Jesus' sacrifice had been accepted in the Most Holy?
52. (a) How was it foreshadowed that the Greater Melchizedek has underpriests? (b) When was the Aaronic priesthood installed, and what "holy sign" was put on Aaron's head?

to be the high priest of Israel and his sons to be under-priests to him. On the first day of the spring month of Nisan of the year 1512 B.C.E., the prophet Moses obeyed God's command and proceeded to install Aaron and his sons in the priesthood. (Exodus 40:1, 2, 12-16; 29:4-9; Leviticus 8:1-13) Among the articles of dress of the high priest "they made the shining plate, the holy sign of dedication, out of pure gold and inscribed upon it an inscription with the engravings of a seal: 'Holiness belongs to Jehovah.'"—Exodus 39:30.

⁵³ So, when dressing his brother Aaron for installation as high priest, Moses carried out Jehovah's command: "And you must set the turban upon his head and put the holy sign of dedication upon the turban. And you must take the anointing oil and pour it upon his head and anoint him." (Exodus 29:6, 7) Because this "holy sign of dedication" was the "shining plate" of pure gold, many translators of the Hebrew Scriptures prefer to render this expression "the holy diadem," "the diadem of holiness." (See Exodus 29:6, footnote; *Jerusalem Bible*) Of course, the regular Hebrew words for "diadem" and "crown" are different from the Hebrew word here rendered "sign of dedication." In Leviticus 21:12 this latter Hebrew word is applied to the anointing oil upon the high priest's head, for we read: "He should also not go out from the sanctuary and not profane the sanctuary of his God, because the sign of dedication, the anointing oil of his God, is upon him." The Hebrew word is derived from the verb *na·zar'*, which is translated "dedicate" in Hosea 9:10.—*An American Translation; NW*.

⁵⁴ Unquestionably, the high priest Aaron and his successors in office were men dedicated to Jehovah God by reason of their official installation. (Exodus 29:30, 35) Because of being anointed with the holy anointing oil, the high priest was called "the anointed one," or Messiah (Leviticus 4:3, 5, 16; 6:22), the same

---

53. (a) In thus adorning the turban of High Priest Aaron, what command of Jehovah did Moses obey? (b) From what Hebrew verb is the term for "sign of dedication" derived?
54, 55. (a) What was the anointed high priest called, and what did the anointing of him typify? (b) Did John the Baptist anoint Jesus with holy spirit, or who did?

as later for the anointed kings of Israel. (1 Samuel 24:6, 10; 26:9-11; Lamentations 4:20) So, after our being told the names of the four sons and underpriests of High Priest Aaron, we read: "These were the names of Aaron's sons, the anointed priests whose hands had been filled with power to act as priests." (Numbers 3:1-3) When Moses, the mediator between Jehovah God and the nation of Israel, anointed his older brother Aaron to be high priest, it had a typical meaning. It typified that God would anoint his Son Jesus with the holy spirit after Jesus came up from the waters of baptism.

⁵⁵ John the Baptist was the son of a Levite priest, namely, Zechariah of the priestly division of Abijah. However, John merely baptized Jesus in the Jordan River; he did not anoint Jesus to be a spiritual high priest. (Luke 1:5-17; 3:21-23; Mark 1:9-11) God alone could anoint Jesus with the holy spirit.

⁵⁶ With reference to Jesus, John the Baptist had said: "After me someone stronger than I am is coming; I am not fit to stoop and untie the laces of his sandals. I baptized you with water, but he will baptize you with holy spirit." God had told John of the coming of this one, for John said: "Even I did not know him, but the very One who sent me to baptize in water said to me, 'Whoever it is upon whom you see the spirit coming down and remaining, this is the one that baptizes in holy spirit.'" (Mark 1:7, 8; John 1:33) So Jesus was not only himself anointed with holy spirit to be the spiritual high priest, but was also to be empowered to baptize others with holy spirit. But when would he baptize with holy spirit? Not before his death as a perfect human sacrifice.

⁵⁷ After his resurrection from the dead, he made materialized fleshly bodies and made visible appearances to his disciples who were still in Jerusalem. What did he then tell them about the holy spirit? Acts 1:4, 5 tells us: "And while he was meeting with

---

56, 57. (a) What did John the Baptist say that Jesus would be empowered to do? (b) Before Jesus left his disciples, what did he tell them about baptism with holy spirit?

them he gave them the orders: 'Do not withdraw from Jerusalem, but keep waiting for what the Father has promised, about which you heard from me; because John, indeed, baptized with water, but you will be baptized in holy spirit not many days after this.'

[58] This proved to be ten days after his ascension to heaven. It proved to be Sivan 6 of the year 33 C.E., the Day of the Festival of Weeks (or Pentecost), when the Jewish high priest at the temple in Jerusalem presented to God two loaves of leavened bread as first-fruits of the wheat harvest. (Leviticus 23:15-21) On this same day, in antitypical fashion, the heavenly High Priest Jesus Christ presented to Jehovah God the Christian congregation as a firstfruits to Him. (Revelation 14:4) He did this by serving as a channel for the pouring out of holy spirit upon his waiting disciples in Jerusalem. It was a beginning of the ful-fillment of the prophecy of Joel 2:28, 29, and the spirit-filled apostle Peter explained it this way, saying to thousands of Jewish spectators:

[59] "This Jesus God resurrected, of which fact we are all witnesses. Therefore because he was exalted to the right hand of God and received the promised holy spirit from the Father, he has poured out this which you see and hear. Actually David did not ascend to the heavens, but he himself says, 'Jehovah said to my Lord: "Sit at my right hand; until I place your enemies as a stool for your feet."' Therefore let all the house of Israel know for a certainty that God made him both Lord and Christ, this Jesus whom you impaled.'" —Acts 2:14-21, 32-36.

[60] In this way Jesus Christ baptized his faithful dis-ciples with the holy spirit. This had been foreshad-owed long previously, on Nisan 1, 1512 B.C.E. This was when Moses carried out Jehovah's orders and anointed with holy anointing oil the sons of High Priest Aaron. About this we read: "Then Jehovah

58, 59. (a) When did this baptism occur, and how did Jesus Christ fulfill antitypically what the high priest did that day at the temple? (b) What prophecy of Joel began fulfilling there, and how did Peter connect Jesus with the matter? 60. How had Jesus' thus pouring out holy spirit been foreshadowed by Moses' action on Nisan 1, 1512 B.C.E.?

spoke to Moses, saying: 'On the day of the first month, on the first of the month, you are to set up the tabernacle of the tent of meeting. Then you must bring Aaron and his sons near to the entrance of the tent of meeting and wash them with water. And you must clothe Aaron with the holy garments and anoint him and sanctify him, and so he must act as priest to me. After that you will bring his sons near and you must clothe them with robes. And you must anoint them just as you anointed their father, and so they must act as priests to me, and their anointing must serve continually for them as a priesthood to time indefinite during their generations.' And Moses proceeded to do according to all that Jehovah had commanded him. He did just so.'—Exodus 40:1, 2, 12-16.

[61] Thus the four sons of Aaron were anointed as the first underpriests of Israel. But thereafter, their successors on being inducted into office as underpriests were not given an individual anointing with the holy anointing oil. Their just being invested with the official garments of an underpriest was considered sufficient. The anointing of the first four underpriests served as a representation for them. However, each successor to the high priest Aaron was individually anointed. (Numbers 3:1-3; Exodus 29:29, 30; Numbers 20:23-29; Deuteronomy 10:6) Nevertheless, the entire priesthood of Israel was to be considered as an anointed class according to the anointing of the original members.

[62] In the antitypical fulfillment, by anointing the 144,000 faithful disciples with holy spirit, the heavenly Jesus Christ acts as God's Representative and makes them spiritual priests, his underpriests over whom he is High Priest. That is why the apostle John could write with reference to Jesus Christ as follows: 'Jesus Christ, 'the Faithful Witness,' 'The firstborn from the dead,' and 'The Ruler of the kings of the earth.' To him that loves us and that loosed us from our sins

by means of his own blood—and he made us to be a kingdom, priests to his God and Father—yes, to him be the glory and the might forever. Amen.' Also: "You were slaughtered and with your blood you bought persons for God out of every tribe and tongue and people and nation, and you made them to be a kingdom and priests to our God, and they are to rule as kings over the earth."—Revelation 1:5, 6; 5:9, 10.

⁶³ There is another inspired witness to the fact—the apostle Peter. Writing a few years before the temple at Jerusalem was destroyed by the Romans (in 70 C.E.) and the Levitical priests there were to lose their jobs, Peter said to the spirit-anointed Christians with a heavenly hope: "These are stumbling because they are disobedient to the word. . . . But you are 'a chosen race, a royal priesthood, a holy nation, a people for special possession, that you should declare abroad the excellencies' of the one that called you out of darkness into his wonderful light."—1 Peter 2:8, 9.

⁶⁴ Their being now a priesthood meant a new standing with relation to the "true tent" or temple, which was put up, not by human hands, but by Jehovah God. It meant that they were now in the priestly spirit-begotten condition that was typified by the Holy compartment of the ancient "tent of meeting" set up by Moses. This was just as in the case of the High Priest Jesus Christ during the time from his anointing with holy spirit down to the time of his death as a perfect human creature. So, like him, they enjoy, while still on earth in their fleshly bodies, the spiritual enlightenment as shed by the antitypical golden lampstand; they eat from the spiritual food as typified by two stacks of loaves of presentation on the golden table; they offer up prayers and fervent service to God as though offering up incense at the golden incense altar in the Holy of the tent of meeting.

63. How did the apostle Peter by letter testify to the priesthood of the anointed disciples of Jesus?
64. So, in what condition are those anointed disciples as typified in the ancient "tent of meeting," and, like Jesus, what privileges do they enjoy in that condition?

⁶⁵ To these in the spirit-begotten condition pictured by the typical Holy, it is written: (You have an anointing from the holy one; all of you have knowledge. These things I write you about those who are trying to mislead you. And as for you, the anointing that you received from him remains in you, and you do not need anyone to be teaching you; but, as the anointing from him is teaching you about all things, and is true and is no lie, and just as it has taught you, remain in union with him.)—1 John 2:20, 26, 27.

⁶⁶ To those in the spirit-begotten priestly condition typified by the Holy compartment in which the Aaronic priests were permitted to enter and serve, it is further written by the apostle Paul: (He who guarantees that you and we belong to Christ [Anointed One] and he who has anointed us is God. He has also put his seal upon us and has given us the token of what is to come, that is, the spirit, in our hearts,)' —2 Corinthians 1:21, 22.

⁶⁷ Inasmuch as these 144,000 are spiritual priests under the heavenly High Priest Jesus Christ, they have the authority to eat from the sacrifice of Jesus Christ on the "altar" of God's "will," and those who unbelievingly rejected Jesus as being the true Messiah or Christ had no authority to eat of his sacrifice on God's antitypical "altar." Without presumption the inspired writer could say to the believing Christianized Hebrews, in Hebrews 13:10-15: (We have an altar from which those who do sacred service at the tent have no authority to eat. For the bodies of those animals whose blood is taken into the holy place by the high priest for sin are burned up outside the camp. Hence Jesus also, that he might sanctify the people with his own blood, suffered outside the gate [of Jerusalem]. Let us, then, go forth to him outside the camp, bearing the reproach he bore, for we do not have here a city that continues, but we are earnestly

65. To those in the condition pictured by the Holy, what did the apostle John write about their anointing?
66. To such ones in the condition pictured by the Holy, what did the apostle Paul write concerning their anointing?
67. To the Christianized Hebrews, what did the inspired writer say about eating from an altar and about sacrificing?

seeking the one to come. Through him let us always offer to God a sacrifice of praise, that is, the fruit of lips which make public declaration to his name.

⁶⁸ Since these spiritual underpriests have the divine authority and eat of the sacrifice upon God's true "altar," this means that they are also in the condition pictured by the courtyard in which the copper altar of sacrifice was located. This is the condition of being declared righteous or justified by God through their faith in the sacrificed Jesus Christ. When the High Priest Jesus Christ took the value of his sacrificial "blood" and entered into the heavenly Most Holy and presented this directly to Jehovah God, then, from the day of Pentecost of 33 C.E. onward, the benefits of his perfect human sacrifice began to apply to the disciples on earth because of their faith. By faith, with a heart of appreciation, they ate of Christ's sacrifice that was offered on the basis of God's will. In this way they gained the forgiveness of their sins. By granting them this forgiveness and thereby counting them as being sinless in the flesh, God declared them righteous or justified them. In this way he brought them into the antitypical courtyard. In proof that they have this standing, we read:

⁶⁹ "We believe on him who raised Jesus our Lord up from the dead. He was delivered up for the sake of our trespasses and was raised up for the sake of declaring us righteous. Therefore, now that we have been declared righteous as a result of faith, let us enjoy peace with God through our Lord Jesus Christ, through whom also we have gained our approach by faith into this undeserved kindness in which we now stand; and let us exult, based on hope of the glory of God. Much more, therefore, since we have been declared righteous now by his blood, shall we be saved through him from wrath."—Romans 4:24 through 5:2, 9.

68, 69. (a) Their eating from the altar indicates that they are in what location antitypically, and how did they get there? (b) In proof that they have this standing, what was written to Roman Christians?

[70] Giving further assurance that these spiritual underpriests are reckoned by God as being sinless, without condemnation, in the flesh while yet on this earth, it is written: "Thanks to God through Jesus Christ our Lord! So, then, with my mind I myself [the apostle Paul] am a slave to God's law, but with my flesh to sin's law. Therefore those in union with Christ Jesus have no condemnation. For the law of that spirit which gives life in union with Christ Jesus has set you free from the law of sin and of death." (Romans 7:25 through 8:2) This righteous, uncondemned standing before God while they are still in the imperfect, sin-laden flesh is what is pictured by the ancient courtyard in which the copper altar of sacrifice stood and at which the Aaronic priests served. They can add nothing to the value or merit of Christ's sacrifice for sins by any fleshly sacrifices of their own. That is why they offer to God through Christ the "sacrifice of praise" and the doing of Christian good. They see the absolute valuelessness of performing what is called the "sacrifice of the Mass" in some church.

[71] While still on the earth in the flesh, these underpriests, clad in the robes of imputed righteousness, are also in that spirit-begotten condition pictured by the Holy compartment of the typical tent or temple. Yet, like their High Priest Jesus Christ, they entertain the hope of entering into the heavenly Most Holy where God thrones in person. What now prevents them from entering directly into that true Most Holy is the fleshly barrier, their yet living in the flesh. This fleshly barrier was pictured by the inner curtain that screened off the Holy compartment of the tent from the Most Holy where the golden Ark of the Covenant with its Shekinah Light was located. Jesus Christ pioneered the way for them "through the curtain" and into the

70. (a) Giving further assurance of their uncondemned condition before God while they are still in the flesh, what is written in Romans? (b) By any sacrifices on their part, can they add anything to the value or merit of Christ's sacrifice?
71. (a) The Christians thus declared righteous are also in what location antitypically? (b) What separates them from the heavenly Most Holy, and who has pioneered a way for them thereinto?

real Most Holy. He entered as a "forerunner" for them into the Most Holy "within the curtain." (Hebrews 6: 19, 20) So he inaugurated this new way into heavenly life.

⁷² Hence these 144,000 spiritual underpriests are told to take courage in their efforts to prove worthy to be admitted to "within the curtain" by faithfulness until death of the fleshly body and a resurrection from the dead to life in the spirit. "Therefore, brothers," says the inspired writer in Hebrews 10:19-22, "since we have boldness for the way of entry into the holy place by the blood of Jesus, which [way] he inaugurated for us as a new and living way through the curtain, that is, his flesh, and since we have a great priest over the house of God, let us approach with true hearts in the full assurance of faith."

⁷³ When, after faithfully carrying out their earthly duties as spiritual underpriests even to the death, they are brought to life in the "first resurrection," they will have passed the fleshly barrier, the antitypical "curtain," and will be admitted into the heavenly Most Holy and see the indescribable glory of the living God. They will enter into his presence, not to do like the High Priest Jesus Christ, in presenting the merit of a perfect human sacrifice, but to serve with their High Priest in extending the benefits of Christ's sacrifice to needy mankind. (Revelation 20:6) Although there is a thousand years of heavenly priesthood to carry out, they will not need successors to serve after them. Like their glorified High Priest, they will have the "power of an indestructible life" and can fully accomplish their priesthood for a millennium without successors.—Hebrews 7:16, 24.

SYMPATHETIC, UNDERSTANDING PRIESTS

⁷⁴ What a blessed time that thousand years of this heavenly priesthood will be for sinful and dying man-

72. The 144,000 underpriests are encouraged to prove worthy of an entry into what, and how?
73. Passing the fleshly barrier, the spiritual underpriests will enter into what, and to do what?
74. (a) The propitiatory sacrifice of Christ paved the way for the 144,000 to gain what? (b) Why will that sacrifice make the thousand years of Christ's priesthood a blessed time for mankind?

kind! The High Priest thereof offered up to God the perfect sacrifice, not just for his 144,000 underpriests, but for *all* mankind. As one of those spiritual underpriests, John wrote nineteen centuries ago: "My little children, I am writing you these things that you may not commit a sin. And yet, if anyone does commit a sin, we have a helper with the Father, Jesus Christ, a righteous one. And he is a propitiatory sacrifice for our sins, yet not for ours only but also for the whole world's." (1 John 2:1, 2) The propitiatory sacrifice of Jesus Christ paved the way for the 144,000 underpriests to get free from sin and its condemnation to death and to gain everlasting life with their High Priest in heaven. That same propitiatory sacrifice carries enough merit to benefit the whole race of mankind; it is for the world's sins. As John the Baptist, pointing to the baptized Jesus Christ, cried out: "See, the Lamb of God that takes away the sin of the world!" —John 1:29.

[75] Jesus Christ the High Priest was able to help the congregation of his 144,000 underpriests to overcome sin and to be relieved of its condemnation to death. He can do the same thing for all the rest of mankind, especially the willing ones, who crave everlasting life with a good conscience toward God. Christ has a thousand years in which to do this. He is willing and desires to do it. He will absolutely make no failure of his millennial priesthood "according to the manner of Melchizedek." He will then help more than just the living, the "great crowd" that survive and come out of the great tribulation with which this worldly system of things ends. He will also help the unnumbered thousands of millions who are now sleeping the sleep of death in the graves of earth. (2 Timothy 4:1; Revelation 7:9-15; Acts 24:15) He will not let any of the precious merit of his perfect human sacrifice go unused, unapplied to the needy.

75. (a) Christ's ability to help the 144,000 underpriests while on earth is assurance of his ability to help whom else? (b) Who besides the great crowd of tribulation survivors will benefit from the merit of Christ's sacrifice?

[76] "While we were yet sinners, Christ died for us." (Romans 5:8) This evidenced that he had a sympathetic, merciful, self-sacrificing attitude toward fallen mankind, the inheritors of sin and death from wayward Adam and Eve. He was kind, patient, compassionate, helpful and understanding when he was on earth for thirty-three and a half years. Being a man himself and under temptation, he could understand man, and this enabled him to appreciate more keenly the kind of treatment that imperfect, sin-plagued mankind needed. Even when dying an innocent death on the execution stake at Calvary, he took uncomplainingly the abuse and reviling of misguided men. If, now, he was that way when on earth under the worst of conditions, we can be sure that he will be just the same way during his millennial priesthood toward mankind. This is the heartwarming argument that the inspired writer makes:

[77] "He is really not assisting angels at all, but he is assisting Abraham's seed. Consequently he was obliged to become like his 'brothers' in all respects, that he might become a merciful and faithful high priest in things pertaining to God, in order to offer propitiatory sacrifice for the sins of the people. For in that he himself has suffered when being put to the test, he is able to come to the aid of those who are being put to the test."—Hebrews 2:16-18. Compare Hebrews 5:1, 2.

[78] What Jesus Christ went through in order to prove himself a successful, faultless high priest on earth for the pure worship of God and for our sakes is described briefly for us in Hebrews 5:7-10, in these words: "In the days of his flesh Christ offered up supplications and also petitions to the One who was able to save him out of death, with strong outcries and tears, and he was favorably heard for his godly fear. Although he was a Son, he learned obedience from the things he suffered; and after he had been made perfect he became

---

76, 77. (a) How did Jesus, when on earth under test, comport himself toward men, and what does this ensure regarding his treatment of mankind during his millennial priesthood? (b) Thus why is Jesus Christ better able to come to the aid of those being put to the test? 78. What does Hebrews 5:7-10 show that Jesus went through for the sake of pure worship and for our sakes?

responsible for everlasting salvation to all those obeying him, because he has been specifically called by God a high priest according to the manner of Melchizedek.'

[79] His having the "power of an indestructible life" will enable him to carry through his millennial priesthood without successors to a God-honoring conclusion. He can help mankind clear through to a total elimination of sin and its terrible penalty death. He can do what the many Aaronic priests in succession could never do in the more than a millennium and a half of their sacred service. As it is written, in Hebrews 7:23-28:

[80] 'Furthermore, many had to become priests in succession because of being prevented by death from continuing as such, but he because of continuing alive forever has his priesthood without any successors. Consequently he is able also to save completely those who are approaching God through him, because he is always alive to plead for them. For such a high priest as this was suitable for us, loyal, guileless, undefiled, separated from the sinners, and become higher than the heavens. He does not need daily, as those high priests do, to offer up sacrifices, first for his own sins and then for those of the people: (for this he did once for all time when he offered himself up;) for the Law appoints men high priests having weakness, but the word of the sworn oath that came after the Law appoints a Son, who is perfected forever.'

[81] And what about the 144,000 spiritual underpriests, who "will be priests of God and of the Christ . . . for the thousand years"? (Revelation 20:6) Well, God foreordained them "to be patterned after the image of his Son." (Romans 8:29) They also have been born and grown up as men and women, as humans, but sinful, imperfect, badly disposed because of inheritance from rebellious Adam and Eve. They know therefore

---

79, 80. (a) Having the "power of an indestructible life" enables Christ to do what in behalf of mankind during his millennial priesthood? (b) What kind of priesthood did God's sworn oath produce in contrast with that produced by the Law?
81. (a) Why will the 144,000 underpriests be able to show sympathy and understanding toward mankind? (b) What will their having the "power of an indestructible life" enable them to do?

what it means to be a weak sinful human creature. So, too, like their High Priest Jesus Christ, they can be sympathetic and kindly disposed toward sinful, dying mankind. They were that way when yet on earth as spiritual underpriests. They will be just the same way when they share in the "first resurrection" and become heavenly underpriests. They will not have to die and regretfully leave their work uncompleted. No, but by having the "power of an indestructible life," they can join and keep up with their High Priest in carrying on the sin-removing work to a perfect completion. With what result? All the willing ones of mankind restored to sinless human perfection.

[82] The awe-inspiring accomplishment by this priesthood for a millennium without scheming priestcraft is described for us in these marvelous words: "Death will be no more, neither will mourning nor outcry nor pain be anymore. The former things have passed away." (Revelation 21:4) Yes, sin, which is the "sting producing death," will be gone! The sinfulness of mankind inherited from our self-seeking first human parents will be wiped out, with all its mournful, God-dishonoring effects. The Most High God Jehovah will again have a clean, pure and holy universe.

82. How does Revelation 21:4 describe the awe-inspiring accomplishment of that millennial priesthood, and what kind of universe will God again have?

CHAPTER 7

What to Expect of Judges
→ *   for a Thousand Years*

WHEN giving his preview of the thousand-year period soon to bring in almost unbelievable marvels, the inspired apostle John wrote: "And I saw thrones, and there were those who sat down on them, and power of judging was given them."—Revelation 20:4.

2 "Thrones," occupied by those to whom the power of judging was given! Is this a hopeful, consoling prospect, or does it cast a gray shadow over what would otherwise be a bright picture of the coming Millennium of millenniums? How did the apostle John himself view such a prospect? How are we today to view it? Are we not deeply disappointed in the judicial system that obtains today, even in Christendom? In our time, as at no previous time, is when the words of Psalm 82:5 have come true as a prophecy with respect to men in a judicial capacity who are like "gods" but who have proved false to their office: "They have not known, and they do not understand; in darkness they keep walking about; all the foundations of the earth are made to totter." Or, as the Roman Catholic Jerusalem Bible puts this Bible verse: "Ignorant and senseless, they carry on blindly, undermining the very basis of earthly society."

3 What mankind wants today is relief! And, happily, what the apostle John saw concerning those "thrones" of judgment was something to bring us great relief of mind, not something to stir up dark misgivings. Let us recall that, in prophetic vision,

---

1. What was given to those who sat on the thrones seen by John?
2. Why does the thought of "judgment," here introduced, tend to take away from what is otherwise a bright picture?
3, 4. (a) However, after what John saw just previously, what feeling should the sight of those thrones give us? (b) Why is it proper to expect relief for misjudged mankind from those "thrones"?

117

John had foreseen the war between the heavenly King of kings and the "kings of the earth" with their "armies" and the worldwide political organization. There were defeat and destruction of all those kings and their earthly supporters. This left vacant the thrones or seats of power from which the political rulers rendered judgment. Immediately after this, the apostle John saw the descent of God's angel to the vicinity of the earth and then the chaining of Satan the Devil and his demons and the hurling of them into the abyss, to be imprisoned under divine seal therein for a thousand years.—Revelation 19:11 through 20:3.

⁴ Such a destruction of the Devil-controlled system of things certainly called for a change in judgeships over mankind. Especially now that the heavenly control over mankind had passed over into the hands of the victorious King of kings, who "is called Faithful and True, and he judges and carries on war in righteousness." (Revelation 19:11-16) In the proper course of things, then, new thrones of judgment come into existence. Nothing else but a better body of judges could be expected to occupy those new thrones of judgment, which are set up by God's authority in the heavens. Judicial relief could thenceforth be expected to come to misruled, misjudged mankind.

⁵ This new set of judges over mankind, who are they? The words of Jesus Christ to a representative group of those prospective judges indicate who are to belong to that set of heavenly judges.

⁶ On the night of his betrayal and arrest and unjust trial by the highest court of Jerusalem, Jesus said to his remaining faithful apostles: "You are the ones that have stuck with me in my trials; and I make a covenant with you, just as my Father has made a covenant with me, for a kingdom, that you may eat and drink at my table in my kingdom, and sit on thrones to judge the twelve tribes of Israel." (Luke 22:28-30) Those faithful apostles were the foremost ones of the 144,000 who are taken by Jesus Christ into

---

5, 6. Who will be the judges occupying those "thrones," according to Jesus' words to his eleven faithful apostles before his betrayal?

the covenant for the heavenly kingdom, with its thrones of judgment. (Matthew 19:27, 28) Over these 144,000 associate judges will, of course, be the Presiding Judge, Jesus Christ.

[7] Here there come to mind the words of the apostle Paul, when he was haled before the Areopagus Court of Athens, about the year 51 C.E. In the course of his explanation of his case to these judges who seemed "to be more given to the fear of the deities than others are," Paul finally said: "True, God has overlooked the times of such ignorance, yet now he is telling mankind that they should all everywhere repent. Because he has set a day in which he purposes to judge the inhabited earth in righteousness by a man whom he has appointed, and he has furnished a guarantee to all men in that he has resurrected him from the dead." (Acts 17:22-31) So the judging of the inhabited earth will be "in righteousness," and the principal one by whom God will do the judging will be his resurrected Son, Jesus Christ.

[8] Designating by name the one appointed to do the judging, the apostle Paul, when writing his final letter to his fellow missionary Timothy, said: "I solemnly charge you before God and Christ Jesus, who is destined to judge the living and the dead, and by his manifestation and his kingdom." (2 Timothy 4:1) This divinely appointed Judge will act as a judicial officer in a way that no human judge on earth has ever acted or could act; he will judge more than just the living humans. He will also judge the dead humans. No mere human judge appointed by men could call back the dead in order to judge them. But this Judge of God's appointment can do so. And these human dead will have this millennial judgment even though it requires bringing them back from the dead in order that they may have this judgment to which they as

7. According to Paul's words to the Areopagus Court of Athens, how will the inhabited earth be judged in God's appointed time?
8, 9. (a) How will this appointed Judge be able to judge mankind as no human judge has done so? (b) According to Jesus' words in John 5:27-30, how will he see to it that everyone gets judged?

well as "the living" are entitled, through Christ's sacrificial death. Note Jesus' words:

⁹ "Just as the Father raises the dead up and makes them alive, so the Son also makes those alive whom he wants to. For the Father judges no one at all, but he has committed all the judging to the Son, in order that all may honor the Son just as they honor the Father. He that does not honor the Son does not honor the Father who sent him. And he has given him authority to do judging, because Son of man he is. Do not marvel at this, because the hour is coming in which all those in the memorial tombs will hear his voice and come out, those who did good things to a resurrection of life, those who practiced vile things to a resurrection of judgment. I cannot do a single thing of my own initiative; just as I hear [from the Father], I judge; and the judgment that I render is righteous, because I seek, not my own will, but the will of him that sent me."—John 5:21-23, 27-30.

¹⁰ Think of it! This Judge, who was known as the Son of man on earth, will glorify his millennial judgeship by liberating all those who are dead in the memorial tombs. The millennial Judgment Day will be resurrection day for all those in the memorial tombs, for whose sakes the Son of man died as a perfect human sacrifice. This means all the redeemed mankind aside from the 144,000 associate judges who have part in the "first resurrection," a heavenly resurrection. (Revelation 20:4-6) Are we now to think that this loving act of liberating the buried dead, this earthly resurrection, is to be used for a hurtful purpose toward the resurrected ones? Is a loving act done to lead to the hurt of one toward whom the act is performed? What we mean is this: This resurrection will be not only of those reckoned as righteous but also of those who are called "unrighteous" in comparison. "There is going to be a resurrection of both the righteous and the unrighteous." (Acts 24:15) We have no fears for the righteous, but what of the unrighteous?

---

10. (a) In behalf of that judgment, from what will the Judge liberate the dead? (b) What kind of act led to that liberation, and so what question arises about the purpose of the resurrection?

[11] Are the "unrighteous" ones to be shown the undeserved kindness of being resurrected only to face a stern, harsh judge who will rehearse all their past unrighteousness in their ears and show them in that way just why he is now sentencing them to the punishment of utter destruction from all existence? Of what practical benefit would resurrection be to these "unrighteous" ones if that was the objective in their case? Is that the purpose of resurrecting them in the case of that one of the "evildoers" who hung on an execution stake alongside Jesus Christ at Calvary and who said to him: "Jesus, remember me when you get into your kingdom"? His saying those sympathetic words to Jesus did not convert him from an evildoer into a saint, did it? Jesus' consoling reply to him did not mean that the evildoer was declared righteous or justified by faith, already forty-two days before the resurrected Jesus ascended to the presence of his heavenly Father to present the merit of his human sacrifice, did it? (Luke 23:39-43) The man still died as a condemned evildoer and must be counted as one of the "unrighteous" due to be raised up.

JUDGES OF PRE-CHRISTIAN TIMES

[12] What will the resurrection of the dead mean for those called "unrighteous" as well as for those called "righteous"? All of them died because of inheriting sin and its penalty death from the disobedient Adam and Eve. So they all died without having any righteousness of their own. (Romans 5:12; 3:23) So when they come back in the resurrection, untransformed as to their personal characteristics, even the "righteous" ones will not be humanly perfect, or free from imperfection and sinfulness. This was true in the cases of those men and women whom the prophets Elijah and Elisha and the Lord Jesus Christ and his apostles resurrected, brought back to life on earth. (Hebrews

11. (a) What question arises as to the objective of the resurrecting of the "unrighteous"? (b) How does the case of the dying evildoer sympathetic to Jesus have a bearing on the matter?
12. Why will the "righteous" as well as the "unrighteous" need more than liberation from the memorial tombs by resurrection?

11:35) In view of that, the "righteous" just as well as the "unrighteous" will need more than just liberation from the memorial tombs by resurrection from the dead. The "righteous" also will need liberation from sinfulness and human imperfection. Consequently, the heavenly Judge Jesus Christ cannot pronounce them at once actually innocent, perfect, free from condemnable sinfulness and hand down the decision on their very day of resurrection that they are worthy of eternal life on earth.

[13] If the matter of carrying out the duties of a judge were limited to just pronouncing decisions on the day that the resurrected "righteous" and "unrighteous" ones appear before him, why is it that a thousand years are assigned to him to serve as judge in behalf of humankind? Such a long period is assigned for a work to be done and not merely for a pronouncing of verdicts and sentences. In the Bible the ones whom God raised up as judges for his chosen people of pre-Christian times did more than merely settle disputes between individuals or hand down and execute judicial decisions. Those "judges" from God were deliverers of his chosen people. There is a book in the Bible that is specifically named "Judges." As a book it is a thriller! Therein we read of the courageous exploits of those men whom God, "the Judge of all the earth," raised up for the deliverance of his oppressed people. Hail the day of judgment that began when God raised up a judge to execute judgment for his afflicted ones!

[14] We read of Ehud who began his judgeship by lone-handedly killing the unusually fat King Eglon of the Moabites in his own conference room and then escaped, organized the Israelites and then led them to victory over Moabite oppressors. We read of Barak who demonstrated his being chosen for the judgeship of his nation by defeating the mighty military forces of Jabin the king of Canaan who made his military

---

13. (a) Why does God assign a thousand years for Jesus Christ to be Judge of mankind? (b) What does the book of "Judges" show regarding what to expect of God's millennial Judge?
14. Briefly, what do we read of Judges Ehud and Barak?

forces fearsome by equipping them with nine hundred war chariots that had iron scythes on their wheels.

[15] Then there was Gideon, an unassuming man, who with just three hundred men of faith in God put to rout the Midianites and Orientals who had swarmed into the land of Israel like numberless locusts. In the dead of the night, when Gideon and his three hundred almost encircled the sleeping enemy camp, they crashed unitedly their jars to the ground, held aloft their exposed torches, blew on their trumpets, and shouted, "Jehovah's sword and Gideon's!" The suddenly disturbed camp panicked and fled, slaughtering one another, and Gideon and his three hundred went in pursuit of the survivors. Many years afterward another crisis arose in the Promised Land, and Jehovah raised up Jephthah, an outcast man, to confront the arrogant Ammonites. Jephthah's zeal for God's cause was so fervent that he vowed of his own accord to sacrifice to God whatever came to meet him on his return home if he were given the victory. When, flushed with victory, he was met first by his lone child, his daughter, he showed his devotion to God by offering her for the divine service.

[16] Who, though, has not heard of Samson, the man whose birth was foretold to his parents and who proved to be the physically strongest man ever on earth! All alone he delivered his people Israel from the oppressive Philistines, but, in the day of death, as a blind prisoner of the Philistines, he caused the collapse of the temple of Dagon at Gaza, Philistia, upon more than three thousand celebrators, thereby killing more Philistines in this day of his death than he had put to death during his lifetime.

[17] Including these judges among the men of triumphant faith in God, the inspired Christian writer says, in Hebrews 11:32-34: "And what more shall I say? For the time will fail me if I go on to relate about Gideon, Barak, Samson, Jephthah, David as well as

---

15. Likewise, what do we read of Gideon, also Jephthah?
16, 17. (a) How did Samson serve as judge of Israel? (b) What does the inspired writer say about the judges in Hebrews 11:32-34?

Samuel and the other prophets, who through faith defeated kingdoms in conflict, effected righteousness, obtained promises, stopped the mouths of lions, stayed the force of fire, escaped the edge of the sword, from a weak state were made powerful, became valiant in war, routed the armies of foreigners."

[18] Of course, the Israelites in the days of those judges were responsible for their afflictions at the hand of the enemy, because they departed from the pure worship of Jehovah as the living God. But when they returned to him in sincere repentance and worship, He showed them favor. As the record in Judges 2:16-19 says:

[19] "So Jehovah would raise up judges, and they would save them out of the hand of their pillagers. And even to their judges they did not listen, but they had immoral intercourse with other gods and went bowing down to them. They quickly turned aside from the way in which their forefathers had walked by obeying the commandments of Jehovah. They did not do like that. And when Jehovah did raise up judges for them, Jehovah proved to be with the judge, and he saved them out of the hand of their enemies all the days of the judge; for Jehovah would feel regret over their groaning because of their oppressors and those who were shoving them around. And it occurred that when the judge died they would turn around and act more ruinously than their fathers by walking after other gods to serve them and bow down to them. They did not refrain from their practices and their stubborn behavior."

IMMORTAL HEAVENLY JUDGES

[20] However, the judges whom this same Jehovah God raises up in Jesus Christ and his 144,000 judicial associates will not die off and leave the inhabitants on

18, 19. (a) Who were responsible for the afflictions that came upon the Israelites after settling in the Promised Land? (b) Why was it necessary for a series of judges to be raised up for them?
20. (a) During the millennium, why will not mankind be left to itself again and again, as during the time of Israel's judges? (b) Why will even the "great crowd" of tribulation survivors need further deliverance?

earth to themselves, even though Satan the Devil and his demons have been removed from the vicinity by being abyssed. Possessed of the "power of an indestructible life," they will all serve continuously for the full judicial term of a thousand years. They will not just sit on thrones and hand down decisions and rulings, but they will act as deliverers, just as did the faithful judges who gained Jehovah's approval in ancient times. Even "the living," who survive the "great tribulation" under divine protection and live on after Satan and his demons are abyssed, will still need a further deliverance. Because of their righteous standing with God they are preserved alive on earth into the millennial day of judgment, but there is more in their case from which to be delivered. What is that? It is their sinfulness, imperfection, weakness and dying state with which they have been preserved clear through the destruction of this system of things and the hurling of Satan and his demons into the abyss.

[21] Likewise, in the case of "the dead," who need to be restored from the memorial tombs: Whether counted "righteous" or "unrighteous" on being awakened from the sleep of death, they all need to be freed from sinfulness, shortcomings, faultiness, human frailties, and proneness to death. The fact that any are counted as "righteous" does not mean that they are humanly and morally perfect in the flesh. Their being righteous in God's eyes, however, means that they are men and women of integrity toward God, as the patient Job of the land of Uz was. (Job 2:3, 9; 27:5; James 5:11; Ezekiel 14:14, 20) Or, like King David of Jerusalem who was not afraid to be judged by his God, for in Psalm 26:1-3, 11, David said:

[22] "Judge me, O Jehovah, for I myself have walked in my own integrity, and in Jehovah I have trusted, that I may not wobble. Examine me, O Jehovah, and put me to the test; refine my kidneys and my heart. For your loving-kindness is in front of my eyes, and

---

21, 22. (a) Why will the human dead, when resurrected, need further deliverance? (b) For what reason will some, like Job and David, be counted "righteous" when resurrected?

I have walked in your truth. As for me, in my integrity I shall walk. O redeem me and show me favor."

²³ Other men of pre-Christian times who died in their integrity, refusing to prove disloyal to Jehovah God by any sort of bargain or compromise with the ungodly, were the men and women named or spoken of in chapter eleven of the book written to Christianized Hebrews. They looked forward to a resurrection to life under better earthly conditions, under a better government, under which they could live forever in perfect peace and happiness and integrity to the living God. In expression of this it is written in Hebrews 11:35-40:

²⁴ "Women received their dead by resurrection; but other men were tortured because they would not accept release by some ransom, in order that they might attain a better resurrection. Yes, others received their trial by mockings and scourgings, indeed, more than that, by bonds and prisons. They were stoned, they were tried, they were sawn asunder, they died by slaughter with the sword, they went about in sheepskins, in goatskins, while they were in want, in tribulation, under ill-treatment; and the world was not worthy of them. They wandered about in deserts and mountains and dens and caves of the earth. And yet all these, although they had witness borne to them through their faith, did not get the fulfillment of the promise, as God foresaw something better for us, in order that they might not be made perfect apart from us."

²⁵ Dying in their integrity to God, these "righteous" ones will be raised in their integrity toward God, even though not raised in human perfection and faultlessness of conduct. They will not fear the great Judgment Day of a thousand years into which they have been ushered by resurrection. Their integrity that they de-

---

23, 24. (a) For the sake of what kind of resurrection did those pre-Christian men of integrity refuse to bargain with the ungodly? (b) What does Hebrews 11:35-40 have to say about such ones?
25, 26. (a) Why will those "righteous" ones, when resurrected, not fear Judgment Day? (b) Why will those "unrighteous" ones, when resurrected, be under a handicap in comparison with the "righteous"?

veloped before death and with which they will be raised up will give them an advantage over the "unrighteous" in advancing to actual human perfection in complete freedom from sinfulness. They will, as it were, have a head start over the "unrighteous" in that direction.

26 To this effect it is written: 'Anyone of little means who is walking in his integrity is better than the one crooked in his lips, and the one that is stupid.' Also: 'The righteous is walking in his integrity. Happy are his sons after him.' (Proverbs 19:1; 20:7) On the other hand, it will go much harder for the "unrighteous" ones, who down till death cultivated sinful tendencies and bad habits and evil cravings. These will be handicaps, disadvantages, encumbrances, to work against them in the race to win everlasting life in sinless human perfection on a paradisaic earth. Also, in this life many of these "unrighteous" ones have failed to take advantage of the spiritual opportunities and provisions that were at hand, but which they ignored, disdained, despised, or resisted. They thus have an unappreciative, obstinate disposition to master. Hence, it will be woeful for them. Jesus Christ gave examples of cases of this kind, when he said to the unrepentant cities of Chorazin, Bethsaida and Capernaum:

27 'Woe to you, Chorazin! Woe to you, Bethsaida! because if the powerful works had taken place in Tyre and Sidon that took place in you, they would long ago have repented in sackcloth and ashes. Consequently I say to you, It will be more endurable for Tyre and Sidon on Judgment Day than for you. And you, Capernaum, will you perhaps be exalted to heaven? Down to Ha'des you will come; because if the powerful works that took place in you had taken place in Sodom, it would have remained until this very day. Consequently I say to you people, It will be more endurable for the land of Sodom on Judgment Day than for you.' —Matthew 11:20-24.

27. How did Jesus illustrate the foregoing by the use of Chorazin, Bethsaida and Capernaum?

[28] Speaking to the generation of Jews who were adulterating their relationship with God by worldliness and basing their belief on visible signs, Jesus said: "Men of Nineveh will rise up in the judgment with this generation and will condemn it; because they repented at what Jonah preached, but, look! something more than Jonah is here. The queen of the south will be raised up in the judgment with this generation and will condemn it; because she came from the ends of the earth to hear the wisdom of Solomon, but, look! something more than Solomon is here."—Matthew 12:38-42.

[29] What surprises, then, there will be for many self-righteous religionists, self-satisfied, complacent formal religionists, who were sure in themselves that they were more righteous than those whom they called pagans or heathens! They will find that they were religious hypocrites, whereas the heathens whom they looked down upon were more sincere, more teachable, more appreciative, and less reprehensible because of their ignorance. Then the sincerity and attitude of persons less favored religiously will condemn the privileged people who neglected their opportunities indifferently or willfully. So there will be a just counter-balancing of matters as between the present-day advantaged persons and the disadvantaged ones.

THE ADVANTAGES OF JUDGMENT DAY

[30] There is no denying the truthfulness of the statement, in Romans 3:22, 23: "There is no distinction. For all have sinned and fall short of the glory of God." Hence, all on Judgment Day, "the living and the dead," urgently need to be delivered, by the help of the heavenly judges whom Jehovah God raises up, from all traces of sin and moral weakness and bodily imperfection with which they are ushered into the Judgment Day.

28, 29. (a) Why will the ancient Ninevites and the queen of the south condemn the Jewish generation of Jesus' day? (b) On Judgment Day, how will matters be counterbalanced as between the now advantaged ones and the religiously disadvantaged ones?
30, 31. (a) On Judgment Day, do all humans need to have their previous condition rehearsed before them to see whether they are innocent or guilty? (b) By the use of the Jews under the Law, what was demonstrated about all mankind?

The evidence and testimony are all against mankind, as comprehensively stated in Romans 3:23 and other scriptures, and this does not need to be rehearsed before those on judgment to see whether they are innocent or guilty. By the failure of the natural Jews to keep the Law that God gave them through Moses, it was demonstrated that no part of humankind, not even the favored Jews themselves, could keep God's law perfectly. Thus by this practical demonstration with the Jews under the Law, every human mouth was silenced from defending its user and all the world of mankind was proved guilty before God. It is just as the apostle Paul wrote long ago:

[31] "Now we know that all the things the Law says it addresses to those under the Law, so that every mouth may be stopped and all the world may become liable to God for punishment."—Romans 3:19.

[32] Because of being born sinful and condemned to death, mankind never had "a chance." It could never justify itself before the God of absolute perfection by doing perfect works of righteousness and ridding itself of sinfulness. So, Judgment Day does not offer mankind what is called "a second chance." Rather, it affords to mankind its first real opportunity to gain eternal life in human perfection and absolute innocence in an earthly Paradise. Judgment Day affords mankind the opportunity that Christ's perfect human sacrifice provides for them to be cleansed from sin and to be uplifted to the full "glory of God" from which they now fall short. In view of this fact it depends upon what "the living and the dead" do on Judgment Day as to whether they will possess the Paradise earth forever or not. Their past record is already made and is irreversible, with good effects or bad effects to themselves. Judgment Day will allow them to prove their sincere heart's desire to be done, finished, through with sin forevermore. The heavenly judges will be in office to help them with instructions and guidance.

32. (a) What should be said about humans having a "second chance" on Judgment Day? (b) On whom, then, will it depend as to whether they will live on the Paradise earth or not, and why?

[33] This opportunity on Judgment Day is pictured for us in Revelation 20:11-15, in this symbolic language: "And I saw a great white throne and the one seated on it. From before him the earth and the heaven fled away, and no place was found for them. And I saw the dead, the great and the small, standing before the throne, and scrolls were opened. But another scroll was opened; it is the scroll of life. And the dead were judged out of those things written in the scrolls according to their deeds. And the sea gave up those dead in it, and death and Ha'des gave up those dead in them, and they were judged individually according to their deeds. And death and Ha'des were hurled into the lake of fire. This means the second death, the lake of fire. Furthermore, whoever was not found written in the book of life was hurled into the lake of fire."

[34] This symbolic picture does not involve those who share in the "first resurrection," and who were already spoken about in Revelation 20:4-6 as being in no danger of the "second death." This picture refers to those who share in a resurrection to existence on earth, and who will be adjudged worthy of everlasting life only at the end of the thousand years, when they will be able to show their fully acquired righteousness in human perfection. The "scrolls" that are opened and according to the things written in which they are judged favorably or adversely are not scrolls containing the record of all their past imperfect, sinful deeds in this present life under this system of things. The heavenly judges do not need to spend a thousand years in going through the records of past human lives in order to determine the guiltiness or innocence of each individual resurrected. They are not so ignorant or ill-informed about mankind's past. What the judges are looking to is, not mankind's past, but mankind's future. Mankind needs guidance for the future!

33. How, in symbolic language, is the opportunity of the Judgment Day pictured in Revelation 20:11-15?
34. (a) Does the resurrection there pictured include those sharing in the "first resurrection"? (b) Of what do the "scrolls" then opened not contain a record, and why?

[35] So those "scrolls" that are opened are the new set of instructions, directions and orders that will be given out by the judges acting for God to mankind. Thus all mankind will be informed of the contents of those opened "scrolls," in order to know the standards by which they are to be judged and what is to be expected of them as to their future conduct and work. Mankind will not be left in ignorance, and everybody will be obliged to know what is the law according to the judgment scrolls. There will be no Satan the Devil and none of his demons around in the invisible vicinity of the earth to blind people, to mislead people, to pervert the published law and instructions. No, indeed; for those old "heavens" will have fled away from before the face of God who set the time for this Judgment Day. Accordingly, there will be no witch doctors around, no spirit mediums or clairvoyants, no astrologers with horoscopes, no sale of Ouija boards and suchlike demonistic contrivances. There will be only the "new heavens" in existence and they will drop down righteousness. As we read:

[36] "O you heavens, cause a dripping from above; and let the cloudy skies themselves trickle with righteousness. Let the earth open up, and let it be fruitful with salvation, and let it cause righteousness itself to spring up at the same time. I myself, Jehovah, have created it."—Isaiah 45:8.

EARTHLY "PRINCES"

[37] How the invisible heavenly judges will communicate the contents of the opened "scrolls" to earth's inhabitants is not specifically stated to us in the Bible. But there will be direct representatives of the heavenly kingdom of God on the earth. Their presence among mankind will be an official evidence that a "new earth" has come into existence with its new human society.

35, 36. (a) What, then, do those "scrolls" picture, and who will know the contents of them? (b) Why will there be no excuse for anyone on earth not to know?
37. (a) How will the heavenly judges communicate to mankind the contents of those "scrolls"? (b) How will mankind know when God's laws and rulings are being executed?

The old "earth" dominated invisibly by Satan the Devil has fled away from before God's face and no place has been found for it except in destruction. The law courts and lawyers and attorneys and judicial system are a thing of the past; the law of God is the thing now for a person to be well versed in, to judge by and to apply. And when the Kingdom's earthly representatives act, the people will know and distinctly understand that it is God's law and rulings that are being executed.

[38] Indications of this arrangement for the thousand-year Judgment Day are given us in the prophetic Scriptures. Take, for example, Psalm 45, which is a lyric concerning God's anointed King, Jesus the Messiah or Christ. After telling prophetically about the heavenly marriage of Jesus Christ and his bridal congregation and those who are attending upon the bridal class, the psalm says: "They will enter into the palace of the king. In place of your forefathers there will come to be your sons, whom you will appoint as princes in all the earth." (Psalm 45:15, 16) Of course, the heavenly King Jesus Christ has had illustrious ancestors, of whom the list is given in the Bible record, whether these have served on the earthly throne of King David at Jerusalem or not. But the heavenly King will not have to depend upon them for illustriousness. He will have his own, even though on earth as a perfect man Jesus Christ refused to sit upon any material throne at Jerusalem or elsewhere.

[39] The heavenly King Jesus Christ will surpass even David in fame, honor and illustriousness. He will extend his kingdom far beyond the boundaries of all the territory that King David conquered in his day according to God's promise to Abraham. (Genesis 15:17-21) Yes, to where East meets West and North meets South, even all around the planet, "all the earth." As it is written "Regarding Solomon" as a prophetic type of the King Jesus Christ: "O God, give your own judi-

---

38. Will the heavenly King Jesus Christ have to depend upon his earthly ancestors for illustriousness or have his own?
39. How will the King Jesus Christ exceed in illustriousness even King David as regards territory?

cial decisions to the king, and your righteousness to the son of the king. May he plead the cause of your people with righteousness and of your afflicted ones with judicial decision. And he will have subjects from sea to sea and from the River to the ends of the earth.)—Psalm 72: superscription, 1, 2, 8.

[40] However, does a problem seem to arise here? This King who is greater and wiser than Solomon the son of King David did not marry when he was here on earth as a perfect man with the reproductive power in his loins to bring forth a perfect human family. How, then, can the prophecy be fulfilled that, "in place of your forefathers," notice, "there will come to be your sons, whom you will appoint as princes in all the earth"? Moreover, the heavenly Jesus Christ is the Permanent Heir of King David, and because of his "power of an indestructible life" he will reign without successors, without the need of a son to succeed him. As the angel Gabriel said to Mary concerning her prospective Son Jesus: (Jehovah God will give him the throne of David his father, and he will rule as king over the house of Jacob forever, and there will be no end of his kingdom.)—Luke 1:32, 33.

[41] We know that the 144,000 joint heirs of Jesus Christ are not his spiritual sons, but are sons of God, "heirs indeed of God, but joint heirs with Christ." (Romans 8:17) Who, then, are these ones spoken of as "your sons, whom you will appoint as princes in all the earth"? Manifestly these are not heavenly sons of the King Jesus Christ. They must be earthly sons, who, being on earth, can be appointed princes "in all the earth." These will be the sons of His by the resurrection of the dead, specifically of the "righteous" dead. His promised title, according to the prophecy of Isaiah 9:6, 7, namely, Eternal Father, will be no mere empty honorary title. He will really be a father to the resurrected human family. He is "the last Adam," who

---

40. As regards princely sons, what problem seems to arise here because of Jesus' earthly childlessness and his being Permanent Heir to King David?
41, 42. (a) Why are the 144,000 joint heirs not the "sons" to be appointed on earth? (b) How will the heavenly Jesus Christ have earthly "sons," in fulfillment of what prophetic title?

became "a life-giving spirit." (1 Corinthians 15:45, 47) The first man Adam sold all his human offspring into sin and death, but the "second man," who is "out of heaven," laid down his perfect human life in order to purchase them back from such an Adamic inheritance. So we read:

"There is one God, and one mediator between God and men, a man, Christ Jesus, who gave himself a corresponding ransom for all." (1 Timothy 2:5, 6) "We behold Jesus, who has been made a little lower than angels, crowned with glory and honor for having suffered death, that he by God's undeserved kindness might taste death for every man."—Hebrews 2:9.

[43] By his self-sacrifice according to God's will, Jesus Christ gained the right to impart life to the dying race of mankind, in this way becoming their father. He will transmit life to the "dead," both the "righteous" and the "unrighteous," by calling them out of their memorial tombs or watery graves and then lifting up all the willing ones to perfection of human life. As for the "living" who survive the "great tribulation" into Christ's millennial reign, he will likewise lift these "righteous" survivors up to a level of life "in abundance," life as human creatures in glorious perfection. (John 10:10; 2 Timothy 4:1; Acts 24:15) He will have all this accomplished by the end of the thousand years. But this abundant life of his earthly children can go on forever, and there will be those who by keeping integrity in perfection will prove deserving of eternal life. These will be his eternal children, and he will be literally their Eternal Father.

[44] At the beginning of his millennial reign the illustrious King Jesus Christ will begin to take suitable ones from among his earthly children to be "princes in all the earth." The "living" who have survived the "great tribulation" and the abyssing of Satan and his

43. (a) How will the King become the father of the "great crowd" of tribulation survivors who need no resurrection? (b) How will his fatherhood of mankind become eternal?
44, 45. (a) How will the King begin his reign with sufficient princes on the earth, and why will all the appointed ones rank as "princes"? (b) However, is royal lineage necessary for a chief over others to be called a prince (sar)?

demons will furnish a number of these "princes." The "righteous" ones of the "dead" who are resurrected from the sleep of death will furnish others, sufficiently so in order to have the appointed "princes in all the earth." Psalm 45:16 appears to mean that such "princes" will include the "righteous" men from among his resurrected "forefathers." Once these were his ancestors, but now they become his "sons" by resurrection. Being the sons of the heavenly King, these appointed ones will rank as "princes."

45 However, it is to be noted that the Hebrew word in Psalm 45:16 for "princes" is *sarim*. Among the ancient Israelites not everyone who was called a "sar" had royal connections. Among them a chief of a thousand, a chief of a hundred, a chief of fifty, and even a chief of ten men was called a "sar." Even a chief of the royal butlers or chief of the royal bakers could be called a "sar."—Exodus 18:21, 25; Deuteronomy 1:15; 20:9; 1 Samuel 8:12; Genesis 40:2. Compare Genesis 23:5, 6.

46 Not all those appointed to be "princes in all the earth" need to be the royal or patriarchal ancestors of Jesus Christ as a man. Basically, they need to be men of integrity, "capable men," "men wise and experienced," such as the prophet Moses appointed to be judges, concerning whom we read: ("Moses proceeded to choose capable men out of all Israel and to give them positions as heads over the people, as chiefs [*sarim*] of thousands, chiefs [*sarim*] of hundreds, chiefs [*sarim*] of fifties and chiefs [*sarim*] of tens. And they judged the people on every proper occasion. A hard case they would bring to Moses, but every small case they themselves would handle as judges.") (Exodus 18:25, 26; Deuteronomy 1:15) The earthly princes appointed by the King Jesus Christ will really be interested in the welfare of the people and in settling difficulties peacefully and amicably. They will be coura-

46, 47. (a) Will all those appointed have to be royal or patriarchal ancestors of the King, and what kind of men will they have to be? (b) In whose interests will they really have to be interested, as described in Isaiah 32:1, 2?

geous and protective of what is right, like the princes described in Isaiah 32:1, 2, which says:

[47] "Look! A king will reign for righteousness itself; and as respects princes [*sarim*], they will rule as princes for justice itself. And each one must prove to be like a hiding place from the wind and a place of concealment from the rainstorm, like streams of water in a waterless country, like the shadow of a heavy crag in an exhausted land."

[48] In those days of the heavenly Prince [*Sar*] of Peace the dealing out of justice and of bringing offenders to account will not be a slow, dragging process, without sufficient judges and officers to try all the offenders promptly. The taking of a long time, years of time in many cases, to bring wrongdoers to trial and to right injustices and enforce justice, has encouraged criminals who are led to believe that they can get away finally unpunished. Crime has increased tremendously during the last half of this twentieth century, but already in the eleventh century before our Common Era began to count, the wise inspired writer of sharp observations wrote:

[49] "Because sentence against a bad work has not been executed speedily, that is why the heart of the sons of men has become fully set in them to do bad. Although a sinner may be doing bad a hundred times" —think of that! But the inspired writer goes on to say: "and continuing a long time as he pleases, yet I am also aware that it will turn out well with those fearing the true God, because they were in fear of him. But it will not turn out well at all with the wicked one, neither will he prolong his days that are like a shadow, because he is not in fear of God."—Ecclesiastes 8:11-13.

[50] The present slow process of bringing the wrongdoers to justice or of never bringing them to account

48, 49. (a) There has been an increase of crime because of what belief encouraged in criminals because of present legal processes? (b) According to Ecclesiastes 8:11-13, with whom will it go well—with a repetitious criminal or with whom?
50. (a) The present slow operation of justice is due to what on high above mankind? (b) How will the "new earth" respond to the "new heavens" as to righteousness?

is because we are living in the 'old earth' under the 'old heavens' and Satan the Devil and his "wicked spirit forces in the heavenly places" are in control over human society. The destruction of the old corrupt human society and the abyssing of Satan and his demons will remove all obstruction of justice during the millennial judgeship of the Prince [Sar] of Peace with his 144,000 associate judges. As a result of the dripping and trickling down of righteousness from the "new heavens," the human soil of the "new earth" will respond and become fruitful in a corresponding way. Jehovah has foretold this, saying: "Let the earth open up, and let it be fruitful with salvation, and let it cause righteousness itself to spring up at the same time. I myself, Jehovah, have created it."—Isaiah 45:8.

[51] Do we not yearn for such an age of righteousness and justice as that? During that time the path of the righteous person will not be such rough going as now but will be smoothed out. In anticipation of that desirable epoch, the prophet Isaiah, who looked forward to an earthly resurrection, wrote under inspiration: "The path of the righteous one is uprightness. You being upright, you will smooth out the very course of a righteous one. Yes, for the path of your judgments, O Jehovah, we have hoped in you. For your name and for your memorial the desire of the soul has been. With my soul I have desired you in the night; yes, with my spirit within me I keep looking for you; because, when there are judgments from you for the earth, righteousness is what the inhabitants of the productive land will certainly learn. Though the wicked one should be shown favor, he simply will not learn righteousness. In the land of straightforwardness he will act unjustly and will not see the eminence of Jehovah."—Isaiah 26:7-10.

[52] The millennial "land of straightforwardness," of straightforward dealing with the people and among

51. For what epoch, then, do we, along with Isaiah, long with our souls?
52, 53. (a) Even in the land of straightforwardness, under divine favor, for whom will it be difficult to learn righteousness? (b) In their case, what principle stated by the apostle Peter seems fitting?

the people, will be a place where great favor is shown to all mankind in their inborn human imperfection. Some members of the human family have gone down more deeply into sinful degradation than others and have been hardened in an unjust personality because of long failing to be brought to account. Their accustomed bent is toward injustice. It is easy to see how wicked ones of that kind would find it difficult to learn righteousness and uprightness even when all around them there is straightforwardness and divine favor is being shown to them through the King Jesus Christ. In spite of all the help proffered to them, they will be inclined to do unjustly. They will not want to recognize the eminence of Jehovah as the rightful Lawgiver nor the rightness of His standards for living. Respecting them the principle set forth by the apostle Peter seems fitting:

[53] "For it is the appointed time for the judgment to start with the house of God. Now if it starts first with us, what will the end be of those who are not obedient to the good news of God? 'And if the righteous man is being saved with difficulty, where will the ungodly man and the sinner make a showing?'"—1 Peter 4:17, 18.

[54] Persons who, in the "land of straightforwardness," receive the "favor" of God in vain, missing its loving purpose, and who prove unreformable, need not necessarily be preserved to the end of the thousand years before being executed as unfit for eternal life in the Paradise restored to earth. Without any injustice to such who prove to be beyond correction, they may be executed by the one whom God has appointed to judge the inhabited earth in righteousness. These do not get their names written "in the book of life" and hence they are fit for nothing but the "second death," as symbolized by the "lake of fire" that causes a complete destruction. (Revelation 20:14, 15) How wise and prudent it is, then, to be obedient now to the "good news of God" and to cultivate a love of righteousness in view of that coming Judgment Day!

54. Do those who receive the favor of God in vain, missing its purpose, need to be preserved till the end of the Judgment Day, and what is the reason?

CHAPTER 8

What to Expect When the Millennial Judgment Day Ends

>

FOR the thousand years of the imprisonment of Satan the Devil in the abyss there will be world wide the judgments from God for the earth and its inhabitants. The heavenly judges will render decisions and act for Jehovah God. The princely representatives on earth will do likewise. They will conduct themselves as judges whom King Jehoshaphat of Jerusalem stationed throughout the land to bring the people back to God. Jehoshaphat said to them: "See what you are doing, because it is not for man that you judge but it is for Jehovah; and he is with you in the matter of judgment. And now let the dread of Jehovah [not of man] come to be upon you. Be careful and act, for with Jehovah our God there is no unrighteousness or partiality or taking of a bribe." (2 Chronicles 19:4-7) With such heavenly judges and their judicial princes on the earth it is nothing too extraordinary to expect that the inhabitants of the productive Paradise land will learn righteousness, all together for a thousand years.—Isaiah 26:9.

[2] What a qualified, reliable Chief Judge all mankind will have in the "new heavens" during all that Judgment Day of ten centuries! Glowing with warmth is the prophetic description of the Judge as given by Isaiah in the eighth century before our Common Era. This foretold Judge is the Lord Jesus Christ, the Messianic Descendant of King David the son of Jesse of Bethlehem. Could Jehovah God provide and appoint a better judge to straighten out human affairs and to

1. Why will it be nothing extraordinary to expect that during the thousand years that Satan is abyssed earth's inhabitants will learn righteousness?
2, 3. (a) Through David, Jesus was the Descendant of what Bethlehemite, and so Isaiah compares Jesus at his earthly start to what with reference to that one? (b) A spirit with what qualities will rest upon him, and how will he judge?

x

139

see that the people get justice and that righteousness is forever established in the earth? Give all due attention, then, as the prophet under inspiration tells of the qualities of this future Judge who descended from the Bethlehemite Jesse through King David. Comparing this Descendant at his earthly start to a small twig that grows out of the trunk of a cut-down tree, Isaiah prophesies:

[3] "And there must go forth a twig out of the stump of Jesse; and out of his roots a sprout will be fruitful. And upon him the spirit of Jehovah must settle down, the spirit of wisdom and of understanding, the spirit of counsel and of mightiness, the spirit of knowledge and of the fear of Jehovah; and there will be enjoyment by him in the fear of Jehovah. And he will not judge by any mere appearance to his eyes, nor reprove simply according to the thing heard by his ears. And with righteousness he must judge the lowly ones, and with uprightness he must give reproof in behalf of the meek ones of the earth. And he must strike the earth with the rod of his mouth; and with the spirit of his lips he will put the wicked one to death. And righteousness must prove to be the belt of his hips, and faithfulness the belt of his loins."—Isaiah 11:1-5.

[4] This Chief Judge takes an actual delight, finds a real enjoyment in fearing Jehovah, so that he will without fail do his judging for Jehovah and not for man. So he is only God-fearing in making his decisions, not man-fearing. Surely he must be wise due to this wholesome fear of the one living and true God, Jehovah. He did not remain like a mere "twig" or "sprout" out of the firmly rooted "stump of Jesse," but grew up into a stalwart "big tree" of heavenly royalty, as the Greater David the Son of the Living Jehovah. (Isaiah 61:3; compare Ezekiel 17:22-24.) Upon this exalted one in his royal majestic position the mighty spirit of Jehovah rests, endowing him with knowledge, understanding and wisdom so much needed for his

4. (a) In the fear of whom will he judge mankind? (b) How will he become more than a mere "twig" or "sprout" out of the "stump of Jesse" and not be a disappointment or irritation?

responsible office. Consequently, as the King enthroned at the right hand of God he will be a credit to Jehovah; and as a divinely appointed Judge, he will not be a disappointment or an irritation to earth's inhabitants.

[5] Justice will be established in the earth. The heavenly Judge will exercise greater discernment than did his prototype King Solomon, who rendered such splendid decisions, such as in the stiff case submitted to him by the two harlots. They both disowned a dead child and laid claim to a live child. Concerning Solomon's unique way of bringing the true mother of the live child to the fore, it is written: "And all Israel got to hear of the judicial decision that the king had handed down; and they became fearful because of the king, for they saw that the wisdom of God was within him to execute judicial decision." (1 Kings 3:16-28) In like manner the Greater Solomon will not judge according to the surface appearance of things nor according to mere hearsay, but will see to it that the true facts are unearthed and that the true account is reported, to the end that a just decision may be rendered and executed. He will not favor the high ones as against the lowly ones, nor the arrogant ones as against the meek ones.

[6] In order to show what his thousand years of judgeship promises to be, this Judge so filled with the spirit of Jehovah will show himself to be a Liberator of the lowly and meek ones in the coming "great tribulation" that culminates in the "war of the great day of God the Almighty" at Har-Magedon. (Matthew 24:21; Revelation 7:14; 16:14, 16) His orders and directions to his heavenly armies will be like a "rod" out of his mouth, for, in fulfillment of what he says as Commander, the 'old earth' of unrighteousness will be struck and broken to pieces. The lips of his mouth will be moved by the spirit of Jehovah and will express his attitude and feeling toward the wicked ones on earth, and these will accordingly be put to death. Our whole earthly globe will be cleansed of the lofty, arrogant,

5. In favor of strict justice, how will he show himself impartial and discerning, even more so than Solomon as judge?
6. How will he, by his procedures in the "great tribulation," show that his thousand years of judgeship will be righteous?

wicked ones. And, of course, the unseen ruler of these, Satan, will be chained and abyssed.

[7] Of a truth, mankind has nothing to expect of the millennial judgeship of Jehovah's appointed Judge, Jesus Christ, but righteousness and faithfulness to their interests. It will be as if this heavenly Judge is belted, sustained by righteousness, as if he girdles himself for the work of righteousness. Yes, it is as if he belts, girds himself with the quality of faithfulness, or girdles himself in support of the faithful care for the interests of the people whom he judges according to God's standards. Oh, what peace and tranquillity this will result in for the earth! What altering there will be of attitudes of persons toward one another, what a changing of personalities for the good of others! This is delightfully pictured in the prophetic words of Isaiah, as he says:

[8] "And righteousness must prove to be the belt of his hips, and faithfulness the belt of his loins. And the wolf will actually reside for a while with the male lamb, and with the kid the leopard itself will lie down, and the calf and the maned young lion and the well-fed animal all together; and a mere little boy will be leader over them. And the cow and the bear themselves will feed; together their young ones will lie down. And even the lion will eat straw just like the bull. And the sucking child will certainly play upon the hole of the cobra; and upon the light aperture of a poisonous snake will a weaned child actually put his own hand. They will not do any harm or cause any ruin in all my holy mountain; because the earth will certainly be filled with the knowledge of Jehovah as the waters are covering the very sea."—Isaiah 11:5-9.

PERSONALITY TRANSFORMATIONS

[9] Imagine the human personalities that are likened to the wolf, the leopard, the bear, the maned young lion, the cobra, the poisonous snake! There have been

7, 8. (a) For the good of mankind, how will it be as if the Judge were belted with righteousness and girded with faithfulness? (b) What effects will this have upon mankind in producing changes in them?
9. Since when, and upon whom, have such transformations of personal characteristics been brought about by God's spirit?

many people with suchlike personalities who have responded finally to the message of God's kingdom and who have changed their personalities so that they could get along with other persons who are meek and inoffensive like the lamb, the kid, the little boy, the sucking child or the weaned child. Ever since the outpouring of God's holy spirit through Christ upon the Christian congregation when gathered together on the Festival Day of Pentecost of 33 C.E., the spirit of God has been working to transform members of the congregation to be Christlike. As a consequence the faithful members of the congregation have been able to put up with one another and to get along together, even though formerly they could be likened in personality to those dreaded wild animals. (Acts 2:1-33) True to Isaiah's prophecy, they have done no harm to fellow Christians nor caused any ruin to the congregation in the "holy mountain" of Jehovah's worship.

[10] This personality transformation has taken place not only with those who finally make up the 144,000 associate judges of the Chief Judge Jesus Christ, but also with the numberless "great crowd" of worshipers of Jehovah who are today being gathered together from all nations, tribes, peoples and languages. These prospective inhabiters of the earthly Paradise are assured of God's protection during the "great tribulation" and will be preserved through it into the divine new order under the millennial judgeship of Jesus Christ. (Revelation 7:9-17) Naturally they will carry their transformed personalities directly into the divine new order. This will result to them very favorably, for they will be the "living" toward whom the heavenly Judge Jesus Christ will begin expressing his millennial judgments. (2 Timothy 4:1) Under such circumstances fear of harm and ruin will be gone from the "holy mountain" of Jehovah's worship. They already know Jehovah, and so with these survivors all around the globe the

10. (a) Upon whom else, besides the 144,000 associate judges of Christ, have such personality transformations been wrought? (b) How will this transformation result favorably toward them at the start of Christ's millennial judgeship?

earth will indeed be filled with the knowledge of Jehovah. But this knowledge will increase.

[11] At this juncture, we remember what was said to the eight human survivors of the deluge of Noah's day, after they came out of the ark and offered sacrifice to God. Jehovah said to them: "And a fear of you and a terror of you will continue upon every living creature of the earth and upon every flying creature of the heavens, upon everything that goes moving on the ground, and upon all the fishes of the sea. Into your hand they are now given." (Genesis 9:2) May this not have its modern counterpart? As the coming "great tribulation" will be directed against ungodly humans of the earth, it will not kill off the land animals, birds and fishes of the sea. It is reasonable to expect that God will put upon those lower earthly creatures any lost measure of fear and dread of human creatures, who will be commissioned to convert the ruined earth into a Paradise. Certainly since God by his spirit was able to transform beastly personalities into Christian personalities among the 144,000 and the "great crowd" of today, he will be able to do something similar in the case of the wild animals. For a fact, they will do no injury to Jehovah's worshipers in the earth.

[12] In accordance with this, we can look for the charming description of animal life as set out in Isaiah 11:6-9 to have a literal fulfillment with the birds, fishes and land creatures of earth during the millennial reign of the Prince of Peace, the Son of the Greater Jesse, Jehovah God. Away back in the original Paradise of Pleasure or Garden of Eden, the woman Eve did not have any fear of the serpent, not fleeing from it when it was made to speak to her. (Genesis 3:1-4) Before this, Adam had had the wild animals and the flying creatures brought before him and he named them, manifesting no fear of them. (Genesis 2:19, 20) That Edenic condition of freedom of fear of the lower crea-

---

11. What did God assure the eight deluge survivors regarding the lower earthly creatures, and how will this have a modern counterpart?
12, 13. (a) Back in the original Paradise, what was the attitude of man and woman toward the lower earthly creatures? (b) What kind of relationship will there be between the lower earthly creatures themselves, in more than a figurative way?

tures of the earth and security from harm by them will be reintroduced in the restored Paradise.

[13] Also, these land animals, flying creatures and fish will be at peace among themselves as well as with man. It would be inconsistent for God to inspire such a prophecy as that of Isaiah 11:6-9, and Ezekiel 34:25 and Hosea 2:18 to have only a figurative or spiritual meaning and not have a true copy of these things in actual life, as though the literal fulfillment were an impossible ideal.

[14] However, the taming of the animal, bird and fish creation is not the main objective. Such earthly creatures existed long before mankind did. It is mankind's continued existence on earth that is in question or at stake. All descendants from Adam and Eve were born sinners and so have fallen "short of the glory of God." (Romans 3:23) In many cases humans have taken on, not godly qualities, but qualities of now ferocious wild beasts. So mankind needs to be brought back to that "glory of God," so as to prove worthy of everlasting life to the praise of God the Creator. The members of the human family need to be brought together into peaceful, harmless relations with one another, doing justice and righteousness perfectly. This is what the thousand-year judgeship of Jesus Christ will bring about.

[15] At present, the crime rate of men is increasing at a rate faster than that of the growth of earth's population. In strong contrast with this, during the millennium earth's population will regularly increase because of the resurrection of the dead, of the "righteous" and the "unrighteous." And yet the rate of wrongdoing will decrease till at last it reaches the vanishing point. Why so? Because the heavenly judges over mankind will be absolutely righteous and will teach all mankind true righteousness according to God's standards. As an aid in this direction, "the earth will certainly be filled with the knowledge of Jehovah as the waters are

14. However, what is more important than the taming of the lower earthly creatures, and why?
15. How will the heavenly judges over mankind bring about that the rate of wrongdoing goes down as the rate of population goes up?

covering the very sea." (Isaiah 11:9) Only the worship of Him will be permitted in this theocratic millennium. Mankind will be brought to the earthly courtyards of Jehovah's "true tent," his spiritual temple. There they will be made to know the truth of what Jesus said in prayer to his heavenly Father: "This means everlasting life, their taking in knowledge of you, the only true God, and of the one whom you sent forth, Jesus Christ."—John 17:3; Hebrews 8:2.

[16] The millennial Judgment Day will not fail of its purpose. By the time of its end all the willing and obedient will have been trained in true justice and righteousness to perfection. Their physical and mental infirmities inherited from Adam and Eve will be done away with. They are now capable in all respects to measure up to God's absolute standards of righteousness, in themselves. Does Jesus Christ as the Chief Judge now bestow upon them the right to eternal life in a peaceful earth all glorious in paradisaic beauty? No! In this regard he does not act for God, for he knows that it is written: "God is the One who declares them righteous." (Romans 8:33) What, then, does God's Judge do?

16. (a) In view of what results will Christ's millennial judgeship not fail of its purpose? (b) Why will Christ not bestow eternal life in Paradise upon restored mankind?

CHAPTER 9

The Post-Millennial Test
of All Mankind

A T THE end of the thousand-year-long Judgment
Day the righteously judged human family stands
perfect before its Judge and Liberator, Jesus Christ.
But not yet are they adjudged worthy of eternal life
on the Paradisaic earth. They must yet face the
Supreme Court of the universe, that of the Most High
God, Jehovah the Sovereign Lord. In harmony with
this final requirement the Deputy Judge Jesus Christ
must hand the human race, now capable of perfect
righteousness, over to his God and Father for Him to
render his decision toward all those who, under test,
will prove worthy or unworthy of the priceless gift
of eternal life in peace and happiness. Despite their
perfection they are yet mortal.

[2] The dying condition that had attached to mankind
because of the sin of their first human father Adam
in Eden has now been undone, destroyed, just as if
hurled into the "lake of fire" to its own death. (Revelation 20:14, 15) However, will mankind, now liberated
from Adamic death and imperfection, do anything of
its own accord, willfully, to deserve eternal death under
Jehovah's judgment? Which individuals will prove
worthy of "second death"? This is what the Supreme
Judge Jehovah must determine as Final Arbiter.

[3] Now applies what the apostle Paul foretold in
1 Corinthians 15:24-28: 'Next, the end, when he
hands over the kingdom to his God and Father, when
he has brought to nothing all government and all

---

1. At the end of the millennial Judgment Day, what is the final requirement for restored mankind, and so what will the Deputy Judge
Jesus Christ do with them?
2. By then what will have happened to Adamic death, and hence what
will Jehovah determine regarding individuals of mankind?
3. According to 1 Corinthians 15:24-28, what transfer of things takes
place?

authority and power. For he must rule as king until God has put all enemies under his feet. As the last enemy, death is to be brought to nothing. For God 'subjected all things under his feet.' But when he says that 'all things have been subjected,' it is evident that it is with the exception of the one [Jehovah God] who subjected all things to him. But when all things will have been subjected to him, then the Son himself will also subject himself to the One who subjected all things to him, that God may be all things to everyone.' —NW; Ro.

⁴ As a result of the Son's handing over the kingdom to his God and Father, the kingdom becomes the property of Jehovah God. There thus remains no subsidiary kingdom between the Sovereign Lord Jehovah and mankind. How, now, will mankind react to God's direct Kingship over them? Will they all declare themselves his loyal subjects to all eternity? Will they all determine personally that He is their choice as God forever? This declaring of a person righteous on his own account and conferring upon him the right to everlasting life is a serious thing, that calls for unswerving loyalty on the part of the recipient of such a precious right. How will God determine whose name should stand on the "book of life"? It will be by a test of heart allegiance and integrity, as in the case of the patriarch Job of the land of Uz.

⁵ For a thousand years now under the kingdom of the Son of God mankind has enjoyed the undeserved kindness of God and they find themselves in a beauteous planetary paradise. As in the case of Job, the question is, Do they love and worship God only for all the good that he has done for them or because of what He is in himself, the one living and true God and the Rightful Sovereign of the universe? In the case of Job, his integrity toward Jehovah God was tested by permitting the Devil Satan to harass him short of taking his life away. So now, by permitting Satan the Devil to put

4. What questions must the Sovereign Lord Jehovah now determine toward perfected mankind, and by what means will he do so?
5. How will the test then made of perfected mankind correspond with that of Job, and for the purpose of proving what?

restored mankind to the test to the extent that God Almighty permits, perfected mankind can be tested and proved as to individual integrity to God in a perfect sense. Such a test would call for Satan and his demons to be loosed from their thousand years of imprisonment in the abyss. This is what will take place.

⁶ What takes place after the end of the millennial reign of Jesus Christ and his 144,000 royal associates, Revelation 20:7-10 tells us, in these words: "Now as soon as the thousand years have been ended, Satan will be let loose out of his prison, and he will go out to mislead those nations in the four corners of the earth, Gog and Magog, to gather them together for the war. The number of these is as the sand of the sea. And they advanced over the breadth of the earth and encircled the camp of the holy ones and the beloved city. But fire came down out of heaven and devoured them. And the Devil who was misleading them was hurled into the lake of fire and sulphur, where both the wild beast and the false prophet already were; and they will be tormented day and night forever and ever."

⁷ The loosing of Satan and his demons from the abyss means letting them come again into the vicinity of the earth where they can exercise an invisible control over those of mankind who succumb to them. Satan the Devil will be confident of himself, in spite of the mental, moral, spiritual, physical perfection of mankind. True, he did fail in the case of the patriarch Job, but he did succeed more than twenty-four centuries earlier in the case of Adam and Eve in spite of their human perfection in Eden. In both cases, however, the point in dispute was the same, namely, the rightful sovereignty of Jehovah God, which requires absolute obedience of human creatures to God's laws and prohibitions.

6. How does Revelation 20:7-10 describe what will happen at the end of the millennial reign of Christ?
7. When loosed, why will Satan and his demons be confident respecting perfected mankind, and what will again be the point in dispute?

[8] That the same issue is forced upon all mankind after the end of the thousand years is shown by the fact that those who are now misled by Satan and his demons advance over the earth and encircle the "camp of the holy ones and the beloved city." Yes, there will be "holy ones" on the earth then. These are encircled by Satan and his earthly hordes because they refuse to be misled by Satan and his demons. Such "holy ones" are those of restored mankind who keep their integrity to God under this all-deciding test. They are like in a war camp under attack by enemy warriors. The "holy ones" are put as separate from "the beloved city." They are not in it but are in the "camp." Evidently, then, this "city" is not any city constructed on earth as a global capital. This must be the city that is spoken of by the glorified Jesus Christ to his followers, in Revelation 3:12, and that he calls "the city of my God, the new Jerusalem which descends out of heaven from my God."

[9] This "city" is one "beloved" by God and also by the "holy ones." The 144,000 joint heirs of Jesus Christ have written upon them the name of this "new Jerusalem." It is not on earth like some material city, but is a heavenly city that descends by extending its influence and authority to the inhabitants of the earth.

[10] This "city" is not disorganized and demolished at the end of the thousand years of its rule over mankind, but its good, righteous effects still remain on earth with the "holy ones." By making war upon this "beloved city" Satan the Devil aims at undoing all this good that the New Jerusalem has wrought. He does not want these benefits to remain with mankind forever. Being restrained to the earth's vicinity, with no place for him any longer up in heaven out of which he and his demons have been cast, he cannot get directly at the "beloved city" up there. So he wars against

8. (a) How is it here shown that the issue forced upon all mankind is that of universal sovereignty? (b) Who are the "holy ones," and what is the "beloved city"?
9. To whom is the city "beloved," and how does it descend out of heaven from God?
10. Is the unloosed Satan able to get at the "beloved city" direct, and so what is the purpose of his attack upon it?

it to the extent of trying to bring to nothing all the righteousness that it has established on the earth.

[11] It is hardly to be expected that this "war" will be carried on with the scientific weapons such as the nuclear bombs and other implements of warfare of this twentieth century. The inhabitants of the earth during the millennium will not have stockpiled such weapons or have learned such war anymore. (Isaiah 2:2-4) It will not be a warfare of military might of that sort. Deceit, misleading propaganda, appeals to selfishness in disloyalty to the Universal Sovereign could be mighty weapons with which to overcome people. That the issue will be over the rightfulness of Jehovah's universal sovereignty rather than God's almightiness is shown in that Satan's being imprisoned a thousand years in the abyss and now being released proves God's superior might in comparison with the power of Satan the Devil. Still a rebel himself against Jehovah's sovereignty, he is intent on making mankind rebels likewise.

EXTENT OF THE POST-MILLENNIAL REBELLION

[12] The number of those whom Satan and his demons succeed in misleading on the prime issue is said to be "as the sand of the sea," that is to say, appearing to be numberless. (Revelation 20:8) This by no means signifies the vast majority of mankind. For instance, the combined armies that warred against Judge Joshua were said to be as numerous as the grains of sand of the seashore. (Joshua 11:4) The camels of the enemies who invaded the land of Israel in the days of Gideon the son of Joash were said to be "without number, as numerous as the grains of sand that are on the seashore." (Judges 7:12) So, too, those who will be misled by Satan are an indefinite number, how many of them not being foretold, but enough of them to make an impression as of a large crowd. So Satan the Devil has only limited success.

11. (a) How will the "war" then be carried on? (b) How is, not God's almightiness, but the rightness of his universal sovereignty, shown to be the issue?
12. What is indicated by the fact that those whom Satan misleads are said to be "as the sand of the sea"?

¹³ Those whom Satan succeeds in misleading are spoken of as "those nations in the four corners of the earth, Gog and Magog." Their appearing on the Paradise earth is not by a resurrection of the dead including the "unrighteous" ones, but is as a result of Satan's misleading an unpredicted number of restored mankind.

¹⁴ During the millennial Judgment Day there have been no national divisions of mankind, nor has the judgment of the people been influenced by any national extractions. The fact that these who are misled by the loosed Satan are called "nations" indicates that, like Satan, they refuse to recognize Jehovah's universal sovereignty and that they choose to establish an earthly sovereignty of their own, like a national sovereignty. They may not have a united sovereignty over them, but, because of division among themselves, they may have group sovereignties. However that may be, they are all united in being against Jehovah's sovereignty. Their being called "those nations in the four corners of the earth" suggests that they are far away from the "beloved city." Hence, in their attitude toward sovereignty, the misled ones have moved far away from sovereignty by Jehovah God. Jehovah God does not become "all things to everyone" in their case.

¹⁵ These misled nationalistic ones are called "Gog and Magog" quite appropriately. In the case of the original "Gog of the land of Magog," as foretold in Ezekiel's prophecy, he made a final attack upon the worshipers of Jehovah God. He did so after these worshipers had been restored to their proper earthly estate and their land had become like the "garden of Eden." (Ezekiel 36:35) They were dwelling as in "open rural country" and "having no disturbance, dwelling in security, all of them dwelling without wall" and not having "even bar and doors." (Ezekiel 38:11) Also,

---

13. Is the appearing on the Paradise earth of "those nations in the four corners of the earth, Gog and Magog," by a resurrection?
14. In what sense, then, can they be called "nations," and in what way can they be said to be "in the four corners of the earth"?
15, 16. (a) In what ways are those misled nationalistic ones like "Gog and Magog" as respects timing of matters and the object of attack? (b) How are those misled ones also like Gog in being maneuvered by Jehovah into making their attack?

the people of the "land of Magog" backed their head chieftain in making this attack upon the seemingly defenseless worshipers of Jehovah. But Gog comes to the attack from far off really because, as Jehovah says: "I shall certainly turn you around and put hooks in your jaws and bring you forth with all your military force, . . . In the final part of the years you will come to the land of people brought back."—Ezekiel 38:4-8.

[16] Those misled by Satan the Devil after the millennial Judgment Day is over will follow this invisible chieftain who has just been released by Jehovah God from the abyss for the very purpose of letting him make an attack upon restored mankind. In being let loose from the abyss Satan the Devil and his demons are allowed to invade the vicinity of the earth again and be in close contact with mankind on the Paradise earth now like the Garden of Eden. So in making his attack, the released Satan the Devil is as if being led along by hooks in his jaws under the maneuvering of Jehovah. And the ones on earth who are now misled by Satan the Devil are, like him, led along as by hooks in their jaws to make this attack upon the "camp of the holy ones and the beloved city." (Revelation 20:7-9) So the names of Gog and Magog can fittingly be appropriated and applied to these misled nationalistic ones of mankind who assail and try to despoil those who loyally adhere to the universal sovereignty of Jehovah God.

[17] These misled ones of mankind, being mere humans on the earth, can no more directly assault the heavenly New Jerusalem than their invisible leader, Satan the Devil, can do so. But they can get into contact with those on earth who have faithfully represented the heavenly Messianic government, namely, the "princes in all the earth." These being appointed to be such princes by the King of the New Jerusalem, the Eternal Father Jesus Christ, they have served as the visible princely representatives of the "beloved city." And

when, at the end of his millennial reign, the kingly
Son of God "hands over the kingdom to his God and
Father," these princely sons on earth must take corresponding action. They must imitate the Son of God
who will "subject himself to the One who subjected
all things to him," the heavenly Father.

[18] Hence these princely "sons" of the Eternal Father
Jesus Christ rightly imitate him and subject themselves
to his God and Father as the rightful Exerciser of
universal sovereignty. Instead of proudly rebelling
against what their changed situation calls for, they act
Christlike and subject themselves to Jehovah's universal sovereignty. The ones misled by Satan the Devil
attack them with arguments and pressures to dissuade
the visible earthly representatives of the "beloved
city," but these decidedly refuse to do so. They maintain their integrity to the Most High God and loyally
cleave to his rightful sovereignty over all the earth and
all the universe. They unhesitatingly choose to let
Jehovah God be "all things to everyone" in their own
case.—1 Corinthians 15:24-28.

DISPOSAL OF "GOG AND MAGOG" AND THEIR MISLEADER

[19] In this "war" for which Satan the Devil has
gathered his misled ones on earth together, the "camp
of the holy ones" and the earthly representatives of
the "beloved city" do not fight back with fleshly
weapons. They, of course, cannot kill off Satan the
Devil and his demon angels, whom they cannot see
or reach. But even though they can see on earth the
misled ones who make up "Gog and Magog," the loyal
choosers of Jehovah's universal sovereignty do not kill
off the misled ones, in such a way acting as execu-
tioners of the misled ones. Choosing the side of Jehovah
God, they let him make expression of his universal
sovereignty and prove it to the misled disloyal ones.
They let the battle be Jehovah's and so do not assume

19. Under attack by the misled ones, how do the loyal ones display,
not only faith in God, but also integrity toward his universal sovereignty?

to act as His executional forces and fight with lethal weapons. This displays, not only faith on their part, but also perfect integrity toward Jehovah God and his universal sovereignty. Let Him himself save them and destroy the disloyal ones! Trustfully they stand still and see the "salvation of Jehovah" in their behalf. —2 Chronicles 20:15-17.

[20] Lodging "under the very shadow of the Almighty One," those who keep allegiance to Jehovah's universal sovereignty will, only with their eyes, "look on and see the retribution itself of the wicked ones." (Psalm 91:1, 8) They will behold the fulfillment of what was foretold in Revelation 20:9 regarding the post-millennial "Gog and Magog": "And they advanced over the breadth of the earth and encircled the camp of the holy ones and the beloved city. But fire came down out of heaven and devoured them." These disloyal ones of mankind get a baptism of fire, which means their everlasting destruction. God does not justify them or declare them righteous and enter their names on the "book of life." (Romans 8:33) This is no abuse of Jehovah's universal sovereignty but is a rightful expression of it toward his enemies.

[21] However, the eternal destruction of these lawless haters of what is good does not remove Satan the Devil and his demon angels from the vicinity of the earth. He has now been let loose from the abyss long enough. God's purpose in letting him loose has been served in full; there is no further reason for letting him and his demons on the loose any longer. We remember that it is written respecting his being hurled into the abyss for a thousand years: "After these things he must be let loose for a little while." (Revelation 20:3) The "little while," in which Satan the Devil has tried to mislead as many of restored mankind as he can into thinking that Jehovah is exercising his sovereignty over the earth in a wrongful, arrogant

---

20. (a) Under divine protection, what will the loyal ones be privileged to see? (b) What does this divine action signify for the disloyal ones? 21. (a) How long was Satan to be loosed from the abyss, and has its purpose now been served? (b) What would returning him to the abyss mean?

way, is now up. What now? Are Satan and his demons hurled back into the abyss? To do so would imply that they were to be let loose again, just as Jesus Christ himself was let loose from an abyss, and the symbolic locusts were let loose from the abyss, and the "wild beast" upon which Babylon the Great rides ascended out of the abyss.—Romans 10:7; Revelation 9:1-3; 17:8; compare Revelation 11:7.

[22] The chaining and imprisoning of Satan the Devil and his demons in the abyss was a temporary torment for them. Is the torment of restraint again to be temporary for them, or for all time? What happens to them after they have seen the ones whom they have misled on earth punished with fiery destruction? The Devil has now had answered the accusation that he has all along made, that men on earth serve Jehovah God merely for what they can get out of him, and that no man will remain loyal to Jehovah out of pure love for him, even under wicked temptation by Satan the Devil. Those men and women of integrity who remain alive on earth after the fiery annihilation of the disloyal ones stand as a living answer to the Devil, proving his accusation to be false and that he is a liar. The controversy of seven millenniums of time has ended in favor of the God of truth, and so there is no reason for letting Satan the Devil and his demons live on any longer. God's patience toward them is now at its end. For these reasons he does not return these rebel angels to the abyss. So what befalls them?

[23] "And the Devil who was misleading them was hurled into the lake of fire and sulphur, where both the wild beast and the false prophet already were; and they will be tormented day and night forever and ever."—Revelation 20:10.

[24] The torment of Satan the Devil in the lake of fire and sulphur signifies the same for him and his demons as it does for the symbolic wild beast and the false

22, 23. (a) How has Satan's accusation with reference to man been answered, and in whose favor has the long controversy been settled? (b) What now befalls Satan and his demons?
24, 25. (a) Being hurled into the lake of fire symbolizes what for Satan and his demons? (b) Why is this another kind of death?

prophet. And what is that? Destruction forever and ever. (Revelation 19:20) Satan the Devil and his demons will no more live again than that symbolic wild beast and false prophet will live again. Their names are not written on any divine "book of life." Life is life, whether spent in pleasure or in suffering pain. So their being plunged into the symbolic "lake of fire and sulphur" does not mean their being preserved in life in order to suffer conscious torment in their bodies and minds.

25 That symbolic "lake" does not symbolize what is called "a living death." It symbolizes another kind of death, different from that suffered by all mankind through birth inheritance from the sinful Adam and Eve and which apparently was the first form of death to enter the realm of creation, among creatures in God's image. Such inherited death proved to be temporary, it being turned into a 'sleep of death' by the resurrection that results from the death and resurrection of Jesus Christ.—1 Corinthians 15:20-22.

26 The death symbolized by the "lake of fire and sulphur" is different from the death inherited by mankind from Adam in that it is not like a sleep terminated by an awakening but is a total destruction, an endless death. Death received from Adam as an inheritance was the 'first death.' This *different* kind of death as symbolized by the "lake of fire and sulphur" is therefore fittingly called "the second death." This is what it stands for in the case of those humans on earth who enter into the thousand-year Judgment Day and who later do not get their names written in God's "book of life." The inspired Scriptures give the significance of the "lake of fire" for such ones unworthy of everlasting life, saying: "And death and Ha'des were hurled into the lake of fire. This means the second death, the lake of fire. Furthermore, whoever was not found written in the book of life was hurled into the lake of fire."—Revelation 20:14, 15.

---

26. Why is this different kind of death fittingly called "the second death," and the humans that suffer it do not have their names written where?

²⁷ This divine explanation of what the "lake of fire" symbolizes is borne witness to a second time, a few verses later, where we read: "Anyone conquering will inherit these things, and I shall be his God and he will be my son. But as for the cowards and those without faith and those who are disgusting in their filth and murderers and fornicators and those practicing spiritism and idolaters and all the liars, their portion will be in the lake that burns with fire and sulphur. This means the second death." (Revelation 21:7, 8) All such references to the "lake of fire" being so close together, in the same context in Revelation, chapters 19-21, then what the "lake of fire" means for those humans not found written on the "book of life" it means *also* for Satan the Devil and his demons. It means "the second death." It does not mean necessarily dying a second time, but dying the second kind of death that the Bible speaks about, and that is an endless death.

²⁸ Accordingly, Satan and his demons can die this kind of death, even though they have never died before. There was not a bit of life in the first kind of death that came in by the sin of the first man. Likewise there is not even a spark of life in the "second death" that is the everlasting punishment for those who willfully disobey God, even ruining their perfection in order to do so. By all Scriptural rules, then, the torment of Satan and his demons in the lake of fire and sulphur forever and ever means their being brought to nothing, their being made nonexistent, their being blotted out of spirit life forever. As a result, God will have a demon-free universe, with demons never being allowed to appear again.

COMING TO LIFE AFTER THE MILLENNIUM ENDS

²⁹ What a glorious eternity, therefore, awaits mankind! Look! Jehovah God permits the "camp of the

27, 28. (a) Why is it possible for Satan and his demons to suffer the "second" death? (b) What, then, does their being tormented in the lake of fire forever mean?
29. God's permitting the camp of the holy ones and also the princely representatives of the beloved city to survive signifies that he has taken what action toward them?

holy ones" and the princely representatives on earth of the "beloved city" to survive the destruction of "Gog and Magog" and of Satan the Devil and his demons! What does this mean but that God has written their names on the "book of life" or has let their names stand written on the "book of life"? This means that He has declared them righteous, justified them, because of their maintaining their integrity to him, thus joining in with the Son of God, Jesus Christ, and the 144,000 joint heirs in vindicating the universal sovereignty of the Most High God, the Creator of all things good. Their being declared righteous by Jehovah God signifies that he has bestowed upon them the right to everlasting life in their Paradise home.

[30] It was the heavenly King, Priest and Judge, Jesus Christ, who, by his loving dealings with mankind during the thousand years, brought the willing and obedient ones up to this perfect righteousness in the flesh. If he had not done so by the end of the thousand years, then he would have been hesitant to turn them over to the final test by the Supreme Judge, Jehovah God. Why? Because he would have known that, lacking perfect righteousness, they could never undergo the divine test with success and gain eternal life. So, in complete righteousness and sinlessness in the flesh they stand in the earthly courtyards of Jehovah's "true tent" or temple as his worshipers. There they keep standing forever by passing the divine test with irreproachable integrity and unswerving allegiance to the Sovereign Lord Jehovah. Forever they remain indebted to the Son of God, Jesus Christ, who lovingly lifted them up to this perfect righteousness as evidence of the completed work of their Ransomer and Savior, the Lord Jesus. So at that time they really *live!*

[31] In the light of that fact we can appreciate the correctness of that parenthetical statement in Revelation 20:5: "(The rest of the dead did not come to

30. (a) To whom will these who successfully pass the final test be ever indebted, and where will they stand forever? (b) When will they really "live"?
31. Thus by the end of the thousand years of Christ's reign, to what do the "rest of the dead" attain, and what happens to the Adamic death?

life until the thousand years were ended.)" If they had not had the preliminary work of the thousand years performed upon them by Jesus Christ and his 144,000 joint heirs who participated in the "first resurrection," this state of perfect life would not have been the portion of the "rest of the dead" at the close of the thousand years. It is really by then that 'death (as inherited from Adam) gave up the dead that were in it and that death was hurled into the lake of fire so as to suffer "second death" or extinction.' (Revelation 20:13, 14) Then it becomes true, as foretold in 1 Corinthians 15:25, 26: "He must rule as king until God has put all enemies under his feet. As the last enemy, death is to be brought to nothing."

[32] Then, with reference to the death inherited from the sinful Adam, it will be fully true: "And God himself will be with them. And he will wipe out every tear from their eyes, and death will be no more, neither will mourning nor outcry nor pain be anymore. The former things have passed away."—Revelation 21:3, 4.

[33] Will all those who have come to life in this perfect sense by the end of the thousand years choose to prolong that abundant life forever? They can do so by proving themselves worthy to receive the right to everlasting life from the Great Source of all life, Jehovah God. For passing the thoroughgoing test of their whole-souled integrity to Him, the faithful and loyal ones are rewarded with that precious right to have their lives protected and prolonged to all eternity in happiness. Thus they will realize in their own selves that "the gift God gives is everlasting life by Christ Jesus our Lord." (Romans 6:23) If it had not been for God's use of his beloved only-begotten Son, this would not have been possible for the human family.

---

32. How will Revelation 21:3, 4 then be fully true?
33. (a) How will those attaining to that abundance of life prove worthy of having their lives prolonged forever? (b) How will they then appreciate in themselves the truth of Romans 6:23?

[34] How soul-satisfying it will then be to worship and serve the God whose name is Jehovah in the earthly courtyards of his spiritual temple! Already at the beginning of the glorious millennium it was true of the "great crowd" of survivors of the "great tribulation" that "they have washed their robes and made them white in the blood of the Lamb. That is why they are before the throne of God; and they are rendering him sacred service day and night in his temple." (Revelation 7:9, 14, 15) It is hoped that the members of this clean-robed "great crowd" will abide in those courtyards of God's spiritual temple clear through the thousand years and the test of absolute integrity to the Sovereign Lord Jehovah after the millennium is ended. Those who are raised from their graves during the millennium will be brought to the earthly courtyards of Jehovah's spiritual temple to take up his worship and service there. By entering with proper appreciation into Jehovah's service there, even the resurrected "unrighteous" ones will feel as did the sons of the Levite Korah:

[35] "For a day in your courtyards is better than a thousand elsewhere. I have chosen to stand at the threshold in the house of my God rather than to move around in the tents of wickedness. For Jehovah God is a sun and a shield; favor and glory are what he gives. Jehovah himself will not hold back anything good from those walking in faultlessness."—Psalm 84: superscription, 10, 11.

[36] The ones who are determined to maintain wholehearted integrity to the one living and true God will cultivate the appreciation of spiritual things that David expressed, when he said: "One thing I have asked from Jehovah—it is what I shall look for, that I may dwell in the house of Jehovah all the days of my life,

34, 35. (a) What is our hope concerning the "great crowd" who already before the "great tribulation" were serving white-robed in Jehovah's spiritual temple? (b) What feelings of the sons of Korah toward Jehovah's courtyards will even the "unrighteous" resurrected ones be enabled to develop?
36. What appreciation of God's temple as expressed by David will those who are determined to keep integrity cultivate?

to behold the pleasantness of Jehovah and to look with appreciation upon his temple."—Psalm 27: super-scription, 4.

[37] All the earth will then be a place of worship of its wondrous Creator. It is his "footstool," whereas the heavens are his "throne." (Isaiah 66:1) His heavenly throne is glorious; his earthly footstool will be made glorious as a suitable place for his feet. Everywhere on earth it will be paradisaic, like the Garden of Eden, like the Garden of Jehovah. (Genesis 2:8; 13:10) It will be a place of delight and joy, for it will be a place of life in unmixed happiness for all his worshipers who no longer "fall short of the glory of God." They will have all the godly qualities in beauteous bloom and enjoy the fullness of sweet re-lationship with God, so that they will find themselves in a spiritual Paradise as well as an earthly Paradise. What a soul-stirring cause all this for praising the Grand Creator and Provider of all this unspeakable goodness! With melodious voices and all their musical skills that they have developed they will gratefully praise Him. They will forever join the heavenly throngs in responding to the enthusiastic call of the last one of the inspired Psalms:

[38] "Praise Jah, you people! Praise God in his holy place. Praise him in the expanse of his strength. Praise him for his works of mightiness. Praise him according to the abundance of his greatness. Praise him with the blowing of the horn. Praise him with the stringed instrument and the harp. Praise him with the tambourine and the circle dance. Praise him with strings and the pipe. Praise him with the cymbals of melodious sound. Praise him with the clashing cym-bals. Every breathing thing—let it praise Jah. Praise Jah, you people!"—Psalm 150:1-6.

37, 38. (a) To what natural state will Jehovah's "footstool" eventually be brought? (b) Will inhabitants of his "footstool" enjoy only a natural paradise, and in what way will they respond to the call of the last of the Psalms?

CHAPTER 10

→ *The "Sign" of Its Approach*

WHEN we look at it according to what the Bible says about it, the Millennium is a thing very much to be desired for all mankind, the living and the dead. That is why the announcement that it has approached is most welcome news for all who understand. We ought to be excitedly interested in knowing what valid reasons we have for being convinced that it has approached. What are they? Shall we take time to consider some of them?

[2] From our consideration of the Millennium thus far, we are aware of the fact that it must be preceded immediately by the most destructive war in all human history, "the war of the great day of God the Almighty" at Har–Magedon. We can now see the political rulers or "kings of the entire inhabited earth" being gathered, under forces beyond human control, for that War of all wars. This fact should in itself be a clear evidence that the hoped-for millennium that follows the War has also approached. (Revelation 16: 13-16) Taking an active part in that war, on the side of God the Almighty will be the Leader of God's heavenly armies, the one called Faithful and True, the Word of God. Already, before this Har–Magedon war begins, this heavenly Leader is a King. "Upon his head are many diadems," and, "upon his outer garment, even upon his thigh, he has a name written, King of kings and Lord of lords." (Revelation 19: 11-16) So he is already reigning as King before he enters upon that thousand-year-long period of reigning with his 144,000 Christian joint heirs.—Revelation 12:5; 14:1-4; 20:4-6.

---

1. Why should we be excitedly interested in knowing about the nearness of the Millennium?
2. (a) What gathering that we see going on is, in itself, clear evidence that the Millennium has approached? (b) Who leads the "war" on God's side, and in what capacity is he already serving?

³ The reference to the beginning of this premillennial reign of this King of kings, Jesus Christ, is made in an earlier picture of world events of our twentieth century. This picture is given in chapter six of Revelation, in which the apostle John tells us about what he saw when the Lamb of God, Jesus Christ, starts opening up the seven seals that seal shut the "scroll" that he has received from the hand of God who sits on the heavenly throne. Says John: "And I saw when the Lamb opened one of the seven seals, and I heard one of the four living creatures say with a voice as of thunder: 'Come!' And I saw, and, look! a white horse; and the one seated upon it had a bow; and a crown was given him, and he went forth conquering and to complete his conquest. And when he opened the second seal, I heard the second living creature say: 'Come!' And another came forth, a fiery-colored horse; and to the one seated upon it there was granted to take peace away from the earth so that they should slaughter one another; and a great sword was given him."—Revelation 6:1-4.

⁴ Here we see the symbols that depict the first world war, which broke out in the year 1914 C.E., but which was merely a forerunner to the second world war that took peace away from the earth for six more years. That first of world wars marked the time when the righteous warrior, Jesus Christ, received the heavenly crown and went forth against his enemies on the earth, to win the fight, to conquer completely his earthly enemies. This meant that he would later be fighting on God's side in the "war of the great day of God the Almighty" at Har–Magedon. His being crowned as King in heaven at the time of the first world war sets the stage for the fulfillment of the words of Psalm Two:

⁵ "Why have the nations been in tumult and the national groups themselves kept muttering an empty

3. With reference to the beginning of Christ's premillennial reign, what did John see when the first two seals of the scroll were opened (Revelation 6:1-4)?
4, 5. (a) In that rider on the fiery-colored horse, what do we see symbolized? (b) Who went forth at that time to conquer completely, and how did this set the stage for Psalm 2:1-6 to be fulfilled?

thing? The kings of earth take their stand and high officials themselves have massed together as one against Jehovah and against his anointed one [his Christ, Greek *Septuagint Version*], saying: 'Let us tear their bands apart and cast their cords away from us!' The very One sitting in the heavens will laugh; Jehovah himself will hold them in derision. At that time he will speak to them in his anger and in his hot displeasure he will disturb them, saying: 'I, even I, have installed my king upon Zion, my holy mountain.'"
—Psalm 2:1-6; compare Acts 4:24-30.

⁶ In spite of all the tumult that has disturbed the nations since the first world war of 1914-1918 C.E., Jehovah has had his King, his Son Jesus Christ, seated upon the heavenly seat of royal government, Zion. (Revelation 14:1; Hebrews 12:22) Neither World War I nor World War II nor the United Nations organization succeeded in unseating this Messianic King. The "war of the great day of God the Almighty" at Har–Magedon will confirm him in his heavenly throne, and he will be on hand there to begin his millennial reign with his loyal 144,000 joint heirs. (Revelation 19:19-21) For this vital reason the promised Millennium with life-giving blessings for mankind is assured to us. It has approached!

⁷ Despite the above-presented evidence, many skeptical persons will demand a "sign" before they decide to be convinced that the Millennium has really approached, yes, will begin within our generation. We are not of that "wicked and adulterous generation" of religious scribes and Pharisees of nineteen centuries ago, who wanted a sign from Jesus Christ, to convince them that he was the Messiah. (Matthew 12:38, 39) However, we do have the description of a "sign" that was given by Jesus Christ himself, and since he made it available for us, we would be keeping ourselves

---

6. Have world wars and the United Nations unseated Jehovah's King on Mount Zion, and what will the outcome of the war at Har–Magedon assure to us?
7. Why are we not like that ancient "wicked and adulterous generation," and yet where do we find a "sign" given by Jesus for us to consider?

in serious ignorance by refusing to consider it. The description is made available for us in chapters twenty-four and twenty-five of Matthew, chapter thirteen of Mark and chapter twenty-one of Luke. The description of the sign was given to his apostles upon request, not to prove that he was the Messiah or Christ but to indicate that certain promised future events were near at hand, about to be fulfilled. It was given on the eleventh day of the spring month of Nisan of the year 33 C.E., three days before his violent death.

THE PROPHECY OF THE "SIGN"

[8] Jesus had just predicted something that sounded very terrible to Jewish ears, namely, the destruction of their temple at Jerusalem. There he had declared to his religious opposers: "Look! Your house is abandoned to you. For I say to you, You will by no means see me from henceforth until you say, 'Blessed is he that comes in Jehovah's name!'" (Matthew 23:38, 39) This indicated that he was going away. When he returned, there would be those who would take up the prophetic words of Psalm 118:26 and say: "Blessed is he that comes in Jehovah's name!"

[9] Evidently it was not at the material temple in Jerusalem that the worshipers of Jehovah would welcome with those prophetic words the one coming in Jehovah's name. This is what Jesus made to appear very plainly, according to the account that follows his portentous words: "Departing now, Jesus was on his way from the temple, but his disciples approached to show him the buildings of the temple. In response he said to them: 'Do you not behold all these things? Truly I say to you, By no means will a stone be left here upon a stone and not be thrown down.'"—Matthew 24:1, 2.

[10] The twelve apostles made no inquiry about this

8. How did Jesus indicate that he would go away, and what words would be said on his return?
9. How did Jesus indicate that those words welcoming his return would not be used by worshipers at Jerusalem's temple?
10. On the Mount of Olives overlooking the temple, what question did four apostles ask Jesus, and how do various translations render their question?

frightful prophecy until they got over onto the Mount of Olives, which overlooks Jerusalem and from which a fine view could be got of that temple that had been renovated by King Herod the Great. The view seems to have stirred a momentous question among four of the apostles, which also aroused the interest of the others, for we read: "While he was sitting upon the Mount of Olives, the disciples approached him privately, saying: 'Tell us, When will these things be, and what will be the sign of your presence [pa·rou·si′a, Greek] and of the conclusion of the system of things?' " (Matthew 24:3) Young's Literal Translation of the Holy Bible translates their words from the Greek to read: "Tell us, when shall these be? and what is the sign of thy presence, and of the full end of the age?" Rotherham's The Emphasised Bible reads similarly: "Tell us when these things shall be,—and what the sign of thy presence and the conclusion of the age." Archbishop Newcome's New Translation (Corrected Text) reads: "What will be the sign of thy appearance, and of the end of the age?"—1808 edition.

[11] We today know when the destruction of the literal temple of Jerusalem took place. It was nineteen hundred years ago, in the summer of the year 70 C.E., when the Roman legions under General Titus destroyed the whole city. (Luke 21:20-24) But what about those other things, the "sign" of Christ's Parousia (presence, appearance) and of the conclusion of the age or system of things (or, the state*), as included in the disciples' question? True, the full end or conclusion of a Jewish state or system of things was reached in the year 70 C.E., but not the conclusion of the larger system of things of which that Jewish system was merely a prophetic pattern or type. Also, the Parousia, presence or appearance of the Lord Jesus Christ did not occur in that year. Since we are living in this

---

* The Sacred Writings of the Apostles and Evangelists of Jesus Christ Commonly called the New Testament, by Campbell, Macknight and Doddridge, of 1828 C.E.

11. (a) When did destruction of Jerusalem's temple take place, but what else did not also occur then? (b) Hence, what would it be natural for us to do respecting history?

twentieth century C.E., the most natural thing to do would be to look into the history of this twentieth century of ours to determine whether the foretold "sign" has appeared during our own generation.

[12] We should note that the disciples asked about the Parousia of the Lord Jesus Christ. In so doing, were they asking about his "coming"? His "Advent," as some call it? This question deserves to be raised, because the Christian martyr Stephen, when speaking about the first "coming" of the Lord Jesus, said to the Jewish Sánhedrin in Jerusalem: "Which one of the prophets did your forefathers not persecute? Yes, they killed those who made announcement in advance concerning the coming [e'leu·sis, Greek] of the righteous One, whose betrayers and murderers you have now become." (Acts 7:52) We notice that, when speaking about Christ's first coming, Stephen used, not the word pa·rou·si'a, but the Greek word e'leu·sis. These two Greek words are not only different in form and derivation but also different in meaning.

[13] The word pa·rou·si'a literally means "a being alongside," it being drawn from the Greek preposition para' ("alongside") and ousia (a "being"). Liddell and Scott's A Greek-English Lexicon, Volume II, page 1343, column 2, gives as the first definition of parousia the English word "presence." It gives as the second definition thereof arrival, and then adds: "Especially visit of a royal or official personage." In agreement with this the Theological Dictionary of the New Testament (by Gerhard Friedrich), in Volume V, gives as "The General Meaning" the English word "Presence." (Page 859) Then, as "The Technical Use of the Terms," in Hellenism, it gives "1. The Visit of a Ruler." On page 865 it says concerning "The Technical Use of pareimi [verb] and parousia in the N.T.": "In the N.T. the terms are never used for the coming of Christ in the flesh, and parousia never has the sense of return.

12. In view of what Stephen said about Christ's first coming, why should we ask whether the apostles were inquiring about Jesus' "coming" or "Advent"?
13. By derivation, what does the word parousia literally mean, but what do authorities on Greek words explain it to mean?

The idea of more than one *parousia* is first found only in the later Church."

¹⁴ So, then, Jesus' disciples were asking, not about his "arrival," but about *after* his arrival. They were asking about his "presence." And if, instead of using the word "presence," we resort to "the technical use of the terms" in Hellenism, the disciples would be understood to ask Jesus: "What will be the sign of your [visit as a royal personage] and of the conclusion of the system of things?" A "visit" includes more than an "arrival." It includes a "presence." In the so-called New Testament the Greek word *parousia* occurs twenty-four times, and in all its occurrences there, not only the *New World Translation of the Holy Scriptures* translates the word every time as "presence," but also other translations do so, as *Young's Literal Translation of the Holy Bible,* of 1862 C.E.; Wilson's *The Emphatic Diaglott,* of 1857-1863 C.E.; and Rotherham's *The Emphasised Bible,* of 1897 C.E. We note how fittingly "presence" and "absence" are contrasted, in Philippians 2:12, where the apostle Paul says: "You have always obeyed, not during my presence only, but now much more readily during my absence."

→   **THE PARABLE OF THE TEN VIRGINS**

¹⁵ The meaning of "presence" for *parousia* is called for in a number of features of Jesus' prophecy on the "sign" of the Parousia and the conclusion of the system of things. For instance, let us consider that portion of the prophecy which is generally spoken of as the parable of the wise and foolish virgins. Jesus had just prophesied about the "faithful and discreet slave" and the "evil slave," and now he prophesies of another feature in connection with his Parousia. "Then," says he, "the kingdom of the heavens will become like ten virgins that took their lamps and went out to meet the bridegroom. Five of them were foolish,

14. (a) According to the technical use of the Greek term in Hellenism, what expression would be used instead of "presence"? (b) In what translations is *parousia* consistently rendered "presence," with what contrast shown in Philippians 2:12?
15. A number of features of the "sign" foretold by Jesus call for Parousia to be rendered how, as in, for instance, which parable?

and five were discreet. For the foolish took their lamps but took no oil with them, whereas the discreet took oil in their receptacles with their lamps."—Matthew 25:1-4; 24:45-51.

[16] First of all, we should note that this parable involves a class of people and so is not to be applied in its completeness to the life and death of each individual. Those involved are "virgins" in a particular sense, inasmuch as they represent the "kingdom of the heavens," because "then," as Jesus said, "the kingdom of the heavens will become like [what?] ten virgins." This is the "kingdom" of which Jesus spoke earlier in his prophecy, saying: "This good news of the kingdom will be preached in all the inhabited earth for a witness to all the nations; and then the end will come."—Matthew 24:14.

[17] The number "ten" being Scripturally a number signifying perfection as regards earthly things, the "virgins" in being ten in number would picture all Christians who are in line or who profess to be in line for the heavenly kingdom in joint heirship with Jesus Christ. When, therefore, did the prophetic parable begin to have its fulfillment? On Sunday, Sivan 6, the Festival Day of Pentecost, of the year 33 C.E. How so? Because then the virgin class came into existence. This was because the faithful disciples of Jesus Christ, who were gathered together in an upper room in Jerusalem, were on that day baptized with the holy spirit. They were thereby begotten of God to be his spiritual sons in a position to be 'heirs of God' and "joint heirs with Christ." (Romans 8:17) But, in the Bible, heirs are usually the sons; and why is it that, in the parable, all the members of the spirit-begotten congregation of Christ's disciples are pictured as females, as virgin girls who, on a wedding night, go out to meet the bridegroom? and who is this "bridegroom"?

16. In what sense are the women "virgins," according to the introduction of the parable?
17. (a) Whom do the "virgins," being ten in number, picture? (b) When did the parable begin to be fulfilled, and why then?

[18] First of all, this "bridegroom" is the resurrected, glorified Lord Jesus Christ. John the Baptist spoke of him from that standpoint and accordingly compared himself with the "friend of the bridegroom." In those days the "friend of the bridegroom" generally arranged for the marriage between the bridegroom and the bride. On the night of union of the two engaged persons, more attention was focused on the bridegroom than on the friend of the bridegroom. And so John the Baptist said to his disciples whom he was preparing for Jesus Christ as their figurative "bridegroom": "I am not the Christ, but, I have been sent forth in advance of that one. He that has the bride is the bridegroom. However, the friend of the bridegroom, when he stands and hears him, has a great deal of joy on account of the voice of the bridegroom. Therefore this joy of mine has been made full. That one must go on increasing, but I must go on decreasing." (John 3:28-30) Rightly, then, John directed his disciples to Jesus.

[19] On his own part, Jesus compared himself with a bridegroom in another parable that he spoke. This was the parable of the "marriage feast" that a king prepared for his son, and this son stood for the Son of the great King of Eternity, Jehovah God. (Matthew 22:1-14) And in the Revelation, which Jesus Christ received from God and transmitted to the apostle John, Jesus as the Lamb of God is likened to a bridegroom who gets married to the congregation of his disciples, in these words: "Let us rejoice and be overjoyed, and let us give him the glory, because the marriage of the Lamb has arrived and his wife has prepared herself. Yes, it has been granted to her to be arrayed in bright, clean, fine linen, for the fine linen stands for the righteous acts of the holy ones. . . . Write: Happy are those invited to the evening meal of

18. In connection with marriage matters, to whom did John the Baptist compare himself and Jesus, and to whom did John direct his own disciples?

19, 20. (a) How does Jesus, in parable and in Revelation, compare himself with a bridegroom? (b) Correspondingly, what is the New Jerusalem called?

the Lamb's marriage." Furthermore, the apostle John tells of an angel who came to him and says:

²⁰ "He spoke with me and said: 'Come here, I will show you the bride, the Lamb's wife.' So he carried me away in the power of the spirit to a great and lofty mountain, and he showed me the holy city Jerusalem coming down out of heaven from God and having the glory of God."—Revelation 19:7-9; 21:9-11.

²¹ The apostle Paul compares the relationship between Jesus Christ and his congregation of 144,000 joint heirs to that of a husband and wife. He writes: "A husband is head of his wife as the Christ also is head of the congregation, he being a savior of this body. In fact, as the congregation is in subjection to the Christ, so let wives also be to their husbands in everything. Husbands, continue loving your wives, just as the Christ also loved the congregation and delivered up himself for it, that he might sanctify it, cleansing it with the bath of water by means of the word, that he might present the congregation to himself in its splendor, not having a spot or a wrinkle or any of such things, but that it should be holy and without blemish."—Ephesians 5:23-27.

²² The marriage of the Bridegroom Jesus Christ and his congregational "bride" is, of course, to take place in heaven, where they will be united together with the blessing of Jehovah God, the heavenly Father. However, it is to be noted that in the parable of the ten virgins there is no mention made of the bride. This is done in order to avoid confusion of thought. It is, in fact, because the "bride" is drawn or selected from the "ten virgins" themselves. The selected "virgins" are the "happy" ones who are "invited to the evening meal of the Lamb's marriage." (Revelation 19:9) In harmony with this, Jesus' parable shows the qualified "virgins" as going through the door into the wedding feast chamber. Just how they qualify, the parable goes on to illustrate.

21. In Ephesians 5:23-27, to what does Paul compare the relationship between Jesus Christ and his congregation?
22. Where does the marriage take place, and why does Jesus' parable make no mention of the bride of the bridegroom?

[23] The members of Christ's bridal congregation are likened to "virgins" for more than the reason that they are betrothed to a virgin Bridegroom. They are "virgins" in a further spiritual sense. Just as a virgin girl is clean, chaste, untouched sexually, so these faithful members of the Christian congregation must be pure and clean by separateness from this world, not having any connections with the religious and political organizations of this world. They do not join in any union of Church and State. They maintain their spiritual virginity by not involving themselves with the affairs of this world. (2 Timothy 2:3, 4) This is what is meant when it is said concerning the 144,000 who are seen standing with the Lamb of God on the spiritual Mount Zion: "These are the ones that did not defile themselves with women [like the religious harlot, Babylon the Great, and her daughters]; in fact, they are virgins. These are the ones that keep following the Lamb no matter where he goes."—Revelation 14:4; 17:3-5.

[24] As regards the required cleanness, the disciple James says: "If any man seems to himself to be a formal worshiper and yet does not bridle his tongue, but goes on deceiving his own heart, this man's form of worship is futile. The form of worship that is clean and undefiled from the standpoint of our God and Father is this: to look after orphans and widows in their tribulation, and to keep oneself without spot from the world."—James 1:26, 27.

GOING OUT TO MEET THE "BRIDEGROOM"

[25] On the Festival Day of Pentecost of the year 33 C.E., when the holy spirit descended as a baptism upon the faithful disciples of Jesus Christ as they waited in Jerusalem, the Christian congregation started out with the "form of worship that is clean and undefiled

23. The fact that the members of Christ's congregation are likened to "virgins" puts what requirements upon them?
24. What does James 1:26, 27 say about the required cleanness of those likened to virgins?
25. How did Christ's congregation, at Pentecost of 33 C.E., start out with the religion pure and undefiled from God's standpoint, and what evidence did they have of this?

from the standpoint of our God and Father." They were spiritually a virgin class, separated from the religious organization that had rejected Jesus Christ and brought about his impalement by the Roman governor Pontius Pilate. (Acts 2:1-42) They started out with the teachings of the Messiah Jesus and the teachings of his twelve apostles, and kept themselves from that "crooked generation" that was steeped in unscriptural religious traditions handed down from misguided forefathers. (Acts 2:40; Galatians 1:13-17; Matthew 15:1-9) The baptism of the holy spirit along with the gift of tongues was an evidence that they had the true religion, and they knew it. Now they must remain "virgin" in it.

²⁶ It was on that day (Sivan 6, 33 C.E.) that the Christian congregation became espoused, betrothed, promised in marriage to the heavenly Bridegroom, Jesus Christ. All those who thereafter became additions to that original congregation of 120 disciples at Jerusalem became part of that betrothed class and were obliged to keep themselves "virgin." To this fact the apostle Paul refers, when he warns the Christians at Corinth against breaking their engagement to Jesus Christ and getting married to a false Christ. Somewhat like a "friend of the bridegroom," Paul says:

²⁷ "I am jealous over you with a godly jealousy, for I personally promised you in marriage to one husband that I might present you as a chaste virgin to the Christ. But I am afraid that somehow, as the serpent seduced Eve by its cunning, your minds might be corrupted away from the sincerity and the chastity that are due the Christ. For, as it is, if someone comes and preaches a Jesus other than the one we preached, or you receive a spirit other than what you received, or good news other than what you accepted, you easily put up with him. For I consider that I have not in a single thing proved inferior to your superfine apostles." —2 Corinthians 11:2-5.

26, 27. (a) In a spiritual way, to whom did the Christian congregation become betrothed on Pentecost of 33 C.E.? (b) How did Paul, like a "friend of the bridegroom," speak to Christians in 2 Corinthians 11: 2-5?

[28] Their marriage to the virgin Bridegroom in heaven was to be in the indefinite future, some time distant from that espousal day of Pentecost of 33 C.E. Fifty-two days before that, on the night of his betrayal by the unfaithful apostle Judas Iscariot, Jesus had said to his faithful apostles: "In the house of my Father there are many abodes. Otherwise, I would have told you, because I am going my way to prepare a place for you. Also, if I go my way and prepare a place for you, I am coming again and will receive you home to myself, that where I am you also may be. And where I am going you know the way." (John 14:2-4) Forty-two days after that, when he was ascending from the Mount of Olives and into the sky before the eyes of a number of his disciples, two angels appeared to them and said: "Men of Galilee, why do you stand looking into the sky? This Jesus who was received up from you into the sky will come thus in the same manner as you have beheld him going into the sky." (Acts 1:9-11) Hence, the disciples knew that, like a Jewish bridegroom on the wedding night, the departed Jesus would come to take them to his heavenly Father's home, even as Jesus had previously assured them. —John 14:1-3.

[29] With that prospect of the wedding occasion, the espoused-virgin class set out to meet the Bridegroom, to welcome him and to rejoice with him. They had to keep on the watch, for they knew "neither the day nor the hour." (Matthew 25:13) How many of those who started out on the day of Pentecost of 33 C.E. and the thousands of those who joined them later would prove to be like the "discreet" virgins of the parable, and how many like the "foolish" or indiscreet virgins? The parable pictures the number of the discreet and the number of the foolish as being equal, to indicate that there was an equal opportunity for all who really start out, and also in order not to indicate that there would

28. How were the disciples told, both by Jesus and by angels, that he would come like a Jewish bridegroom to take them home?
29. (a) When did the "virgin" class start out to meet the Bridegroom? (b) What question now arose, and what is indicated in the fact that both kinds of virgins were equal in number?

be more of the one kind than of the other kind; the matter was left indefinite. But the parable did foretell that not all of those setting out as "virgins" would prove worthy of being admitted to enter in and enjoy the "evening meal of the Lamb's marriage."—Luke 12:35-38.

30 What, then, was it that distinguished the discreet or prudent virgins from the foolish or imprudent virgins? This: "The foolish took their lamps but took no oil with them, whereas the discreet took oil in their receptacles with their lamps." (Matthew 25:3, 4) Yet all of them knew that their having lighted lamps clear to the end of the welcoming procession would be an identification of them, a proof of their worthiness to be admitted to the wedding feast. In view of this they needed enough oil to last them until the wedding procession reached the home of the bridegroom. What, in the fulfillment of the parable, was pictured by the oil? They started out to meet the bridegroom before his arrival was announced, and their lamps were burning when they started out. So at least there was then oil in their lamps. But was it enough to keep their lamps burning till the wedding procession entered the bridegroom's house?

31 The oil was an illuminating liquid. Without it the wick in the lamp would not give a steady, continuous light. What did their carrying a lighted lamp to the wedding feast symbolize? In answer to this question, we must remember the purpose for which Jesus gave this parable. The purpose was to show that those who desired to gain admittance to the heavenly marriage would have to bear a certain identification, a certain personality, and they would have to retain this clear down to the finish, no matter at what time the wedding procession began and carried on until it finally reached the Bridegroom's home for his "bride." For one thing, the "kingdom of the heavens" class, while on earth

---

30. (a) What distinguished the discreet virgins from the foolish ones? (b) Did all start out with burning lamps, and so what was the vital question in this respect?
31, 32. (a) The purpose of the parable was to show what with respect to those symbolic "virgins"? (b) What waiting attitude must they maintain, as expressed by Paul in Philippians 3:20, 21?

amid this bedarkened world, would have to remain "virgin" in a spiritual way. They had their hopes fixed on the heavenly Bridegroom, and this attitude allowed for no contamination of themselves with the unclean world. They must "keep following the Lamb no matter where he goes." (Revelation 14:4) They must keep like the apostle Paul, who said:

[32] "Our citizenship exists in the heavens, from which place also we are eagerly waiting for a savior, the Lord Jesus Christ, who will refashion our humiliated body to be conformed to his glorious body according to the operation of the power that he has, even to subject all things to himself."—Philippians 3:20, 21.

[33] So their sustained spiritual virginity is because of their desire and determination to prove worthy to be accepted by the heavenly Bridegroom as his "bride." Their daily lives must reflect this amid the darkness of this world of mankind. In his Sermon on the Mount in the year 31 C.E., Jesus Christ the Bridegroom said to his disciples: "You are the light of the world. A city cannot be hid when situated upon a mountain. People light a lamp and set it, not under the measuring basket, but upon the lampstand, and it shines upon all those in the house. Likewise let your light shine before men, that they may see your fine works and give glory to your Father who is in the heavens."—Matthew 5:14-16.

[34] The apostle Paul also said to fellow Christians: "Keep doing all things free from murmurings and arguments, that you may come to be blameless and innocent, children of God without a blemish in among a crooked and twisted generation, among whom you are shining as illuminators in the world, keeping a tight grip on the word of life, that I may have cause for exultation in Christ's day, that I did not run in vain or work hard in vain."—Philippians 2:14-16.

---

33. (a) How long must they retain this spiritual virginity, in order to prove worthy of what? (b) How did Jesus speak of their reflecting this acceptable condition?
34. According to Paul's words in Philippians 2:14-16, how were the Christians to shine?

[35] For the "kingdom of the heavens" class to shine as "the light of the world," they must engage in "fine works" that glorify the heavenly Father; they must do all things without murmuring and arguments, keep themselves blameless and innocent as far as their Christian lives are concerned, proving themselves to be without blemish as children of God. They must do this in expectation of the Bridegroom's coming to take them to his heavenly Father's home. Their doing all this is pictured by the virgins' holding up their lighted lamps. It is something that will delight the Bridegroom amid the world's night of darkness.

THE SYMBOLIC OIL AND RECEPTACLES

[36] What, then, does the oil, the illuminating liquid, picture? It symbolizes that which keeps the "kingdom of the heavens" class shining as illuminators amid a bedarkened world. Accordingly, it would picture the "word of life," on which they must keep a "tight grip"; for it is written: "Your word is a lamp to my foot, and a light to my roadway." (Psalm 119:105) "The very disclosure of your words gives light, making the inexperienced ones understand." (Psalm 119:130) As a picture, the "oil" would also include the holy spirit of God, for this holy invisible active force of God aids one in understanding God's Word. (John 16:13) Also, this holy spirit in a Christian manifests itself in fruitage, in the fruits of the spirit such as love, joy, peace, long-suffering, kindness, goodness, faith, mildness, self-control. (Galatians 5:22, 23) Such spiritual "oil" has illuminative power.

[37] In the parable, the "virgins" had to have a supply of oil in receptacles, from which they could pour it into the lamps that they carried. They could not make their own bodies "receptacles" by drinking the oil and then, as it was needed, regurgitating it into the lamps to keep them burning. However, having "re-

35. So what, then, is pictured by the virgins' holding up their lighted lamps, and this in expectation of what?
36. What does the "oil," as an illuminating liquid, picture?
37. What does the virgins' having a supply of oil in their "receptacles" picture, and why so?

ceptacles" filled with oil meant that they had an oil supply in their possession, not, of course, in their personal bodies, as containers. So the "kingdom of the heavens" class does have in its possession, yes, has within itself, a supply of God's Word and his holy spirit. Fittingly, then, the "receptacles" pictured in the parable stand for the members of the "virgin" class themselves as possessors of the symbolic "oil." They certainly do need an ample supply of such "oil" as they go forth to meet the Bridegroom and join his procession.

[38] In the parable, the ten virgins used oil lamps for brightening up the night scene. What, then, do those lamps picture in the fulfillment of the parable today? The same thing as the oil "receptacles" do, for the ancient lamps carried illuminating oil the same as the supply "receptacles" did. The members of the "kingdom of the heavens" class are themselves the symbolic lamps. Not that they swallow oil to the full and then pour oil all over themselves and set fire to themselves so as to become "living torches" lined up along the procession route like self-sacrificing martyrs in honor of the Bridegroom. No, but they are filled with God's enlightening Word and his holy spirit, and this makes them shine in a spiritual way to the honor of the glorious heavenly Bridegroom. They themselves, because of their spiritual qualities, are "illuminators in the world." Because of the kind of lives that they live under the influence of God's Word and spirit, they shine to His glory.

[39] Inasmuch as no hour of the night was set for the bridegroom to leave the house where his bride was given to him and thereafter to lead a procession back to his own home for married life, the virgins of the parable did not know exactly how long they might have to wait for the bridegroom to put in appearance. So they did not know how long they might have to

38. What, then, is symbolized by the virgins' lamps, and in what way is there a shining?
39. (a) Why did the "virgins" not know how long they would have to wait for the bridegroom? (b) What did the discreet virgins therefore find it advisable to do?

keep their lamps burning. It would be advisable therefore for them to have not only filled lamps but also a receptacle filled with additional oil. The "discreet" or prudent virgins saw this and "took oil in their receptacles," along with their lighted lamps. The "foolish" or indiscreet, imprudent virgins did not do so, and their foolishness in this regard became evident in course of time.

⁴⁰ In the fulfillment of the parable, those pictured by the "discreet" five virgins take along extra oil in their receptacles, so to speak, by filling themselves up with the Word of God, having it in their minds and their hearts by means of private personal study, by attending Christian meetings where God's Word is taught and discussed and by making use of that Word of God through sharing it with others. They pray for God's spirit and seek to be continually "filled with spirit." (Ephesians 5:18) In any future time of emergency this fullness of the spiritual "oil" would help them to renew their powers of endurance and to keep on shining as the "light of the world" in proof that they were holding true to their betrothal to their heavenly Bridegroom.

"WHILE THE BRIDEGROOM WAS DELAYING"

⁴¹ In the autumn of the year 36 C.E., the door was opened for uncircumcised non-Jews, Gentiles, to be converted to the Christianity that is the "form of worship that is clean and undefiled" from the standpoint of God. These believing Gentiles received God's holy spirit and its gifts the same as the Jewish believers had on the day of Pentecost in 33 C.E. (Acts 10:1 to 11:18; 15:7-19) Thus these also became part of the "chaste virgin" class that is 'promised in marriage' to Christ. (2 Corinthians 11:2) From then onward they had a part in the fulfillment of the parable

40. (a) In fulfillment of the parable, how do the "discreet" virgin class take along oil in their receptacles? (b) How does this aid them to prove true to their betrothal to their Bridegroom?
41. (a) When did Gentiles first become part of the "chaste virgin" class that went out to meet the Bridegroom? (b) Because of what happened to the Jews in 70 C.E., did the "virgins" meet the Bridegroom then?

of the "ten virgins" and, to use the language of the parable, they "took their lamps and went out to meet the bridegroom." In the year 70 C.E. the city of Jerusalem and its gorgeous temple were destroyed by the Roman legions, but, although that horrible destruction was an expression of God's judgment against the unbelieving, antichristian Jews, the "chaste virgin" class did not meet up with the heavenly Bridegroom whom they had gone out to welcome.—Luke 21:20-24; Matthew 24:15-22; Mark 13:14-20.

⁴² Years went by, and toward the end of the first century C.E., about the year 96 C.E., the apostle John received the marvelous Revelation with what it had to reveal about the heavenly Bridegroom Jesus Christ and his "bride," who was pictured as the New Jerusalem. (Revelation 21:1 to 22:17) This must have been of untold encouragement to the "chaste virgin" class who were still persisting in their hopes of meeting the returning Bridegroom. However, the heavenly Bridegroom closed that Revelation, saying: "He that bears witness of these things says, 'Yes; I am coming quickly.' " In response, the aged apostle John replied: "Amen! Come, Lord Jesus," and then John added in closing: "May the undeserved kindness of the Lord Jesus Christ be with the holy ones." (Revelation 22:20, 21) Possibly two years after that, about 98 C.E., the apostle John wrote the first of his three letters, and in it he said:

⁴³ "Young children, it is the last hour, and, just as you have heard that antichrist is coming, even now there have come to be many antichrists; from which fact we gain the knowledge that it is the last hour." "We know that every person that has been born from God does not practice sin, but the One born from God watches him, and the wicked one does not fasten his hold on him. We know we originate with God, but the whole world is lying in the power of the wicked one." —1 John 2:18; 5:18, 19.

⁴⁴ Shortly after writing his three letters and also the life account of Jesus known as the Gospel of John, the aged apostle must have died, doubtless the last of the "twelve apostles of the Lamb." John's passing would therefore allow for the gradual opening of the door to the incoming, not of Christ the Bridegroom, but of the antichrist, concerning whom John had warned. (2 Thessalonians 2:7, 8) Then the "light of the world" was almost snuffed out. The symbolic "lamps" of the class pictured by the "ten virgins" must have burned very low. In fact, the number of true "virgins" must have become very few. Other interests, mundane material interests, rather than the desire for the return of the Lord Jesus, must have occupied the attention of those who were merely professing Christians. So long a time was passing, and yet he did not put in appearance.

⁴⁵ This was what the parable of the ten virgins foretold in these words: "While the bridegroom was delaying, they all nodded and went to sleep." (Matthew 25:5) Likewise, within the religious group that professed to be the Christian congregation, the members were growing tired of waiting for the Bridegroom's coming. In fact, with the so-called "conversion" of Constantine the Great and his making the professed Christianity of his day the State Religion of the Roman Empire, there appeared to be no need for the return of Christ. Christendom was now established, many of the religious bishops of the churches became allied with the Roman State and began reigning in a religious sense. Not only were the genuine apostles of Jesus Christ asleep in death, but these professed Christian bishops fell asleep to Christian responsibility and the need to keep the Christian congregation pure, free from the philosophies and traditions of men, and the need to keep absolutely pure and spotless from

44. (a) John's death thereafter opened up the way for the coming of whom? (b) By then how brightly must the lighted lamps of the "ten virgins" class have been burning, and what hope was there of meeting the Bridegroom?
45. How was it fulfilled that, "while the bridegroom was delaying, they all nodded and went to sleep," especially by Constantine's time?

the world in a clean, undefiled form of worship before God.

[46] This religious situation seems to parallel that which was pictured in Jesus' parable of the wheat and the weeds, in which he said: "The kingdom of the heavens has become like a man that sowed fine seed in his field. While men were sleeping, his enemy came and oversowed weeds in among the wheat, and left." (Matthew 13:24, 25) Only after a long growing season would the harvest come and the time for the parabolic "man" to come to the harvest work and order the weeds to be pulled out and the pure "wheat" to be gathered into his storehouses. Interestingly, in explaining all this parable, Jesus used the same expression that his apostles used when asking him the question recorded in Matthew 24:3. Jesus said: "The harvest is a conclusion of a system of things." (Matthew 13:39) Till the conclusion of the worldly system of things was yet a long time, and the sleep foretold in the parable of the "ten virgins" proved to be a long one. The fulfillment of the final features of the parable of the virgins was to be part of the "sign" that we are in the "conclusion of the system of things."

46. (a) How does this sleeping of the "ten virgins" class parallel what Jesus foretold in the parable of the wheat and the weeds? (b) How long was the spiritual sleeping to last, and at what time was fulfillment of the parable's final feature to be located?

CHAPTER 11

"Here Is the Bridegroom!"

DURING that indefinitely long sleep as foretold in Jesus' parable, there must have been some stirrings on the part of the symbolic "virgins," especially on the part of the "discreet" virgins who had brought along an extra supply of oil in their recep-

1. During this indefinitely long sleep of the "ten virgins," there would be stirrings on whose part, and especially after what religious awakening?

tacles. This was so particularly after there was a religious awakening in the early sixteenth century C.E. and an effort was strenuously put forth in Europe to return to the inspired Holy Scriptures as the sole book of divine truth, the true inspired guide for the followers of Christ the Bridegroom. Christ's promise to come again made quite an impression on sincere Bible readers and students. They saw that this second coming would be premillennial, that is to say, before the promised Millennium began, this millennium to be marked by Satan's being bound and imprisoned in the "bottomless pit" or "abyss."

[2] For instance, in the first half of the eighteenth century there arose a Lutheran theologian named Johann Albrecht Bengel, who was born at Winnenden in Wuerttemberg, Germany, in 1687 and died in 1752 C.E. He wrote a number of books on the Sacred Scriptures. Says the *Encyclopædia Britannica* (eleventh edition) concerning them:

> The more important are: *Ordo Temporum* [Order of the Times], a treatise on the chronology of Scripture, in which he enters upon speculations regarding the end of the world, and an *Exposition of the Apocalypse* which enjoyed for a time great popularity in Germany, and was translated into several languages.—Volume 3, page 737.

Says M'Clintock and Strong's *Cyclopædia* concerning Bengel:

> His chronological works, endeavoring to fix the "number of the beast," the date of the "millennium" (he was positive in fixing the beginning of the millennium at the year 1836), etc., have rather detracted from his reputation for solidity of judgment.—Volume 1, pages 749, 750.

[3] However, the published writings of Bengel in the first half of the eighteenth century did not prove to be the midnight cry: "Behold, the bridegroom! Come out to meet him." "Here is the bridegroom! Be on your way out to meet him." (Matthew 25:6, *Revised Standard Version; New World Translation*) Those who fol-

2. How did the Lutheran theologian J. A. Bengel play a part in such stirrings religiously?
3. (a) Why did those published writings of Bengel not prove to be the midnight cry about the Bridegroom? (b) How did another stirring come with William Miller of Pittsfield, Massachusetts?

lowed up Bengel's publications and acted according to them did not meet the heavenly Bridegroom in the year 1836 by a visible return of Him in the flesh. In course of time there came other stirrings among those Christians who professed to be of the "chaste virgin" class, particularly that in connection with a man born in Pittsfield, Massachusetts, U.S.A., in the year 1781. This man was William Miller, who became the founder of the so-called *Millerites* or *Adventists*. Says M'Clintock and Strong's *Cyclopœdia,* Volume 6, page 271:

> About 1833, when a resident of Low Hampton, N.Y., he began his career as an apostle of the new doctrine, which taught that the world was coming to an end in 1843. The main argument on which his belief rested was that relative to the termination of the 2300 days in Daniel 8:14, which he regarded as years. Then considering the seventy weeks in Daniel 9:24, as the key to the date of the 2300 days of the preceding chapter, and dating the periods B.C. 457, when Artaxerxes, king of Persia, sent up Ezra from his captivity, to restore the Jewish polity at Jerusalem (Ezra 7), and ending the seventy weeks, as commentators generally do, in A.D. 33, with the crucifixion of Christ, he found the remainder of the 2300 days, which was 1810, would end in 1843. For ten years he held forth to this purport, and succeeded in gathering a large number of followers, which is said to have reached fifty thousand, who awaited, with credulous expectation, the appointed day. The result, however, turning out contrary to the teaching of their apostle, the Adventists, as they are sometimes termed, gradually forsook Miller. He died at Low Hampton, Washington County, N.Y., December 20, 1849.

[4] Evidently, then, the launching of the Millerite movement did not turn out to be the midnight cry, "Here is the bridegroom!" The heavenly Bridegroom did not appear in the flesh visibly to those Adventists and take them in a rapture to their desired heavenly home, in 1843. And yet Bible study continued on. Thirty years later found a small group of men, not associated with the Adventists or affiliated with any of the religious sects of Christendom, studying the Holy Scriptures at Pittsburgh (Allegheny), Pennsylvania,

---

4. (a) How did the Miller movement not prove to be the midnight cry? (b) Thirty years later, what did an independent group of Bible students discover about Christ's second coming?

U.S.A. They studied independently so as to avoid looking at the Bible through sectarian spectacles. Among these men was one Charles Taze Russell, just entered into his twenties. They were, of course, intensely interested in the second coming of the heavenly Bridegroom, Jesus Christ. However, their Bible studies led to their discovery that Christ's return would be an invisible one, not visibly in the flesh as a materialized man, but invisibly in the spirit, inasmuch as he was no longer flesh and blood. His arrival would therefore be unseen to men, and this arrival would begin an invisible presence or parousia on his part. But it would be made manifest by evidences.

→ **"SEVEN TIMES"—**
"THE TIMES OF THE GENTILES"

[5] In the course of their Bible studies, these searching students took up a consideration of the "times of the Gentiles," as spoken of by Jesus at Luke 21:24 (*AV*), and they associated those Gentile Times with the "seven times" mentioned four times in Daniel, chapter four, verses 16, 23, 25, 32. What did those Bible students determine to be the date for those "seven times" of Gentile domination of the earth to end legally before God? Well, at that time there was a monthly magazine being published in Brooklyn, New York, by one George Storrs, and it was called "Bible Examiner." In the year 1876 the twenty-four-year-old Russell made a contribution on the subject to this magazine. It was published in Volume XXI, Number 1, which was the issue of October, 1876. On pages 27, 28 of that issue Russell's article was published under the title "Gentile Times: When Do They End?" In that article (page 27) Russell said: "The seven times will end in A.D. 1914."

[6] In the following year (1877) Russell joined with one Nelson H. Barbour, of Rochester, New York, in

5. In the course of their studies, what time period mentioned by Jesus did they consider, and, in 1876, what did Russell have published about the end of that period?
6. (a) In 1877, what book did Russell join in publishing, and what did it say about the end of the Gentile Times? (b) When did the chronology then followed end six thousand years of man's existence, but in what year was the seventh millennium figured to begin?

publishing a book entitled "Three Worlds, and the Harvest of This World." In this book it was set forth that the end of the Gentile Times in 1914 C.E. would be preceded by a period of forty years marked by the opening of a harvest of three and a half years, beginning in 1874 C.E. This harvest was understood to be under the invisible direction of the Lord Jesus Christ, whose presence or parousia began in the year 1874. Shortly afterward was understood to be the beginning of the great antitypical Jubilee for mankind, that had been foreshadowed by the ancient "jubilee" observances of the Jews under the law of Moses. (Leviticus, chapter twenty-five) According to the Bible chronology that was thereafter adopted, the six thousand years of man's existence on the earth ended in the year 1872 but the Lord Jesus did not come at the end of those six millenniums of human existence, rather, at the start of the antitypical Jubilee in October of 1874. The year 1874 was calculated as being the end of six millenniums of sin among mankind. From this latter date mankind was understood to be in the seventh millennium.—Revelation 20:4.

[7] From that understanding of matters, the "chaste virgin" class began going forth to meet the heavenly Bridegroom in the year 1874, as they believed him to have arrived in that year and to be from then on invisibly present. They felt that they were already living in the invisible presence of the Bridegroom. Due to this fact, when Charles T. Russell began publishing his own religious magazine in July of 1879, he published it under the title "Zion's Watch Tower and Herald of Christ's Presence." He had already become familiar with Wilson's *The Emphatic Diaglott*, which translated the Greek word *pa·rou·si'a* as "presence," not "coming," in Matthew 24:3 and elsewhere. The new magazine was heralding Christ's invisible presence as having begun in 1874. This presence was to continue until the end of the Gentile Times in 1914, when the Gentile nations

7. (a) Why did Russell's religious magazine when published in 1879 include in its title "And Herald of Christ's Presence"? (b) What was to happen when that "presence" reached the end of the Gentile Times in 1914?

would be destroyed and the remnant of the "chaste virgin" class would be glorified with their bridegroom in heaven by death and resurrection to life in the spirit. Thus the class pictured by the five wise virgins would enter through the door into the wedding.

[8] As the years passed by and the time drew closer, the remnant of the "chaste virgin" class looked ahead with intensifying interest to that critical date, October 1, 1914. These were a class of Christians separated from this unclean world and fully "consecrated" to God through Christ, and they had symbolized their "consecration" to God by water immersion. They were endeavoring to let their light shine as they approached the time when they expected to meet their Bridegroom in the heavens. Finally the day arrived, October 1, 1914, and on the morning of that day Charles T. Russell as president of the Watch Tower Bible and Tract Society announced to the headquarters staff of workers in Brooklyn, New York: "The Gentile Times have ended and their kings have had their day."

C. T. Russell

[9] However, with that end of the Gentile Times there did not also come the anticipated glorification of the remnant of the church in the heavens. It was first on October 31, 1916, that Russell himself died, leaving the Society's presidency to another. Something must have been miscalculated.

8. (a) What did the remnant of the "chaste virgin" class look forward to eagerly, and why? (b) On the morning of that day, what did Russell announce to the headquarters staff of workers in Brooklyn, N.Y.?
9. However, when did Russell himself die, and what conclusion must be drawn therefrom?

[10] Instead of seeing the glorification of the Christian church in heaven, the date of October 1, 1914, saw great trouble shaping up for those who were desirous of meeting the heavenly Bridegroom. As the years of World War I dragged on in a horrifying fashion there came a climax to the persecution that continued to be heaped upon the "chaste virgin" class. This came in the summer of 1918, when the Watch Tower Society's new president, Joseph F. Rutherford, and the secretary-treasurer thereof, W. E. Van Amburgh, and six other Christian men connected with the headquarters staff in Brooklyn, New York, were unjustly convicted in a Federal court and imprisoned in the Federal penitentiary in Atlanta, Georgia. From his cell there, President Rutherford addressed a letter to his fellow Christians who were undergoing persecution outside prison bars and walls. A portion of this letter was printed on the fourth page of the program of the four-day convention of the International Bible Students Association, August 30 to September 2, 1918, at Milwaukee, Wisconsin.* This letter revealed the heart-yearning of the "chaste virgin" class for an early union with the Bridegroom in the heavens, especially in these lines that we quote therefrom:

TO THE ISRAEL OF GOD

"Dearly Beloved in Christ:—

"Prison life seems strange; and yet every experience is attended with joy, since we look at all such from the heavenly viewpoint. Truly now we can sing:

'Fade, fade, each earthly joy,
    Jesus is mine!'

"In fact, there are now no earthly joys; but we are looking with joyful anticipation to our gathering home. . . . We often feel in a strait betwixt two—whether we would prefer to depart or to come and serve you a season before we go home. His will be done! I feel sure that all these experiences are ripening the church pre-

---

* See the book *"Then Is Finished the Mystery of God,"* page 274, last paragraph. See also *The Watch Tower* under date of August 15, 1918, page 249, on Milwaukee convention and Rutherford's letter.

10. (a) What did October 1, 1914, see shaping up for the remnant of the "chaste virgin" class on earth? (b) When did the persecution reach a climax, and what letter shows a heart yearning for union with the heavenly Bridegroom?

paratory to the final ingathering. The letters from the dear ones elsewhere show how sweetly they are yielding to the fire that is consuming the sacrifice. . . .

" . . . Do all you can to encourage the dear sheep of the flock. Comfort them with the sweet promises of an early and glorious home-coming. Never have I loved you all so much as now. How sweet it will be to gather around our Father's throne and rejoice with joy unspeakable forevermore! . . .

"I thank our dear Father for being so good as to send seven brethren with me, that we may have these privileges together. . . .

"Know of a certainty that we greatly love you all. The grace of our Lord Jesus Christ be with you all.

"Your brother and servant by His grace,
"J. F. RUTHERFORD."

[11] During all these hard experiences amid the darkness of World War I the suffering remnant of the "chaste virgin" class did not appreciate that the year 1874, then over forty years in the past, had not been the time of the Bridegroom's return and the time for announcing: "Here is the bridegroom! Be on your way out to meet him." The time of the midnight cry was yet ahead, but close at hand. The time spent in prison by President Rutherford did not prove to be twenty years, according to the sentence that had been imposed upon him by the court on June 21, 1918, but turned out to be only nine months. On March 25, 1919, he and his seven companions were released from the Atlanta Penitentiary and returned to Brooklyn, New York, where, on March 26, they were all admitted to bail and an appeal was granted to them. They were again free to take up their postwar work with all other members of the remnant of the "chaste virgin" class. This remnant had experienced no ingathering to their heavenly Father's throne away from the increasing darkness of this wicked world. A new period of Christian service on earth was opening up!

[12] It was at this critical juncture that they ex-

11. (a) During that persecution, what did the remnant of the "chaste virgin" class not appreciate regarding 1874? (b) How long did the Society's representatives serve in penitentiary, and what opened up on their release?
12. What part of Jesus' parable of the "ten virgins" did they then experience?

perienced what was foretold by the heavenly Bridegroom in his parable of the "ten virgins," in these words: "Right in the middle of the night there arose a cry, 'Here is the bridegroom! Be on your way out to meet him.' Then all those virgins rose and put their lamps in order."—Matthew 25:6, 7.

[13] In the parable the announcement of the bridegroom's being there was not made by the "ten virgins." It was evidently made by the bridegroom's attendants. The virgins merely heard the cry. Likewise, in the year 1919 C.E., the fact of the heavenly Bridegroom's invisible presence was thrust upon all those who claimed to be like the virgins awaiting the coming of the Bridegroom to lead them to the spiritual wedding feast inside his Father's home.

[14] Hence, the year 1919 proved to be a rousing year for all the professed "virgins," the foolish ones and the discreet ones. The first global war was over, and the League of Nations was pushed forward as an international organization for world peace and security. Since the outbreak of that world war in 1914 a sufficient number of features of Jesus' prophecy concerning his parousia and the conclusion of the system of things had been fulfilled to make up a composite "sign" that Jesus Christ had indeed come into his heavenly kingdom at the end of the Gentile Times in 1914. So the promised Messianic kingdom of God had been established in the heavens. World history and Church history now really proved that the Christ was present!

PUTTING THEIR "LAMPS" IN ORDER

[15] Now at last the *Watch Tower* magazine could rightly bear the subtitle "And Herald of Christ's Presence." The eight Christian Bible students released from the Federal penitentiary in March were privileged to attend the annual celebration of the Lord's Supper on Sunday night, April 13, 1919, and, according to an

13, 14. (a) In the parable, by whom was the bridegroom's presence announced, and how was this fulfilled? (b) Since 1914, what evidence was there to prove that the heavenly Bridegroom was really present? 15. (a) What subtitle could the *Watch Tower* magazine now correctly bear? (b) *Watch Tower* readers world wide were stirred by what announcement in the issue of April 15, 1919?

incomplete report of the total attendance published in
The Watch Tower as of May 15, page 151, there were
upward of 17,961 who celebrated. Pages 117, 118 of
the *Watch Tower* issue of April 15, 1919, announced
the release on bail of $10,000 each of the eight falsely
accused men, and the grand reception that was given
to them at the Brooklyn Bethel home by hundreds of
fellow Christians. This announcement, published world
wide, had a stimulating effect on readers of *The Watch
Tower and Herald of Christ's Presence*.

[16] It was now no time for spiritual drowsiness and
sleep. It was a time for action when, as Isaiah 60:2
foretold, "darkness itself will cover the earth, and thick
gloom the national groups; but upon you Jehovah will
shine forth, and upon you his own glory will be seen."
The world situation called for courageous action on the
part of all the "consecrated" Bible students. No time
was lost in strengthening the Christian courage of
those who had been looking for the Bridegroom, for,
in the *Watch Tower* issues of August 1 and 15, 1919,
there were published the two articles on the theme
"Blessed Are the Fearless," together with announcements of arrangements for a "General Convention:
Cedar Point, Lake Erie," for eight days, September
1-8, and on an international scale. Vigorously shaking
themselves free of spiritual sleepiness, thousands of
God's "consecrated" people flocked to the convention
location, around 6,000, particularly from Canada and
the United States, attending the daily sessions. That
stirring convention was an occasion for the "consecrated" ones to renew their resolves to be wide awake
and active in God's service that lay ahead.

[17] Tremendous enthusiasm was evoked on "Co-
laborers Day," Friday, September 5, when President
J. F. Rutherford announced the publication of a new
magazine from October 1, 1919, onward, to be en-

16. (a) According to Isaiah 60:2, for what was it then the time? (b) How
was the courage of the "consecrated" Bible students strengthened, and
what international gathering was held?
17, 18. (a) On "Co-laborers Day" of that General Convention, what was
announced for publication, and with what prospect? (b) In what way
were the instructions on how to proceed with the work encouraging,
and were the happenings of that convention day merely of passing
interest?

titled "The Golden Age." This was to be a companion of the *Watch Tower* magazine for publishing the good news of God's Messianic kingdom, and God's "consecrated" people were encouraged to take part in getting subscriptions for it, looking to the time for the circulating of 4,000,000 copies of an issue. Later, additional instructions on how to proceed in this world-wide publicity work appeared in the two-and-a-half-page article entitled "Announcing the Kingdom," on pages 279-281 of *The Watch Tower* as of September 15, 1919.

[18] What an energizing call to all readers was the statement in the third-last paragraph of this article: "Enter it quickly. Remember as you go forth in this work you are not soliciting merely as the agent of a magazine, but you are an ambassador of the King of kings and Lord of lords, announcing to the people in this dignified manner the incoming of the Golden Age, the glorious kingdom of our Lord and Master, for which true Christians have hoped and prayed for many centuries"! There was an instantaneous response to that invitation into this new feature of the Kingdom work, and today, more than fifty-three years later, that same magazine bearing now the name "Awake!" has a printing of 7,500,000 copies of each issue. Certainly the presence of those 6,000 "consecrated" Christians there at Cedar Point, Ohio, and their hailing of the announcement of the *Golden Age* magazine on Friday, September 5, 1919, were not by any means things of passing interest, that were of no consequence in the history of God's "chaste virgin" class in this true time of Christ's parousia. That virgin class has not gone asleep again!

[19] That was truly the time when "all those virgins rose and put their lamps in order." (Matthew 25:7) In the parable, this required the virgins to refill their lamps with oil, for their lamps were "about to go out." But, alas! the foolish virgins found that they were unable immediately to refill their lamps; they had

19. The putting of the lamps in order called for what action, and why did this lead to a division between the virgins?

brought no receptacles filled with oil along with them, whereas the discreet virgins had done so. This led to a division among the virgins. Why? Matthew 25:8, 9 explains, saying: "The foolish said to the discreet, 'Give us some of your oil, because our lamps are about to go out.' The discreet answered with the words, 'Perhaps there may not be quite enough for us and you. Be on your way, instead, to those who sell it and buy for yourselves.'"

[20] We can imagine what difficulty that would entail upon those foolish virgins, to go at that hour of the night and try to locate an open oil shop or oil dealers who would accommodate them with the needed oil. Well, then, was that not selfish on the part of the discreet virgins, not to share their supply with the indiscreet virgins? No! for had they done so, then none of the ten virgins would have got to the door of the bridegroom's house and entered into the wedding feast. The divided supply of all the ten would have given out before they got there. The discreet virgins showed that they felt obligated to get there by bringing along an emergency supply of oil. This showed, also, that they all had determined to get there, and now these discreet virgins were not allowing themselves to be frustrated and come short of their good purpose to the honor of the bridegroom. Furthermore, oil was still available for the foolish virgins from other sources without their hindering or endangering the success of the discreet virgins.

[21] How does this work out in the fulfillment of the parable in this time of the parousia or presence of the heavenly Bridegroom? Does it mean that, if some honest person who heard about the invisible presence of the Lord Jesus Christ desired to have the "discreet" virgin class study the Bible with him and share in honoring the Bridegroom, the "discreet" virgin class would refuse to do so but would tell the person to

20. Was it selfish on the part of the discreet virgins to refuse to share their oil with the foolish ones, and what was the resolve of the discreet ones?
21. What does this not mean as to the "discreet" virgin class' treatment of one who desired to study the Bible and learn about the Bridegroom?

shift for himself? If he wanted to get filled with God's Word and holy spirit, would it be violating the lesson of the parable to do so? Not at all.

²² Why, then, in the fulfillment, do the "discreet" virgin class refuse to divide their "oil" with the "foolish" virgin class? We must bear in mind that the having of oil in one's receptacle is the same as having the symbolic "oil" in oneself. Also, the holding aloft of the lighted lamp is the same as one's letting one's light shine, the same as one's shining as a luminary, in order for people in this dark, benighted world to see our good works and to glorify God because thereof. (Matthew 5:14-16; Philippians 2:15) It is the symbolic "oil" that gives the illuminating power, and this "oil" pictures both God's Word, which is as a lamp and a light to a worshiper of God (Psalm 119:105), and also God's holy spirit, which illuminates God's Word to us and produces in all its possessors the fine godly qualities that are called the "fruitage of the spirit." (Galatians 5:22, 23; Ephesians 5:18-20) Well, then, should the "discreet" virgins reduce the amount of this "oil," this illuminative power, in themselves? Finally, cease shining? .

²³ This is what the "foolish" virgin class would like the "discreet" ones to do. The "foolish" ones desire the "discreet" ones to compromise with them. The announcement of the heavenly Bridegroom's invisible presence in 1919 C.E. posed a challenge to all those who professed to be "virgins" with a desire to meet and share the joy of that Bridegroom. Those who are like the "foolish" virgins have merely a profession of Christianity; they are largely nominal Christians, but do not meet the requirements of true Christianity. They may have some knowledge of the Bible, especially knowledge with a sectarian understanding of such Bible knowledge. They may have been influenced by what knowledge of Scripture that they have, but not

22. In considering the question of sharing the "oil," what should we remember that holding aloft the lighted lamp signifies, and the "oil" symbolizes what?
23. (a) What do the "foolish" virgin class desire the "discreet" class to do toward them? (b) What kind of "Christians" are the "foolish" virgin class?

to the point of having God's powerful spirit in them for producing the "fruitage of the spirit." Their conduct does not conform to the true Christian pattern. They shine merely as nominal or professed Christians in the religious formalisms of their sect in Christendom. They expect to go to heaven when they die!

[24] However, their religious development does not enable them to meet the challenge when the midnight cry is made, "Here is the bridegroom! Be on your way out to meet him." In fact, they do not discern, they do not accept the provable fact of the Bridegroom's presence since the year 1914. They profess to believe in the Bridegroom and that the church is his bride, but they insist on meeting the Bridegroom and entering into his joy in their own way, their sectarian way. So, if there is to be a sharing of company between them and the "discreet" virgin class, there has to be a compromise. There needs to be an interfaith amalgamating of them all as professed Christians and heirs of heaven. The "discreet" class must take away from their own supply of spiritual "oil" and bring down their level of Christian development to that of the indiscreet religionists. Thus the "discreet" ones should make themselves religiously foolish in order to keep company with the "foolish," indiscreet, imprudent professors of Christianity.

[25] The issue is clear: Are those of the "discreet" virgin class to be influenced by mere religious sentiment such as is found in Christendom? Are they going to let themselves be drained of their spiritual "oil" and become incapacitated to shine as true Christians down to the end, obliged in course of time to drop out of the procession of light bearers who are accompanying the Bridegroom to the door of the wedding-feast chamber? They need, as 2 Peter 1:10 says, to "do your utmost to make the calling and choosing of you sure for yourselves." They need to imitate the apostle Paul, who,

---

24. (a) Does the religious development of the "foolish" virgin class enable them to accept the provable evidences of the Bridegroom's presence? (b) To what level of Christian profession do the foolish want the discreet to bring themselves so as to keep together?
25. (a) What, then, is the issue as respects the "discreet" virgin class? (b) To meet the requirements finally, what words of Peter and Paul do they need to carry out?

toward the finish of his earthly life, wrote: "I have run the course to the finish, I have observed the faith. From this time on there is reserved for me the crown of righteousness, which the Lord, the righteous judge, will give me as a reward in that day." They must measure up to the full Christian requirements when they reach that door to the wedding feast of the Bridegroom. —2 Timothy 4:7, 8.

[26] For that reason the "discreet" virgin class parted company with mere professors of Christianity, like the weeds in the parable of the wheat and the weeds or tares (darnel). During World War I they had been brought into bondage to Babylon the Great, the world empire of false religion, and her military, political and judicial paramours. Not only were they under restraints due considerably to the fear of men in powerful positions but they were in literal captivity through imprisonments and confinement in military camps and other places of detention. In 1919 they acted upon the call from heaven regarding Babylon the Great: "Get out of her, my people, if you do not want to share with her in her sins, and if you do not want to receive part of her plagues." (Revelation 18:4) They could not compromise with the "foolish" virgin class on that issue. They must obey God rather than Babylon the Great and her worldly paramours. They could not go along, also, with Babylon the Great in worshiping the image of the wild beast, the League of Nations, which Babylon the Great made her riding mount in the year 1919 C.E.—Revelation 13:14, 15; 14:11, 12; 17:1-18.

[27] The position taken by the "discreet" virgin class on this issue was unequivocal from the start. In evidence of this, on Sunday afternoon, September 7, 1919, at the Cedar Point convention, President Rutherford gave his public address on "The Hope for Distressed Humanity," in which he pointed out God's disapproval of the League of Nations. To quote from the report

26. How did the "discreet" virgin class come under restraint during World War I, and why did it part company with the "foolish" virgin class in 1919?
27. How was the position of the "discreet" virgin class unequivocal from the start, as evidenced by the public statement made on Sunday, September 7, 1919?

published in the Sandusky (Ohio) *Star-Journal* on Monday, September 8, 1919:

> President Rutherford spoke to nearly 7,000 persons under the trees Sunday afternoon. He declared a League of Nations formed by the political and economic forces moved by a desire to better mankind by establishment of peace and plenty would accomplish great good, and then asserted that the Lord's displeasure is certain to be visited upon the League, however, because the clergy —Catholic and Protestant—claiming to be God's representatives, have abandoned his plan and endorse the League of Nations, hailing it as a political expression of Christ's kingdom on earth.—*The Watch Tower,* under date of October 1, 1919, page 298, column 1.

[28] The "discreet" virgin class had the faith that the kingdom of God's dear Son had been established in the heavens at the close of the Gentile Times in 1914, and they stood uncompromisingly for it and refused to recognize and worship any substitute. They could not afford to give away any of their spiritual "oil" and reduce the full measure of their devotion to God's Messianic kingdom. This staunch attachment to the Kingdom did not make them popular with this world or friends with this world. It intensified the hatred of this world toward them. But this hatred and enmity from the world made it all the more apparent that they were holding true to their relationship to the heavenly King-Bridegroom. Not to them could be applied the reproachful term "adulteress" for the reason for which the disciple James directed the term to certain members of the congregation of the first century, saying:

[29] "Adulteresses, do you not know that the friendship with the world is enmity with God? Whoever, therefore, wants to be a friend of the world is constituting himself an enemy of God."—James 4:4.

[30] So by uncompromisingly keeping their full supply of spiritual "oil" and using it to keep themselves as "lamps" continually burning with a bright flame, the

28, 29. Why did the "discreet" virgin class take this stand, and what reproachful term used by James could not be applied to them?
30, 31. To whom did the "discreet" virgin class thereby show the qualities of a betrothed virgin, and how is such bridal beauty described in Isaiah's prophecy?

"discreet" virgin class were honoring their heavenly Bridegroom, to whom they were betrothed or promised in marriage. They were letting shine forth in themselves the loyal, chaste, clean, pure qualities that are looked for in those who are to be made the heavenly bride of their "one husband," the Lord Jesus Christ. They rejoice with him that God's time for his beloved Son to lead his "bride" home to himself has come; they share in his exultation, just as it is written: "With the exultation of a bridegroom over a bride, your God will exult even over you." (Isaiah 62:5) To match the glory of his appearance, they also want to look beautiful like the bride on the wedding day, accepting the adornment that the heavenly Father gives to them. This lovely balance of beauty between bridegroom and bride is described in Isaiah 61:10:

[31] "For he has clothed me with the garments of salvation; with the sleeveless coat of righteousness he has enwrapped me, like the bridegroom who, in a priestly way, puts on a headdress, and like the bride who decks herself with her ornamental things."

[32] Nothing on the part of the "discreet" virgin class on earth should reflect against the glory of the heavenly Bridegroom, who is all radiant like the sun: "It is like a bridegroom when coming out of his nuptial chamber." (Psalm 19:4, 5) It is therefore incumbent upon the "discreet" virgin class to shine in their Bridegroom's honor like luminaries by displaying those Christlike qualities that distinguish them from that religious harlot, Babylon the Great, and all her religiously immoral "daughters." By thus shining they do not misrepresent their beloved Bridegroom to mankind.

BUYING LAMP OIL FROM THE SELLERS

[33] For lack of the spiritual "oil" the "foolish" virgin class could not shine in honor of the Bridegroom who had arrived and was present and proceeding to the

---

32. How does the "discreet" virgin class shine in honor of its Bridegroom?
33. According to Jesus' parable, what only could the "discreet" virgins say to the "foolish" ones, and what did the "discreet" thus show?

wedding feast. They were not entitled to any of the "oil" that the "discreet" ones had brought along with them and that they needed to follow in the steps of the Bridegroom. So, according to the parable, all that the "discreet" could say to the "foolish" was: "Perhaps there may not be quite enough for us and you. Be on your way, instead, to those who sell it and buy for yourselves." (Matthew 25:9) In taking this position, the "discreet" virgins further showed their discreetness, and the foolishness of the indiscreet, imprudent virgins turned out to be disastrous for them. They were obliged to seek out oil dealers and get their lamps refilled.

[34] Similarly, in the fulfillment of the parable, the "foolish" were obliged to get their own needed supply of spiritual "oil." They went to where they religiously felt that they could get the "oil" that would pave the way for their entry into heaven, according to their religious creeds. Accordingly, they sought out their denominational, religious sectarian systems for the type of "oil" that these sold and from such dealers they got the kind of "oil" that they were willing to pay for, without the right kind of devotion to the heavenly Bridegroom. But will the religious "oil" that is bought from the oil dealers at their price prove to be effective toward gaining admission to the marriage feast? On this we read:

[35] "While they were going off to buy, the bridegroom arrived, and the virgins that were ready went in with him to the marriage feast; and the door was shut." —Matthew 25:10.

[36] The "discreet" virgins and the "foolish" virgins went in opposite directions—the "foolish" away from the Bridegroom, and the "discreet" to the arriving Bridegroom. There was a distance from where the "discreet" virgins met the bridegroom to the "door" of the house where the marriage feast was to be held. Between those two points there was for a time a lighted

34, 35. In the parable's fulfillment, how was this buying of oil accomplished, but what does the parable show would happen in the meantime? 36. Which virgins enjoyed the bridegroom's presence in the procession, and what enabled these to pass inspection at the "door"?

procession, and during that period of time the "discreet" virgins were with the bridegroom and the bridegroom was present with them. When the joyful procession reached its destination and proceeded through the door of the bridegroom's residence, the lamps of the "discreet" virgins were brightly burning. Their oil supply had not run out before they reached the "door." Then the "discreet" virgins proved that they were part of the procession that followed in the steps of the bridegroom. This entitled them to admission to the marriage feast. The importance of their being prepared for the inspection is emphasized when the parable says: "And the virgins that were ready went in with him to the marriage feast." The door was not shut in their faces but was shut behind them!

[37] In the parable's fulfillment in our time, the "discreet" virgin class continue in the procession that honors and magnifies the glorious Bridegroom down to the end. When they reach the inspection point at the "door," they prove to be worthy of admission into the marriage festivities. The inspecting of them by the heavenly One to whom they are promised in marriage brings to light that they are shining with the Christian personality that the Bridegroom approves for his heavenly "bride." They present themselves "as a chaste virgin to the Christ." They have not let themselves be "corrupted away from the sincerity and the chastity that are due the Christ." (2 Corinthians 11:2, 3) The Bridegroom can accept these "discreet" virgins of today as part of the Christian congregation, concerning which it is written: "That he might present the congregation to himself in its splendor, not having a spot or a wrinkle or any of such things, but that it should be holy and without blemish."—Ephesians 5:27.

→ **"AND THE DOOR WAS SHUT"**

[38] Of course, no more will be admitted through the "door" to the marriage feast except those who will

---

37. At the inspection point, the "virgins" of today prove themselves to be shining in what way, and the Bridegroom admits them to the "bride" class for being in what condition?
38. How many, eventually, will be admitted to the wedding festivities, and when will the "door" be officially shut? And why?

complete the number of the 144,000 members of the heavenly "bride" class. (Revelation 7:4-8; 14:1-5) But when is it that the "door" is officially shut? This would be when the "great tribulation" breaks forth at God's appointed time and destruction starts to come upon Christendom and all the rest of that religious harlot, Babylon the Great, the world empire of false religion. Then it will be too late for any professed Christians to get out of Babylon the Great in order not to be sharers in her sins and to receive part of her deadly plagues. (Revelation 18:4) Since the number of the days of the "great tribulation" will be "cut short" on account of the "chosen ones," it is evident that the full number of the "chosen ones," namely, 144,000, will be completed by the time of the outbreak of the "great tribulation." This brings about the shutting of the door.

[39] What is due to happen then? The parable of the "ten virgins" indicates, when it concludes with the words: "Afterwards the rest of the virgins also came, saying, 'Sir, sir, open to us!' In answer he said, 'I tell you the truth, I do not know you.' "—Matthew 25: 11, 12.

[40] The five "foolish" virgins procured what oil they could get from what oil dealers they could locate at that hour of the night, and they came to the door with their lamps burning. But their lamps had not shone in honor of the bridegroom. They were not part of the procession that met him and accompanied him with joy on his account. What basis, then, did the bridegroom have for recognizing them as part of his celebrators? None at all! They had not added any brilliance to *his* marriage procession. Truthfully, therefore, he could say to them: 'I do not know you.' This justified him in keeping the door locked in their faces.

[41] Likewise, when the "great tribulation" begins

---

39. In the parable of the "ten virgins," what finally happens?
40. Why was the bridegroom justified in saying to the "foolish" virgins: "I do not know you"?
41. When the "great tribulation" strikes Christendom, what will those of the "foolish" virgin class find out about themselves?

upon Christendom as the most prominent part of the religious harlot, Babylon the Great, their hopes of going to heaven when they die will be greatly shaken and put in doubt. They will discern that they have not been associated with the correct religious organization that makes up the "chaste virgin," "the bride, the Lamb's wife." They will not find themselves being "caught up" in their physical bodies into the clouds, in a bodily rapture, "to meet the Lord in the air," according to the interpretation placed by their religious instructors on 1 Thessalonians 4:17. True, they have been shining as members of this or that religious sect of Christendom, but they were merely nominal or professed Christians and not the real thing. What now counts as they enter into the "great tribulation" is, not what their priest or preacher thought or said about them, but what the heavenly Bridegroom says that they are!

[42] Too late, as "shutouts," they approach the situation that betokens a closed door for them, as the religious basis on which they have stood is wrecked by the "great tribulation." Their religious organization that acted as a mediator for them being destroyed, they will have to deal directly with the Bridegroom Head of the true congregation. His parousia or presence being invisible and he being concealed from their eyes as if he were behind a shut door, they will call out to him to see whether their mere profession of Christianity without the right works will save them and get them to heaven. They have recognized him, by word of mouth, and ought he not to now reciprocate and recognize them? "Sir, sir," or, "Lord, Lord!" they will call out in hope of being heard by him. That ought to cause the door to be opened to them. But does it do so?

[43] They have not taken seriously what the heavenly Bridegroom said on earth in his Sermon on the Mount:

42. With their religious organization then gone as a mediator, they will make an appeal for recognition by the Bridegroom on what basis?
43. (a) What words of Jesus' Sermon on the Mount have those "foolish" virgin class members not taken seriously about calling him "Lord"? (b) What will happen to them when Jesus finally takes those words seriously?

'Not everyone saying to me, 'Lord, Lord,' will enter into the kingdom of the heavens, but the one doing the will of my Father who is in the heavens will. Many will say to me in that day, 'Lord, Lord, did we not prophesy in your name, and expel demons in your name, and perform many powerful works in your name?' And yet then I will confess to them: I never knew you! Get away from me, you workers of lawlessness.' (Matthew 7:21-23) But then, in the "great tribulation," the "foolish" virgin class will know that the Bridegroom said those words very seriously as a principle for his guidance. He will not open the door to the heavenly marriage feast to them. He will leave them outside in the blackness of the world's deepest night, to perish with all other "workers of lawlessness." From their destruction they will experience no resurrection to heavenly life.

[44] Consequently, Jesus' words with which he emphasized the point of the parable of the "ten virgins" are particularly timely for us who live at the "conclusion of the system of things," namely, ('Keep on the watch, therefore, because you know neither the day nor the hour.') (Matthew 25:13) It is the occasion now for the ones who desire to be like the five "discreet" virgins to shine continually with an active Christian personality that meets the requirements for membership in the heavenly "bride" class. They dare not make any compromise with those who seek to make them share the burden of the others' foolishness and so to take away some or much of their supply of the spiritual "oil."

[45] We dare not expose ourselves to the danger of having our light burn down and put ourselves in their religious company. We require all the spiritual "oil" with which we can supply ourselves. Our faith in the Bridegroom's arrival and presence must continue bright, and we need to continue as a part of the shin-

44. With what words did Jesus close the parable of the "ten virgins," and what do the "discreet" ones not dare to allow about their supply of spiritual oil?
45. In whose religious company do the "discreet" ones not dare to put themselves, and in whose honor should they shine continually, and why?

ing procession that follows his steps until he brings his bridal congregation completely home. The long delay in the Bridegroom's arrival is ended. He is here, in his glorious parousia. The time for drowsiness and sleep is past! It is a time to shine in his honor and to rejoice with him in this joy that the heavenly Father set before him, of taking his spiritual "bride" to himself and celebrating this with a marriage feast. It is vitally necessary now to keep on the watch, for we do not know the day or the hour when that "door" of opportunity will be shut, never to be reopened.

A PART OF THE "SIGN" OF HIS PAROUSIA

[46] The parable of the "ten virgins" was given as part of the answer to the question of Jesus' apostles: "What will be the sign of your presence [pa·rou·si'a] and of the conclusion of the system of things?" (Matthew 24:3) The climax of that parable has been undergoing fulfillment since the year 1914 C.E. All the world can see the final features of that parable being realized today. The events set out in detail above were not performed in a corner, out of sight in an obscure spot, but have been taking place in the open where observing persons could take note of them, regardless of whether they understood their significance or not. At least, those who are of the "discreet" virgin class have observed these meaningful happenings, and in them they have strong proof that the heavenly Bridegroom arrived in 1914 C.E. and that his parousia or presence is now in progress invisibly. They discern his presence with their eyes of faith because of the evidence supplied in the fulfillment of the parable of the "ten virgins." They are assured that the "conclusion of the system of things" began in the year 1914 C.E.

[47] Yes, too, the Greek word used by the apostle

46. (a) The parable of the "ten virgins" is part of Jesus' answer to what question of his apostles? (b) How do the "discreet" class see the climax of the parable's fulfillment, and of what facts does this convince them?
47. How is the proper meaning of the Greek word pa·rou·si'a borne out by what the "discreet" virgins of the parable did after the midnight cry announcing the bridegroom?

Matthew in his Gospel, chapter twenty-four, verse three, means "presence," not "coming," as many translators render the Greek word. This is borne out by what is described in the parable. The "ten virgins" rise up from slumber and sleep when they hear the midnight cry, 'Here is the bridegroom!' When their eager eyes, watching for his lighted procession discern his reaching their location, then they go with him in his train. From that point on it consumed time before they all reached the Bridegroom's residence where the marriage feast awaited all the worthy ones invited. Consequently, there was a period of the Bridegroom's presence or parousia after he arrived until he brought his bride into the house prepared for her.

THE CORRECTING OF A MISUNDERSTANDING

[48] It is true that the editor and publisher of *Zion's Watch Tower and Herald of Christ's Presence* calculated that the "presence" or parousia of the heavenly Bridegroom began in the year 1874 C.E. Also, that the date of the first man's creation by Jehovah God was in the year 4128 B.C.E., which meant that six thousand years of man's existence on the earth ended in the year 1872 C.E., as calculated by Russell and his associates. This reckoning began to be announced on the front page of *Zion's Watch Tower and Herald of Christ's Presence* beginning with the issue of July 1, 1906, and this practice continued down through the issue of September 15, 1928. For instance, on the first of such mentioned issues appeared the date of issue: "July 1, A.D. 1906—A.M., 6034"; whereas the dating of the last mentioned issue was: "Anno Mundi 6056—September 15, 1928." The *Anno Mundi* or "Year of the World" date was calculated to be the year 4128 before our Common Era.

[49] Two years, however, were allowed for the inno-

---

48. (a) The editor and publisher of *Zion's Watch Tower* calculated that Christ's presence began in what year? (b) Also, what was the date of man's creation, as published on the cover page of *The Watch Tower* for some years?
49. (a) When was sin's entrance calculated to have occurred? (b) When, therefore, was the millennium to begin for Satan's casting into the bottomless pit and for Christ's reign?

cence of the perfect man and woman in the Garden of Eden before sin entered, and hence the year of sin's entrance was calculated as 4126 B.C.E. This resulted in their calculating six thousand years of sin as ending in 1874 C.E., in which year also, in the autumn, the seventh millennium began, for the instigator of sin, Satan the Devil, to be bound and cast into the bottomless pit and for Christ to start reigning for the foretold thousand years. This meant that the year of the start of Christ's reign was also the year of his return and the beginning of his invisible presence or parousia.

⁵⁰ The above chronology followed the suggestion that was made in Wilson's *The Emphatic Diaglott*, in its footnote on Acts 13:20, which verse read: "And after these things, he gave Judges about four hundred and fifty years, till Samuel the prophet." The footnote on this reading of the verse said:

> A difficulty occurs here which has very much puzzled Biblical chronologists. The date given here is at variance with the statement found in 1 Kings 6: 1. There have been many solutions offered, but only one which seems entirely satisfactory, i.e., that the text in 1 Kings 6:1 has been corrupted, by substituting the Hebrew character *daleth* (4) for *hay* (5) which is very similar in form. This would make 580 years (instead of 480) from the exode to the building of the temple, and exactly agree with Paul's chronology.

⁵¹ Accordingly, on page 53 of the book entitled "The Time Is at Hand," author C. T. Russell wrote, referring to 1 Kings 6:1:

> It evidently should read the five-hundred-and-eightieth year, and was possibly an error in transcribing; for if to Solomon's four years we add David's forty, and Saul's space of forty, and the forty-six years from leaving Egypt to the division of the land, we have one hundred and thirty years, which deducted from four hundred and eighty would leave only three hundred and fifty years for the period of the Judges, instead of the *four* hundred and fifty years mentioned in the Book of Judges, and by Paul,

50. That chronology followed what footnote on Acts 13:20 as found in Wilson's *Emphatic Diaglott?*
51. (a) Accordingly, what did author C. T. Russell say on page 53 of *"The Time Is at Hand"* regarding 1 Kings 6:1? (b) According to that, when was man created, when did 6,000 years of sin end, and when did the Grand Jubilee begin?

as heretofore shown. The Hebrew character *"daleth"* (4) very much resembles the character *"hay"* (5), and it is supposed that in this way the error has occurred, possibly the mistake of a transcriber. I Kings 6:1, then, should read *five* hundred and eighty, and thus be in perfect harmony with the other statements.

Thus, by inserting 100 years into the Bible chronology during the period of the Judges, man's creation was pushed back 100 years to 4128 B.C.E., and the six thousand years of man's existence on earth ended in 1872 C.E. (*The Time Is at Hand,* page 42) Then the allowance of two years before the entry of sin led to the year 1874 as the year in which six thousand years of human sin terminated and the seventh thousand years for the elimination of sin by Christ's reign began. So the Grand Jubilee was then due to begin.

[52] According to the oldest manuscripts of the Christian Greek Scriptures, however, the reading of Acts 13:20 is different from that given in *The Emphatic Diaglott* and the King James Authorized Version of the Bible. So, according to the most ancient manuscripts, the four hundred and fifty years are not applied to the period of the Judges. In verification of this, *The New English Bible* (of the year 1970) renders Acts 13:20 as follows: "for some four hundred and fifty years, and afterwards appointed judges for them until the time of the prophet Samuel." *The Jerusalem Bible* (English translation of 1966) reads: "for about four hundred and fifty years After this he gave them judges, down to the prophet Samuel." The Revised Standard Version Bible of 1952 reads similarly, and so does the American Standard Version Bible of 1901 C.E.

[53] Furthermore, the oldest Hebrew manuscripts extant, like those of the Dead Sea Scrolls, spell out the numbers of the Bible and do not use alphabetic charac-

---

52. According to the oldest Greek manuscripts, the 450 years of Acts 13:20 apply before or during the period of the Judges, as shown by modern Bible translations?
53. Did the ancient Hebrew Bible manuscripts use alphabetic characters to stand for numbers?

ters for numerals, thus not allowing for a transcriber's visual error at 1 Kings 6:1.*

⁵⁴ The insertion of 100 years into Bible chronology during the period of the Judges is thus seen not to rest upon Scriptural grounds. The insertion should therefore be dropped and the Bible should be accepted just as it reads concerning its chronology. Unavoidably, then, this would affect the date for the parousia of the Bridegroom Jesus Christ to begin. With the *Watch Tower* magazine's issue of January 1, 1939, the title was changed to *The Watchtower and Herald of Christ's Kingdom*, and with the issue of March 1, 1939, to *The Watchtower Announcing Jehovah's Kingdom*. This did not mean that the publishers of the magazine no longer believed in the presence or parousia of Christ as being then in progress. It meant, rather, that more importance was given to the Kingdom, to the kingdom of Jehovah God by Jesus Christ, for it is Jehovah's kingdom by Christ that will vindicate Jehovah's universal sovereignty.

⁵⁵ In the year 1943 the Watch Tower Bible and Tract Society published the book *"The Truth Shall Make You Free."* In its chapter 11, entitled "The Count of Time," it did away with the insertion of 100 years into the period of the Judges and went according to the oldest and most authentic reading of Acts 13:20, and accepted the spelled-out numbers of the Hebrew Scriptures. This moved forward the end of six thousand years of man's existence into the decade of the 1970's. Naturally this did away with the year 1874 C.E.

---

* When, after Bible times, the Hebrews used alphabetic letters for numbers, they had no symbol for zero, as their system had no zero. Hence 400 was not represented by the letter *daleth* followed by two zeros, and 500 by the letter *he* followed by two zeros. The number 400 was represented by one Hebrew letter (*taw*), and the number 500 was represented by two Hebrew letters (*taw qoph*). The number eighty was represented by the Hebrew letter *pe*, whereas ten was represented by the one letter *yod*. So there was no likelihood of mistaking *taw pe* (480) as distinguished from *taw qoph pe* (580).

54. (a) The accepting of Bible chronology just as written would affect the beginning of what period here under discussion? (b) Did dropping of "Presence" from the *Watchtower* title mean that Christ's presence was no longer believed in?
55. (a) When and how was the insertion of 100 years into the period of the Judges done away with, so that 6,000 years of man's existence ended when? (b) How did this affect the date 1874 C.E., and what question arose?

as the date of return of the Lord Jesus Christ and the beginning of his invisible presence or parousia. The millennium that was to be marked by the detaining of Satan the Devil enchained in the abyss and by the reign of the 144,000 joint heirs with Christ in heavenly glory was therefore yet in the future. What, then, about the parousia (presence) of Christ? Page 324 of the above book positively says: "The King's presence or *parousia* began in 1914." Also, in the *Watchtower* issue of July 15, 1949 (page 215, paragraph 22), the statement is made: " . . . Messiah, the Son of man, came into Kingdom power A.D. 1914 and . . . this constitutes his second coming and the beginning of his second *parousia* or presence."

[56] In the year 1950, there was published the *New World Translation of the Christian Greek Scriptures*, with the most authentic reading of Acts 13:20, and translating *pa·rou·si'a* every time as "presence." Immediately afterward appeared the book *"This Means Everlasting Life."* Its chapter 21 was entitled "Second Presence of Life's Chief Agent." Here was a whole chapter on the subject according to the straight Bible timetable. On pages 220-222, we read:

> The evidence already considered proves that A.D. 1914 God's kingdom was born and his Son was enthroned with authority to rule with an iron rod amid his foes. Eventually he will dash them to pieces and rid the universe of all fighters against God's rightful sovereignty.—Psalm 2:8, 9.
>
> So A.D. 1914 marks the time of Christ's invisible return in spirit. . . . His coming into the Kingdom in 1914 marks the beginning of his second presence or *par·ou·si'a*. This Greek word means *presence*.
>
> . . . Although invisible in spirit, his second presence is of such importance to people over all the earth that it must not be kept secret, and it will not be. . . . "For just as the lightning comes out of eastern parts and shines over to western parts, so the presence [*par·ou·si'a*] of the Son of man will be."—Matthew 24:26, 27, *NW*.
>
> Since 1914 the present Christ has been making the evidences of his second presence or *par·ou·si'a* manifest and understandable to men everywhere.

---

56. (a) In 1950, what new Bible translation was published, and with what rendering of Acts 13:20? (b) Also, what statement was made about Christ's presence according to straight Bible chronology?

[57] How harmonious with the inspired Scriptures it is, then, that Christ did not begin reigning forty years before the end of the Gentile Times in 1914! Rather, he waited till then at his heavenly Father's right hand to begin ruling in the midst of his earthly enemies, whom Jehovah places as a stool for his feet! (Psalm 110:1, 2; Hebrews 10:12, 13) Rightly, then, his royal presence or parousia began in that year. In the year 1919, as history proves, he caused the midnight cry to sound on earth and roused the sleeping "virgins" to the urgency of the situation. "Here is the bridegroom! Be on your way out to meet him." That cry assured them of the heavenly Bridegroom's presence. The "discreet" virgin class has since been on its way out to meet him. They are seen shining as luminaries in this benighted world. This in itself is an evidence that the promised presence of Christ is upon us. It is also an evidence that God's kingdom by Christ of a thousand years has approached!

[58] Fulfillment of the parable of the "ten virgins" is not all there is to the "sign" of the approach of that blessed millennial kingdom. We cannot, therefore, stop with this parable, but must go on to consider other features of that wondrous "sign."

---

57. (a) Did Christ begin reigning amidst his enemies before the end of the Gentile Times in 1914? (b) When did the Bridegroom cause the midnight cry to be heard, and what has taken place since is evidence of what important facts?
58. Why can we not stop here with the parable of the "ten virgins" in considering the "sign" of the Kingdom's approach?

CHAPTER 12

> ## → *Increasing the King's Belongings*

SINCE all the evidence indicates that God's kingdom of a thousand years has approached, this question arises: What should we expect of those who are to be joined with God's millennial King in the heavenly government? While they are among us, we should expect to observe them when they are being tested and inspected on how they handle that which belongs to the heavenly King with whom they are called to rule as kings. How do they take care of all the concerns that the heavenly King has on earth? If we observe a testing and inspecting of the joint heirs of that Kingdom taking place among us, it furnishes strong evidence that God's Messianic King is ruling. He is present on his royal throne!

[2] This interesting development that has been taking place under observation of human eye during this twentieth century was pictured for us in a parable or illustration that Jesus Christ included in his remarkable prophecy as he sat on the Mount of Olives overlooking Jerusalem, on the eleventh day of the spring month of Nisan in the year 33 C.E. He was still giving his detailed answer to the questions submitted by his apostles: "When will these things be, and what will be the sign of your presence [pa·rou·si′a, Greek] and of the conclusion of the system of things?" (Matthew 24:3) He had just finished giving to his apostles the parable of the "ten virgins" and drawing a lesson therefrom, and now he gives them a further parable by the fulfillment of which it will be signified that his invisible parousia has begun and is in prog-

---

1. (a) What question arises regarding the Kingdom joint heirs still among us? (b) If we observe such things going on with them, this gives evidence of what fact?
2, 3. (a) What we see developing is in fulfillment of what parable of Jesus, and part of his answer to what question of his apostles? (b) How did that parable begin?

212

ress. This parable is quite commonly called "the parable of the talents." It begins:

³ 'For it is just as when a man, about to travel abroad, summoned slaves of his and committed to them his belongings. And to one he gave five talents, to another two, to still another one, to each one according to his own ability, and he went abroad.' —Matthew 25:14, 15.

⁴ What is it, though, that is "just as when" a wealthy man commits his belongings to his slaves before his departure abroad? Why, it is the circumstances connected with the Kingdom about which Jesus Christ has been speaking. This is apparent from his preceding parable, that of the "ten virgins," which he introduced with these words: 'Then the kingdom of the heavens will become like ten virgins that took their lamps and went out to meet the bridegroom.' (Matthew 25:1) It is also apparent from the parable that Jesus gives after his parable concerning the "talents." (Matthew 25:31-34) In the parable now under consideration the wealthy man traveling abroad is, of course, the Lord Jesus Christ himself. It was concerning the "sign" of *his* presence that he was asked.

⁵ This parable of the "talents" resembles in a number of features an earlier parable that Jesus gave and that is commonly called "the parable of the pounds" (or, minas). Curiously, the parable of the "talents" was meant to prove by its fulfillment in our day that the royal presence or parousia of the Lord Jesus Christ was in progress, whereas the parable of the "pounds" or minas was given by the Lord Jesus to show his listeners that, at that time, the Messianic kingdom was yet a long time in the future. Hence, the account that introduces the parable of the minas says: 'While they were listening to these things he spoke in addition an illustration.' Why? "Because he was near Jerusalem and they were imagining that the kingdom

4. (a) According to the context of this parable, what is it that is "just as when" a wealthy man traveled abroad and committed valuables to his slaves? (b) Whom does this "man" picture, and why?
5. What earlier parable resembles in some features the parable of the "talents," but how do the two parables differ in what they were meant to show?

of God was going to display itself instantly. Therefore he said: 'A certain man of noble birth traveled to a distant land to secure kingly power for himself and to return. Calling ten slaves of his he gave them ten minas and told them, "Do business till I come."' " (Luke 19:11-13) A long journey to a distant land and a return therefrom were involved, and this would mean a long time before the noble man got back with his kingdom power.

[6] Likewise, indeed, when the Lord Jesus gave his parable of the "talents" the Messianic kingdom of God was yet a long way off; it was not due to appear instantly. Just two days previously, Sunday, Nisan 9, 33 C.E., Jesus had made his triumphal ride on a colt of an ass into Jerusalem and the jubilant multitudes had cried out, "Blessed is he that comes in Jehovah's name! Blessed is the coming kingdom of our father David! Save, we pray, in the heights above!" And yet the Kingdom had not displayed itself then. (Mark 11:9, 10) Is that Kingdom displaying itself in our day? That is the vital question for us now! A long time has passed since Jesus was here in the flesh.

[7] The parable of the "talents," the fulfillment of which has to do with Jesus' parousia or presence, began to go into reality in the days of the apostles nineteen centuries ago. The certain "man" of the parable, Jesus Christ himself, was still with them personally until the day of his ascension to heaven, ten days before the Festival of Pentecost was observed at Jerusalem. The parable opens with the man being "about to travel abroad" and summoning his slaves and committing to them his belongings. The resurrected Jesus did not start to "travel abroad" to a "distant land" until the day that he ascended into the sky and disappeared. So, before that event, he must have summoned the "slaves of his," his then faithful disciples, and must have committed to them his belongings. That

6. (a) What had happened just two days before Jesus gave the parable of the "talents," and what did not display itself then? (b) So what question arises now?
7, 8. (a) How do we determine when the parable of the "talents" began fulfillment? (b) How does Acts 1:2-5 confirm this?

is why, too, the parable must have begun between the time of his resurrection from the dead and his ascension to his heavenly Father's presence. In harmony with this we read, in Acts 1:2-5:

8 "Until the day that he was taken up, [Jesus had business to do with his disciples. He was taken up] after he had given commandment through holy spirit to the apostles whom he chose. To these also by many positive proofs he showed himself alive after he had suffered, being seen by them throughout forty days and telling the things about the kingdom of God. And while he was meeting with them he gave them the orders: 'Do not withdraw from Jerusalem, but keep waiting for what the Father has promised, about which you heard from me; because John, indeed, baptized with water, but you will be baptized in holy spirit not many days after this.'"

9 The land "abroad" to which the "man" of the parable was to travel was heaven itself, where the heavenly Father of the Lord Jesus Christ resides. Luke 19:12 properly speaks of it as a "distant land." In the parable of the "talents," Jesus does not tell us the purpose for which the "man" traveled abroad. He indicates, nonetheless, that it was to obtain a special "joy" and really increase his "belongings" to "many things" more. So, when the man realized the purpose of his traveling abroad, he entered into his "joy" as Lord of those "slaves" whom he left behind. The parallel or corresponding parable of the minas indicates that the purpose of the traveling abroad was to "secure kingly power for himself and to return." The possession of the kingdom was therefore his "joy." In indication of this being the purpose of his going away to heaven, Jesus said to his faithful apostles after he had showed them how to celebrate annually the Lord's Supper: "I make a covenant with you, just as my Father has made a covenant with me, for a kingdom, that you may eat and drink at my table in my king-

9. (a) In the "talents" parable, how is the purpose of the man's traveling abroad indicated? (b) In the corresponding parable of the minas, what was the purpose of the man's going to a distant land, and how did Jesus confirm this at the Lord's Supper?

dom, and sit on thrones to judge the twelve tribes of Israel."—Luke 22:29, 30.

[10] In the parable, the "slaves of his" were those baptized disciples of Jesus Christ who were in line for a throne in the "kingdom of the heavens." Even the apostles did not blush to confess themselves to be the "slaves" of the Lord Jesus. For example, the second letter of Peter is opened up with the words: "Simon Peter, a slave and apostle of Jesus Christ." (2 Peter 1:1) In introducing the last book of the Bible, Revelation, the apostle John says that Jesus Christ "sent forth his angel and presented it in signs through him to his slave John." (Revelation 1:1) The disciple Jude begins his letter by saying: "Jude, a slave of Jesus Christ, but a brother of James." (Jude 1) The disciple James starts his letter with the words: "James, a slave of God and of the Lord Jesus Christ, to the twelve tribes that are scattered about." (James 1:1) The apostle Paul opens his letter to the Philippians: "Paul and Timothy, slaves of Christ Jesus, to all the holy ones in union with Christ Jesus who are in Philippi."—Philippians 1:1.

THE COMMITTING OF "HIS BELONGINGS"

[11] The disciples who were in line for the heavenly kingdom were the "slaves" whom the departing Jesus Christ summoned before he left the earth and to whom he committed "his belongings." (Matthew 25:14) What were these *belongings?* He did not leave any material belongings behind for his disciples, such as houses, lands, clothing, moneys in the bank. He left his aged mother Mary and his half brothers and half sisters behind when he died on the torture stake at Calvary, and to these any physical properties were left to avail themselves of according to the Law of Moses. And during his activity in preaching and teaching God's kingdom for about three years and a half he was not storing up for himself "treasures upon the earth," but was seeking first the kingdom of his heav-

10. In the parable, whom did the "slaves of his" picture, and how was their acceptance of this designation shown?
11. The "belongings" that Jesus as the "man" of the parable left behind with his "slaves" were not of what kind?

enly Father. (Matthew 6:19, 20, 33; 12:46, 47; 24: 3-47; Acts 1:14) What, then, did he leave behind that he could commit to his "slaves"?

[12] It was a foundation for further Christian work, a cultivated field in which further preaching of the good news of God's Messianic kingdom and making of Christian disciples could be carried on with results. It was a way prepared for his disciple "slaves." Already in the year 30 C.E., when he was on his way through the land of Samaria and after he had preached to a Samaritan woman at "Jacob's fountain" near Sychar, Jesus said to his apostles:

[13] "Look! I say to you: Lift up your eyes and view the fields, that they are white for harvesting. Already the reaper is receiving wages and gathering fruit for everlasting life, so that the sower and the reaper may rejoice together. In this respect, indeed, the saying is true, One is the sower and another the reaper. I dispatched you to reap what you have spent no labor on. Others have labored, and you have entered into the benefit of their labor." —John 4:35-38.

[14] For about six months John the Baptist had served as a forerunner of Jesus and had proclaimed: "Repent, for the kingdom of the heavens has drawn near." And after John's imprisonment in the year 30 C.E., Jesus had taken up the same message. For the following three years Jesus persisted in preaching that message and teaching the people wherever the opportunity offered itself. The free public activity of John the Baptist was therefore quite short, only about a year, but Jesus' public and private activity was three times as long. Both men could be said to have done a sowing work, Jesus taking up where John left off. Jesus began to reap disciples, but not all those possible to be reaped from his field of activity. (Matthew 4: 12-23; 3:1-7) Moreover, Jesus had, by means of his public career that included his violent death and resur-

12, 13. (a) What was it, then, that Jesus Christ left behind as his "belongings"? (b) How is this view of it borne out by what Jesus said to his apostles near Jacob's well in Samaria?

14. (a) How did the public careers of John the Baptist and Jesus Christ compare? (b) Among whom and in what way did Jesus leave a cultivated field capable of further productivity?

reaper - slaves disciples

sower. Jesus

rection from the dead, fulfilled the Bible prophecies concerning the promised Messiah, and this was all public knowledge. This had an effect upon the Jewish people living in the territory in which Jesus Christ became the most controversial public figure of the times. This resulted in a cultivated field for the producing of Christian disciples.

15 Jesus thus put into the field of people in which he worked a potentiality, a latent power and capacity to bring forth disciples, a prepared condition of the field that was ready to react favorably or respond to the future work of Jesus' disciples. This prepared field of potentialities (Christian possibilities) for the cultivating and reaping of Christian disciples was what constituted the "belongings" of the resurrected Lord Jesus Christ. This was what he committed to his disciple slaves. After his resurrection from the dead he had appeared to "upward of five hundred brothers at one time," but thereafter on the Festival Day of Pentecost there were only about one hundred and twenty disciples gathered in the upper room in Jerusalem who were the first to receive the holy spirit when poured down from heaven. (1 Corinthians 15:6; Matthew 28:16-18; Acts 1:13-15) Hence, there were at least more than a hundred Christian "slaves" to whom he committed his "belongings" before he traveled abroad by ascending to his heavenly Father.

16 How was the distribution of his "belongings" made, and upon what basis? We read: 'And to one he gave five talents, to another two, to still another one, to each one according to his own ability, and he went abroad.' (Matthew 25:15) Thus eight (8) silver talents represented his "belongings" that he distributed to his slaves. This stood for a lot of wealth back there in the first century of our Common Era, for each silver talent equaled sixty (60) minas or around $850 of American money. The slave who received one

15. (a) So what valuable thing with potentiality did Jesus Christ leave with his disciples? (b) With how many at the start did he leave those "belongings"?
16. The "belongings" of the man of the parable amounted to how much money, and how did he distribute these "belongings" to his "slaves"?

silver talent got this amount of money to use; the
slave who got two talents received twice that amount
of money; the one who got five talents received five
times that amount. Each slave received the amount
of money that corresponded with "his own ability" to
handle such an amount and do business with it. The
wealthy man was familiar with his slaves and their
abilities.

[17] In the parable, the abilities were natural abilities
or abilities that the slaves had cultivated and developed. In the fulfillment of the parable of the "talents,"
the "ability" is not a mere physical or mental ability,
although such kind of ability can be valuable and
helpful. Rather, the "ability" represents the spiritual
possibilities that are to be found in the Christian
slave who is in line for the heavenly kingdom. The
zeal, the willingness, the eagerness that the Christian
slave has contributes to his possibilities for use of
the spiritual wealth committed to him. The one who
receives what resembles five talents according to his
own ability bears, of course, the greatest responsibility.
The Lord Jesus Christ thus laid upon his apostolic
slaves the greatest responsibility, and they had a pioneering work to do on a large scale, as well as to be
secondary foundations of the Christian congregation.
—Revelation 21:14; Ephesians 2:20-22.

[18] The Lord Jesus Christ has, of course, more than
three spiritual "slaves" for whom he has covenanted
for the heavenly kingdom. So the three "slaves" of the
parable stand for three respective classes of prospective heirs of the heavenly kingdom. We must remember
that the spirit-begotten Christian congregation contains
many believing women. On the Festival Day of Pentecost of 33 C.E. Jesus' mother Mary was one of such
women, and likely Mary and Martha of the town of
Bethany near Jerusalem were among the "some wom-
en" mentioned in Acts 1:14, who received the holy spir-

17. (a) What kind of abilities did the "slaves" of the parable have, but
what about the parable's fulfillment? (b) Who received the greatest
responsibility in the parable, and in the fulfillment?
18. (a) What did the "slaves" in being only three represent? (b) In the
parable the "slaves" were all men, but how about the fulfillment?

it on that notable day of Pentecost. (John 11:1-45) Also, when under the pressure of persecution at Jerusalem the evangelizer Philip went north to Samaria, he found believing Samaritan women, for we read: "But when they believed Philip, who was declaring the good news of the kingdom of God and of the name of Jesus Christ, they proceeded to be baptized, both men and women."—Acts 8:12.

[19] In the parable, the traveling man expected his slaves to do business with those talents during his absence and bring increase on them. He did not desire them to let the money lie idle and unproductive. Likewise the Lord Jesus Christ when committing to his disciple "slaves" all his belongings on earth expected them, in fact, commanded them, not to let the prepared, cultivated field that he committed to them go without further attention and development so as not to produce more. Nor was the field to be left to its original proportions without being added to, spread out, enlarged. No, but increase was expected by the absent Lord Jesus Christ, and, consequently, failure to bring increase would result in punishment for the one not living up to his responsibility.

DOING BUSINESS WITH THE "TALENTS"

[20] The slaves of the parable, if not specifically told, realized that increase was expected of them. The parable makes this apparent, for we read: "Immediately the one that received the five talents went his way and did business with them and gained five more. In the same way the one that received the two gained two more." (Matthew 25:16, 17) Evidently, these two slaves did not deposit the money in a bank and let it gain interest by the operations of the bankers; but they themselves engaged in business ventures with skill and discernment and sharp astuteness. Their personal efforts paid off, for their respective moneys doubled in amount. Each one made use of "his own

19. (a) In the parable, what did the "man" expect the slaves to do about his "belongings"? (b) What does Jesus Christ expect about the "belongings" that he left with his disciple "slaves"?
20. What did the "man" expect of the slaves entrusted with the talents, and how did the meeting of those expectations pay off for the slaves?

ability," with loyalty and devotion for his owner, as well as a desire to win his approval.

²¹ How, now, is that portion of the "belongings" of the Lord Jesus Christ that is committed to the prospective Kingdom heir doubled in amount in the fulfillment of the parable? The Lord Jesus told how it was to be done and the Bible account furnishes illustrations of how it was done nineteen centuries ago. Some days before his ascending to heaven the Lord Jesus materialized and appeared to his disciples at a prearranged place on a mountain in the province of Galilee. There he said to them: "All authority has been given me in heaven and on the earth. Go therefore and make disciples of people of all the nations, baptizing them in the name of the Father and of the Son and of the holy spirit, teaching them to observe all the things I have commanded you. And, look! I am with you all the days until the conclusion of the system of things." (Matthew 28:16-20) But on the day of his ascending to heaven he was more specific about the course that the work of increasing his "belongings" was to take. About this we read:

²² "When, now, they had assembled, they went asking him: 'Lord, are you restoring the kingdom to Israel at this time?' He said to them: 'It does not belong to you to get knowledge of the times or seasons which the Father has placed in his own jurisdiction; but you will receive power when the holy spirit arrives upon you, and you will be witnesses of me both in Jerusalem and in all Judea and Samaria and to the most distant part of the earth.' "—Acts 1:6-8.

²³ During his earthly activity as a Kingdom preacher and teacher Jesus had restricted his efforts to Jerusalem and the provinces of Galilee and of Judea (including Samaria) and to Perea on the eastern banks of the Jordan River. In those areas Jesus had produced a prepared, cultivated condition among the Jews and

21, 22. How were the "belongings" of Jesus Christ to be increased in quantity, and to what extent? Over what area?
23. (a) To what areas had Jesus restricted his preaching and teaching, and with what result? (b) Where, then, did the disciples find Christ's "belongings," to work with until whose due time?

Samaritans for the making of more disciples. This condition in those areas was what the disciples were to take advantage of in increasing the number of Christian disciples; it was the "belongings" that Jesus their Lord committed to them as "slaves." So, first of all, they were to work in those prepared areas until the time or season that the heavenly Father held within his own jurisdiction. This they must do, remembering that ("Christ actually became a minister of those who are circumcised in behalf of God's truthfulness, so as to verify the promises He made to their forefathers.")—Romans 15:8.

[24] In harmony with this the disciple "slaves" back there capitalized on the prepared, cultivated estate that the Lord Jesus had committed to them as his "belongings" for which he had worked, and they put that spiritual estate to work in order to produce an increase of the disciples. They did that at once, right there on that Festival Day of Pentecost of 33 C.E., at Jerusalem, and at once there was a production of about three thousand baptized who were put in line for the Kingdom by their being baptized with holy spirit. These were all circumcised persons, whether natural Jews or proselytes to the Jewish faith. The belongings of the Lord Jesus that had been committed to the disciples continued to be used still more, Christian business being done with those "belongings," so that sometime later the number of disciples in Jerusalem had gone up to "about five thousand." (Acts 4:4) Doubtless, hundreds of those Jews and proselytes who left Jerusalem after the celebration of Pentecost and returned to their homes in various parts of the earth found a field for activity in behalf of Christianity among their home Jewish neighborhoods.

[25] Possibly, many of those returning Jews and proselytes had come in contact with Jesus Christ and had

24. (a) After receiving holy spirit, how did the disciples at once put the "belongings" of their Lord to work, and with what amount of production? (b) What field for productivity did the Jewish believers find on returning home after Pentecost?
25. (a) How had Jesus already worked for some "belongings" in the case of Jews and proselytes attending the Jerusalem festivals? (b) How did persecution cause the Christian faith to be spread to distant Jewish communities?

heard him on previous visits to Jerusalem to attend all the festivals. That being so, Jesus had even produced a prepared, cultivated condition in the case of those visiting Jews and proselytes, and the apostles and fellow disciples at Jerusalem took advantage of this part of Jesus' belongings and put such "belongings" to work. (John 12:20-29; Acts 2:5-11) So it came about that, before ever the apostle Paul got to Rome, Italy, there was a congregation of many Christians there. (Romans 1:1-7; 15:22-24) Also, the persecution that arose at Jerusalem against Christ's disciples there resulted in the spread of the Christian faith to many Jews outside the Jewish provinces. In Acts 11:19 it is written: "Consequently those who had been scattered by the tribulation that arose over Stephen went through as far as Phoenicia and Cyprus and Antioch, but speaking the word to no one except to Jews only."

[26] This holding down the increasing of the "belongings" of the absent Lord Jesus Christ to only the Jews and Jewish proselytes continued till the autumn of the year 36 C.E. Then the time of increasing the number of Christian disciples in other areas arrived, just as Jesus himself had commanded, saying: "Go therefore and make disciples of people of all the nations, baptizing them," and, "you will be witnesses of me . . . to the most distant part of the earth." (Matthew 28:19, 20; Acts 1:8) Then it was God's due time for the Jewish disciples, to whom Jesus had committed his spiritual "talents," to use those "belongings" of his in order to make more spiritual "talents." This began by the action on the part of the five-talents class, when the apostle Peter was sent to the Roman capital of Judea at Caesarea to convert Cornelius to the discipleship of Jesus Christ. (Acts 10:1 to 11:18) By this the whole Gentile or non-Jewish world of humankind was opened up for disciple-making. This was an area that had not 'belonged' to Jesus Christ on earth by

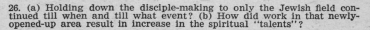

assignment from Jehovah God for him to sow and reap and make disciples.—Matthew 15:24.

²⁷ Here now was a vast area in which there had been no conditioning of the people by Jesus Christ himself, no prepared, cultivated state left by Jesus as a pioneer for his disciples to use to advantage toward increasing the Christian congregation. With the benefit and the advantage and the impetus of what Jesus had done in providing the original field under cultivation, they could now as experienced, qualified workers sow the seed and cultivate the possibilities of growth and thereby add other fields for the producing of disciples of Jesus the Messiah. This required pioneering efforts on their own part, and called for courage, sincere effort, careful attention and perseverance to be exercised by them that no loss might be suffered. They were no longer building on another man's foundation, but were themselves doing all the preliminaries to disciple-making in a brand-new area. This showed obedience to their Lord.—Romans 15:17-21.

²⁸ The apostles and other first-century disciples of Jesus Christ set the pattern as to how to 'do business' with the figurative "talents" that were committed to them. They increased the number of their Lord's talents one hundred percent. The class of Christian "slaves" entrusted with "five talents" of the Lord's "belongings" made five talents more. The class of Christ's "slaves" that were made responsible for two talents of what belonged to their Lord made two talents more. It was a hundred-percent increase, proportionately, for each class, so that each one did up to the extent that was possible for him, and no one was better than anyone else. He did as much as could be expected of him. Each one did his utmost according to "his own ability." However, the increase made with the belongings of their Lord did not owe itself wholly to the use of the "ability" of each "slave." There was

27. This opening up of a worldwide area for productivity called for what on the part of the Jewish disciples?
28, 29. (a) Following the pattern set by the first-century disciples, how have the later disciple "slaves" of Christ done according to their ability? (b) What has been the most vital factor involved in the bringing in of increase?

another factor that entered into the matter, and this was the most essential factor of all. The apostle Paul refers to this factor when he speaks comparatively of his own service and that of the eloquent disciple Apollos, saying:

[29] "What, then, is Apollos? Yes, what is Paul? Ministers through whom you became believers, even as the Lord granted each one. I planted, Apollos watered, but God kept making it grow; so that neither is he that plants anything nor is he that waters, but God who makes it grow. Now he that plants and he that waters are one, but each person will receive his own reward according to his own labor. For we are God's fellow workers. You people are God's field under cultivation, God's building."—1 Corinthians 3:5-9.

[30] God, therefore, is the One to be credited with the increase, and Christ's "slaves" are merely the instruments that he is pleased to use in effecting the increase. He helps the "slaves" to meet their responsibilities. He equips the "slaves" with what they need for carrying on successfully the work of making disciples from people of all the nations. Thus the prepared, cultivated disciple-producing area that the departing Son of God left to his faithful disciples is added to, because other areas of this kind are brought into existence all around the globe through the obedience of Christ's "slaves" to his commands and their imitation of his example. What evidence of this was there in the first century of our Common Era? This: congregations of disciples who were heirs of the kingdom of the heavens sprang up outside of Jerusalem and of all Judea and Galilee and Samaria. Congregations were established in Asia, Africa, Europe and islands of the Mediterranean Sea.

[31] For instance, take the apostle Peter. He was one of the four apostles who, after hearing Jesus predict

30. (a) Who, then, is to be credited primarily with the increase? (b) In the first century, what evidence was there of the increase in the area cultivated by disciples?
31. As an example of the foregoing, what does the location from which Peter wrote his first letter indicate about him?

the destruction of the magnificent temple in Jerusalem, put the question to him: "When will these things be, and what will be the sign when all these things are destined to come to a conclusion?" (Mark 13:1-4) Well, about thirty years later, around 62-64 C.E., or several years before "these things" did occur with the siege and destruction of Jerusalem along with its temple, the apostle Peter was doing missionary work outside the Roman Empire. Yes, the first letter that he wrote to fellow Christians inside the Roman Empire was written in the city of Babylon on the Euphrates River in Mesopotamia, and in this letter he refers to the Christian congregation there at the close of his letter, saying: "She who is in Babylon, a chosen one like you, sends you her greetings."—1 Peter 5:13.

[32] Then there was also the apostle Paul. He had at last reached the imperial capital of Rome, but as a prisoner who had appealed to Caesar for a fair trial. From his place of custody in Rome he wrote to the Christian congregation in Colossae, Asia Minor, about 60-61 C.E. This was almost ten years before "these things" predicted by the Lord Jesus Christ, and yet as early as that before the end of the Jewish system of things as centered in Jerusalem, the apostle Paul spoke of the worldwide increasing of the figurative "talents" that Jesus had committed to his "slaves." As Paul is referring to the 'telling of the good news' to them he writes:

[33] "We heard of your faith in connection with Christ Jesus and the love you have for all the holy ones because of the hope that is being reserved for you in the heavens. This hope you heard of before by the telling of the truth of that good news which has presented itself to you, even as it is bearing fruit and increasing in all the world just as it is doing also among you, from the day you heard and accurately knew the undeserved kindness of God in truth. That

32-34. (a) About when and from where did Paul write his letter to the Colossians? (b) How does Paul therein indicate the worldwide increase of the "talents" committed to the disciples?

is what you have learned from Epaphras our beloved fellow slave, who is a faithful minister of the Christ on our behalf, who also disclosed to us your love in a spiritual way.

[34] "Indeed, you who were once alienated and enemies because your minds were on the works that were wicked, he now has again reconciled by means of that one's fleshly body through his death, in order to present you holy and unblemished, and open to no accusation before him, provided, of course, that you continue in the faith, established on the foundation and steadfast and not being shifted away from the hope of that good news which you heard, and which was preached in all creation that is under heaven."—Colossians 1:4-8, 21-23.

[35] What a testimony those inspired words of the apostle Paul were to the zeal of those first-century "slaves" of the Lord Jesus Christ in 'doing business' with the "talents" that he had committed to them! What an accomplishment that was for them in such a short period of time—the good news "bearing fruit and increasing in all the world," the good news already "preached in all creation that is under heaven"! Think of it: Jesus Christ had "manifested himself once for all time at the conclusion of the systems of things," in the years 29-33 C.E., and yet even before the conclusion of the Jewish system of things was finished in the year 70 C.E., by the annihilation of their religious capital, the Jews throughout the then known world had received a witness concerning the Messianic kingdom of God. Indeed, all the Gentile nations had also received such a witness, in a typical fulfillment of Jesus' prophecy on the "sign" of the "conclusion of the system of things," namely: "This good news of the kingdom will be preached in all the inhabited earth for a witness to all the nations; and then the end will come."—Matthew 24:14; Hebrews 9:26.

---

35. This testimony to the zeal of the first-century disciples was effected during what limited period of time, and in fulfillment of what prophecy of Jesus?

CULMINATION OF THE PARABLE'S
FULFILLMENT TODAY

[36] Those first-century "slaves" who increased the precious "talents" to such a worldwide extent in spite of wars, pestilences, famines, earthquakes and persecutions all died off, but their departed Lord and Owner did not return in their day, either before or after the destruction of Jerusalem by the Roman legions. About twenty-six years after that horrible event shocked the Jewish religious world, the apostle John had his prison term on the Isle of Patmos brightened by receiving the divine Revelation, in which he pointed to the future and said: ('Look! He is coming with the clouds, and every eye will see him, and those who pierced him.') And John closed the Revelation account with the prayer: (' 'Amen! Come, Lord Jesus.' May the undeserved kindness of the Lord Jesus Christ be with the holy ones)' (Revelation 1:7; 22:20, 21) That fervent prayer for the Lord's coming was not actually answered before more than eighteen centuries had passed.

[37] Only with the return of the Lord Jesus Christ and his parousia or presence would the culmination come in the fulfillment of the parable of the "talents." In the latter half of the past nineteenth century it was thought that the Lord had returned in the year 1874 C.E. and that with that year his invisible presence in spirit had begun. But really the "sign" of his presence and of the conclusion of the system of things did not present itself during the succeeding four decades. Not until the end of the Gentile Times in the year 1914, about October 4/5 or the middle of the Jewish lunar month Tishri. At that time the preaching of the good news of a coming Messianic kingdom of God turned into the preaching of the good news of the *established* kingdom of God. World events that followed piled up evidence that in the aforesaid critical

36. Did the Lord of the disciple "slaves" come again before or after Jerusalem's destruction, and what did John's closing words of the Revelation indicate about Christ's coming?
37. (a) Contrary to what expectation, when did the Lord Jesus Christ return? (b) From then on, the Kingdom-preaching took on what new meaning, and why?

year God's kingdom of the heavens was born by the enthronement and crowning of his Messiah, Jesus the son of David the son of Abraham. (Matthew 1:1) The one had come who has the "legal right" to it. In fact, he had *returned!*—Ezekiel 21:25-27.

[38] The parable of the "talents" was given by Jesus Christ as being a part of the many-featured "sign" for indicating the fact of his parousia or presence. So the bringing of the fulfillment of the parable to a head in our time ought to add to the testimony that he has returned in spirit and that his presence is upon us. Certainly if we say that the royal presence of the Lord Jesus Christ began at the close of the Gentile Times in 1914, then there ought to be facts available to verify that the fulfillment of the parable is undergoing its culmination in our day. What are the facts?

[39] First, we look to see how the parable turned out. So we take up reading further in Jesus' parable, as follows: "But the one that received just one went off, and dug in the ground and hid the silver money of his master. After a long time the master of those slaves came and settled accounts with them."—Matthew 25: 18, 19.

[40] When the "master of those slaves" came, he came back with what he had traveled abroad to gain. His own words later show that he had gained a "joy" to share with his faithful slaves; he came back with "many things" that he had not had when he committed the eight silver talents to them. An earlier parable given by Jesus, the parable of the "ten minas," specifies that what he came back with was "kingly power." (Luke 19:12-15) The Gentile Times, or "the appointed times of the nations," have to do with "kingly power," particularly the "kingly power" of the family of King David of Jerusalem, the kingly power of which Davidic family Nebuchadnezzar the king of Babylon over-

---

38. The parable of the "talents" was given as part of what prophecy, and so how should the culmination of its fulfillment in our day be indicated?
39. What did the slave with the one talent do, and when did settling of accounts with the slaves begin?
40. (a) In the parable, with what did the "master of those slaves" return? (b) The year 1914 C.E. had to do with what "kingdom power" in particular, and how so?

threw in the year 607 B.C.E. That disastrous year was the date when the 2,520 years of the Gentile Times began their count down to the year 1914 C.E. So the end of those Gentile Times about October 4/5 of 1914 should logically witness a reversal of the situation of such long standing. It was therefore not without significance that October 4/5, 1914, found the Gentile nations in trouble, already for two months embroiled in the first world war of human history.

[41] What, though, about the Christian "slaves" of the heavenly Master Jesus Christ to whom he had committed his valuable "talents"? To this day there is still a small number of those faithful "slaves" who were on the earthly scene at that marked time and who discerned from the Holy Scriptures the meaning of World War I. This international conflict that finally dragged in twenty-eight nations and empires in total warfare did not kill off those loyal "slaves" of the newly enthroned heavenly King, Jesus Christ. The earthly enemies, who did not want Jesus Christ to rule over them as King of all the earth, would have liked to kill off these "slaves" of his," but did not succeed in doing so. They tried, in effect, to take away from them those figurative "talents" that they had received from their heavenly Master and Owner. They tried to undo all the fine accomplishments and spiritual gains that these "slaves" had made for the newly enthroned heavenly King. To this end they tried to kill the influence of these with the people of all the nations. They tried desperately to undermine the prepared, cultivated foundation of these for future Kingdom witnessing.

[42] The end of World War I on November 11, 1918, found "slaves" of the reigning heavenly King practically killed as respects that good reputation with the people inside and outside of Christendom. The favor with the people as Christians was practically dead

41. (a) Did World War I kill off the small number of the disciple "slaves" of the Lord Jesus Christ then on earth? (b) What did the nations seek to do to them as respects further witnessing by them?
42, 43. (a) The end of World War I in 1918 found the "slaves" of the heavenly Master in what state? (b) To all appearances, what had happened to the "talents" entrusted to them?

under a shroud of misrepresentation and vilification
by nationalistic patrioteers and war-minded fanatics.
Violent mobbings had taken place against them. Either
their Bible literature was banned or they themselves
were proscribed. Many of them were in prison, most
outstandingly of all these being the president of the
Watch Tower Bible and Tract Society, also the secretary-treasurer thereof, and six other prominent associates under false charges from which they could be
exonerated only after the war madness had died down.

[43] Seemingly, these "slaves" of the Rightful Ruler of
this earthly globe were stripped of everything. His
"talents" committed to them seemed to have been
wiped out. Their enemies rejoiced at having put those
"slaves" out of the service of their heavenly Master
for all time to come, for the ability of these to start
all over again appeared to have been put in doubt.

[44] It was not till more than four months later, after
the war ended, that the enemies were surprised, startled
at a reversal that started to set in. This was when
those eight representatives of the Watch Tower Bible
and Tract Society were released from imprisonment
in the Atlanta (Georgia) Federal Penitentiary on
March 25, 1919, and admitted to bail the next day in
Brooklyn, New York. Exoneration from the grossly
false accusations against them came shortly in due
course. But how much did this count with the war-
prostrated people who carried with them the preju-
diced, distorted viewpoint respecting the "slaves" of
Jesus Christ because of war propaganda and war fever?
It was something for the "slaves" to consider. Could
they pick up and go forward again in the face of such
forbidding circumstances? Did they have the courage
and the confidence of their heavenly Master to do so?
It was indeed a time of test for these Christian slaves.

[45] The parable of the "talents" pictured that when
the traveler returned from abroad he would settle

44. (a) When did a reversal of matters set in, and how? (b) What question now arose as to the surviving "slaves,"—and why?
45. (a) According to the parable, what was due to be carried on by the
"master of those slaves"? (b) As regards their possession of "talents,"
what needed to be done in behalf of those Christian slaves?

accounts with them. This meant an inspection of them. Quite logically, with that turn of events in the spring of 1919, it would be the due time for the heavenly "master of those slaves" to inspect them. But what account could they render with respect to his "talents" that had been committed to the slave class? Any increase that they may have gained prior to the climax of wartime persecution in 1918 seemed to have been wiped out. They were as if they had no figurative "talents" in their possession at all. If, now, they were to show any increase in their Master's "talents," they must produce this increase in the postwar period and render such increase of his belongings to him in the future. They must be given a new and further opportunity to 'do business' with his precious "talents." This is just how it worked out historically, due to the merciful considerateness of their heavenly Master.

[46] The year 1919 was the vital time to dispel the fear of men that had been created among the slave class during the violence and hysteria of the first world war and that had caused the slave class to withdraw considerably from doing business as responsible slaves of the reigning King, Jesus Christ. It was then high time for them to begin reorganizing their broken, crippled ranks for the biggest endeavor of their lives in their service of their Master now possessed of kingly power. Now, as never before, their Master had the rightful claim to all the earth as his field at his disposal for the producing of further disciples favored with the hope of the heavenly kingdom. He could commit this opportune situation to them for 'doing business' in his service. It was the auspicious time for the "slave" class of disciples to arise as pictured by the slave to whom "five talents" were entrusted, and also for the class pictured by the slave who had two talents committed to him. They did so, for the parable of the "talents" could not fail of its fulfillment, especially at its culmination.

46. (a) What was it the time for them to dispel, and for what did they need to reorganize? (b) In view of their heavenly Master's being possessed of "kingdom power," for what was the situation opportune and the time auspicious?

⁴⁷ No time was lost. In 1919 those two classes of "slaves" got busy. They received strong reassurance from the *Watch Tower* articles of August 1 and 15, 1919, on the theme "Blessed Are the Fearless." They hailed the announcement of the eight-day convention to be held at Cedar Point, Ohio, on September 1-8, 1919. They did not shrink back from attending that general convention for fear that they might be confronted with a postwar work that would require great energy and courage on their part, with further persecution.

⁴⁸ With eagerness to learn how Jehovah purposed for them to do the work that lay ahead of them, six thousand who came particularly from Canada and the United States of America daily attended the sessions of this convention of the International Bible Students Association. With surprise and yet hearty appreciation they received the announcement of a new magazine to be published beginning October 1, 1919, *The Golden Age,* as a companion to *The Watch Tower and Herald of Christ's Presence.* This new magazine would be an additional adjunct in announcing God's established Messianic kingdom. It would be another instrument for them to use in doing the planting, watering and cultivating of new areas for the production of more disciples of the Lord Jesus Christ. Side by side with *The Watch Tower* that new magazine (now *Awake!*) has worked in an increasing circulation until now, arousing new interest in honest-hearted persons and readying them to receive the deeper things of God's Word. It has done an excellent preparing work.

⁴⁹ Also, communications between the headquarters of the Watch Tower Bible and Tract Society and its branch organizations around the globe that had been disrupted by the world war were reestablished and strengthened, and, as time and circumstances revealed

47. In 1919, how were they strengthened not to fear but to present themselves for the postwar work?
48. (a) How did the Cedar Point conventioners receive the announcement of a new magazine as a companion of *The Watch Tower?* (b) How has this additional magazine been used till now?
49. What was done with regard to branches of the Watch Tower Society, and to what extent have areas thereby brought under cultivation been increased?

the need, new branches were set up in various lands. This increased the areas that were brought under closer supervision of the "slaves" of the heavenly Master Jesus Christ and aided greatly in intensifying the work for cultivating such areas for the gathering of more disciples of people of all the nations. From the few branches that then existed the number has soared to ninety-five branches today. These have the oversight over the seeding and cultivating operations that are being carried on in two hundred and eight countries and islands of the sea.

50 In September of 1922 these Christian slaves who are in line for the heavenly kingdom were forcefully made aware that they are indeed now under inspection of the King of kings and Lord of lords, the reigning Lord Jesus. In fulfillment of Malachi 3:1, he has accompanied Jehovah God when coming to his spiritual temple for judgment work with regard to his spirit-begotten "slaves" at the temple. Those attending the second convention of the International Bible Students Association in Cedar Point, Ohio, on its fourth day, September 8, 1922, designated as "The Day," now saw themselves to be in the position of the prophet Isaiah, when he had a vision of Jehovah God at his temple. Isaiah felt the need for being spiritually cleansed, and he was mercifully given the needed cleansing. This put him in the favorable position to respond to Jehovah's invitation with the eager cry: "Here I am! Send me." (Isaiah 6:1-8) So the question was, Would the I.B.S.A. conventioners respond similarly to Jehovah's invitation to service then being extended to them?

51 In the second-last paragraph of his speech that dealt with Isaiah's vision, the Watch Tower Society's president, J. F. Rutherford, put a number of questions to the conventioners, including these final ones: "Do you believe that the Lord is now in his temple, judging the nations of the earth? Do you believe that the King

of glory has begun his reign?') With high enthusiasm the thousands of conventioners shouted affirmatively. At this the speaker climaxed his speech by saying: ("Then back to the field, O ye sons of the most high God! Gird on your armor! Be sober, be vigilant, be active, be brave. Be faithful and true witnesses for the Lord. Go forward in the fight until every vestige of Babylon lies desolate. Herald the message far and wide. The world must know that Jehovah is God and that Jesus Christ is King of kings and Lord of lords. This is the day of all days. Behold, the King reigns! You are his publicity agents. Therefore advertise, advertise, advertise, the King and his kingdom.')—See *The Watch Tower* under date of November 1, 1922, pages 332-337.

[52] With greater zeal and effort than ever before the "slaves" of the returned Lord Jesus Christ went forth to advertise him as reigning King, preaching publicly both from house to house and from the public platform. Since 1920 they had begun operating their own printing establishment in Brooklyn, New York, and this enabled them to come into possession of greater quantities of Bible literature, magazines, booklets, tracts, hardbound books, and finally Bibles themselves, at greater economy, to use in advertising the Messianic King and his kingdom. From Sunday, February 24, 1924, radio stations owned by legal corporations of these "slaves" began to be used in broadcasting the Kingdom message to a numberless invisible audience at their radio receivers. In course of time scores of radio stations were brought into use, either on rented time or on free time, in a number of lands to sound out the Kingdom good news to the very ends of the earth. To these publicity means were added, some years later, sound cars with loudspeakers and portable phonographs carried by Christ's "slaves" from door to door to advertise the Kingdom to the householders.

52. (a) In 1920, what did the Society do for increasing the distribution of Bible literature? (b) In 1924, what other means for advertising the Kingdom did the Society start using, enlarged later by what other publicity means?

→ [53] It was a thrill for the readers of *The Watch Tower and Herald of Christ's Presence* when they received their issue of March 1, 1925, and read the leading article entitled "Birth of the Nation." Why? Because they received therein a closer understanding of Revelation, chapter twelve. Their eyes of spiritual discernment were opened to see that the symbolic birth of the man child, so excitingly presented in that chapter so long a mystery to them, pictured the birth of God's Messianic kingdom in the year 1914, at the end of the Gentile Times. The article concluded, on page 74, saying: "The kingdom of heaven is here. The day of deliverance is in sight. Let this good news be heralded to the peoples of earth. Victory is with our King. Faithful now to the end of the war; and we shall forever bask in the sunshine of his love, where there is fulness of joy and pleasures for evermore."

[54] The annual celebration of the Lord's Supper on the following date, Wednesday, April 8, 1925, brought something encouraging to light. Because of the planting, watering and cultivating work that had gone on till then in additional areas of activity, with the newly provided instruments for Kingdom publicity, the number of congregations of disciples with heavenly hopes increased. The membership of congregations increased. So at this celebration of the Lord's Supper the number of participants therein indicated this growth and production of disciples of Christ. How many, then, did participate that year? The September 1, 1925, issue of *The Watch Tower,* page 263, under "Memorial Reports," says:

[55] "We are pleased that the number participating in the Memorial is so great, because it manifests much interest in the truth everywhere, and this is as it should be. The grand total reported to date is 90,434, which is 25,329 more than were reported a year ago."

[56] Truly the "slaves" of Christ, the class pictured

---

53. Why did the readers have reason to be thrilled at the leading article of the issue of March 1, 1925, of *The Watch Tower?*
54, 55. How did the number of those participating in the Lord's Supper in 1925 indicate an increase in the areas of activity?
56. What did this indicate with regard to the "business" transactions of the disciple "slaves" who were entrusted with the "talents"?

by the slave entrusted with "five talents," and the class pictured by the slave to whom two talents were committed, were prompt and early in 'doing business' with them, so as to add other areas that would be fruitful with more disciples of Christ. The published facts prove that these "slaves" were being blessed in their efforts and were rewarded with increase. This encouraged them on still more.

JOY

[57] However, now historically another factor comes to plain view in the matter. In Jesus' parable, the man who possessed the eight silver talents and three slaves did not go traveling abroad simply for pleasure as on a sight-seeing trip. He had a serious reason for traveling abroad; he desired to secure something valuable. What he went abroad for, as the parable shows, was to gain a certain "joy," along with "many things." Consequently, he had to travel a long distance, requiring a long stretch of time, in order to apply to the one who could impart to him that particular "joy." This is implicit in Jesus' parable, although the parable of the "talents" does not explicitly say so. Since the wealthy man in the parable pictures the Lord Jesus Christ, the man's traveling abroad for a long trip pictures the Lord Jesus going to the one Source of the special joy that he had in view. To whom, then, did he go? Who was that Source of joy?

[58] This is indicated for us in Hebrews 12:2, which reads: "We look intently at the Chief Agent and Perfecter of our faith, Jesus. For the joy that was set before him he endured a torture stake, despising shame, and has sat down at the right hand of the throne of God."

[59] Ah, yes, Jehovah God is the Source of that "joy." It was to him that the resurrected Jesus Christ went away, leaving his faithful disciples here on earth, en-

57. (a) Why did the wealthy man of the parable travel abroad? (b) So what questions arise as to Jesus Christ in the parable's fulfillment?
58, 59. (a) To whom did the resurrected Jesus Christ go to obtain that "joy"? (b) To whom else is He the Source of joy, as indicated in Romans 15:13?

trusted with his "belongings," his "talents." The heavenly Father was the Source of Jesus' special cause for "joy." Jehovah God is the Source of joy also to the disciples of his beloved Son. Accordingly, one of those disciples, when writing to fellow Christians in Rome, said: "May the God who gives hope fill you with all joy and peace by your believing, that you may abound in hope with power of holy spirit." (Romans 15:13) God was able to answer that proper prayer.

⁶⁰ In the proper course of things it would be good timing to have God, the heavenly Source of joy, given due prominence in the eyes of the "slaves" of the Lord Jesus Christ after his joyful return, now that God's Messianic kingdom had been born in the heavens. The time had come for this divine Source of joy to make a name for himself, and this required that first His personal name be made known. That Name was duly made known. Deservedly, it went into regular use among his reverent worshipers on earth and it has been published throughout the whole earth as it had never been publicized at any previous time. When the year 1926 opened up, the first issue of *The Watch Tower* presented its leading article entitled "Who Will Honor Jehovah?" From then forward, the divine name, which appears thousands of times in the original Hebrew text of the Holy Bible, was exalted to its rightful elevation among the "slaves" of the Son of God. They began to be witnesses for Him foremost, but not diminishing their witness for his Son Jesus Christ. They lovingly acted on their obligation to be witnesses for the Only One who bears the name Jehovah.

⁶¹ Five and a half years of such witnessing for the divine Name followed. Then came the time for the Christian "slaves" to identify themselves, to differentiate themselves from all the professed Christians of religious Christendom. To this end, action was taken by the "slaves" of Jesus Christ on Sunday afternoon,

---

60. (a) To whom was it timely to give due prominence, now that Jesus Christ had returned with his "joy"? (b) How was this due prominence given to Him as respects his name?
61. (a) By a resolution in 1931, the disciple slaves of Jesus Christ declared themselves opposed to being called by what names? (b) By what name did they henceforth desire to be called?

July 26, 1931, at the international convention held in Columbus, Ohio, U.S.A. At 4:00 p.m., there was presented and read to the thousands of conventioners a resolution, the fourth, fifth and sixth paragraphs of which we are here pleased to quote:

Now, THEREFORE, in order that our true position may be made known, and believing that this is in harmony with the will of God, as expressed in his Word, BE IT RESOLVED, as follows, to wit:

THAT we have great love for Brother Charles T. Russell, for his work's sake, and that we gladly acknowledge that the Lord used him and greatly blessed his work, yet we cannot consistently with the Word of God consent to be called by the name "Russellites"; that the Watch Tower Bible and Tract Society and the International Bible Students Association and the Peoples Pulpit Association are merely names of corporations which as a company of Christian people we hold, control and use to carry on our work in obedience to God's commandments, yet none of these names properly attach to or apply to us as a body of Christians who follow in the footsteps of our Lord and Master, Christ Jesus; that we are students of the Bible, but, as a body of Christians forming an association, we decline to assume or be called by the name "Bible Students" or similar names as a means of identification of our proper position before the Lord; we refuse to bear or to be called by the name of any man;

THAT, having been bought with the precious blood of Jesus Christ our Lord and Redeemer, justified and begotten by Jehovah God and called to his kingdom, we unhesitatingly declare our entire allegiance and devotion to Jehovah God and his kingdom; that we are servants of Jehovah God commissioned to do a work in his name, and, in obedience to his commandment, to deliver the testimony of Jesus Christ, and to make known to the people that Jehovah is the true and Almighty God; therefore we joyfully embrace and take the name which the mouth of the Lord God has named, and we desire to be known as and called by the name, to wit, *Jehovah's witnesses.*—Isa. 43:10-12; 62:2; Rev. 12:17.

[62] The eighth and last paragraph of the Resolution said:

We humbly invite all persons who are wholly devoted to Jehovah and his kingdom to join in proclaiming this good news to others, that the righteous standard of the

62. What invitation was extended in the last paragraph of the resolution?

Lord may be lifted up, that the peoples of the world may know where to find the truth and hope for relief; and, above all, that the great and holy name of Jehovah God may be vindicated and exalted.

[63] This resolution was enthusiastically adopted, not only by those in convention assembled at Columbus, Ohio, but also, later on, by the congregations of the "slaves" of Jesus Christ all around the globe. Thus they voluntarily embraced the name "Jehovah's witnesses." This Resolution on the name was also published in the booklet released at the convention entitled "The Kingdom, the Hope of the World." That title was also the subject of the public address by the Society's president J. F. Rutherford to both the visible convention audience and the invisible audience listening in by means of a vast radio network, from twelve o'clock noon onward. Thereafter this booklet containing both the public address and the Resolution was placed directly by personal bearers into the hands of the religious clergymen, Catholic and Protestant, and afterward into the hands of prominent political and professional men. There was also a wider circulation among the people in general. In this way notice was served on all the world that these justified and spirit-begotten worshipers of the Most High God would walk in the name of their God and acknowledge only the name Jehovah's witnesses.—Micah 4:5.

[64] Inasmuch as there were also witnesses of the one living and true God before the first coming of the Lord Jesus Christ, they recognize themselves to be Jehovah's *Christian* witnesses.—Isaiah 43:10-12; 44:8; Hebrews 11:1 to 12:1. See also *The Watch Tower* as of September 15, 1931, pages 278, 279.

---

63. (a) By whom, altogether, was this resolution on the New Name adopted? (b) How was the resolution thereafter publicized and thereby notice served on the world?
64. Why do they recognize themselves to be Jehovah's *Christian* witnesses?

CHAPTER 13

Settling Accounts with the Slaves of Today

THE bearing of the divine name from the year 1931 onward added a new joy to the remnant yet on earth of the "slaves" of the Lord Jesus Christ. Their joy came from the same Source as that from which their Lord and Owner had obtained his joy, namely, from Jehovah God. The Lord Jesus Christ referred to this joy of his when he was settling accounts with his slaves in fulfillment of the parable of the "talents." We note this in Matthew 25:20-23, where we read:

2 "So the one that had received five talents came forward and brought five additional talents, saying, 'Master, you committed five talents to me; see, I gained five talents more.' His master said to him, 'Well done, good and faithful slave! You were faithful over a few things. I will appoint you over many things. Enter into the joy of your master.' Next the one that had received the two talents came forward and said, 'Master, you committed to me two talents; see, I gained two talents more.' His master said to him, 'Well done, good and faithful slave! You were faithful over a few things. I will appoint you over many things. Enter into the joy of your master.'"

3 This settling of accounts with the slaves certainly required time and attention. So it would picture a period of presence or parousia on the part of the heavenly Master, Jesus Christ, in the fulfillment of the parable in its final features. (Matthew 24:3) Never

1, 2. (a) The bearing of the divine name added what to the remnant of Christ's "slaves," and who was the source of it? (b) How is this joy referred to in the parable of the "talents"?
3, 4. (a) Do the three "slaves" picture individuals, or what? (b) How does the settling of accounts with what is pictured by the "slaves," in the fulfillment of the parable, argue for the proper meaning of parousia?"

let us forget that the three slaves in the parable stood for classes and that these classes are made up of individuals. It takes more time and attention to deal with a class or group than with a single individual. In the case of a class or group, each member thereof must be dealt with. In Romans 14:9, 10 the apostle Paul wrote:

⁴ "For to this end Christ died and came to life again, that he might be Lord over both the dead and the living. . . . For we shall all stand before the judgment seat of God."

⁵ In the fulfillment of the parable of the "talents," the Lord Jesus Christ judges for Jehovah God. Not all his "slaves" to whom "talents" were committed are found alive in the flesh here on earth in this twentieth century. For instance, those of the first century during the days of the twelve apostles, down to John the receiver of the Revelation, died long ago, falling asleep in death and awaiting the parousia of their heavenly Lord and Owner, when they would receive the reward from him as the righteous Judge. As the apostle Paul, shortly before his martyrdom, wrote to Timothy his missionary companion: "I have fought the fine fight, I have run the course to the finish, I have observed the faith. From this time on there is reserved for me the crown of righteousness, which the Lord, the righteous judge, will give me as a reward in that day, yet not only to me, but also to all those who have loved his manifestation." (2 Timothy 4:7, 8) Yes, indeed, the apostle Paul looked forward to "that day," the day of the Lord's parousia, for a resurrection from the dead and the receiving of the prize of immortal heavenly life. All dying before his parousia had to wait.

⁶ During his invisible parousia in spirit, all those faithful "slaves" who were sleeping in death were awakened at the time for the beginning of the judg-

---

5. (a) For whom does Jesus Christ judge when judging the living and the dead? (b) Those of the classes pictured by the "slaves" who died before Christ's parousia had to do what with regard to their reward?
6. When are those "slaves" sleeping in death resurrected, and over whom do these take precedence as to resurrection?

ment, to heavenly life in the spirit realm. Thus the rewarding of the living "slaves" did not take precedence over the rewarding of the sleeping faithful "slaves." This is not our imagination; for the apostle Paul writes to the Christian congregation in Thessalonica and says: "If our faith is that Jesus died and rose again, so, too, those who have fallen asleep [in death] through Jesus God will bring with him. For this is what we tell you by Jehovah's word, that we the living who survive to the presence of the Lord shall in no way precede those who have fallen asleep [in death]; because the Lord himself will descend from heaven with a commanding call, with an archangel's voice and with God's trumpet, and those who are dead in union with Christ will rise first. Afterward we the living who are surviving will, together with them, be caught away in clouds to meet the Lord in the air; and thus we shall always be with the Lord." —1 Thessalonians 4:14-17.

7 This means that during the Lord's parousia there occurs, at the time for the judgment to begin, an invisible resurrection of the sleeping faithful "slaves" to heavenly life in the spirit. This is, of course, not visible to the surviving "slaves" yet on earth with their fleshly eyes, just as it is also invisible to worldly people who are not "slaves" of the invisibly present Lord Jesus.

8 The meeting by the resurrected "slaves" with the "Lord in the air" is also invisible to all fleshly eyes on the earth, so that humans on earth do not know that it is going on except by faith in God's Word and the indications of the times. Those "slaves" who were sleeping in death were all resurrected together at the same time to "meet the Lord in the air." However, those "slaves" on earth who survived until the time for the judgment or settling of accounts to begin were not caught up literally in their visible physical bodies

---

7. What kind of resurrection is it that the sleepers get?
8, 9. (a) What does the evidence show as to whether the meeting of the "slaves" with the Lord in the air means a catching up of physical bodies into the atmosphere? (b) What, as pointed out in 1 Corinthians 15:50-54, has a bearing on this matter?

into earth's atmosphere to meet a visible Lord in the air, for modern history does not record any such happening. Members of this surviving group of "slaves" died off from time to time during the now more than fifty years that have elapsed, but, according to Bible promise, they had an instantaneous resurrection to life in the spirit in the invisible heavens. Since the parousia of the Lord had already begun, they did not need to sleep in death in waiting for his arrival. What Paul said applied to them:

[9] "Flesh and blood cannot inherit God's kingdom, neither does corruption inherit incorruption. Look! I tell you a sacred secret: We shall not all fall asleep [in death], but we shall all be changed, in a moment, in the twinkling of an eye, during the last trumpet. For the trumpet will sound, and the dead will be raised up incorruptible, and we shall be changed. For this which is corruptible must put on incorruption, and this which is mortal must put on immortality. But when [this which is corruptible puts on incorruption and] this which is mortal puts on immortality, then the saying will take place that is written: 'Death is swallowed up forever.' "—1 Corinthians 15:50-54; Isaiah 25:8.

[10] To those anointed slaves who survived on earth until and into the parousia or presence of the Lord and who died thereafter in faithful union with the Lord, the promise of Revelation 14:13 applies: "Happy are the dead who die in union with the Lord from this time onward. Yes, says the spirit, let them rest from their labors, for the things they did go right with them." They are "happy" because at their death in the flesh they experience that instantaneous change from corruption to incorruption, from mortality to immortality, from human to spirit, so that, without any sleep in death, they cease from their earthly labors and enter right into heavenly work with their Lord with whom they are joint heirs.

10. In what way are those "slaves" referred to in Revelation 14:13 "happy"?

[11] Take, for instance, the case of Robert J. Martin. He was one of those eight consecrated Christian men, including the Society's president J. F. Rutherford, who suffered about nine months of unjust imprisonment in the federal penitentiary in Atlanta, Georgia, from July 5, 1918, to March 25, 1919. When this "slave" was set free on bail in Brooklyn, New York, on Wednesday, March 26, 1919, he had practically nothing as far as "talents" from his heavenly Lord was concerned. World War I with its persecution of the Lord's "slaves" was now in the past for more than four months, and R. J. Martin had to begin practically anew. He was still in faithful union with the Lord Jesus, and he was glad to accept "talents" with which to 'do business' for his heavenly Lord, in order to enlarge the field that would prove fruitful in producing disciples of the Lord Jesus Christ. In the year following his release from imprisonment he was made the factory manager of the printing plant newly established in Brooklyn for the Watch Tower Bible and Tract Society. On November 1, 1926, he was made one of the directors of this Society, which post he held to his earthly end.

R. J. Martin

[12] So the years passed, with R. J. Martin faithfully doing business in increasing the "talents" committed to him in the field of disciple-making. He died at his post on September 23, 1932, at the age of fifty-four years. (Born March 30, 1878) His death "in union with

11. Who was this R. J. Martin who was taken as an example of the foregoing?
12. When did Martin die, and what comment did *The Watch Tower* make thereon?

the Lord" was announced in the issue of October 1, 1932, of *The Watch Tower and Herald of Christ's Presence*, page 304, which said, in part:

J. F. Rutherford

> It was just past midnight, or the beginning of the morning of September 23, 1932, that Robert J. Martin, a soldier in the organization of Jehovah, folded his earthly tent and peacefully went away. This good and faithful witness has finished his course on earth. There is every reason to believe that he immediately passed into the kingdom and is now for ever with the Lord in the capital organization of Jehovah.
>
> . . . The hope of the faithful comrades of Brother Martin is that they too may see the Lord in all his glory and beauty and participate ever thereafter in carrying out Jehovah's purposes. The devotion of Brother Martin to Jehovah's cause is an inspiration to those of the remnant to continue to press the battle to the gate. . . .

[13] His fellow prisoner, J. F. Rutherford, finished his earthly course at the age of seventy-two years, while still president of the Watch Tower Bible and Tract Society, on Thursday, January 8, 1942. Under the heading "A Faithful Witness," his death was announced on page 45 of the issue of February 1, 1942, of *The Watchtower Announcing Jehovah's Kingdom*. The history of more than thirty years since then shows that his death marked the end of an epoch in the modern activities of Jehovah's Christian witnesses.

[14] Certainly the career of Christian "slaves," such as the two aforementioned, indicates that they "did

13. When did Martin's fellow prisoner, Rutherford, die, and what did his death mark historically?
14. (a) What is there Scriptural reason to believe regarding such two "slaves" as to their reward for doing business with Christ's "talents"? (b) Have the "slaves" still remaining alive on earth entered into any "joy," and what about the matter of rulership?

business" with the Lord's "talents" committed to them and thereby increased the earthly field of operation for the producing of more disciples of Christ. There is Scriptural reason to believe that, when appearing before the judgment seat of their Lord Jesus Christ, they heard his words of commendation: "Well done, good and faithful slave! You were faithful over a few things. I will appoint you over many things. Enter into the joy of your master." (Matthew 25:21, 23) But now, many years later, there is still a small remnant of those loyal Christian "slaves" on earth who are lovingly seeking to increase the "talents" of their heavenly Master. They expect, in due time, to finish their earthly career and appear before the heavenly judgment seat of Jesus Christ and happily hear those same words of commendation. But even now on earth, to the extent that they are increasing the "talents" of their heavenly Owner, they have already entered into a goodly measure of the joy of their Master. They have not, however, entered into any rulership but merely look forward to sharing in his millennial reign in heaven.

THE "WICKED AND SLUGGISH SLAVE"

[15] We are now interested to learn what happens to the slave in Jesus' parable who received but one talent and concerning whom it was said: "But the one that received just one went off, and dug in the ground and hid the silver money of his master." (Matthew 25: 15, 18) Not exerting himself and not showing courage to 'do business' as the slave with the five talents and the slave with the two talents did, this third slave could not expect to increase the silver talent of his master. He had the proportionate "ability" to handle that one silver talent and make increase with it, but he failed to show his ability. At the coming and during the presence or parousia of his master he would have no increase to show when accounts were settled. So what

---

15, 16. (a) How did the slave with the one talent fail to use his "ability," with what consequences? (b) What excuse did he give for handing back only what he had received?

excuse would he have for presenting no increase to his master? In the parable, Jesus tells us:

[16] "Finally the one that had received the one talent came forward and said, 'Master, I knew you to be an exacting man, reaping where you did not sow and gathering where you did not winnow. So I grew afraid and went off and hid your talent in the ground. Here you have what is yours.' "—Matthew 25:24, 25.

[17] This slave knew that increase was expected of him. But he lacked the courage to take the risk by 'doing business' with his master's silver talent. He did not have the love for his master so as to act, in spite of his fears, and take the risk and make the efforts to expand the "belongings" of his master. He likened his master to a farming landowner, who not only got crops from his own land but also harvested products from the land that he did not own and did not cultivate and gathered grain that he had not winnowed clean of its chaff. The slave did not approve of his master's making increase in that way. At least he charged his master with making increase in such a way. So, consistent with his professed belief and attitude, he handed back just the one silver talent that his master had entrusted to him. So, as *he* thought, since his master had suffered no loss, why should he complain? He was receiving back what was his very own. The slave did not appreciate that money is for circulation and is for use in a profit-making way.

[18] The slave's master answered him according to his own argument, for we read: "In reply his master said to him, 'Wicked and sluggish slave, you knew, did you, that I reaped where I did not sow and gathered where I did not winnow? Well, then, you ought to have deposited my silver monies with the bankers, and on my arrival [literally, and having come] I would be receiving what is mine with interest.' "—Matthew 25:26, 27.

---

17. (a) Did this slave approve of his master's being like the landowning farmer that he described? (b) Why did the slave think his master had no right to complain at getting no increase?
18. According to what line of reasoning did the master answer the slave, and so why did he call the slave what he did call him?

¹⁹ This unprofitable slave was "wicked," in that his failure to bring increase to his master was deliberate, willful. He was not interested in the increase of his master's belongings. Not that he did not know that his master required increase. He did know this, and he could have taken the easy way and deposited the silver talent in his care with the bankers, that these might make investments therewith and make gain and therefore pay due interest on the money deposited with them. In this way, the slave's master on his coming back would have received not only the silver talent but also the interest that was paid on the deposit of the money with the bankers. Not only did he not imitate the slave with the five talents and the slave with the two talents, but he did not cooperate with them. Although he returned the original silver talent that was committed to him, he caused really a loss to his master. His purposely causing his master such a loss made him "wicked."

²⁰ The unprofitable slave was also "sluggish." He was lazy, unwilling to 'do business' with alertness, in the way that the fellow slaves did. He had the ability to work gainfully, otherwise his master would not have entrusted him with, at the least, a talent. His being given one talent made him the least responsible of all three slaves, but this least amount of money was not more than "his own ability" could care for. Yet, instead of directing his ability in profitable channels, he dug in the ground and hid his master's talent and rendered it unproductive. He was so sluggish that even his sizing up his master as an "exacting man" did not drive him to get to work with the precious talent during the long time that his master would be gone. The slave had plenty of opportune time. His failing to bring increase resulted disastrously for him.

²¹ This "wicked and sluggish slave" has a modern counterpart in the fulfillment of the parable at its

19. Why did the slave deserve to be called "wicked," and how could he have taken the "easy way" to meet his master's requirements?
20. In what way was this slave "sluggish," this resulting how to him?
21. What is the counterpart of the slave in the modern-day climax of the parable's fulfillment?

climax in our day. As in the case of the two fellow slaves, the unproductive slave also stands for a class or group of Christian slaves who are actually in the service or who are committed to the service of the heavenly Master, the Lord Jesus Christ. This unprofitable class put in appearance after the settling of accounts began in that first postwar year of 1919 C.E.

[22] Of course, the sectarian church members of Christendom professed to be in the service of the heavenly Lord Jesus Christ. Well, then, did they go cultivating the field that lay wide open before them at the close of World War I on November 11, 1918, and go producing disciples for the reigning King Jesus Christ, now in his parousia? No; they took a compromising course with the politicians and militarists of this world. They neglected the Kingdom "belongings" of the King whose princely rule is to increase without end. They turned their interest and attention to the proposed League of Nations, which the Federal Council of the Churches of Christ in America called "the political expression of the Kingdom of God on earth." (Isaiah 9:6, 7) They tried to increase the number of supporters and worshipers of that man-made international organization for world peace and security. At present the religious sects and denominations of Christendom are advocating the successor organization, the United Nations.

[23] In the settling of accounts during this time of examination by the returned Lord Jesus Christ, those professed "slaves" in Christendom can present to him no increase in his belongings. They have not cultivated the world field for the benefit of God's Messianic kingdom, for they have turned their backs upon it and have left the people in ignorance of Jehovah's established Messianic kingdom.

[24] However, even among those in contact with the faithful "slaves" of the returned, reigning King Jesus

22. Who else claimed to be in the service of the heavenly Master, but how did they neglect his "belongings" after World War I ended?
23. Their not cultivating the world field for the benefit of God's Messianic kingdom has had what result?
24. How do those described in paragraph three of the "New Name" resolution fit the picture of the "sluggish slave"?

Christ there has appeared a class of anointed Christians who fit the picture of the "wicked and sluggish slave." Evidently this class is referred to in the third paragraph of the Resolution entitled "A New Name," that was adopted Sunday afternoon, July 26, 1931, at the international convention held in Columbus, Ohio, under the auspices of the Watch Tower Bible and Tract Society. This paragraph we now quote:

> WHEREAS shortly following the death of Charles T. Russell a division arose between those associated with him in such work, resulting in a number of such withdrawing from the Watch Tower Bible and Tract Society, and who have since refused to cooperate with said Society and its work and who decline to concur in the truth as published by the Watch Tower Bible and Tract Society in *The Watch Tower* and the other recent publications of the said above-named corporations, and have opposed and do now oppose the work of said Society in declaring the present message of God's kingdom and the day of the vengeance of our God against all parts of Satan's organization; and said opposing ones have formed themselves into divers and numerous companies and have taken and now bear such names as, to wit, "Bible Students," "Associated Bible Students," "Russellites teaching the truth as expounded by Pastor Russell," "Stand-Fasters," and like names, all of which tends to cause confusion and misunderstanding . . ."

²⁵ Factually, those uncooperative and even opposing ones mentioned above did not embrace that "new name," Jehovah's witnesses, and become known as the Christian witnesses of Jehovah. They have shared neither in the terrible sufferings that the bearers of the "new name" have experienced since then nor in the work of announcing Jehovah's established kingdom in the hands of his Messiah in all parts of the earth. For these reasons they have not shared in the marvelous expanding of the field for the cultivating and producing of disciples of Christ, to include at present 208 lands and islands or island groups, and requiring the publication of the Kingdom message in more than 160 languages. Despite vicious persecution in various lands, this cultivating of the field (which is the world

25. Consequently, the above-mentioned ones have not shared in what experiences and accomplishments of those bearing the "new name"?

of mankind) for the bringing forth of additional disciples of Christ moves forward to its culmination! It is presently being carried on under the supervision of the ninety-five branch organizations of the Watch Tower Bible and Tract Society of Pennsylvania.

²⁶ Evidently, then, this increasing of the Messianic King's "belongings," his "talents," has the approval and blessing of the Most High God Jehovah and his Son Jesus Christ. The anointed "slaves" engaged in the use of the King's "talents" are finding it a joyful responsibility, and they are striving to qualify as a "good and faithful slave" from the standpoint of their heavenly Master. They do not care to have any of the "wicked and sluggish slave" class associated with them. Rather, they try to help all those who meet the Scriptural qualifications to associate with them, to become productive ministers of the Word of God. In evidence of the divine blessing upon their loving endeavors, during this past service year of 1972 there were 163,123 taught ones who were baptized in water as disciples of the Lord Jesus Christ. During the past five service years, 1968-1972, there were more than half a million, actually 680,871, who were thus baptized in lands all around the globe. So the remnant of anointed "slaves" who increase the Lord's "belongings" do not believe that he is improperly reaping where he himself, when personally on earth, had not sown.

THE UNUSED "ONE TALENT" TAKEN AWAY

²⁷ In the parable, how does the master decide regarding the slave who failed to present to him what belonged to this master along "with interest"? "Therefore," says the indignant master concerning the "wicked and sluggish slave" who proved unprofitable, "take away the talent from him and give it to him that has the ten talents. For to everyone that has, more will be given and he will have abundance; but as for

---

26. What evidence is there that the remnant of anointed "slaves" have had Heaven's blessing in using the Master's "talents" by cultivating the world field?
27. What decision did the master make regarding the unprofitable slave?

him that does not have, even what he has will be
taken away from him. And throw the good-for-nothing
slave out into the darkness outside. There is where
[his] weeping and the gnashing of [his] teeth will
be."—Matthew 25:28-30.

[28] This slave is not invited to enter into the joy of
his master. He is not appointed to be ruler over many
things because of having been found faithful over a
few things. He is not called a "good and faithful slave,"
but is spoken of as "the good-for-nothing slave." He
is not retained as a slave in the service and household
of the master, but is thrown out of the house "into
the darkness outside." Evidently the returned master
settled accounts with his slaves in the nighttime, and
thus there would be "darkness outside" into which the
slave could be thrown. In place of finding the joy of
his master out there, he would weep and gnash his
teeth because of the conditions into which he had
been cast.

[29] This sets forth a solemn lesson for the remnant
of the anointed "slaves" today. They must continue
to work for the increase of the "belongings" of their
heavenly Master. Otherwise, that set of values with
which they have been entrusted by their Master will
be taken away from them. Then, too, they will be
thrown into the "darkness outside," to join the
"wicked and sluggish slave" class there. Ever since the
close of the Gentile Times in the year 1914 it has been
a nighttime for the world of mankind outside the
lighted house of the heavenly Master Jesus Christ,
even Christendom being shrouded in such nighttime
darkness. But that darkness will blacken intensely
when the time arrives according to God's schedule for
the "great tribulation" to break suddenly upon this
generation of mankind. (Matthew 24:21, 22; Luke
21:34-36) Into that death-dealing darkness the "wicked
and sluggish slave" class will be thrown, there to

---

28. What considerations granted to the profitable slaves were denied
to this slave, and what did his being cast into the darkness outside mean
for him?
29. Why does this set forth a solemn lesson for the at-present faithful
anointed "slaves" in the darkening world situation?

weep and gnash their teeth with religious hypocrites until they perish.

[30] In this time of the Master's parousia, when he is settling accounts with his "slaves," whether with those who die individually or with the respective slave classes yet on earth, one thing is already apparent. The "wicked and sluggish slave" class are not doing business with their "one talent" and bringing him interest on his "monies." Accordingly, he is already taking that "one talent" away from this unfaithful class that survives as a *class* till now. He is not letting them have any assignment from him in the way of territory that is to be cultivated and made productive of additional disciples of Christ. They are no longer treated as His slaves; he does not recognize and accept their religious activities. He does not let them share the gladdening light of his household. Their "one talent" is taken away from them, and their assigned field of potential disciple-making is given to the "good and faithful slave" class that has increased or is increasing the King's "belongings" to "ten talents," exercising the greatest ability in the field of disciple-making.—Matthew 28:19, 20; Psalm 2:8.

[31] Thus there is being exemplified today the divine principle or rule of procedure that "to everyone that has, more will be given and he will have abundance; but as for him that does not have, even what he has will be taken away from him." (Matthew 25:29) In the parable the "wicked and sluggish slave" had the "one talent," but he did not have what should be stirred up and manifested by the possession of this "one talent." That something extra should be loyal zeal for his master, an appreciation of the trust that had been committed to him, a belief in the deservedness of his master to have an increase to the "one talent" that had working power, gainful power. His failure to present an increase when accounts were settled elo-

---

30. How is the "one talent" taken away from the "sluggish slave" class, and to whom is it given, and why?
31. (a) What rule of procedure on the Master's part is thus exemplified? (b) The "sluggish slave" class did not have what extra, besides "ability," and so what was done to him?

quently testified, in addition to his own excuse, that he did not have that something extra on his own part. Therefore, the "one talent" was taken away from him as a "good-for-nothing slave." He had disappointed his master's confidence in him. He was dismissed from his master's service and cut off from his house.

[32] The same principle is applied to the modern-day "wicked and sluggish slave" class. To those of this class there was committed that which corresponds to the "one talent." This came from their heavenly Master, especially from the first postwar year of 1919. But they had to have something on their own part, which would complement or be a fitting companion of that "one talent." This complementary thing that their possession of the "one talent" should have roused in them was zeal and devotion toward Jehovah's Messianic kingdom, a belief in the worthiness of their heavenly Master to receive an increase in the disciple-producing field, a courageous and loving motive to have as large a share as possible in the proclamation of God's established Messianic kingdom and in the making of disciples of people of *all* the nations, not merely the Jewish nation to whom Jesus Christ on earth confined his public and private ministry. Because they do not have that which they themselves should apply toward using the Master's "one talent," this "talent" is taken away from them, as present-day facts indicate.

[33] On the other hand, the "good and faithful slave" classes do have that which should complement their being entrusted with the "talents" of their celestial Master. True to the parabolic picture, more is being given to them, at the expense of the "wicked and sluggish slave" class, and opportunities and privileges are added to them as being responsible, reliable, profitable "slaves." In consequence of this, they have indeed an "abundance" in the increased field of disciple-making. As they make the heart of their Master glad,

32. What is the something extra that the "sluggish slave" class do not have since 1919, and so what is taken away from them?
33. (a) So, at whose expense do those of the "good and faithful slave" class receive an "abundance"? (b) What joy do they experience, and what rulership do they await?

their own joy overflows and they have a foretaste of the joy that their Master feels in his now established kingdom. This joy strengthens them to press on in the service to him down to the end of their earthly career. And when this occurs, they expect to enter by resurrection from the dead into the fullness of his joy and to be made ruler over many things in his millennial kingdom. They will then fully know the happiness of those "slaves" who have part in the "first resurrection." —Revelation 20:6.

[34] In the afore-related way the climactic part of the parable of the "talents" has been going on since the year 1919 C.E. This has been observable by people and nations all around the inhabited earth. Especially are the "good and faithful slave" class aware of it. It all goes to prove that the parousia or invisible presence of the King Jesus Christ has been in progress since the Gentile Times ended in 1914. It is therefore a part of the grand "sign" of Christ's "presence" and of the "conclusion of the system of things," this parable of the "talents" being a part of his detailed prophecy concerning that "sign."—Matthew 24:3.

[35] Yet there is more to the "sign" of Christ's invisible presence in spirit than the parables of the "ten virgins" and of the "talents" that we have already considered. A further parable constitutes an important part of his prophecy on the "sign," and the fulfillment of it in our startling time adds to the proof that the presence, the parousia, of the Lord Jesus Christ is in progress to yet wonderful things. Shall we consider further our Lord's great prophecy?

---

34. Observable fulfillment of these climactic parts of Jesus' parable proves that what is in progress, and why?
35. Why do we desire to continue further the consideration of Christ's prophecy, and in order to prove what fact?

CHAPTER 14

Earthly Subjects of the Kingdom of God

IN THE marked year of 1914 C.E. the world population was estimated as well over one thousand million persons.* The growth was on its way to reaching 1,859,892,000 inhabitants by the year 1920, in spite of the many millions who were cut down by World War I and the Spanish influenza. This world population was fragmented into many nations and empires, the greatest empire in 1914 being the British Empire, which embraced one fourth of the earth's surface and one fourth of the world's population. But there were other empires at the time, such as the Turkish Empire, the Chinese Empire, the Dutch Empire, the French Empire, the German Empire, the Austro-Hungarian Empire, and the Portuguese Empire. These nations and empires made a very impressive sight on the world stage, but how did they look to the earth's Owner, the Great Creator, the Most High God? Can he make a survey of them all with just one sweep of his eyes? In exaltation of the Creator's superhuman ability the prophet Isaiah says:

2 "Who has taken the proportions of the spirit of Jehovah, and who as his man of counsel can make him know anything? With whom did he consult together that one might make him understand, or who teaches him in the path of justice, or teaches him knowledge, or makes him know the very way of real understanding? Look! The nations are as a drop from a bucket; and as the film of dust on the scales they have been accounted. . . . There is One who is dwelling

---

* On page 494, *The World Almanac* for 1915 listed 64 distinct countries under the heading "Statistics of the Countries of the World" and gave their total population as being 1,691,741,383.

1, 2. (a) What was the world population estimated to be in 1914 C.E., and into what was it fragmented? (b) What kind of sight did those nations and empires make on the world stage, but how did they look to the Creator?

above the circle of the earth, the dwellers in which are as grasshoppers."—Isaiah 40:13-15, 22.

³ Logically, then, it is very simple for the Creator God to gather all the nations before him and to judge them and execute sentence upon them. Likewise, it is an easy thing for this to be done by the mighty Son of God, Jesus Christ, whom Jehovah has appointed to act as his Deputy Judge. (Acts 17:31) That he would do this very thing at the due time, the Son of God himself foretold in his parable of the sheep and the goats. With this parable the apostle Matthew brings to a close the prophecy that the Lord Jesus Christ uttered on the Mount of Olives concerning the "sign" of his presence (parousia) and the "conclusion of the system of things." (Matthew 24:3) In the parable just preceding this, namely, the parable of the "talents," the Lord Jesus illustrated that the faithful disciples who would reign with him in his heavenly kingdom must work while here on earth for an increase in his "belongings." Quite appropriately, then, in the next succeeding parable he illustrates what is required of those today living who will become subjects of his heavenly kingdom. He opens the parable, saying:

⁴ "When the Son of man arrives in his glory, and all the angels with him, then he will sit down on his glorious throne. And all the nations will be gathered before him, and he will separate people one from another, just as a shepherd separates the sheep from the goats. And he will put the sheep on his right hand, but the goats on his left."—Matthew 25:31-33.

⁵ Prior to this parable, Jesus had already referred to himself seven times as "the Son of man." (Matthew 24:27, 30, 37, 39, 44; 25:13, AV) Since this designation was used in connection with the Messianic kingdom, its use here was most fitting. Its use here was a reminder of the prophecy of Daniel 7:9, 10, 13, 14, where we read:

3, 4. (a) Is the gathering of all nations before him a hard thing for God's Deputy Judge, Jesus Christ, and in what parable is such a thing foretold? (b) This parable shows what is required of people with what prospect?
5, 6. (a) In his prophecy, how had Jesus been designating himself? (b) Why does this remind us of Daniel's prophecy, chapter seven?

[6] "There were thrones placed and the Ancient of Days sat down. . . . There were a thousand thousands that kept ministering to him, and ten thousand times ten thousand that kept standing right before him. The Court took its seat, and there were books that were opened. I kept on beholding in the visions of the night, and, see there! with the clouds of the heavens someone like a son of man happened to be coming; and to the Ancient of Days he gained access, and they brought him up close even before that One. And to him there were given rulership and dignity and kingdom, that the peoples, national groups and languages should all serve even him. His rulership is an indefinitely lasting rulership that will not pass away, and his kingdom one that will not be brought to ruin."

[7] Although it occurred invisibly to our human eyes in the heavens, yet it was in the year 1914, at the close of the "times of the Gentiles" (or, "the appointed times of the nations"), that the "son of man" gained access to the Ancient of Days, Jehovah God, and there were given to the "son of man" all that "rulership and dignity and kingdom." So it was then, at the end of the Gentile Times in 1914, that the Lord Jesus as the Son of man came accompanied by all the angels and sat down "on his glorious throne." Thus the Messianic kingdom of God was born in the heavens. (Revelation 12:5, 10) It was a restoration of the kingdom of David, which had formerly held sway at Jerusalem but which had been overthrown by Nebuchadnezzar the king of Babylon in 607 B.C.E. So what took place in the year 1914 C.E. was the reverse of what took place in 607 B.C.E. Now, once again, a descendant of David reigned.

[8] At that time the "presence" or parousia of the Lord Jesus Christ began. Hence, what is described in the parable of the sheep and the goats happens during his parousia. This includes the gathering of all the

7. When did Jesus Christ come accompanied by angels and sit down "on his glorious throne," and thereby there was a restoration of what?
8. In view of what took place in 607 B.C.E., why was it the fitting thing for all the Gentile nations to be gathered before the enthroned Son of man in 1914 C.E.?

nations before him as the King who is present on his throne. This was quite the right thing to happen. Why? Because the 'appointed times of the Gentile nations' had ended. (Luke 21:24) For seven prophetic "times" those Gentile nations had held domination of all the earth without interruption from any Messianic kingdom of God. Biblically, a prophetic time means 360 days or, symbolically, years. Now there were to be seven of such prophetic "times." That meant a total of 2,520 years (7 × 360 years). For that long the Gentile nations held earth-wide domination. During all that time they had trampled on the right of God's Messianic kingdom to exercise world rulership. Counting back 2,520 years from 1914 C.E. gives us the year 607 B.C.E. That was when Babylon's king Nebuchadnezzar became world ruler by overthrowing King David's reigning family in Jerusalem.—Ezekiel 21:27.

⁹ Thus the "seven times" of Gentile domination began in 607 B.C.E., and yet it was more than a year afterward that King Nebuchadnezzar of Babylon got his dream about those "seven times." (Daniel 4:16, 23, 25, 32) Another thing: this dream had a typical fulfillment upon Nebuchadnezzar when he became mad for seven literal "times" (years) and chewed grass like a bull in the field. Does this mean that the "seven times" of Gentile domination could not have begun in 607 B.C.E., before the prophetic dream? Did those Gentile Times first have to begin when the king was recovered from those seven years of madness? No! So, the year of his recovery not being known, this does not require that the "seven times" of Gentile domination of the world must begin first at the fall of Nebuchadnezzar's dynasty in the year 539 B.C.E. If we count the prophetic "seven times" (2,520 years) from Babylon's fall to the Medes and Persians in 539 B.C.E., then those "seven times" would end in the fall of the year 1982 C.E., still in the future. On

9. (a) Since Nebuchadnezzar's dream of "seven times" occurred more than a year after he got world power, does this mean that the Gentile Times could not begin until after the dream was typically fulfilled? (b) Where would the "seven times" end if counted from Babylon's fall to the Medes and Persians, and what would be the logical thing to take place then?

that basis, what would be the logical thing to expect in that coming year? The opposite of what took place in 539 B.C.E., namely, the restoration of the dynastic throne of King Nebuchadnezzar, the restoration of the Babylonian Empire with a descendant of Nebuchadnezzar on the throne!

[10] However, that is absolutely contrary to what the inspired Word of God foretells. Ancient Babylon on the Euphrates River has perished forever! The dynasty of King Nebuchadnezzar has been overthrown forever. The Babylonian Empire has ceased eternally as the third world power. But what is it that Jehovah God, whose representative throne was at Jerusalem, promised to restore? It is the Messianic kingdom in the hands of a descendant of David that the God of the heavens has promised to restore. (Ezekiel 21:27; Luke 1:30-33) The desolating of Jerusalem and the land of Judah by the Babylonians in 607 B.C.E. marked the overthrow of the Messianic kingdom of David, and hence this is what marked the beginning of the "seven times" of the Gentile domination of the world of mankind. Unalterably, then, the 2,520 years of the Gentile Times began then, and, because of beginning there, they ended in early autumn of the year 1914 C.E.

[11] So, the fact that King Nebuchadnezzar had his seven years of madness after he overthrew David's throne at Jerusalem in 607 B.C.E. served to show how long those Gentile Times, already begun, were to last. World events indicated that they lasted till 1914 C.E.

[12] When, in that year, the "seven times" of uninterrupted Gentile domination of the world ended and then the "son of man" was brought before the Ancient of Days, it was the due time for the heavenly Son of man to act upon the prophetic invitation given

---

10. (a) What does the Bible say about the restoration of ancient Babylon, Nebuchadnezzar's dynasty and the Babylonian Empire? (b) When, therefore, did the "seven times" begin, and what is it that is to be restored?
11. Nebuchadnezzar's having seven years of madness after overturning David's throne showed what regarding the Gentile Times?
12. When the "seven times" ended in 1914, it was the time for Jesus Christ to act upon what divine invitation?

in Psalm Two, verses seven to nine: "Let me refer to the decree of Jehovah; he has said to me: 'You are my son; I, today, I have become your father. Ask of me, that I may give nations as your inheritance and the ends of the earth as your own possession. You will break them with an iron scepter, as though a potter's vessel you will dash them to pieces.' "—See also Revelation 12:5.

"AS A SHEPHERD SEPARATES THE
SHEEP FROM THE GOATS"

[13] It is not after the reigning "Son of man" dashes the nations to pieces in the great "time of distress" that he separates the people of the nations like "sheep" and "goats." He does not occupy his entire Millennial reign with thus separating the inhabitants of the earth, the vast majority of whom will be resurrected from their earthly graves. (Daniel 12:1) The separating work is an activity that precedes the outbreak of the "great tribulation," in the grand climax of which the nations are dashed to pieces at Har–Magedon. (Matthew 24:21, 22; Revelation 16:14, 16; 19:15) So the gathering of all the nations before the Son of man for him to begin the separating work does not include the resurrection of the earthly dead.

[14] The gathering of the nations does not mean the bringing of them all together to one assembly place on earth, an impractical thing. Rather, the gathering is accomplished when the Creator of heaven and earth delivers over to the Son of man all the nations as his inheritance and all the earth to its very extremities as his possession. From God's hand he accepts authority over all those nations, and he directs his attention to them all and uses "all the angels with him" in dealing with those nations. Thus the "people" of all the nations become his flock, figuratively speaking, only it is like a flock with a mixture of sheep

---

13. The separating of the people of the nations begins when with reference to the "great tribulation," and so what does it not include?
14. Are the nations gathered to one assembly place on earth for the dividing work, or how does the heavenly Son of man deal with them?

and goats. Such mixed flocks are a common thing over in the Middle East.

15 The separating of the goats from the sheep is not done with any discredit to the goat kind of animal. In Jesus' day on earth a young male goat could be used just as well as a lamb in the celebration of the annual Passover meal. (Exodus 12:1-5) Also, on the annual Day of Atonement it was the blood of Jehovah's goat that was taken within the curtain into the Most Holy of the temple in order to "make atonement . . . in behalf of the entire congregation of Israel." (Leviticus 16:7-9, 15-17) So, in the parable, the goats are merely used to picture one class of people, whereas the sheep are used to picture another class; and as the time comes for a shepherd to separate the two kinds of animals, so during the parousia of the Son of man and before the "great tribulation" the time comes to separate the two classes of people.

16 Of course, the separating of the sheep and goats of a literal flock could be accomplished in a portion of a day, but the separating of people with free moral agency as sheep and goats would take a much longer time earth wide. This fact, in itself, requires that the Greek word *pa·rou·si'a* means "presence" rather than "coming" or "arrival."

17 In the parable, the separation is made on the basis that the animals are of two distinct kinds, and a shepherd would not want goat's milk mixed with sheep's milk for household uses. The hair of the one class of animals differs also from that of the other class, and these were not to be blended. (Leviticus 19:19; Deuteronomy 22:11; Exodus 36:14; Proverbs 27:27) In the fulfillment of the parable, the separating of the people is based on the difference of personalities and courses of action. A personality takes time to be fully developed, and a course of action is built up from a

---

15. (a) Is the picturing of the dividing work as being between sheep and goats meant to discredit goats? (b) During what time period does the separating take place?
16. The separating work in the fulfillment of the parable calls for *pa·rou·si'a* to mean what?
17. (a) The separating of sheep and goats is made upon what point of difference? (b) Why would the separating of people with free moral agency take longer than that of literal animals?

series of acts that become the regular thing for a person to do. It therefore takes a longer period of time before a judgment can be made as to the fixed personality and the unvarying habitual conduct of a person. This calls for time to be allowed before a just, irreversible sentence can be pronounced and executed upon a person. It is not a matter of a day of twenty-four hours.

[18] In the parable the shepherdlike Son of man puts the sheeplike ones on his right hand and the goatlike ones on his left hand. The right-hand side turns out to be the side of a favorable sentence, and the left-hand side that of an unfavorable sentence. This outcome makes the situation for the people of all the nations of today a serious one. The question upon which each individual must make his decision is, Am I gaining the favor or the disfavor of the Son of man now seated upon his glorious heavenly throne, attended by all the angels? Each individual will inescapably be called to account. The fact that the reigning Son of man is invisible during his parousia does not excuse anyone, allowing for him to plead, "I did not know." The invisible parousia of the Son of man has been proclaimed world wide, and this obliges each one to consider with deep concern whether what he is or is not doing finds favor or disfavor with the King and Judge.

[19] Who, though, are the symbolic sheep and who are the symbolic goats? On Saturday, August 25, 1923, a startling explanation of who these respectively were was given to Christian students of the Holy Bible. This was the eighth day of a nine-day regional convention held by the International Bible Students Association in Los Angeles, California, U.S.A. That day the Association's president, J. F. Rutherford, addressed an audience of 2,500 on the subject "Parable of Sheep and Goats." This Biblical presentation did

18. (a) In view of what the right hand and the left hand are shown to be, what is the question upon which each one must make a decision? (b) Does the invisibility of the parousia of the Son of man allow for anyone to excuse himself, and why or why not?
19. Where did the speech by President Rutherford at the I.B.S.A. convention at Los Angeles in 1923 locate the fulfillment of the parable of the sheep and goats?

not locate the fulfillment of the parable of Matthew 25:31-46 after the "time of distress" with which this present system of things ends and during the thousand-year reign of Christ. It located the parable's fulfillment now, since 1919 C.E., during the invisible parousia or "presence" of the reigning Son of man and down to the destruction of this system of things. The material of this convention speech was published on pages 307-314 of the October 15, 1923, issue of *The Watch Tower and Herald of Christ's Presence*.—See paragraphs 17-21 of said article under the heading "The Time."

[20] In this manner the readers of *The Watch Tower* and members of the International Bible Students Association were alerted to the fact that the parable was already undergoing fulfillment and the present generation of mankind was vitally involved. This made it advisable for each one to study what kind of personality he was developing and on which side of the reigning Son of man his course of conduct put him.

[21] Over a period of years a special effort was made to help the natural, circumcised Jews of the world to become symbolic "sheep" on the right side of the reigning Messiah. This effort was made by public lectures on the subject "Jews Returning to Palestine," such as delivered to large audiences by the I.B.S.A. president, J. F. Rutherford, during the year 1925, also by the public address on the subject "Palestine for the Jews—Why?" delivered by him on Monday night, May 31, 1926, in the famous Royal Albert Hall of London, England, which seats 10,000 and which was well filled by a Jewish audience. Besides such public lectures there was published the book *Comfort for the Jews*, under the publication date of October, 1925, and, later, the 360-page book entitled "Life," which was released for public distribution on Sunday, August 25, 1929, after a nationwide radio chain broadcast from Station WBBR, Staten Island, New York, on the subject "Health and Life for the People." This special

20. Why, therefore, did it become advisable for each individual to consider what kind of personality he was developing?
21. What efforts were made to help Jews to become symbolic "sheep," and till when did this special interest in Jews continue?

interest in the natural circumcised Jews continued until the release of the book *Vindication*, Volume 2, in 1932, which volume showed that Ezekiel's prophecies concerning Israel applied to spiritual Israel today.

[22] However, interest in the "sheep" class on a wider scale was stirred up in the year 1931. On July 30, at the international convention of the International Bible Students Association in Columbus, Ohio, the Association's president delivered the talk on "The Man with the Writer's Inkhorn," after which Robert J. Martin announced the release of the new book entitled "Vindication," Volume 1. This book gave a detailed, verse for verse discussion of chapter nine of Ezekiel's prophecy, which presents the vision of this linen-clad man with the writer's inkhorn. Both the speech and the book called attention to the fact that a marking work had to be done by the anointed remnant of Christ's disciples in behalf of sheeplike people of the earth, not merely of natural Israelites but also of people of all the nations. This was a lifesaving work, inasmuch as the Holy Scriptures show that only the marked ones will be spared alive with the anointed remnant through the coming "great tribulation." They become earthly subjects of the Kingdom.

[23] For decades of time there had been keen interest in what is called "a great multitude" in Revelation 7:9, King James Authorized Version Bible. Just who were the ones that made up this great crowd? On November 19, 1934, at Brooklyn, New York, there was released to God's devoted people the book entitled "Jehovah." This 384-page book spoke both of that "great multitude" and of the parable of the sheep and the goats. (See page 159 under "Great Multitude"; also pages 354, and 359 regarding "sheep.") However, this then latest publication did not identify the "sheep" of the parable as being the same as that "great multitude" nor as being those who are marked in their

---

22. How was interest in the sheeplike ones on a wider scale stirred by the information given out at the Columbus convention in 1931?
23. For years, what interest had existed regarding the "great multitude" of Revelation, chapter seven, and how did the release of the book *Jehovah* in 1934 fail to clarify matters?

foreheads by the symbolic man clothed in linen with the writer's inkhorn at his side. Nor did it disabuse the minds of the Bible students of the long-held idea that the "great multitude" was a body of spirit-begotten Christian martyrs who are bound for heavenly life even though they were no part of the 144,000 joint heirs of Jesus Christ the King. Those of the "great multitude" were thought to be yet "prisoners" of Babylon the Great, the world empire of false religion.

²⁴ At what time, then, did there come to those who were so eager to know, an explanation of the vision of the "great multitude" that proved satisfying and that agrees with the developing facts? In the year 1935, six months after the release of the book *Jehovah*. This was on the occasion of the Washington (D.C.) convention of Jehovah's witnesses, May 30 to June 3, 1935. The full-page announcement on this on page 127 of the April 15, 1935, issue of *The Watchtower* expressly said: "All persons who are on the side of Jehovah and his kingdom are welcome." It also went on to say: "This is a service convention, and it is expected that all the remnant and the Jonadabs will participate in the service. . . . Arrangements will be made for all who desire to symbolize their consecration by water immersion." Later announcements of the convention said: "Heretofore not many Jonadabs have had the privilege of attending a convention, and the convention at Washington may be a real comfort and benefit to them."

²⁵ It was on Friday afternoon, May 31, that those interested persons who saw a resemblance between themselves and ancient Jonadab the son of Rechab came to realize why they had specially been invited to attend this Washington convention. Why so? Because it was then that the principal convention speaker, J. F. Rutherford, addressed his visible audience there at the Washington Auditorium and a countless invisible audience simultaneously over radio stations

---

24. At what convention did the satisfying, factual explanation of the "great multitude" come, and who especially were invited to attend that convention?
25. (a) When did the so-called Jonadabs realize the special reason why they had been invited to the Washington convention? (b) Whom did the speaker on "The Great Multitude" identify these as being?

WBBR and WHPH (Petersburg, Virginia) on the subject "The Great Multitude." This explanation of Revelation 7:9-15 set forth that the "great multitude" (*AV*) is not a multitude of worshipers who are destined to have a spiritual resurrection and go to heaven. Rather, it is an earthly class of Jehovah's worshipers to whom is held out in God's Word the hope of everlasting life on a Paradise earth under the heavenly kingdom of Jesus Christ and his glorified church or congregation. At that time such worshipers with earthly hopes were likened to Jonadab the son of Rechab and were designated as "Jonadabs." As *The Watchtower* later said:

> These are otherwise called "the Jonadabs." These are being baptized in symbol, thus testifying that they have consecrated themselves to do the will of God and have taken their stand on the side of Jehovah and serve him and his King; thus they have cleaned up and are now "arrayed in white robes." Thus the great multitude is definitely identified, not as a spirit-begotten class whose hopes are for a place in heaven, but . . . they . . . "come out of the great tribulation." . . .—*The Watchtower* as of August 15, 1935, page 248, paragraph 21.

[26] The material of this remarkable address was published in the two-part article entitled "The Great Multitude" in the issues of August 1 and 15, 1935, of *The Watchtower*, for the information of Jehovah's worshipers all around the globe. On the day following the address there were 840 who presented themselves for immersion in water, to symbolize their becoming disciples of the Lord Jesus Christ.* (Matthew 28:19, 20) These 840 baptismal candidates were not Scripturally authorized to put themselves into either the heavenly class of joint heirs of Christ or the earthly class represented by the "great multitude." It was not their will that was to be done, but was Jehovah's will. He was the One to express his sovereign will in placing them in either class according to his good pleasure. If, after their baptism, he begot anyone of

---

* See *The Golden Age,* as of July 17, 1935, page 660, column 2.

26. (a) How was the speech publicized still more, and how many were baptized after the speech? (b) Did the baptismal candidates put themselves in any class, and how would they come to know to which class they belonged?

these with his holy spirit to become a spiritual son of God, he thereby brought such one into the spiritual class with a heavenly inheritance. If He did not beget anyone as a spiritual son and deal with him as He does with spiritual sons, then the one not spirit-begotten was reserved for the earthly great multitude.

27 The Washington (D.C.) speech on the "great multitude" and the material thereafter published on that subject provided a new backdrop against which to view the parable of the sheep and the goats. It made stand out more clearly and fully what are the requirements for membership in the "sheep" class than the requirements that were set out in the speech on the parable of the sheep and the goats twelve years previously in 1923 at Los Angeles, California.

28 For example, those of the "sheep" class must be more than merely kindly disposed, righteously disposed persons who were humanitarian and did some kindness to the anointed remnant of Christ's disciples. They themselves must be Christ's disciples, baptized in "the name of the Father and of the Son and of the holy spirit," and also be acting as Christian witnesses of Jehovah. The "great multitude" of Revelation 7:9-17 (*Authorized Version*) were identical with the "sheep" class of Jesus' parable in Matthew 25:31-46.*

"COME, YOU WHO HAVE BEEN BLESSED BY MY FATHER"

29 The vital requirements that are looked for in those who make up the "sheep" class are indicated by what the Shepherd King gives as the reason for assigning the symbolic "sheep" to a blessed future. The parable pictures the "sheep" class at the right hand of the royal Son of man as he speaks to them. "Then the king will say to those on his right, 'Come, you who

---

* In awareness of this, *The Watchtower* under date of May 1, 1936, identified the "sheep" class with the "great multitude" in its article entitled "Armageddon Survivors," page 140, paragraphs 47, 48.

27. What did this newer information on the "great multitude" provide with respect to the parable of the sheep and the goats?
28. How were the requirements for the "sheep" class shown to be greater than those set forth in 1923?
29. In what words are the vital requirements for getting onto the King's right side set out in what he says to the "sheep"?

have been blessed by my Father, inherit the kingdom prepared for you from the founding of the world. For I became hungry and you gave me something to eat; I got thirsty and you gave me something to drink. I was a stranger and you received me hospitably; naked, and you clothed me. I fell sick and you looked after me. I was in prison and you came to me.'"—Matthew 25:34-36.

30 It was only indirectly that these sheeplike people of "all the nations" did these things to the Lord Jesus Christ. Let it not slip from our memory that, when on earth, Jesus confined his three years and some months of teaching and preaching to the nation of Israel and the Samaritans over there in the Middle East. (Matthew 15:24; 10:6; John 1:11; 4:3-43; Luke 17:15-18) So these sheeplike people are like those Christians in the first century, in the Roman provinces of Asia Minor, to whom the apostle Peter wrote: ("Though you never saw him, you love him. Though you are not looking upon him at present, yet you exercise faith in him.") (1 Peter 1:8) Although never having been able to see him on earth, the sheeplike people who are separated to Jesus' right hand did want to do something in his behalf and made an effort to do so, indirectly.

31 When this part of the prophetic parable is fulfilled, these sheeplike people will not see the Son of man seated on his glorious heavenly throne, neither will he appear visible to their naked eyes and speak to them audibly to their natural ears and say his words of appreciation. During his presence or parousia in the spirit, they see him on his throne only by the eye of faith, and at the time of his handing down his favorable decision to them his words of favor will be transmitted to them through whatever is his chosen channel. The fulfillment of the conversation in the parable between the enthroned Son of man and the "sheep" has to take

---

30. Why could it be only indirectly that those "sheep" did to Jesus the things that he mentions?
31. Will the conversation between King and "sheep," as described in the parable, be direct, and what bearing does 1 Timothy 6:14-16 have on the matter?

into account what is stated in 1 Timothy 6:14-16: "Until the manifestation of our Lord Jesus Christ. This manifestation the happy and only Potentate will show in its own appointed times, he the King of those who rule as kings and Lord of those who rule as lords, the one alone [out of all those whom men serve as kings] having immortality, who dwells in unapproachable light, whom not one of men has seen or can see." So the conversation between this King of kings and the "sheep" will not be direct.

³² On inviting these sheeplike people at his right hand to "come," he is not inviting them to come to heaven and sit with him on his throne. These symbolic "sheep" are not members of the 144,000 spirit-begotten joint heirs of Jesus Christ who experience the "first resurrection" and reign with him for a thousand years over mankind. (Revelation 14:1-3; 20:4-6) Being people of "all the nations" who are gathered during his presence or parousia in the spirit, they come to number many more than 144,000, in fact, many times as many individuals. They compose the "great crowd, which no man was able to number, out of all nations and tribes and peoples and tongues." (Revelation 7:9, 10) Those of this "great crowd" are likened to "sheep" when it is further said of them: "The Lamb, who is in the midst of the throne, will shepherd them, and will guide them to fountains of waters of life." (Revelation 7:17) In fact, they are part of those "other sheep," whom Jesus differentiated from the "little flock" of 144,000 joint heirs, by saying:

³³ "I have other sheep, which are not of this fold; those also I must bring, and they will listen to my voice, and they will become one flock, one shepherd." —John 10:16; Luke 12:32.

³⁴ The "great crowd" of such "other sheep" the enthroned Son of man tells to "come" to him, that is, to approach him at the time of his giving them their

32, 33. (a) What must be said as to whether the King's invitation to the "sheep" to "come" is an invitation to heaven? (b) Why did Jesus speak of these as "other sheep"?
34. When does the enthroned Son of man bid the "great crowd" of "other sheep" to "come," and how are they those who "have been blessed" by his heavenly Father?

reward. He calls them "you who have been blessed by my Father." (Matthew 25:34) True, while they were trying to do something good and helpful to the Lord Jesus Christ during this time of his presence or parousia, his heavenly Father blessed them for this. However, they "have been blessed" by his heavenly Father particularly in that He has reserved such a blessed reward for them. The heavenly Father foresaw this sheeplike class of this time of his Son's presence or parousia, and he accordingly reserved a blessed reward for them. The blessings they have already received do not compare with the blessing they are yet to enjoy. What is that particular blessing reserved for them?

[35] It is indicated in Jesus' words to them: "Inherit the kingdom prepared for you from the founding of the world." (Matthew 25:34) The "great crowd" of the "other sheep" were not in these words being invited by Jesus Christ to a seat with him on his heavenly throne, for they are not of the 144,000 joint heirs. How, then, are the words of invitation to be understood? Under the original Greek word for "kingdom" (Ba·si·lei'a), page 309 of Volume I of Liddell and Scott's *Greek-English Lexicon* states that the Greek word has also a *passive* meaning, namely, one's "being ruled by a king," and also may mean "reign." So it is indeed: the "great crowd" of such "other sheep" inherit a state of "being ruled by a king," namely, the Messianic King Jesus, and they inherit a thousand years of a "reign" by the King of kings, Jesus Christ. Where will they enjoy this millennium of being ruled over by the glorified Son of man? Not in heaven, which they as creatures of "flesh and blood" cannot enter (1 Corinthians 15:50); but down here on earth, which is the earthly realm of Christ's kingdom.—Psalm 2:8; Daniel 2:35-45.

[36] This earth will be a grand place in which to live under such a king as the Lord Jesus Christ, along with his glorified 144,000 coregents. How, though, was the

35. (a) What does Jesus indicate is the special blessing reserved for the "great crowd" of "other sheep"? (b) What, specifically, is the "kingdom" that they inherit, and where do they do so?
36. From the founding of what "world" was this "kingdom" prepared for the "great crowd" of "other sheep," and how?

"kingdom" in this sense "prepared" for that sheeplike "great crowd" all the way "from the founding of the world"? In that the heavenly Father, the Creator, had it in mind for them "from the founding of the world." This does not mean the founding of our earthly planet. It means the world of mankind. This was after the creating of Adam and Eve in their perfection in the Garden of Eden. Adam was not made a king, and Eve was not made his queen. Adam was not made a king over all the animal creation of land animals, amphibious animals, fish and birds. In Job 41:34 Jehovah calls Leviathan the "king over all majestic wild beasts." No more so was Adam to be a king over all his human descendants. Kings came into existence upon the earth first after the flood of Noah's day and beginning with Nimrod the bold hunter who founded Babel or Babylon in the Mesopotamian Valley. (Genesis 10:8-10) Adam's descendants were not born into a kingdom of Adam. Adam and Eve themselves did not constitute a "world."

[37] However, when Adam and Eve, outside the Garden of Eden from which they had been expelled under sentence of destruction, began to have children, then a "world," that is, a world of mankind, was founded. These children, though born in sin and imperfection and under condemnation of death, came under the opportunity that was expressed in Jehovah's words to the serpent in Eden after the inducing of Adam and Eve to sin: "I shall put enmity between you and the woman and between your seed and her seed. He [the woman's seed] will bruise you in the head and you will bruise him in the heel." (Genesis 3:14, 15) As time went on, Jehovah God gave further information concerning this mysterious Seed that would gain the victory over the symbolic Serpent, Satan the Devil. The victorious Seed was to become a King over all mankind. Hence, when children began to be born who had the opportunity of coming under the established kingdom of the Seed, Jehovah's promise took effect toward the world of mankind that had just been

---

37. (a) When and how was that world founded? (b) How was it that from that founding the "kingdom" was prepared?

founded. Thus the "kingdom" was held in reserve, "prepared" for earth's inhabitants "from the founding of the world."—Compare Luke 11:50, 51.

DONE TO "ONE OF THE LEAST OF THESE MY BROTHERS"

[38] In the prophetic parable, when the King invited the "sheep" to "inherit the kingdom prepared" for them from the founding of the world, they gave way to surprise. Jesus tells us: "Then the righteous ones will answer him with the words, 'Lord, when did we see you hungry and feed you, or thirsty, and give you something to drink? When did we see you a stranger and receive you hospitably, or naked, and clothe you? When did we see you sick or in prison and go to you?' And in reply the king will say to them, 'Truly I say to you, to the extent that you did it to one of the least of these my brothers, you did it to me.' "—Matthew 25:37-40.

[39] It is noteworthy that Jesus speaks of these sheeplike persons as "the righteous ones." Their righteous appearance before him is not due solely to the fact that they did all the considerate things to him that he mentions. These sheeplike ones are not justified or declared righteous on the basis of their own works any more than the 144,000 joint heirs of Christ are. The prime thing that counted was the thing that was evidenced by their trying to do what they could in behalf of Christ just as the situation afforded, namely, their faith in him as the Messiah or Christ of God. They recognized that they had no righteousness wholly pleasing to God in themselves. In harmony with this they availed themselves of the propitiatory blood of the sacrificial Lamb of God, Jesus Christ. (John 1:29, 36) To gain a righteous appearance before Jehovah God, they did a washing, as it were, of their symbolic robes. This is called to our attention in John's vision of the "great crowd."

38. How is the surprise of the sheeplike "great crowd" at the king's invitation explained by the words of the king?
39. Is it on the basis of their considerate deeds done to the King that they are called "righteous," or what?

⁴⁰ To bring out the fact that those of this sheeplike "great crowd" are disciples of the Lamb Jesus Christ and are worshipers at the spiritual temple of Jehovah God, the apostle John reports this conversation that arose over the vision of the "great crowd": "And in response one of the elders said to me: 'These who are dressed in the white robes, who are they and where did they come from?' So right away I said to him: 'My lord, you are the one that knows.' And he said to me: 'These are the ones that come out of the great tribulation, and they have washed their robes and made them white in the blood of the Lamb. That is why they are before the throne of God; and they are rendering him sacred service day and night in his temple.'" (Revelation 7:13-15) So it is essential that they wash their bad appearance before God in the shed blood of Christ by their exercise of faith, besides which they render sacred service to God at his spiritual temple by doing what the opportunity offers them in behalf of the Lamb Jesus Christ. Properly, then, Jesus could speak of them as "righteous ones."

⁴¹ By their repeatedly saying, "When did we see you?" when they inquired about the things the King Jesus Christ said they had done to him, the righteous sheeplike ones make it manifest that they did not see him in the flesh. Rightly so, forasmuch as his royal presence or parousia is invisible to human eyes, he being now one "whom not one of men has seen or can see." His parousia had to be an extended invisible presence for them to do to him all the things that he enumerates, in an indirect manner. How, then, was it to *him* that they did all such loving things? Jesus explains:

⁴² "And in reply the king will say to them, 'Truly I say to you, To the extent that you did it to one of the least of these my brothers, you did it to me.'"—Matthew 25:40.

---

40. How do those of the "great crowd" of "other sheep" clean up their bad appearance before God, and where and how do they render sacred service?
41. (a) What do these righteous "sheep" indicate about the parousia by repeatedly asking, "When did we see you?" (b) In this regard, why did the parousia have to be an extended period of time?
42. The king tells the "sheep" that they did such things to him indirectly in what way?

[43] During the time of his invisible parousia or presence as enthroned King, Jesus Christ the Son of man has a remnant of his spiritual brothers visibly in the flesh on the earth. Previously, on the same day on which he gave the parable of the sheep and the goats, Jesus referred to these "brothers," when he said: "Do not you be called Rabbi, for one is your teacher, whereas all you are brothers. Moreover, do not call anyone your father on earth, for one is your Father, the heavenly One. Neither be called 'leaders,' for your Leader is one, the Christ." (Matthew 23:8-10) Five days after telling the parable the risen Lord Jesus appeared to a number of women on his resurrection day and said to them: "Have no fear! Go, report to my brothers, that they may go off into Galilee; and there they will see me."—Matthew 28:9, 10.

[44] On his resurrection day he also appeared to Mary Magdalene and spoke of his spiritual brothers, saying to her: "Be on your way to my brothers and say to them, 'I am ascending to my Father and your Father and to my God and your God.'" (John 20:17) There will finally be 144,000 of these spiritual brothers who will share the heavenly glory with Jesus Christ, their oldest spiritual Brother. The fact that there are these spiritual brothers of Christ is dwelt upon by the inspired writer, in Hebrews 2:10-12, in these words: "It was fitting for the one for whose sake all things are and through whom all things are, in bringing many sons to glory, to make the Chief Agent of their salvation perfect through sufferings. For both he who is sanctifying and those who are being sanctified all stem from one [Father], and for this cause he is not ashamed to call them 'brothers,' as he says: 'I will declare your name to my brothers; in the middle of the congregation I will praise you with song.'" These "brothers" are members of the "seed" of Abraham the Hebrew; and in order to help them to heavenly glory,

43. During his parousia the King Jesus Christ has a remnant of whom on the earth, and how did he speak about them on the day of his prophecy and on resurrection day?
44. (a) How did Jesus speak about these brothers to another woman on resurrection day? (b) What does Hebrews 2:10-12 say regarding Jesus' attitude toward these brothers?

the heavenly Son of God became a man like them. Accordingly, it is written:

[45] "He is really not assisting angels at all, but he is assisting Abraham's seed. Consequently he was obliged to become like his 'brothers' in all respects, that he might become a merciful and faithful high priest in things pertaining to God, in order to offer propitiatory sacrifice for the sins of the people."—Hebrews 2:16, 17.

[46] Just as the King Jesus Christ himself, when on earth as a perfect man, tried to assist his spiritual brothers, so he appreciates all those who put forth some efforts to assist his spiritual brothers who become his heavenly joint heirs. What such kindly assisters do to his "brothers" he counts as being done to him personally. Those offering such assistance he likens to sheep. They are not commended for just being philanthropic or humanitarian in a general sense, doing good to anybody and everybody regardless of who such anybody is, indiscriminately. Often persons who are philanthropic and humanitarian like that are afraid to do good specifically to Christ's spiritual brothers amid the sufferings of these on earth. Any sign of sympathy with Christ's "brothers" brings the frown of disapproval and criticism on the part of those who are against Christ's "brothers" and who cause these "brothers" of Christ much of their suffering, even to imprisonment.

[47] Rather, those whom the parable-teller Jesus designates as "sheep" and calls "righteous" do discriminate fearlessly. They intelligently and deliberately do good to Christ's "brothers" because they recognize these to be such. They believe these "brothers" are imitating Jesus Christ and are doing the work that he commanded them to do. It is for this reason that their acts of assistance to Christ's brothers have a special merit in his sight, for acts of that kind have a real Christian motivation. Such view of matters Jesus made clear

<hr>

45. Jesus was made like his spiritual brothers for what purpose?
46. The King Jesus Christ appreciates those who are the assisters of whom specifically, and why?
47. As stated by Jesus, why do the acts of assistance on the part of the righteous "sheep" have special merit?

to his apostles, when he said: "He that is not against us is for us. For whoever gives you a cup of water to drink on the ground that you belong to Christ, I truly tell you, he will by no means lose his reward." (Mark 9:40, 41) "And whoever gives one of these little ones only a cup of cold water to drink because he is a disciple, I tell you truly, he will by no means lose his reward."—Matthew 10:42.

> ### TAKING THEIR STAND WITH THE KING'S "BROTHERS"

[48] The historical records reveal that during their work of preaching the good news of God's kingdom and making disciples of people of all the nations down to the year 1935 C.E., and thereafter, Christ's spiritual "brothers" have literally hungered and thirsted, they have needed clothing, they have been strangers and homeless, they have got sick and even been put in prison unjustly. Not just their own spiritual "brothers" have come to their assistance, but also others who are not begotten of God's spirit as Christ's "brothers" have done so. These latter ones did not act thus in ignorance of just who these suffering, needy Christians were and of the unpopularity of these persecuted ones. To the contrary, they recognized that these were the "ambassadors" of God's Messianic kingdom, and they wanted to give concrete evidence that they were taking their stand on the side of God's kingdom.

[49] Thereby these sheeplike ones demonstrated their faith in Jesus Christ as the reigning King. They rejoiced at the preaching of the good news of God's now established kingdom, and they desired to give their full support to it. They responded to the disciple-making work of the Kingdom "ambassadors" and got baptized in water as also disciples of Christ, obeying his teachings. (2 Corinthians 5:20; Matthew 24:14; 28:19, 20)

48. (a) Before and after 1935 C.E., did Christ's spiritual brothers on earth go through such experiences as he describes? (b) The "sheep" who rendered assistance did so with what knowledge and appreciation?
49, 50. (a) How do these "sheep" who are not spiritual Israelites respond to the Kingdom-preaching, and to whom do they join themselves? (b) Accordingly, in whose name do these get baptized, thereby attaching themselves to whom?

In that course thus being taken, even until now, by these sheeplike people who are not spiritual Israelites, the prophecy of Zechariah 2:11 is being fulfilled at this time: "Many nations will certainly become joined [or, join themselves] to Jehovah in that day, and they will actually become my people; and I will reside in the midst of you."—*New World Translation; American Standard Version.*

⁵⁰ These sheeplike people from "many nations," 208 countries and islands according to reports thus far, get baptized not only in the name of the Son and of the holy spirit but also in the name of the Father, the Son's Father, who is Jehovah. They do not believe merely in the Son and ignore the Father. Not only do they "believe on the Lord Jesus" to get saved, but they necessarily also recognize that "everyone who calls on the name of Jehovah will be saved." (Acts 16:31; Acts 2:21; Romans 10:13) So they do call upon Jehovah's name and get baptized in the name of Him. They "join themselves," they dedicate themselves, to Jehovah in order to become His people. They abandon the false gods to whom they were formerly dedicated. (Hosea 9:10) They become irrevocably attached to Jehovah God the Father through Jesus Christ.

⁵¹ In their dedication of themselves to Jehovah through Christ these sheeplike ones are further pictured in Zechariah's prophecy, in these words: "This is what Jehovah of armies has said, 'It will yet be that peoples and the inhabitants of many cities will come; and the inhabitants of one city will certainly go to those of another, saying: "Let us earnestly go to soften the face of Jehovah and to seek Jehovah of armies. I myself will go also." And many peoples and mighty nations will actually come to seek Jehovah of armies in Jerusalem and to soften the face of Jehovah.' This is what Jehovah of armies has said, 'It will be in those days that ten men out of all the languages of the nations will take hold, yes, they will actually take

51, 52. (a) In being thus baptized, to whom are these "sheep" likened in Zechariah 8:20-23? (b) Who is the "Jew" upon whose skirt they take hold?

hold of the skirt of a man who is a Jew, saying: "We will go with you people, for we have heard that God is with you people." ' "—Zechariah 8:20-23.

[52] In the fulfillment of this prophecy, the man whose skirt is taken hold of by these men of "all the languages of the nations" is a spiritual Jew, namely, one of the 144,000 spiritual Israelites who are spoken of in Revelation 7:4-8, just before the apostle John's vision of the numberless "great crowd," the members of which come "out of all nations and tribes and peoples and tongues."

[53] During the presence or parousia of the King Jesus Christ since the year 1914 C.E., there has been just a remnant of such spiritual Jews in the flesh on earth. It was particularly from the year 1935 onward, after the identification of who made up the "great crowd" of praisers of God and his Lamb, that "ten men" speaking the tongues of many nations began to humble themselves as if taking hold of the skirt of a person and volunteering to go up with the spiritual Jew to the center of worship of Jehovah of armies. By that year of 1935 these spiritual Jews had been bearing the Bible designation "Jehovah's witnesses" for four years, so that there was no mistaking of what kind of Christians they were.

[54] The fact that in these last days many persons who are *not* a part of the remnant of spiritual Jews or Israelites should join themselves in dedication to Jehovah as God and seek to worship him at his spiritual temple was also foretold in these beautiful words of the prophet Isaiah: "It must occur in the final part of the days that the mountain of the house of Jehovah will become firmly established above the top of the mountains, and it will certainly be lifted up above the hills; and to it all the nations must stream. And many peoples will certainly go and say: 'Come, you people, and let us go up to the mountain of Jehovah, to the house of the God of Jacob; and he will instruct us about

53. (a) Particularly since what year have these "ten men" speaking the languages of many nations taken hold of the skirts of spiritual Jews? (b) By that year these spiritual Jews bore what distinguishing designation?
54. How was the fact that these "sheep" join themselves to Jehovah and seek to worship him foretold in Isaiah 2:2-4?

his ways, and we will walk in his paths.' For out of Zion law will go forth, and the word of Jehovah out of Jerusalem. And he will certainly render judgment among the nations and set matters straight respecting many peoples. And they will have to beat their swords into plowshares and their spears into pruning shears. Nation will not lift up sword against nation, neither will they learn war anymore."—Isaiah 2:2-4.

⁵⁵ When we take all these Bible prophecies that apply at the present time, the time of Christ's presence or parousia, into consideration, along with Jesus' parable of the sheep and the goats, what can we see? This: that it is not a case of unknowingly and by chance doing good to one of Christ's spiritual brothers that makes a person a "sheep" with a "righteous" standing before God and his Messianic King. Those of the "sheep" class know what they are doing, even though they do not see the reigning King, the Son of man, with their literal naked eyes. They give due recognition to his spiritual "brothers," even "to one of the least of these [his] brothers," and for that special reason they endeavor to help them, not only in a material, physical way, but also in a spiritual way by joining with them in preaching "this good news of the kingdom" and in the Bible teaching work that results in making disciples of Christ. They know that Christ's "brothers" are exalting Jehovah's worship above everything else, and with these they go up to Jehovah's spiritual temple to worship, meeting the high requirements for this.

⁵⁶ Because the sheeplike ones desire to help and do good to the spiritual "brothers" of Christ, they do not fight with them on any grounds, national, racial, tribal, political, skin color, cultural, linguistic. With Christ's "brothers" they take their stand for absolute neutrality toward the violent, destructive, sanguinary conflicts and controversies of this heavily armed world. They

---

55. (a) In the light of the foregoing prophecies, what is it that makes a person a "sheep" with a "righteous" standing before God and Christ? (b) How high do they elevate Jehovah's worship?
56. (a) What is the position of these "sheep" regarding fighting with Christ's "brothers" on various divisive grounds? (b) Whose friends do they choose to be, and how do they keep their "robes"?

would rather be friends with Christ's "brothers," who are "no part of the world," than enjoy the "friendship with the world." (John 17:14, 16; James 4:4) So they choose to suffer with Christ's brothers at the hands of this hostile world, so as to maintain their Christian integrity toward God and to prove themselves also to be real disciples of Christ. They keep clean their "robes" washed in Christ's blood.

[57] The fact that Zechariah 8:23 prophesied that "ten men out of all the languages of the nations" would take hold on the skirt of a spiritual Jew or spiritual Israelite indicates that such self-humbling men of all nations would outnumber the remnant of spiritual Jews or Israelites. The ratio would be like ten to one. This has really come about since the year 1935 C.E. In that epochal year the worldwide population for religious bodies, Christian and non-Christian, was estimated as 1,849,185,359. (*The World Almanac and Book of Facts,* for 1936, by the New York *World-Telegram,* page 419) In that same year the number of Jehovah's witnesses who were reporting activity in the field ministry world wide numbered less than 60,000. What has been the growth of the world population since then?

[58] According to *The 1973 World Almanac and Book of Facts,* page 343, the religious population of the world was published as being 2,661,120,100. This means that between 1935 and 1973 the religious population of the world had not doubled. Now, as for the world population in general, in the year 1935 it was an estimate that was published with no change from that given for the year 1927, namely, 1,960,000,000. According to *The 1973 World Almanac and Book of Facts,* page 206, the estimate of the world's population was 3,631,797,000. Thus, between 1935 and 1973, the world population had not quite doubled.

---

57. (a) Zechariah 8:23 put the ratio of Jew to non-Jewish worshipers at what figure? (b) Back in 1935 C.E., what was the estimate for the world's religious population, to compare with how many witnesses of Jehovah?
58. Since 1935, to what extent has the world's religious population increased, and also the world population in general?

⁵⁹ What, though, about the growth in numbers of Jehovah's witnesses? Their ministerial service year begins on September 1 of a calendar year. So, during the 1971/1972 service year, the number associated with Jehovah's witnesses who were regularly active in the field ministry was reported to be 1,596,442, on the average, although during that service year a peak of 1,658,990 Kingdom proclaimers was attained. What an increase this represents in the number of Jehovah's witnesses in comparison with the number of them back there in 1935!

⁶⁰ But how many among these Christian witnesses of Jehovah are spiritual Jews? Only 10,350. These identified themselves as spiritual Israelites by partaking of the emblematic bread and wine at the annual celebration of the Lord's Supper, on March 29, 1972, at which celebration there was a total attendance, world wide, of 3,662,407. In the 208 lands and islands of the sea in which Jehovah's Christian witnesses are active there were 28,407 congregations functioning. From all this, what do we note? This: that during Christ's invisible parousia (presence) a "great crowd" of sheeplike persons out of all nations, tribes, peoples and languages has been gathered to the King's right hand and has joined the small remnant of spiritual Israelites in going up to Jehovah's spiritual temple to worship Him as God. This is a noteworthy feature of the "sign" proving that the unseen "presence" or parousia of the Lord Jesus is in progress and that we are living in the "conclusion of the system of things."—Matthew 24:3.

---

59. In the ministerial service year of 1971/1972, to what extent had the number of Jehovah's witnesses increased?
60. (a) In what way was it determined how many of those were spiritual Jews? (b) From all this, what do we note as respects the going of people up to Jehovah's spiritual temple to worship? (c) Hence, in what vital time must we be living?

CHAPTER 15

Why Goatlike Ones Fail > *to Inherit the Kingdom*

WHAT disposition, however, is to be made of those people of "all the nations" who are likened to "goats" and who are separated to the King's left hand? Jesus continues on in his parable of the sheep and the goats to say: "Then he will say, in turn, to those on his left, 'Be on your way from me, you who have been cursed, into the everlasting fire prepared for the Devil and his angels. For I became hungry, but you gave me nothing to eat, and I got thirsty, but you gave me nothing to drink. I was a stranger, but you did not receive me hospitably; naked, but you did not clothe me; sick and in prison, but you did not look after me.' "—Matthew 25:41-43.

[2] The King Jesus Christ points out that the people like "goats" failed to do the things that the "sheep" class did. For such failure he tells them to get away from him. He does not want them as earthly subjects during his reign of a thousand years. They are "cursed" persons. They are under the divine curse rather than under the blessing that the sheeplike persons gained from the King's heavenly Father. This means that the divine judgment, as foretold in the Bible prophecies, pronounces bad things to come upon them. They are under the divine curse, and there is no provision to lift that curse from them as was the case with the natural circumcised Jews who were under the curse of Jehovah's Law covenant with them. (Galatians 3:13) They are cursed, just as Satan the Devil and his demon angels are. Hence, they deserve an everlasting future like that of the Devil and his angels—"the everlasting fire prepared for the Devil and his angels."

---

1. In the parable of the sheep and the goats, how does the King address himself to those separated to his left?
2. What does being under the "curse" mean for the goatlike ones?

[3] Does this mean everlasting conscious torment in a firelike element in the invisible realm (the spirit realm) where Satan and his demon angels are? This is what religious churches of Christendom have taught for centuries. They will refer to Revelation 20:10 as a support of their teaching, for in that Bible verse it is written: "And the Devil who was misleading them was hurled into the lake of fire and sulphur, where both the wild beast and the false prophet [already were]; and they will be tormented day and night forever and ever." However, sulphur or brimstone does not exist in the spirit realm where Satan and his demon angels are. The language is evidently figurative, just as the "wild beast" and the "false prophet" are. So the "lake of fire and sulphur" is figurative of what? The fourteenth verse of the same chapter explains, saying: "And death and Ha'des were hurled into the lake of fire. This means the second death, the lake of fire." Revelation 21:8 repeats this explanation of the "lake that burns with fire and sulphur," saying: "This means the second death."

[4] This agrees with the plain literal language of Hebrews 2:14, which speaks in no figurative way, saying: "Therefore, since the 'young children' are sharers of blood and flesh, he [Jesus] also similarly partook of the same things, that through his death he might bring to nothing the one having the means to cause death, that is, the Devil." In God's due time the once dead but now resurrected and glorified Jesus brings Satan the Devil "to nothing"; that is, he annihilates that wicked, murderous one. He brings about the destruction of the Devil. The once bruised Jesus, who is primarily the "seed" of God's "woman," is God's appointed one to bruise the Serpent in the head. —Genesis 3:15; Romans 16:20.

---

3. (a) What do the churches of Christendom claim that the "fire prepared for the Devil and his angels" means for the "goats"? (b) What does the Revelation itself explain the 'lake burning with fire and sulphur' to mean?
4. How does this agree with Hebrews 2:14 as to what is to be done to the Devil?

[5] Consequently, the "second death" is what is reserved for the Devil and his angels, and it is this same everlasting destruction, symbolized by "everlasting fire," into which the delinquent "goat" class of people go away from the King Jesus Christ. In his condemnation of these, the King does not say that they directly persecuted and did direct hurt to his spiritual "brothers." But even though they took a negative attitude toward Christ's "brothers," they were taking the side of the Devil and his angels. Jesus, when on earth as a perfect man preaching the good news of God's Messianic kingdom, said: "He that is not on my side is against me, and he that does not gather with me scatters." (Matthew 12:30) The Devil is not on Jesus' side, and so the goatlike people who do nothing helpful to the reigning King Jesus Christ are against him and are on the Devil's side. There is no neutral side in the time of Christ's presence or parousia.

[6] The goatlike people might try to defend themselves and say that if they had seen Jesus Christ himself in person in such needy straits as he describes, they would have come to his help. Such an attempted defense is implied in their response to the King. "Then they also will answer with the words, 'Lord, when did we see you hungry or thirsty or a stranger or naked or sick or in prison and did not minister to you?' " —Matthew 25:44.

[7] However, their seeing him personally in the flesh and recognizing who he was would be no assurance that they would minister to him in a helpful way. Nineteen hundred years ago Jesus Christ was actually visible in flesh on earth and was engaged in God's foreordained work for the Messiah, and yet the majority of Jesus' own people, the natural Jews, did not minister to him nor to his twelve apostles. Rather, before the Roman governor, Pontius Pilate, they howled for Jesus

5. (a) So what is the "everlasting fire" reserved for the Devil and his angels, and into which the goatlike class are sent? (b) Why does the goats' not doing direct injury to Christ's brothers not put them in a neutral position?
6. What is the attempted defense of themselves that is implied in what the "goats" answer back to Jesus the King?
7. Why would the goatlike ones' seeing and identifying Jesus be no assurance that they would have ministered to him in a helpful way?

to be put to death on a torture stake, or they sided with those who took the direct responsibility to have him put to such an agonizing death. Accordingly, the goatlike people of the present time cannot excuse themselves on the ground that they did not know, forasmuch as they did not see him directly when they refused help with respect to him.

[8] A person does not have to see another individual directly in person in order to decide whether to help him or refuse him help. A person does not need to behold another individual directly in front of him in order to determine whether he is in favor of that one or against him. A person can decide and show how he stands with reference to that one by the manner in which he treats someone who acts as a visible representative for that one. The representative identifies himself as acting for the one who is not visibly present to the view of the person with whom he is talking or dealing. This enables the person to make his decision as to whether he wants to help or not, to show favor or not, to take his stand with or against the individual whose personal representative is visibly before him. In this way the person betrays his personal attitude, and this is what counts with the absent, unseen individual just as much as if he were actually there in person.

[9] This is the point that Jesus makes when in his parable he tells how the king answers the self-excusing "goats" at his left hand:

[10] "Then he will answer them with the words, 'Truly I say to you, To the extent that you did not do it to one of these least ones, you did not do it to me.'" —Matthew 25:45.

[11] Hence, it does not matter how unimportant one of Christ's spiritual "brothers" may be. Although being the least important, he is, nevertheless, a "brother" of the King Jesus Christ and is a spirit-begotten son of

---

8. What is it that counts for or against one when another individual is personally absent but has a representative visibly present with one?
9, 10. How did Jesus make that very point in the parable by the way that the King answers the goatlike ones on his left?
11. Why is not even the least important one of Christ's spiritual brothers to be disrespected by those in touch with them?

God, an heir indeed of God and a joint heir with Christ. (Romans 8:17) This is the serious thing about the situation. Not one of Christ's spiritual "brothers" is one of the great, important, prominent ones of this world, either in the political field or in the religious clerical field of Christendom, for Christ's true "brothers" are no part of this world, even as he himself was no part of it. (1 Corinthians 1:26-31; John 15:19; 17:14, 16) But this is no reason for those of the goatlike people to look down upon them. They should be respected in view of whom they represent and what Biblical message they are proclaiming. If they are not respected for this vital reason, then the disrespectful ones disclose that they do not respect the heavenly Brother of these either.

¹² Oh, yes, the goatlike self-excusers may call the King Jesus Christ "Lord," but that is just a hypocritical form of address on their part. If they had really appreciated him as their "Lord," they would not have refused to lend any assistance to his spiritual "brothers," not even to the lowliest one of these "brothers." These "brothers" did not go around incognito like spies or like those who are trying to pull a fast trick at the expense of the people. Particularly since the end of World War I in 1918 and their resuming of public activities in the year 1919, the remnant of Christ's spiritual brothers have been obeying his prophetic command: "This good news of the kingdom will be preached in all the inhabited earth for a witness to all the nations; and then the end will come." (Matthew 24:14) They have publicized Christ's invisible presence or parousia in his established heavenly kingdom. Especially since the year 1926 they have been making known the name of the heavenly Father of the King Jesus Christ, even going to the extent of embracing the name "Jehovah's witnesses" in the year 1931. So there has been no excuse for mistaking who they are.

───────

12. (a) In addressing the King as "Lord," why are the "goats" hypocritical? (b) Since the end of World War I, why has there been no excuse for mistaking whom the King's "brothers" are?

[13] Consequently, the symbolic "goats" refuse to give aid to these when they are literally hungry, thirsty, naked, without lodging, sick or in prison not because of whom these spiritual "brothers" of Christ are in themselves personally. No, but they withhold help from them, if they do not positively persecute them, because of what these represent. There is an issue involved, and the "goats" make an intelligent decision over this issue! This issue with which the "goats" are confronted by the preaching and disciple-making activity of this remnant of Christ's "brothers" is the means by which the invisibly present King Jesus Christ separates the "goats" from the "sheep" today, particularly from the year 1935 onward. There is no in-between or neutral class respecting this universal issue. Either they are for Jehovah's Messianic kingdom in the hands of the Lord Jesus Christ or they are against it. The "goats" take their stand against it. For this they cannot have the blessing of the heavenly Father of Christ. The only thing for them to receive is His curse, the opposite of His blessing.

WHEN THE "GOATS" GO OFF
TO THEIR PUNISHMENT

[14] Jesus declares that what awaits these symbolic "goats" at his left hand of cursedness is the "fire prepared for the Devil and his angels." They have given no moral support to God's Messianic kingdom and have thereby proved themselves to be a part of this world of which Satan the Devil is the invisible "ruler." (John 12:31; 14:30; 16:11) This wicked world under Satan the Devil is doomed to destruction in the "great tribulation" that is just ahead. The "goats" will enter into that "fire" of destruction when they get into that "great tribulation such as has not occurred since the world's beginning until now, no, nor will occur again." (Matthew 24:21; Mark 13:19) They refuse

13. (a) Is it because of what Christ's "brothers" are in themselves personally as humans that the "goats" refuse them help? (b) Why is it that the "goats" get God's curse instead of his blessing?
14, 15. (a) When is it that the "goats" will enter into the "everlasting fire prepared for the Devil and his angels"? (b) How does Paul picture the destruction by means of the same element in 2 Thessalonians 1:7-10?

to acknowledge and recognize God as Jehovah, whose name presents itself thousands of times in the inspired Hebrew Scriptures of the Holy Bible, and they refuse to obey or conform to the good news about the Lord Jesus Christ. At the revelation of the power and authority of the invisibly present Christ in the "great tribulation," the "goats" will experience what the apostle Paul foretold, in 2 Thessalonians 1:7-10:

[15] "The revelation of the Lord Jesus from heaven with his powerful angels in a flaming fire, as he brings vengeance upon those who do not know God and those who do not obey the good news about our Lord Jesus. These very ones will undergo the judicial punishment of everlasting destruction from before the Lord and from the glory of his strength, at the time he comes to be glorified in connection with his holy ones,"—his spiritual "brothers."

[16] Thus there is fulfilled upon the symbolic "goats" what Jesus foretold in the closing words of his parable of the "sheep" and the "goats," with which also Jesus' prophecy on the "sign" of his presence or parousia concludes, according to Matthew's account: "And these shall go away into everlasting punishment: but the righteous into life eternal."—Matthew 25:46, *Authorized Version.*

[17] Let us not jump to a mistaken conclusion respecting what befalls the symbolic "goats" of the parable. Jesus does not say that "these shall go away" into everlasting conscious torment in an invisible spirit realm. For these to suffer eternal torment consciously in any form would require that they gain everlasting life, for without life there is no consciousness of either torment or pleasure. Jesus plainly says that it is only the symbolic sheep, "the righteous," who go "into life eternal." So the "everlasting punishment" into which the unrighteous "goats" go away is the direct opposite of the "life eternal" of the righteous "sheep," namely, death eternal. Because this death lasts eternally it is

16. In closing the parable, Jesus says the "goats" go away into what, and the "sheep" into what?
17. Why does the everlasting punishment of the "goats" not mean everlasting conscious torment in an invisible spirit realm?

an "everlasting punishment." Similarly when an earthly judicial court of today punishes a proved criminal with the sentence of death, the death executed on the convicted criminal is an "everlasting punishment." It does not mean everlasting torment for the executed criminal. Only God Almighty can terminate that everlasting punishment by the resurrection of the unjust. An earthly court of justice cannot do so.—Acts 24:15.

[18] In agreement with that logical and Scriptural understanding of the matter, *The Emphatic Diaglott,* by Benjamin Wilson (1864 edition), renders Matthew 25:46 as follows: "And these shall go forth to the aionian cutting-off; but the righteous to aionian Life." *The New World Translation of the Holy Scriptures* (1971 edition) reads similarly: "And these will depart into everlasting cutting-off, but the righteous ones into everlasting life." On the word "cutting-off" this translation gives the following footnote: "Literally, 'pruning'; hence a curtailing, a holding in check. See 1 John 4:18." How appropriate this translation, for the unrighteous "goats," by suffering everlasting death, are cut off from life in any realm everlastingly. Eternal conscious torment is therefore impossible in their case. They are annihilated, just as the Devil and his demon angels eventually will be. After the "great tribulation" the Devil and his angels will be hurled into the "abyss." But after the end of Christ's thousand-year reign, they will be let loose for a little while to test out restored mankind, after which they will be forever destroyed.

[19] As for the "righteous" sheeplike persons who do good to Christ's spiritual "brothers" down till the outbreak of the "great tribulation," the reigning King Jesus Christ will express his approval of them then. (Matthew 25:34) Like a loving Shepherd toward his "sheep," he will protect them during the "great tribulation" in order that they may enter into the thousand-year period of his blessed reign. As it was said of the

---

18. How do the *Diaglott* and the *New World Translation* translate the Greek word for "punishment," and why is this translation appropriate?
19. How will the righteous "sheep" class be rewarded, as indicated in Revelation 7:14?

"great crowd," in Revelation 7:14, it will be said of these sheeplike survivors of the "great tribulation": "These are the ones that come out of the great tribulation."

[20] Immediately after the "great tribulation" the "Devil and his angels" are bound as in chains and are hurled into the "abyss" of imprisonment. Then the glorious millennial reign of the Shepherd King, Jesus Christ, begins. The "righteous" sheeplike survivors will become the obedient earthly subjects of Christ's millennial kingdom. They will now begin to experience physically and mentally the restorative powers of Christ's kingdom, and this will mark the start for them on the way to perfect human life forever.

[21] For the particular encouragement of the "righteous" sheep class the Lord Jesus Christ included this parable in his prophecy on the "sign" of his presence and of the conclusion of the system of things. What a joy-inspiring prospect this parable sets before these present-day doers of good to Christ's spiritual "brothers"! Their steadfast continuance in such well-doing will pave the way for them to hear those welcoming words of the King: "Come, you who have been blessed by my Father, inherit the kingdom prepared for you from the founding of the world."—Matthew 25:34.

20. Immediately after what event does Christ's millennial reign begin, and, in the case of the surviving "sheep," this marks the start of what? 21. For whose special encouragement now was this parable included in his prophecy on the "sign," and what prospect does it set before them?

CHAPTER 16

Completion of the Foretold "Sign"
Nears

WE TODAY can be thankful that the apostles
of Jesus Christ asked him the question: "Tell
us, When will these things be, and what will be the
sign of your presence and of the conclusion of the
system of things?" (Matthew 24:3) Their question
led to his giving a lengthy, detailed prophecy the
accuracy of which leaves us amazed as we see the
progress of its fulfillment in this eventful twentieth
century. This aids us in determining with certainty
where we are in the outworking of God's purpose
toward suffering mankind. We are strengthened in
our belief that we are actually living during the
invisible "presence" of Christ in the spirit and in the
"conclusion of the system of things," inasmuch as
we do see "the sign" that he foretold.

2 The "sign" in all its details is nearing its stage
of complete clarity with no room for any watching
observers to be mistaken. The "sign" has many features, as set out in Matthew's account, chapters
twenty-four and twenty-five, Mark's account, chapter thirteen, and Luke's account, chapter twenty-one;
and it has been almost the lifetime of a generation
of mankind for all the features of the "sign" to become manifest in their fullness. In preceding chapters we have considered those features of the sign
as described in Matthew's account, chapter twenty-
five. Now we consider those features set out in chapter
twenty-four, along with the comparative accounts
given by Mark and Luke.

1. Why can we be thankful that Jesus' apostles asked him the question
contained in Matthew 24:3?
2. Where is the "sign" in all its features described, and what part of
the account shall we now consider?

293

[3] When Christ's apostles opened up their inquiry by saying, "Tell us, When will these things be?" they were referring to the things that Jesus had said prophetically that same day of Tuesday, Nisan 11, of the year 33 C.E. In Jerusalem's temple, after denouncing the hypocritical religious scribes and Pharisees, Jesus went on to say: ("Here I am sending forth to you prophets and wise men and public instructors. Some of them you will kill and impale, and some of them you will scourge in your synagogues and persecute from city to city; that there may come upon you all the righteous blood spilled on earth, from the blood of righteous Abel to the blood of Zechariah son of Barachiah, whom you murdered between the sanctuary and the altar. Truly I say to you, All these things will come upon this generation. Jerusalem, Jerusalem, the killer of the prophets and stoner of those sent forth to her,—how often I wanted to gather your children together, the way a hen gathers her chicks together under her wings! But you people did not want it. Look! Your house is abandoned to you. For I say to you, You will by no means see me from henceforth until you say, 'Blessed is he that comes in Jehovah's name!'")

[4] Before Jesus left the temple or house of worship, he added further words of solemn prophecy, concerning which we read: ("Departing now, Jesus was on his way from the temple, but his disciples approached to show him the buildings of the temple. In response he said to them: 'Do you not behold all these things? Truly I say to you, By no means will a stone be left here upon a stone and not be thrown down.'")—Matthew 23:34 to 24:2.

[5] Just two days previously, on Sunday, Nisan 9, he had paused in his triumphal ride toward Jerusalem and wept over her because of her coming destruction. Predicting her terrible destruction by the Romans in 70 C.E., he said: ("Because the days will

3, 4. When asking Jesus, "When will these things be?" to what things were the disciples referring?
5. On his triumphal ride toward Jerusalem, what had Jesus said with reference to her?

come upon you when your enemies will build around you a fortification with pointed stakes and will encircle you and distress you from every side, and they will dash you and your children within you to the ground, and they will not leave a stone upon a stone in you, because you did not discern the time of your being inspected."—Luke 19:41-44.

⁶ For natural, circumcised Jews, such as Christ's apostles were, those were disturbing predictions. Upon the generation of which they were a part, the innocent blood spilled in the course of Jewish history and earlier was to be visited. Exactly when would these things be fulfilled? They wanted to know. They believed and confessed Jesus to be the Messiah or Anointed One, the Christ. But Jerusalem's predicted destruction indicated that he would not set up his Messianic kingdom in that doomed city. He spoke of his not being seen "from henceforth," but also of his coming "in Jehovah's name." When would he be present again to carry out his Messianic role? The coming destruction of Jerusalem and her temple must certainly spell the end of the Jewish system of things. With no holy city and no holy temple the Jewish priesthood of the family of Aaron the Levite might be among those of Jerusalem's "children" who would be dashed "to the ground" or would at least be put out of their temple service. No wonder the apostles asked, not only about the destruction of Jerusalem and her temple, but also: "What will be the sign of your presence and of the conclusion of the system of things?"

⁷ Their questions were on proper points of inquiry, for Jesus did come in the "conclusion" of the Jewish system of things. Other scriptures speak of the situation in that same sense. Hebrews 9:26-28 shows that Jesus did not need to make repeated sacrifices of himself and says: "Otherwise, he would have to suffer often from the founding of the world. But now he

6. What kind of predictions were those for the circumcised natural Jewish disciples, and what mental problems were raised for them?
7. Why was the apostles' asking about the "conclusion of the system of things" a question on a proper point of inquiry?

has manifested himself once for all time at the conclusion of the systems of things to put sin away through the sacrifice of himself. . . . so also the Christ was offered once for all time to bear the sins of many." Also, 1 Corinthians 10:11 says: "Now these things went on befalling them as examples, and they were written for a warning to us upon whom the ends of the systems of things have arrived." Counted from the year of Jesus' prophecy on the subject, the Jewish system of things had thirty-seven years yet to go, less than a generation with a life-span of forty years. Jerusalem was taken and destroyed by the Romans on Elul 7 (or, August 30, 70 C.E., Gregorian calendar time). How many of Christ's apostles escaped martyrdom and survived till that horrible event, the Bible record does not say.

A TIME OF TESTING AND DISASTERS

[8] In answer to the inquiry of his apostles, Jesus described first the events leading up to the destruction of Jerusalem within that generation. "And in answer Jesus said to them: 'Look out that nobody misleads you; for many will come on the basis of my name, saying, "I am the Christ," and will mislead many. You are going to hear of wars and reports of wars; see that you are not terrified. For these things must take place, but the end is not yet.'" —Matthew 24:4-6.

[9] Jews would arise, not claiming to be Jesus returned in the flesh, but claiming to be the promised Messiah or Christ. But neither the apostles nor their fellow disciples should be misled by such self-styled Messiahs or Christs, for their operations would not betoken the "presence" or parousia of Jesus Christ nor bring deliverance to the Jewish nation. The Jewish revolt against the Romans in the year 66 C.E. was to be such a Messianic effort, but it led to Jeru-

8. In answering the apostles, what things did Jesus first describe?
9. The rising of Jews claiming to be Messiah would not betoken what as being in progress, and would not lead to what desired event?

salem's destruction and the scattering of the Jewish nation. The Messianic hopes of these misled people were bitterly disappointed.

¹⁰ During this thirty-seven-year period there were to be a number of wars, within earshot of the disciples or merely reported to them in the news. But those wars, while affecting the situation of the Jewish nation, were not the ones that directly brought on the end of the Jewish system of things. So the disciples were not to be terrorized into taking any premature action. "The end is not yet."

¹¹ "For," said Jesus in enlarging upon what he had just said about wars and reports of war, "nation will rise against nation and kingdom against kingdom, and there will be food shortages and earthquakes in one place after another. All these things are a beginning of pangs of distress."—Matthew 24:7, 8. Also, Mark 13:8.

¹² Such calamities being merely a "beginning of pangs of distress," the end was "not yet." Those calamities were merely indications, not the final death throe. These things would affect the people in general, but there were things that would come specifically upon Jesus' disciples because they announced the true Messiah or Christ and followed in his footsteps. Hence, Jesus went on to say:

¹³ "Then people will deliver you up to tribulation and will kill you, and you will be objects of hatred by all the nations on account of my name. Then, also, many will be stumbled and will betray one another and will hate one another. And many false prophets will arise and mislead many; and because of the increasing of lawlessness the love of the greater number will cool off. But he that has endured to the end is the one that will be saved. And this good news of the kingdom will be preached in all the inhabited

10. What about wars, and why were the disciples not to be terrified by such?
11. What did Jesus predict would be a "beginning of pangs of distress"?
12, 13. (a) Were those things making up a "beginning of pangs of distress" to come upon any particular people? (b) What things were to come upon the disciples for announcing Messiah and being his followers?

earth for a witness to all the nations; and then the end will come."—Matthew 24:9-14. Compare Mark 13:9-13.

[14] The Bible book entitled "Acts of Apostles" testifies to the fulfillment of those prophetic words of Jesus Christ even within that generation, for this book was written by the medical doctor Luke about the year 61 C.E. Other Bible books, inspired letters written by apostles and other disciples before the destruction of Jerusalem in 70 C.E., confirm the account in Acts of Apostles and add to the record of Christian suffering under persecution and international hatred toward Christianity. The good news of God's kingdom had penetrated beyond the Middle East into Asia Minor, Continental Asia, Africa, Europe and the islands of the Mediterranean Sea. The preaching of the Kingdom message was being carried on in all the inhabited earth. Although not resulting in world conversion to Christianity, a thing it was never purposed to accomplish, it resulted in a witness to all the nations. (Colossians 1:6, 23) Before this praiseworthy exploit was accomplished by outspoken Christian witnesses, the calamitous end could not come upon Jerusalem and the Jewish system of things.

JERUSALEM'S SECOND DESTRUCTION INDICATED AS AT HAND

[15] Having shown in considerable detail the preliminaries that were to precede "the end," Jesus now specified the particular thing that would indicate the close nearness of the end of Jerusalem and the system of things that was centered in her and her temple. He said: "Therefore, when you catch sight of the disgusting thing that causes desolation, as spoken of through Daniel the prophet, standing in a holy place, (let the reader use discernment,) then let those in Judea begin fleeing to the mountains. Let the man on

14. (a) What confirms that those things occurred within the generation then living? (b) The end could not come upon Jerusalem and the Jewish system before what accomplishment?
15. What did Jesus say would indicate the close nearness of the destruction of Jerusalem and the Jewish system, and what did he say to do thereafter?

the housetop not come down to take the goods out of his house; and let the man in the field not return to the house to pick up his outer garment. Woe to the pregnant women and those suckling a baby in those days! Keep praying that your flight may not occur in wintertime, nor on the sabbath day."

[16] Why the great need for the Christian Jews and proselytes in the Roman province of Judea to get out of it at top speed, with no unnecessary burdens, by direct route, at the opportune time, and take refuge in the mountains outside the mentioned province? "For then," Jesus continues on to say, "there will be great tribulation such as has not occurred since the world's beginning until now, no, nor will occur again. In fact, unless those days were cut short, no flesh would be saved; but on account of the chosen ones those days will be cut short."—Matthew 24:15-22.

[17] This counsel of Jesus the apostles and other disciples should not forget nor disregard. If any of them delayed their flight out of Judea after seeing the disgusting thing standing in a holy place, it might cost them their lives; they might not be among those comparatively few who are spoken of as "flesh" that is saved only because the days of tribulation are cut short. But what is the "disgusting thing" the sight of which standing in the holy place would certify that not much time was left now before the devastating "great tribulation" was right at hand?

[18] Jesus left no doubt as to what it was. He said it was the disgusting thing "as spoken of through Daniel the prophet." (Matthew 24:15) The "disgusting thing" that is foretold by the prophet Daniel in connection with the second destruction of Jerusalem is the one described in Daniel 9:26, 27 (especially according to the Greek Septuagint Version of the Hebrew Bible

16. Why was it, as Jesus advised, that Christian Jews and proselytes should abandon Jerusalem and Judea so quickly?
17. (a) Why was this counsel of Jesus not to be disregarded by his apostles and their fellow Christians? (b) So what vital question now poses itself?
18, 19. (a) By whom had this disgusting thing that causes desolation already been foretold, and where? (b) How did Jesus, according to Luke's account of his prophecy, show what that disgusting thing would be?

text).* Secular history reveals ~~that "disgusting thing"~~ to ~~be the pagan Roman armies~~ under their "leader." That this is the proper explanation of the prophecy is borne out by a comparison of Matthew's account of Jesus' prophecy at this place with Luke's account at the corresponding place in Jesus' prophecy. Luke 21:20-24 says:

¹⁹ "Furthermore, ~~when you see~~ Jerusalem surrounded by ~~encamped armies, then~~ know that the desolating of her ~~has~~ drawn near. Then let those in Judea begin fleeing to the mountains, and let those in the midst of her withdraw, and ~~let those in the country~~ places not enter into her; ~~because these are~~ days for meting out justice [or, days of vengeance], ~~that~~ all the things written [including Daniel 9:26, 27] may be fulfilled. Woe to the pregnant women and the ones suckling a baby in those days! For there will be great necessity upon the land and wrath on this people; and they will fall by the edge of the sword and be led captive into all the nations; and Jerusalem will be trampled on by the ~~nations~~, until the appointed times of the nations are fulfilled."—Compare also with Mark 13:14-20.

²⁰ It was in the year 66 C.E. that the Christian Jews in Jerusalem and Judea began to see the "disgusting thing that causes desolation, as spoken of through Daniel the prophet," take a stand in a "holy place," namely, Jerusalem and its environs. It was in that year that the unchristianized Jews revolted with Messianic aspirations against further rule by the Roman Empire. In reaction to this, the Roman general, Cestius Gallus, came down from Syria and

----

* Daniel 9:26, 27 reads: "And after the sixty-two weeks, the Messiah shall be cut off, though there is no crime in him; and he, with the ruler who is coming, will destroy the city and the sanctuary. They shall be destroyed with a deluge, and even to the end of the war determined on in course, with desolations. Now one week shall confirm a covenant for many and in the half of that week My sacrifice and libation shall be taken away. And upon the temple shall be an abomination of the desolations, and at the end of a time, an end shall be put to that desolation."—*The Septuagint Bible*, by Charles Thomson.

20, 21. (a) When was it that the Christian Jews in Judea saw the disgusting thing standing in a "holy place"? (b) How long did that disgusting thing thus stand?

surrounded Jerusalem with "encamped armies." It
was at the time that the Jews celebrated the Festival
of Booths (or, Tabernacles) from Tishri 15 to 21,
which in that year should have run for the seven
days of October 22-28 (Gregorian calendar). General
Cestius Gallus brought his armies up to within "fifty
furlongs" of the celebrating city. The Jews, well armed,
sallied forth in attack and inflicted some damage on
the Romans.

21 There now followed a "wait for three days." Then
General Gallus, forcing the Jews back to Jerusalem, brought his troops up close to the city.
But it was first on the last day of the month
Tishri (about November 5) that he got his troops
into the city of Jerusalem. He was indeed now in a
place considered "holy" to the Jews. For five days
the Romans made an attack on the temple wall, and
on the sixth day they undermined the wall. This certainly was an assailing of what the Jews considered
most holy. Easily the Romans could have now captured the whole city, but then, suddenly, without any
valid reason for doing so, General Gallus withdrew
from the city and retreated. The elated Jews went in
hot pursuit and harassed the retreating Romans and
inflicted considerable harm, so that the retreat turned
into a rout.* This was a stinging blow at the pride
of the world-conquering Romans. Jerusalem was liberated! And in commemoration the Jews coined some
new silver shekels bearing on one side the inscription
"Jerusalem the Holy."

22 Were the Christianized Jews in Jerusalem and
in the province of Judea deceived by this reestablish-
ing of the independence of this land of the Jews?
Not those who took to heart Jesus' prophecy and
his counsel. They had actually seen the holy city of
Jerusalem surrounded by encamped armies. They had
seen the "disgusting thing that causes desolation,"

* See Josephus' *Wars of the Jews*, Book II, Chapter XIX, sections 1-7.

22. Why were the Christianized Jews not deceived by that reestablishment of Jerusalem's independence, and how did they safeguard themselves?

with its military standards that were idolized as gods by the soldiers, standing "in a holy place," "standing where it ought not." (Mark 13:14) From this they were to "know that the desolating of her [Jerusalem] has drawn near." (Luke 21:20) It was now high time either to get out of Jerusalem or not to enter into her but to flee from all the province of Judea to the mountains outside, for instance, eastward across the Jordan River to the province of Perea. There, outside the doomed territory, these Christianized Jews could continue their preaching of the good news of God's true Messianic kingdom, instead of perishing with the doomed unbelieving Jews.

[23] The independence of the Jews in Judea proved to be of short duration. Roman General Vespasian succeeded to General Gallus and reached Palestine early in the following year, 67 C.E. His endeavors to get the rest of the country under control allowed for the Jews to strengthen their defenses. After the death of Emperor Nero in 68 C.E., Vespasian was elevated to imperial power. Leaving Palestine, he reached Rome about the middle of 70 C.E. He left his son General Titus in charge of Roman military forces in Syria. The Jewish Passover of the year 70 approached, and the non-Christian Jews flocked to the city of Jerusalem for the celebration. It was then that General Titus came with four legions and bottled up the celebrating Jews inside the city. To starve out the rebellious Jews, he did what Jesus had foretold, build a fortified stockade, "a fortification with pointed stakes," about five miles long all around the city, to prevent any Jews from escaping.

[24] The straits of the cooped-up Jews inside Jerusalem became desperate. The first-century Jewish historian, Flavius Josephus, in his writings, vividly describes the horrors resulting from the Roman siege. The loss of Jewish lives was mounting higher and higher. It appeared that, if the siege lasted too long, "no flesh" inside the besieged city would survive. It

23, 24. (a) Why did the independence of Judea not last long? (b) How serious and menacing did the siege of Jerusalem become?

was as Jesus had foretold concerning this "great tribulation" upon Jerusalem and Judea: "In fact, unless Jehovah had cut short the days, no flesh would be saved. But on account of the chosen ones whom he has chosen he has cut short the days."—Mark 13:19, 20.

[25] Providentially, the days of the siege proved to be relatively short, just 142 days, counted from Nisan 14 to Elul 7, or parts of six lunar months. That is to say, according to the Gregorian calendar, by August 30, 70 C.E., it was all over. Some Jewish flesh was permitted to survive, 97,000 Jews, according to Josephus' account, whereas he reports that 1,100,000 perished in the siege. Were those 97,000 survivors the "chosen ones" on account of whom Jehovah had cut short the days? Not unless you would call them chosen for captivity and enslavement. For it was just as Jesus had said: "There will be great necessity upon the land and wrath on this people; and they will fall by the edge of the sword and be led captive into all the nations; and Jerusalem will be trampled on by the nations, until the appointed times of the nations are fulfilled."—Luke 21:23, 24.

[26] No! the "chosen ones" on account of whom the number of days of Jerusalem's "great tribulation" was cut short were not those 97,000 miserable Jewish captives, upon whom Jehovah's great "wrath" rested in those "days for meting out justice." Jehovah's "chosen ones" were the Christianized Jews, to whom he had given the signal to flee without delay from all of Judea, including its capital Jerusalem. He desired all of them to get safely out of the danger zone, by acting in faith on Jesus' counsel to flee promptly after seeing the "disgusting thing that causes desolation, as spoken of by Daniel the prophet, standing in a holy place." After Jehovah got all these "chosen" disciples of his Son Jesus Christ out of the place upon which divine

25. (a) How were the days of that tribulation upon Jerusalem cut short? (b) Were the surviving Jews the "chosen ones" spoken of by Jesus in his prophecy?
26. (a) Who, then, were the "chosen ones" spoken of in Jesus' prophecy? (b) In what way was the number of days of Jerusalem's tribulation cut short on their account?

304 GOD'S KINGDOM OF A THOUSAND YEARS HAS APPROACHED

justice was to be meted out, he could let the execution of his vengeance upon the rebellious Jews be of short duration. As it is written: "Jehovah will make an accounting on the earth, concluding it and cutting it short." (Romans 9:28; Isaiah 10:23) Rightly, then, "on account of the chosen ones" those days of great tribulation on Jerusalem were cut short.

27 Secular history records the accuracy of Jesus' prophecy. But with this account of the destruction of earthly Jerusalem the prophecy of Jesus does not end, for there is more to say concerning the "sign" of his presence and of the "conclusion of the system of things." He looks beyond the destruction of Jerusalem in 70 C.E., for he says, in Luke 21:24: "And Jerusalem will be trampled on by the nations, until the appointed times of the nations are fulfilled." Jesus looked to the fulfilled "end" of those appointed times of the nations, usually called the Gentile Times. That means that he looked forward to the year 1914 C.E., for in that year the right of Jerusalem to have a Messianic kingdom in the hands of the Permanent Heir of King David ceased being trampled on by the nations. Why do we say this, inasmuch as in the year 1914 the rebuilt city of Jerusalem over in the Middle East was still under control of the Mohammedan Turks? It is because, in that year, at the close of the Gentile Times, Jehovah God enthroned the Permanent Heir of King David, not in the Turk-controlled earthly Jerusalem, but in the heavenly Jerusalem.—Hebrews 12:22.

FULFILLMENT UPON ANTITYPICAL UNFAITHFUL JERUSALEM

28 It becomes plain that, in his prophecy, Jesus was using the city of Jerusalem not only in a literal sense but also in a typical sense, as prefiguring something else of greater proportions. Otherwise, he would not have said concerning her destruction in 70 C.E., "then

27. (a) Did Jesus stop his prophecy with the description of Jerusalem's destruction, or did he look beyond that? (b) Why do we say that Jerusalem ceased to be trampled on by Gentile nations in 1914?
28. In speaking about Jerusalem's destruction as being so terrible, in what senses must Jesus have been referring to Jerusalem?

there will be great tribulation such as has not occurred since the world's beginning until now, no, nor will occur again." (Matthew 24:21; Mark 13:19) All informed persons know that Jerusalem's destruction in 70 C.E. was not the worst catastrophe since the world's beginning, for, what about the global deluge of Noah's day? And as for the equal of Jerusalem's destruction by the Romans never occurring after 70 C.E., what about World War I and World War II in this twentieth century? Jesus' language was not exaggerated, but evidently he was thinking of Jerusalem as a prophetic type, as a warning example of something that would embrace the whole world in a similar destruction. He was thinking of the antitypical unfaithful Jerusalem, namely, one of modern times. And what is that? It is Christendom with her hundreds of conflicting religious sects.—1 Corinthians 10:11.

²⁹ This application of Jesus' prophecy holds true, not only as to Christendom's approaching destruction with all her political, commercial, military and judicial paramours, but also as to the world events that immediately lead up to her annihilation. Christendom now lives in a period of time that resembles in her twentieth-century experiences the period of time from Jesus' prophecy given on the Mount of Olives until the Romans destroyed Jerusalem and her temple in 70 C.E. This particular corresponding period of time for Christendom began at the close of the "appointed times of the nations" in the year 1914. Consider world happenings since then.

³⁰ What things did Jesus say would be a "beginning of pangs of distress"? Were they not to be wars, food shortage, earthquakes, pestilences? (Matthew 24:7, 8; Mark 13:8; Luke 21:10, 11) What "wars" in the days of Christ's apostles in the first century can compare with World Wars I and II, not to speak of all the other wars since the close of World War II in 1945 C.E.?

29. (a) To what else, in addition to Christendom's destruction, does Jesus' prophecy apply? (b) To what, then, does the time from Jesus' prophecy to Jerusalem's destruction correspond?
30. Since 1914, has Christendom experienced what Jesus said would be the "beginning of pangs of distress"?

Did the famines, earthquakes, pestilences of the years 33 to 70 C.E. surpass the food shortages, earthquakes and pestilences Christendom and all the rest of the world have had since the end of the Gentile Times in 1914?

[31] Jesus also told his apostles that his disciples would be sorely persecuted, being delivered up to tribulation and being killed, yes, of their becoming an object of hatred by all the nations; also, of the arising of false prophets, false Messiahs, and of the increasing of lawlessness toward God with a consequent cooling off of the quality of love on the part of the great majority of professed religionists; also, of the need of Christian endurance during such a time as that. (Matthew 24:9-13; Mark 13:9-13; Luke 21:12-19) Such developments marked apostolic times of the first century. And what about world developments since the Gentile Times ended in 1914? Has the world become so converted to Christianity that the persecution of Christ's true disciples has ceased? Is there any religious minority that is more the object of "hatred by all the nations on account of my [Christ's] name" than Jehovah's Christian witnesses? Are there any religious persecutions greater than those heaped upon these Christian witnesses of Jehovah all the way from 1914 down to the present time? A record is there for all to consult.

[32] There was another distinguishing feature about that apostolic period of the first century prior to 70 C.E. To his Jewish opposers in Jerusalem, Jesus said: "The kingdom of God will be taken from you and be given to a nation producing its fruits." (Matthew 21:43) Even with their false Messiahs the Jews were not producing the fruits of God's kingdom by proclaiming it to the Gentiles. Before Jerusalem's destruction, they did not take up the message of John the Baptist and proclaim that the kingdom of the heavens was at hand. No, for during his last visit to

31. (a) What did Jesus say would happen to his disciples before Jerusalem's destruction? (b) Whose sufferings today correspond with those of the disciples of that time period?
32. What other feature was to distinguish that apostolic period down to 70 C.E., and through whom was this feature then fulfilled?

the temple in Jerusalem Jesus said to the religious scribes and Pharisees: "You shut up the kingdom of the heavens before men; for you yourselves do not go in, neither do you permit those on their way in to go in." (Matthew 23:13) To whom, then, goes the credit for a fulfillment before the year 70 C.E. of Jesus' dynamic words: "And this good news of the kingdom will be preached in all the inhabited earth for a witness to all the nations"? (Matthew 24:14; Mark 13:10) It goes to those who were the "objects of hatred by all the nations on account of my name"—his own disciples.

33 Similarly, in this corresponding period since the close of the Gentile Times in 1914 C.E., it is those who are outstandingly the "objects of hatred by all the nations on account of [Christ's] name" that are bringing about a modern-day fulfillment of Jesus' prophecy concerning the good news of God's kingdom. They are the ones who, despite hatred and persecution, have filled the inhabited earth with the preaching of the good news of God's Messianic kingdom for a witness to all the nations. This is not the message of God's kingdom such as Christendom has been preaching since the start of her existence in the days of Emperor Constantine in the fourth century—a kingdom within her hundreds of millions of church members, in their hearts, a kingdom that is finally realized by world conversion to Christendom's churches. In stark contrast, the kingdom preached by Jehovah's Christian witnesses since the end of the Gentile Times in 1914 is a real government that was born in the heavens in that year. It is the established kingdom of God in the hands of the Permanent Heir of King David, and it will put an end to all the political governments of this earth and bless earth's inhabitants with everlasting life, peace and happiness.

34 This remarkable accomplishment, the preaching

33. Since 1914, who has correspondingly preached the good news of God's kingdom internationally, and how does this kingdom preached differ from that proclaimed by Christendom?
34. (a) This international Kingdom-preaching was to be part of the "sign" of what fact? (b) What disaster was the accomplishment of this Kingdom-preaching to precede?

of such good news in all the inhabited earth for an international witness, by Jehovah's Christian witnesses is significant. It is a brightly shining feature of the "sign" that was to mark the "presence" or parousia of the reigning King Jesus Christ in spirit. Since the year of his enthronement in the heavens at God's right hand that preaching from door to door and by all other means of modern communication has been carried on by Jehovah's Christian witnesses for well over half a century, notwithstanding world wars and other large-scale calamities. Evidently the completing of the witness to all the nations concerning God's Messianic kingdom that is about to take over all mankind's affairs must be very near. This worldwide Kingdom-preaching was to precede "the end." All the inhabited earth has now heard the Kingdom-preaching. No longer do "all the nations" remain without a witness to them. "And then the end will come," said Jesus, for this system of things!

"THE DISGUSTING THING THAT CAUSES DESOLATION"

[35] Another feature of the "sign" ensures that the long-awaited "end" is near. Although other startling things might occur within the critical period and yet the end would not be right then, Jesus foretold one ominous thing that proved that the hour of calamity was about to strike, that the desolating end was about to overtake all those delaying flight to safety. In the case of the first-century inhabitants of the Roman province of Judea, it was the surrounding of Jerusalem with encamped armies, the standing of the "disgusting thing that causes desolation" in the place where it ought not to stand, "a holy place." Then of all times it was the occasion for Jews believing in Jesus as Messiah to flee clear out of Judea. But do we see anything today like a "disgusting thing" that is a desolator? Its appearing bodes no good for religious Christendom, for

35. (a) What feature of the "sign" proved that Jerusalem's desolation was indeed very near? (b) Inasmuch as that world power of the first century is no more, what question do we ask?

she is the modern-day counterpart of unfaithful Jerusalem of the first century. That holy capital of Jewish worship was desolated by armed forces of the Sixth World Power of Bible history, the pagan Roman Empire. But that imperial world power is now gone!

³⁶ Today, since 1914, the world scene is still dominated by the Seventh World Power, the British-American Dual World Power. With Britain's king or queen claiming to be the head of the Anglican Church, the Church of England, and with the United States of America being declared by its Supreme Court to be a "Christian nation," this Seventh World Power is a prominent part of Christendom and a stout defender of her. So, in its religious aspect, it is due to feel some of the effects produced by that disgusting desolator.

³⁷ However, the last book of the Holy Bible discloses an EIGHTH WORLD POWER. Intriguingly, Revelation 17:9-11 informs us of what the apostle John was told in his vision of a wild beast, scarlet in color, having seven heads and ten horns, and being ridden by the religious harlot, "Babylon the Great." The verses say: "Here is where the intelligence that has wisdom comes in: The seven heads mean seven mountains, where the woman sits on top. And there are seven kings: five have fallen, one is, the other has not yet arrived, but when he does arrive he must remain a short while. And the wild beast that was but is not, it is also itself an eighth king, but springs from the seven, and it goes off into destruction."

³⁸ In the apostle John's day, in the first century, the Sixth World Power was holding him as a prisoner on the penal island of Patmos. The Seventh World Power had not yet arrived, for history verifies that it arrived first in the eighteenth century, when Great Britain became the commercial and naval mistress of the seas. So this Seventh World Power is just more

36. Why is the Seventh World Power of today due to feel the effects produced by the disgusting desolator?
37. What does Revelation 17:9-11 tell us to indicate whether the seventh one was the last world power?
38. In the apostle John's day, which world powers had already fallen, which one then was, and which one was to come, to continue for how long?

than two centuries old today, and this is a "short while" in comparison with the nearly eighteen centuries of domination by the Sixth World Power. So the seventh head of the scarlet-colored wild beast represented this Seventh World Power; the other heads represent the preceding six world powers, the Egyptian, the Assyrian, the Babylonian, the Medo-Persian, the Grecian and the Roman. All these seven world powers have had relations with the religious harlot, "Babylon the Great," who is the world empire of false religion.—Revelation 17:1-6, 18.

[39] Since the wild beast "is also itself an eighth king," it represents an eighth world power. This does not mean Communist Russia or the Communist bloc of nations, for Russia and the Communist bloc did not 'spring from the seven,' that is, from the seven preceding world powers. Concerning the Communist bloc of nations it cannot be said that "the wild beast was, but is not, and yet will be present."—Revelation 17:8.

[40] So what is the Eighth World Power, which the Babylonish world empire of false religion has been riding till now, as the harlot Babylon the Great rode the scarlet-colored wild beast seen in the apostle John's vision? It is the international organization for world peace and security. Prior to World War II this was called the League of Nations, and since World War II it has been called the United Nations. This "world peace and security" agency was organized in the first postwar year of 1919, but it went into the abyss of inaction and incompetency when World War II broke out in 1939. During World War II it 'was not' for all practical purposes as a keeper of world peace. After World War II ended in 1945, it came up out of the abyss, this time under the new name, United Nations. It has been "present" since that time. Today it has a world membership of 132 nations. These are all militarily armed, five of these nations being already armed with nuclear bombs.   152

---

39. Why is Communist Russia or the Communist bloc of nations not the Eighth World Power?
40. (a) What, then, is the Eighth World Power? (b) When was that world power not, and when did it become present?

⁴¹ Well, but why is the symbolic wild beast, the Eighth World Power, the United Nations of today, identified with the "disgusting thing that causes desolation"? Its being likened to a seven-headed wild beast carrying a harlot on its back shows that it is unclean in God's sight, "disgusting" to Him. Since it "springs from the seven" non-Christian world powers, it is not a Christian organization. Half of the member nations of the United Nations do not even profess to be Christian, but here we find nations of Christendom in political union with non-Christian or pagan nations. The United Nations is a part of this world and is a "friend of the world" and, consequently, is an "enemy of God." (James 4:4; John 8:23; 18:36) Messianic hopes are attached to it by its idolizers, and it is accepted by Christendom as a substitute for the established Messianic kingdom of God. Disgusting!

⁴² The United Nations is credited with having done many good things. How possibly could it be called a desolator, a "thing that causes desolation"? Well, the Sixth World Power, the Roman Empire, was trying to preserve the Pax Romana throughout the earth and was trying to hold down peace in the Middle East; but latterly its armed forces turned to becoming the desolator of the religious holy city of Jerusalem. Likewise, the Eighth World Power, the United Nations, has not yet finished its foretold world role before it "goes off into destruction." (Revelation 17:11) It will yet turn out to be a "thing that causes desolation." To whom? Revelation 17:15-18 reveals to us to whom. There we read:

⁴³ "The waters that you saw, where the harlot is sitting, mean peoples and crowds and nations and tongues. And the ten horns that you saw, and the wild beast, these will hate the harlot and will make her devastated and naked, and will eat up her fleshy parts and will completely burn her with fire. For God

41. Why is the United Nations not a Christian organization, and what makes it disgusting to God?
42. What armed forces will the United Nations be like in becoming a "thing that causes desolation"?
43. How does Revelation 17:15-18 symbolically describe the desolating work?

put it into their hearts to carry out his thought, even to carry out their one thought by giving their kingdom to the wild beast, until the words of God will have been accomplished. And the woman whom you saw means the great city that has a kingdom over the kings of the earth."

[44] So the Eighth World Power, the United Nations, will turn into a "thing that causes desolation" when it brings to desolation the symbolic international harlot, Babylon the Great. Ancient Babylon on the Euphrates River was a city, and Babylon the Great is therefore likened to a "great city." And since she has a "kingdom over the kings of the earth," Babylon the Great means the world empire of false religion. The thing for sensible persons to do now is to get out of that Babylonish world empire of false religion before destruction comes upon it, for fear that they might be destroyed with it. This is the very thing that the inspired call from heaven tells persons who desire to be God's people to do, saying: "Get out of her, my people, if you do not want to share with her in her sins, and if you do not want to receive part of her plagues." —Revelation 18:1-4.

[45] This is no time for us to be deceived. Because Christendom claims to be Christian, her church people belonging to her hundreds of religious sects should not think that they have already got out of Babylon the Great. As long as they remain a part of Christendom, they are staying with Babylon the Great and sharing in her sins. Why so? Because Christendom is herself a part of Babylon the Great, in fact, the most dominant part of that world empire of false religion. Furthermore, war-guilty, bloodstained Christendom is the antitypical modern-day unfaithful Jerusalem, from whom all of Jesus' true disciples must flee for their lives. For, when the Eighth World Power (the United Nations) desolates Babylon the Great, it will also

---

44. Of what, then, does the United Nations become a desolator, and what is the sensible thing to do now regarding the thing to be desolated, in order to be God's people?
45. (a) What should be said as to whether people belonging to Christendom's churches have already got out of Babylon, and why? (b) So why must Christendom be destroyed with Babylon the Great?

destroy the most reprehensible part of Babylon the Great, namely, Christendom. Lovers of life in harmony with the true God must flee out of Christendom without delay, just as the Jewish disciples of Jesus Christ fled out of Judea and Jerusalem after they saw the "disgusting thing that causes desolation . . . standing" in the place that was considered very holy by the Jews.

[46] During this "presence" or parousia of the reigning King Jesus Christ since 1914 C.E., God-fearing persons have been warned to get out of Babylon the Great lest they be caught in her destruction. An early warning was given by the publication of the book entitled "The Finished Mystery" by the People's Pulpit Association in July of 1917, after the United States of America had got into World War I. This book presented a verse-for-verse commentary upon the entire book of Revelation, including chapters seventeen and eighteen. This is the book that came under governmental ban early in the following year. Before this, however, that early warning was sounded extensively on Sunday, December 30, 1917. This was done on the morning of that day by a concerted distribution throughout the land of the four-page tract *Bible Students Monthly,* Volume 9, No. 9, entitled "The Fall of Babylon." This simultaneous distribution of this strongly worded tract from coast to coast was followed by public talks on the subject of Babylon that Sunday afternoon.—See *The Watch Tower and Herald of Christ's Presence* under date of December 15, 1917, page 370, under the heading "Volunteer Day—December 30th."

[47] Since modern-day Babylon the Great (including Christendom) is to be destroyed by the "disgusting thing that causes desolation," early postwar thinking by Bible students concerned itself with identifying what that disgusting thing or abomination was in

46. How was an early warning to God-fearing people to get out of Babylon the Great sounded in the year 1917?
47. (a) After World War I, early postwar thinking by Bible students concerned itself with identifying what thing? (b) What did *The Watch Tower* as of January 1, 1921, say about it?

twentieth-century developments. After the League of Nations was established and a mandate over Palestine was given to the British Empire, *The Watch Tower* as of January 1, 1921, page 12, under the heading "Spoken of by Daniel," said:

> ... since the land belongs to Jehovah, it follows that the beasts in question [of Revelation, chapter 13] have no authority to exercise a controlling power over the land of Palestine; and their man-made thing, the League of Nations (under the authority of which the British Empire holds a mandate over Palestine), is an abomination unto the Lord. This abomination, therefore, is standing where it *ought not to stand.* ...
> Mark, then, the further corroborative evidence that we have reached the end of the world; viz., the abomination of desolation standing where *it ought not to stand* —"standing in the holy place", the Holy Land, God's own land; and seeing Jerusalem "compassed with armies" —the armies of the other beast; and let him who is able to *read* understand and know that we have reached the end of the world. ...

⁴⁸ Although being based upon a literal application of Matthew 24:15, and Mark 13:14 (*Authorized Version*), the conclusion proved to be correct, that the "abomination of desolation" (or, "the disgusting thing that causes desolation") was at that time the League of Nations. Years afterward, that international organization for world peace and security was identified as being the Eighth World Power of Bible prophecy. This identification came on Sunday night, May 30, 1926, in the public address delivered in the Royal Albert Hall, London, England, and entitled "Why World Powers Are Tottering—The Remedy." When dealing with the theme "League Foretold," the speaker, President J. F. Rutherford of the Watch Tower Bible and Tract Society, said:

> God foretold the seven world powers, to wit, Egypt, Assyria, Babylon, Medo-Persia, Greece, Rome and the British Empire, and also foretold that out of the seven would grow the eighth. The latter is also symbolized as a "beast", because its purpose is to rule and control

48. In the year 1926 the international organization for world peace and security was identified as being what, and on what occasion?

the peoples of the earth. The Lord foretold its birth, its short existence, and its everlasting end.—Revelation 17:10, 11; Isaiah 8:9, 10.—See *The Watch Tower* as of July 15, 1926, page 215.

⁴⁹ Thus after World War I ended in 1918, the surviving anointed remnant of Jehovah's "chosen" ones began to catch sight of the "disgusting thing that causes desolation" and to get an understanding of it and of what its appearing on the world scene meant. They had come into bondage to Babylon the Great and her political and military paramours during World War I, and now they responded to the heavenly call to get out of her. Those God-fearing persons who were afterward added to His remnant of "chosen" ones also obeyed the divine command and left Babylon the Great (including Christendom). Since the antitypical unfaithful Jerusalem, namely, Christendom, is not confined to earthly Jerusalem and the land of Palestine but is world wide, those fleeing from her did not have to wait until seeing Christendom surrounded by the armed forces of the Eighth World Power (the international organization for world peace and security). The angelic command, "Get out of her, my people, if you do not want to share with her in her sins, and if you do not want to receive part of her plagues," did not wait until that event.

⁵⁰ However, the flight of Jehovah's anointed "chosen" ones before that event was a noteworthy indication that the desolating of unfaithful Christendom and the rest of Babylon the Great was approaching and was due to occur during this generation, during the lifetime of the Eighth World Power, which is short as if for but "one hour." The prompt early flight of Jehovah's "chosen" ones was a reliable example for the "great crowd" of Christ's "other sheep" to follow from the year 1935 C.E. onward till now. The desolating of antitypical unfaithful Jerusalem, Christendom, and

49. Why did the remnant of "chosen" ones not delay about coming out of Babylon the Great until they saw her encircled by encamped armies?
50. (a) That early flight of Jehovah's "chosen" ones was an indication of what, and a good example for whom? (b) After what experience of the "disgusting thing" is Babylon the Great to be destroyed?

the remainder of Babylon the Great by the armed forces of the "disgusting thing" cannot now be far off in the future. Be it noted that the "disgusting thing" does its desolating of Babylon the Great after it, as the Eighth World Power, ascends out of the "abyss." The Eighth World Power, under the form of the League of Nations, took a fall into the "abyss" of deathlike impotency with the outbreak of World War II in 1939, and it came up out of the "abyss" in 1945, but under the form of the United Nations. (Revelation 17:8, 11, 12) That was nearly thirty years ago. It is unsafe to delay flight much longer!

WHY A "GREAT TRIBULATION" WITHOUT EQUAL

[51] The desolating of modern-day antitypical unfaithful Jerusalem, Christendom, will be part of indeed a "great tribulation such as has not occurred since the world's beginning until now, no, nor will occur again." (Matthew 24:21) The realm of Christendom is world wide, much larger than the land of Israel in which the earthly city of Jerusalem is located as capital. The realm of Babylon the Great, which "has a kingdom over the kings of the earth," is still larger in realm than that of mere Christendom. Consequently, when the symbolic "ten horns" and the rest of the scarlet-colored "wild beast" start hating the harlotrous religious Babylon the Great and desolate her, it will be a religious calamity without equal, embracing our entire planet. Christendom will no more get God's protection than will all the rest of immoral, bloodguilty Babylon the Great. If Jerusalem's destruction in 70 C.E. was horrible, and is a prophetic picture, this worldwide religious calamity will also be horrible. Then those religionists who did not heed the divine call to get out, but who selfishly stayed in Babylon the Great, will be counted as sharing in her sins and will justly taste a part of her plagues.

---

51. (a) Why will the tribulation upon the antitypical unfaithful Jerusalem be indeed a "great" one? (b) What will happen to those who delayed their flight out of Babylon the Great?

⁵² The destruction of Babylon the Great is not all there is to the coming "great tribulation." It is merely the first part of it. The political and commercial and social elements of the world have had unclean, pleasure-seeking, materially enriching relations with religious Babylon the Great. They have shared with her in her bloodguiltiness and in her opposition to Jehovah God and in persecuting the true disciples of Jesus Christ and in obstructing their preaching of "this good news of the kingdom" as a witness. For this they have to settle accounts with God. The political elements also lend their support to the Eighth World Power, the United Nations, and their nations make up the members of it. This unchristian Eighth World Power stands in defiant resistance to Jehovah's Messianic kingdom. It assumes on earth, with the approval of Christendom's clergymen, the place of God's rightful kingdom of his Christ. After it desolates its former lover, Babylon the Great, it fights irreligiously, with full militant power, against Jehovah's reigning King, the Lamb Jesus Christ.

⁵³ This final showdown fight the apostle John describes in this symbolic language: "And the ten horns that you saw mean ten kings, who have not yet received a kingdom, but they do [by becoming members of the Eighth World Power] receive authority as kings one hour with the wild beast. . . . These will battle with the Lamb, but, because he is Lord of lords and King of kings, the Lamb will conquer them. Also, those called and chosen and faithful with him will do so." (Revelation 17:12-14) This will mean the climax of the "great tribulation," namely, "the war of the great day of God the Almighty" at Har–Magedon. Fuller description of that universal war is given in Revelation 19:11-21.

⁵⁴ This will involve the more than three thousand

52. (a) Why is the destruction of Babylon the Great not the only part of the "great tribulation"? (b) After the Eighth World Power acts as the desolator, what does it do?
53. Why will what is described in Revelation 17:12-14 be the climax of the "great tribulation"?
54. How many earthly enemies does God Almighty then take on in combat, and how will the slaughter compare with any previous one?

million inhabitants of our earthly globe. Even the deluge of the patriarch Noah's day, although planetary, did not involve that many humans, just 1,656 years from man's creation. God the Almighty, in his "war of the great day," can outmatch all the nuclear bomb power of all the earthly nations and can take on in combat all his earthly enemies combined. (Revelation 16:13-16) It portends to be a slaughter such as this planet has never before experienced, nor will it ever occur again. Little room for surprise, then, that Jesus, looking far beyond ancient Jerusalem's desolation in 70 C.E., remarked: "In fact, unless Jehovah had cut short the days, no flesh would be saved. But on account of the chosen ones whom he has chosen he has cut short the days."—Mark 13:20.

[55] Miraculous though it will have to be, some flesh will "be saved." This will be because Jehovah cuts short the number of the days of the "great tribulation," doing so "on account of the chosen ones whom he has chosen." Not by getting his "chosen ones" off the face of the earth, but by getting them out of all partnership with this condemned system of things and by doing so before his scheduled time for the "great tribulation" to begin, Jehovah sees good to cut short the number of the days of tribulation. Not only does he get his anointed "chosen ones" out to a condition of safety under his protection, but he also gets out the "great crowd" of sheeplike "righteous" ones who do good to even the least ones of Christ's spiritual brothers. (Matthew 25:31-40) Having both his "chosen ones" and the "great crowd" separated from the goatlike people, Jehovah God by his Lamb Jesus Christ can make it a "short" work in executing divine vengeance upon all his enemies who remain a part of the world-wide system of things.—Romans 9:28.

[56] This will ensure that "flesh" will be saved right

---

55. (a) How is it that the cutting short of the days of tribulation is "on account of the chosen ones"? (b) Who take advantage of this arrangement?
56. At Jerusalem's destruction in 70 C.E., who made up the "flesh" that was saved, and in spite of what in their disfavor?

here on earth. Jehovah God the Creator is not going to let the human race be wiped out from the earth, either by man-made nuclear bombs or by his heavenly executional forces. "Flesh" in the form of 97,000 Jews was saved at Jerusalem's destruction in 70 C.E. These 97,000 had seen Jerusalem surrounded by encamped Roman armies in the year 66 C.E. But that short siege and the standing of the "disgusting thing" where it ought not to stand, in the holy place, was not a part of their "great tribulation." The "tribulation" was not in two parts. That siege by General Cestius Gallus was unexpectedly lifted, and the retreat of the Roman armies was turned into a rout, with a joyful victory for the Jews. But when the "great tribulation" did begin in the spring of 70 C.E., then those 97,000 managed to survive only because the number of days of the tribulation was cut short. Those 97,000 were saved alive in spite of their not being Jehovah's "chosen ones." But their lives were spared only for slavery the rest of their days throughout the Roman Empire.

[57] The cutting short of the number of days of the approaching "great tribulation" is a guarantee that again "flesh" will be saved. This time, however, the "flesh" saved will not be that of any of his enemies similar to those rebellious non-Christian Jews cooped up in ancient Jerusalem. This time *all* his enemies are sentenced to destruction. The "flesh," aside from his "chosen ones," will be the "great crowd" of obedient sheeplike persons who have obeyed his commandments and forsaken the doomed system of things (including Christendom) and taken their stand on His side. Saved alive into God's new order under Christ's millennial reign, this "great crowd" of "flesh" will have it said of them: "These are the ones that come out of the great tribulation." (Revelation 7:14) How happy that "great crowd" of survivors will then be! How gracious, too, on Jehovah's part to cut short the tribulation!

---

57. Who will comprise the "flesh" that will be saved in the coming "great tribulation," and what will be said about them?

MESSIAH'S WARNING AGAINST FALSE MESSIAHS

⁵⁸ In Jesus' prophecy on the "sign" of his "presence" (parousia) and the "conclusion of the system of things," Jesus indicated that false Christs would come before the desolating of Jerusalem in 70 C.E. He began his prophecy on this note, saying to his inquiring apostles: "Look out that nobody misleads you; for many will come on the basis of my name, saying, 'I am the Christ,' and will mislead many." (Matthew 24:4, 5) But they proved to be false, impostors, for they did not bring about any deliverance of Jerusalem nor any deliverance at all. After Jerusalem's destruction the Jews that did not believe in Jesus as the Messiah would have to continue looking for a Messiah in the flesh. On the other hand, the Christians, Jewish and non-Jewish, would have to continue looking for the promised "presence" (parousia) of the true Messiah, Jesus the Son of God. The tactics that the deceivers would employ to induce interested persons to go after Messianic pretenders, Jesus described after foretelling the literal desolating of Jerusalem by the Roman legions. He continued on to say:

⁵⁹ "Then if anyone says to you, 'Look! Here is the Christ,' or, 'There!' do not believe it. For false Christs and false prophets will arise and will give great signs and wonders so as to mislead, if possible, even the chosen ones. Look! I have forewarned you. Therefore, if people say to you, 'Look! He is in the wilderness,' do not go out; 'Look! He is in the inner chambers,' do not believe it. For just as the lightning comes out of eastern parts and shines over to western parts, so the presence [pa·rou·si'a] of the Son of man will be. Wherever the carcass is, there the eagles will be gathered together."—Matthew 24:23-28.

⁶⁰ Better than anyone else on earth, Jesus "the Son of man" knew how he would accomplish his coming and presence. He would not locate himself either "here"

58, 59. (a) How did the false Christs whom Jesus foretold prove disappointing, and they left the Jews looking for whom after Jerusalem's destruction? (b) What did Jesus say further regarding the tactics used in connection with false Christs?
60. What would be the reason for a false Christ to be out "in the wilderness" or "in the inner chambers"?

or "there" or in any particular spot on the earth. He would not put in an appearance in some isolated place, "in the wilderness," so that Messiah seekers should resort to him out there away from observation by the governmental authorities of the land, so that they could train under his leadership out there and prepare to strike a political blow, a *coup d'etat,* and install him as the Messianic Ruler of the world. (Acts 5:36, 37; compare 1 Samuel 22:1, 2.) Neither would he conceal himself in some "inner chambers," his location being known to only a select few, that there unobserved and undetected he might conspire and draw up secret plans with accomplices for overturning the world government and have himself anointed as the promised Messiah. (Compare 2 Kings 9:4-14.) To the contrary of this, there was to be nothing to hide about Jesus' having come as King and beginning his royal presence.

[61] His presence or parousia was to resemble the lightning as to its effects. His parousia was to be like the lightning, not in flashing suddenly, unexpectedly and in the fraction of a second. The emphasis here is not on the lightning's striking instantaneously unannounced, but on its shining over a broad area, from eastern parts to western parts. (Luke 17:24) The lightning's illuminative power is like that described in Psalm 97:4: "His lightnings lighted up the productive land; the earth saw and came to be in severe pains." So, too, the inhabitants of the earth were not to be left in darkness respecting the parousia of the Son of man. From horizon to horizon all the people were to be enlightened concerning his regal parousia. It was to be made as public as is a flash of lightning by its illuminative power, its far-extended shining. To Christ's disciples today, who are acquainted with his invisible parousia, his words to his apostles nineteen centuries ago apply:

[62] "Therefore do not fear them; for there is nothing covered over that will not become uncovered, and secret that will not become known. What I tell you

61, 62. (a) In what way was Christ's parousia to be like the lightning? (b) What words of Jesus regarding publicity as given to his apostles apply to his disciples today?

in the darkness, say in the light; and what you hear whispered, preach from the housetops."—Matthew 10:26, 27.

[63] The purpose of the rising up of false Christs and false prophets is to "mislead, if possible, even the chosen ones." (Matthew 24:23-25; Mark 13:21-23) But the faithful "chosen ones" will not let themselves be "sent on a wild-goose chase." They will not let themselves be led in different directions on a search for some visible pretender in the flesh. They will not let themselves be attracted to some visible man in the flesh who claims to be the Christ, making great demonstrations to prove his identity as such. (Luke 17:22, 23) From the Scriptures they know where to look. They are like the eagles whose farsightedness magnifies microscopic things far below on the earth, unerringly. (Job 39:27-29) Hence, they do not gather together to a false Christ only to end up spiritually unfed. Like eagles that can spot the edible carcass from far off and that gather there for a common meal, the "chosen ones" discern where the true spiritual food is to be found, namely, with the true Christ at his invisible parousia, and there is where they gather together and find spiritual nourishment.—Luke 17:37.

[64] By no means is the King Jesus Christ at his parousia to make a visible appearance in the flesh at any location on the surface of the earth. That is all that false Christs, who are mere men of blood and flesh, can do. But with the resurrected, glorified, reigning Lord Jesus Christ it is different. (1 Timothy 6:14-16) It is to this fact that he called the attention of his apostles as he carried his prophecy still forward, saying: "Immediately after the tribulation of those days the sun will be darkened, and the moon will not give its light, and the stars will fall from heaven, and the powers of the heavens will be shaken. And then the sign of the Son of man will appear in heaven, and

63. (a) What is the purpose of the rising up of these foretold false Christs and false prophets? (b) How are the faithful "chosen ones" like the eagles that gather where a carcass really is?
64. (a) Where only can false Christs make an appearance of themselves, and why? (b) Where, as Jesus now said, would the sign of him appear after the tribulation of those days?

then all the tribes of the earth will beat themselves in lamentation, and they will see the Son of man coming on the clouds of heaven with power and great glory. And he will send forth his angels with a great trumpet sound, and they will gather his chosen ones together from the four winds, from one extremity of the heavens to their other extremity."—Matthew 24:29-31; Mark 13:24-27.

CELESTIAL PHENOMENA "IMMEDIATELY AFTER"

[65] By his expression "immediately after the tribulation of those days" Jesus was evidently referring to the days of the "great tribulation" that came upon Middle Eastern Jerusalem at the hands of the Romans in 70 C.E. However, search the historical records as much as we may, we do not find such things as Jesus described occurred "immediately after" in the sense of instantly after, without a break after, following in unbroken sequence like a chain of events. Instantly after the "great tribulation" that ended in Jerusalem's destruction, the "sign of the Son of man" did not "appear in heaven" and the Roman besiegers and the other "tribes of the earth" did not "beat themselves in lamentation" at a visible sight of the Son of man coming in clouds and with "power and great glory." Authentic history records that, after the Roman legions destroyed the holy city of Jerusalem, they laid siege to the last Jewish stronghold, the fortress atop Mount Masada on the west bank of the Dead Sea, and captured it in the year 73 C.E., thereby completing their subjugation of all the province of Judea. Well, then, was Jesus wrong at this point?

[66] No, Jesus was not here a false prophet. Under inspiration of God's holy spirit he could not be wrong. What, then, is wrong here? It is evidently the common understanding of the expression "immediately after." Evidently here the meaning of "immediately" is like

that in John 6:21 (*Authorized Version*) where, after Jesus walks over the waters of the Sea of Galilee and gets aboard the ship in which his disciples were, it says: "And immediately the ship was at the land whither they went." Certainly more than an instant of time elapsed before they landed. It is similar to the word "shortly" in Revelation 1:1, where we read: "A revelation by Jesus Christ, which God gave him, to show his slaves the things that must shortly take place." This word "shortly" widens out in time from when the apostle John got the Revelation about 96 C.E., to the fulfillments of the Revelation in our twentieth century. (Compare the length of time covered by "shortly" in Romans 16:20.)

[67] To harmonize Jesus' prophecy of Matthew 24:29 with the available facts, we must understand Jesus' expression "immediately after" to skip a span of centuries of time down to our twentieth century.* At this time, during the parousia of the Son of man since the year 1914 C.E., we do have things and events that do correspond with what Jesus foretold in that verse.

[68] Historians will agree that since 1914 C.E. mankind has entered into the blackest period of its existence. It is as if the sun had been "darkened" during the daytime, as if the moon did not "give its light" by night, and as if, during the same nighttime with no moonlight, the stars had fallen from heaven and disappeared into the blackness of the night. For the doomed system of things, including Christendom, there is no brightness to the future outlook during either the daytime or the nighttime. The inability of men, even

---

* Compare with *The Watchtower* as of December 1, 1970, page 726, paragraphs 30, 31. Inasmuch as Jesus said, in the same prophecy at Matthew 24:36, that no creature knew "that day and hour" when he would come to destroy this system of things, nobody was able to say how soon after the destruction of Jerusalem the expression "immediately after" meant. We, who live nineteen centuries later, can appreciate how that short expression bridged such a long period of time. We note that the parallel verse in Mark's account does not use the adverb "immediately" before the preposition "after."—Mark 13:24.

---

67. How, then, are we to understand Jesus' words, "immediately after"?
68, 69. (a) How has the world situation since 1914 been like the effects of what Jesus foretold concerning celestial bodies? (b) How, because of lack of self-help, have men been like those described in Isaiah 59:9, 10 and Zephaniah 1:17, 18?

in Christendom, to see their way out of the world's situation by their own human means is well pictured in the ancient Bible prophecies, in these words:

69 "We keep hoping for light, but, look! darkness; for brightness, but in continuous gloom we kept walking. We keep groping for the wall just like blind men, and like those without eyes we keep groping. We have stumbled at high noon just as in evening darkness; among the stout ones we are just like dead people." (Isaiah 59:9, 10) "And I [Jehovah] will cause distress to mankind, and they will certainly walk like blind men; because it is against Jehovah that they have sinned. And their blood will actually be poured out like dust, and their bowels like the dung. Neither their silver nor their gold will be able to deliver them in the day of Jehovah's fury; but by the fire of his zeal the whole earth will be devoured, because he will make an extermination, indeed a terrible one, of all the inhabitants of the earth."—Zephaniah 1:17, 18.

70 The heavens seem to have lost their benign appearance. Modern science informs us of the great flares of atomic energy that shoot up thousands of miles into the sky and that appear like sunspots but that send out tremendous streams of particles that reach and affect our earth. Continually our earth is being bombarded by unseen rays of nuclear energy streaming toward us from unknown regions in outer space. Our radar telescopes pick up radar signals from stars that are unseen to the eye of the most powerful telescopes but that give evidence of their existence in space just the same. Landings have been made on the moon by astronauts six times, which moon some militarists would like to turn into a military base for directing warfare against enemies on the earth. And when we think of the supersonic warplanes and of the intercontinental missiles with warheads loaded with atomic and nuclear bombs of frightful destructiveness, we appreciate all the more the solemn meaning of

70. (a) In the light of scientific observations, how have the heavens lost their benign appearance? (b) In what way have the powers of the heavens been shaken?

Jesus' words: "And the powers of the heavens will be shaken." (Matthew 24:29) Men have invaded the skies and outer space and upset the normal balance of things.

[71] Even the sea, which was formerly a hidden universe, has now become a menacing region. It swarms with man-made submarines modernized with the latest missile-shooting devices to send up from the depths roaring destruction upon the defenseless inhabitants of the dry land. Added to this, the sea is becoming polluted because of the dumping of life-destroying waste products into the briny deep. The sea is threatened with becoming as dead as the lowest spot on earth, the Dead Sea of the Middle East. At the same time, the atmosphere above the sea as well as the dry land is becoming polluted from the increasing discharges of deadly fumes from industrial plants, motor vehicles and continental and overseas airplanes. Not without good foresight of consequences the London (England) *Medical News-Tribune*, under date of March 27, 1970, headlined the warning: "By 1984 the Earth Could Be Dead."

"SIGN OF THE SON OF MAN...IN HEAVEN"

[72] Yet, never will this planet earth be destroyed by man-made nuclear warfare. Never will it come to be entitled "The Late Great Planet Earth." Never will its Creator permit the earth to become void of all creature life, including human life. It is the international system of things that obtains now upon the earth that will be destroyed. Its destruction will come from God by means of his Messianic King, Jesus Christ, with all his holy angels. When he was on earth in the flesh and was called the Son of man, the skeptical Jews asked Jesus "to display to them a sign from heaven" in proof that he was indeed the promised Messiah. But he told them that nothing but an *earthly* sign would

71. (a) How have the seas become something menacing, and the atmosphere been ill affected? (b) What warning did the *Medical News-Tribune* of London publish in 1970?
72, 73. (a) If not the earthly planet itself, then what is to be destroyed, and how? (b) What kind of sign concerning Messiah was given nineteen centuries ago, but what kind did he say will be given during his parousia?

be given to them, "the sign of Jonah." That sign was given when Jesus was dead for parts of three days in the heart of the earth and then was raised from the dead on the third day. (Matthew 16:1-4; 12:39, 40) But now, during his invisible parousia in spirit, earth's inhabitants will be given a "sign . . . in heaven." After telling how the powers of the heavens would be shaken, Jesus went on to say:

[73] "And then the sign of the Son of man will appear in heaven, and then all the tribes of the earth will beat themselves in lamentation, and they will see the Son of man coming on the clouds of heaven with power and great glory."—Matthew 24:30.

[74] This refers, not to the beginning of his parousia or at his arrival in spirit, but to his "coming" (Greek: er·kho'me·non) at the great tribulation such as has not occurred since the world's beginning. His "coming" being described as a coming "on the clouds of heaven" makes it plain that it is an invisible coming, by the turning of his long-range attention to this earth and by his projecting of his power to it with destructive forcefulness. People will be made aware of it as proceeding, not from men, but from heaven, from the glorified Son of man who acts as God's Representative. This is related to the sign in heaven that the prophet Daniel saw, and which he describes, saying:

[75] "I kept on beholding in the visions of the night, and, see there! with the clouds of the heavens someone like a son of man happened to be coming; and to the Ancient of Days he gained access, and they brought him up close even before that One. And to him there were given rulership and dignity and kingdom, that the peoples, national groups and languages should all serve even him. His rulership is an indefinitely lasting rulership that will not pass away, and his kingdom one that will not be brought to ruin.'—Daniel 7:13, 14.

[76] The fulfillment of that vision of Daniel was unseen,

74, 75. (a) In Matthew 24:30 Jesus' word "coming" refers to what, and how is that "coming" effected? (b) This prophecy of the "sign . . . in heaven" is related to what prophecy of Daniel?
76. (a) When did that vision of Daniel begin its fulfillment? (b) How will all the tribes see the Son of man "coming," and who will not join with them then in selfish lamentation?

in the spiritual heavens, from 1914 C.E. onward. So, at God's appointed time, the glorified Son of man proceeds with his authority and power against Babylon the Great (including Christendom) and the hostile nations of this earth. The evidences of his proceeding against them, which they will be able to see and feel, will be as a "sign . . . in heaven" for them. In the face of their impending annihilation, "all the tribes of the earth will beat themselves in lamentation." However, the remnant of God's "chosen ones" and the "great crowd" of sheeplike ones, all of whom have separated themselves from Babylon the Great and her paramours, will not join with those terrified tribes of earth in their selfish lamentation. They will all have been gathered to the right side of the reigning King, Jesus Christ. —Revelation 7:9-17; Matthew 25:31-40.

THE ANGELIC GATHERING
OF THE "CHOSEN ONES"

[77] By that time what Jesus next describes will have been completed, namely: "And he will send forth his angels with a great trumpet sound, and they will gather his chosen ones together from the four winds, from one extremity of the heavens to their other extremity." (Matthew 24:31) This angelic gathering of the "chosen ones" has been going on during his parousia. It was in the postwar year of 1919 that the "chosen ones" began leaving their bondage in Babylon the Great and returning to their God-given spiritual estate on earth, similar to the return of the Jewish remnant from Babylon to their homeland in the year 537 B.C.E. Like a "great trumpet sound" the proclamation has gone forth since then that God's Messianic kingdom has been established in the heavens and that they should take their stand firmly on the side of the heavenly kingdom and preach "this good news of the kingdom" world wide. In the direction of the "four winds" this announcement of good news has been blasted as by a

---

77. (a) By that time, what gathering will have been accomplished, and since when? (b) How has this gathering been accomplished as with the sound of a "great trumpet"?

trumpet. It has been heard from one extremity of the heavens to the other.

[78] In accordance with the inviting tones of the "great trumpet sound" the heavenly angels who attend the Son of man in his parousia have been gathering his "chosen ones" from all quarters of the globe. This gathering has been apparent for all men to see, especially in the series of large-scale assemblies that have been held beginning with the general convention of the I.B.S.A. September 1-8, 1919, down to the international assemblies on the theme "Divine Victory" held by Jehovah's witnesses around the globe during the year 1973. (See announcement of the assemblies world wide, on pages 94 and 95 of the February 1, 1973, issue of The Watchtower.) Particularly is the "great crowd" conscious of the angelic gathering of the "chosen ones" during Christ's parousia, and they also take their stand on the side of Jehovah's Messianic kingdom and assemble and work with the gathered "chosen ones."

[79] From the fulfillment thus far of Jesus' prophecy regarding the "conclusion of the system of things," his disciples know that the time is very near for "all the tribes of the earth" to "beat themselves in lamentation" at what they see threatening them at the hands of the glorified Son of man.

AN ILLUSTRATION
FOR DETERMINING ITS NEARNESS

[80] It is not necessary for us to know the day and the hour of the exact year when the "great tribulation" is to break out against this entire "system of things." In order for us to know that now it is dangerously near, all we have to do is to heed what Jesus said at this critical point in his prophecy: "Now learn from the fig tree as an illustration this point: Just as soon as its

---

78. (a) This angelic gathering of the "chosen ones" has been apparent to all men especially by what occasions? (b) Who, particularly, have been conscious of such a gathering and have acted?
79. From the fulfillment of Jesus' prophecy thus far, it is apparent that what expression of emotion by the earthly tribes is near?
80. In order to know that the "great tribulation" is dangerously near, what observation of Jesus at this critical point of his prophecy do we need to heed?

young branch grows tender and it puts forth leaves, you know that summer is near. Likewise also you, when you see all these things, know that he is near at the doors. Truly I say to you that this generation will by no means pass away until all these things occur. Heaven and earth will pass away, but my words will by no means pass away."—Matthew 24:32-35.

[81] How much more do we, of this generation that saw the outbreak of World War I in 1914, have to see of the fulfillment of Jesus' prophecy to know that "he is near at the doors"? What more could we want in the way of evidence? We are not left in worrisome ignorance of the meaning of things that have been occurring on earth since the close of the Gentile Times in 1914. As intelligent, understanding Bible-studying persons we are convinced that the completion nears for the "sign of [Christ's] presence and of the conclusion of the system of things."—Matthew 24:3.

[82] Does this depress us? Does this take all joy out of living now? It should not, and it does not. For Jesus told his disciples how they should react toward world events during his invisible parousia, saying: "Also, there will be signs in sun and moon and stars, and on the earth anguish of nations, not knowing the way out because of the roaring of the sea and its agitation, while men become faint out of fear and expectation of the things coming upon the inhabited earth; for the powers of the heavens will be shaken. And then they will see the Son of man coming in a cloud with power and great glory. But as these things start to occur, raise yourselves erect and lift your heads up, because your deliverance is getting near."—Luke 21:25-28.

[83] Have we of this generation seen "these things start to occur"? Have we seen "these things" occurring throughout the decades since 1914 C.E.? Inasmuch as we have done so, there is no reason for us to be bowed down with international "anguish." There is no reason

---

81. From what evidence can we of this generation know that the "sign" foretold by Jesus is near completion?
82. How did Jesus say that we should react to world events during his parousia?
83. So this is no time for the "chosen ones" and the "great crowd" to do what, and what does deliverance betoken for them?

for us to bend our backs any longer under the religious enslavement imposed by Babylon the Great, including Christendom. It is a time to raise ourselves erect like free worshipers of the Most High God, the Sovereign Lord Jehovah. No longer is it the fitting time for us to look despairingly down to the ground. It is the time to lift our heads up heavenward and see in the brightening light of the Holy Scriptures that contains Jesus' prophecy the evidences of a most reassuring future for mankind. The meaning of these evidences is unmistakable: Deliverance is at hand! This betokens for God's "chosen ones" and the "great crowd" of their fellow worshipers survival of the "great tribulation" just ahead. When we under divine preservation come out of that "great tribulation," we shall leave behind the irreparable ruins of this present death-dealing system of things. Gloriously opens up before us God's new system of things!

CHAPTER 17

The "Slave" Who Lived to See the "Sign"

MAN'S Creator is a timekeeper. He meant for man to keep time also. In the creative account as found in the first chapter of his inspired Word, we read: "And God went on to say: 'Let luminaries come to be in the expanse of the heavens to make a division between the day and the night; and they must serve as signs and for seasons and for days and years. And they must serve as luminaries in the expanse of the heavens to shine upon the earth.' And it came to be so. And God proceeded to make the two great luminaries, the greater luminary for dominating the day and the lesser luminary for dom-

1. According to the account of the creation of heavenly lights, God desired man to be like him in what respect?

inating the night, and also the stars." (Genesis 1: 14-16) So the Holy Bible keeps a count of time on man's existence, and does so in seasons and days and years.

[2] The Bible's count of time carried on from man's creation in the Garden of Eden until where its chronology connects up with the authentic dates of secular history. The Bible's prophecies that contain chronological features project the count of time still farther into the future, even down to the end of the "seven times" of Gentile domination of mankind without divine interruption, till in the year 1914 C.E. (Daniel 4: 16, 23, 25, 32; Luke 21:24) That year was the time when the parousia or "presence" of the glorified Jesus Christ in heaven began. Jesus prophesied of the unequaled "great tribulation" that was to occur during his parousia, but he did not pinpoint the particular day and hour when that unparalleled time of trouble would break upon the whole world of mankind. He said:

[3] "Concerning that day and hour nobody knows, neither the angels of the heavens nor the Son, but only the Father. For just as the days of Noah were, so the presence of the Son of man will be. For as they were in those days before the flood, eating and drinking, men marrying and women being given in marriage, until the day that Noah entered into the ark; and they took no note until the flood came and swept them all away, so the presence of the Son of man will be. Then two men will be in the field: one will be taken along and the other be abandoned; two women will be grinding at the hand mill: one will be taken along and the other be abandoned. Keep on the watch, therefore, because you do not know on what day your Lord is coming [Greek: *er'khe·tai*]."—Matthew 24:36-42; Mark 13:32, 33.

[4] According to this prophecy, the social conditions

2, 3. (a) How did the Bible project the count of time even down to the year 1914 C.E.? (b) What did Jesus say regarding the time for his coming at the "great tribulation" that occurs during his parousia?
4. So social conditions among mankind during Jesus' parousia were to be like the days of whom, and which particular days?

among men and women on earth during this invisible parousia of the Lord Jesus Christ should be like those in the days of Noah before the planetary deluge. Evidently by the time reference, "the days of Noah," Jesus meant "those days before the flood" when Noah was preparing the ark that God had instructed him to build. Otherwise, there would have been nothing special for the antediluvian people to take note of to indicate that a deluge was scheduled for their generation. This preparing of the ark would locate the particular "days of Noah" within the last hundred years of his life before the deluge, for the deluge started in Noah's six hundredth year, and so we read: "Noah got to be five hundred years old. After that Noah became father to Shem, Ham and Japheth."—Genesis 5:32; 7:11.

⁵ Another limit on the time would be that Noah was told that he must take into the ark his own wife and his three sons and his "sons' wives" with him. (Genesis 6:18) This would indicate that Noah's three sons were married before the work on the ark began. So the time before the deluge during which the people could note that something unusual was going on may have been reduced to around fifty years before the global catastrophe. At any rate, the "days" allowed to the people for taking serious note were a considerable time. Inasmuch as "so the presence [parousia] of the Son of man will be," this proves that the invisible parousia of Christ is an extended period of time and does not mark merely the time of the start of the "great tribulation" at a certain hour of a specific day. In harmony with that view of the parousia, Jesus' parallel statement, in Luke 17:26, says: "Moreover, just as it occurred in the days of Noah, so it will be also in the days of the Son of man." But just as the days of Noah's building the ark led up to the entry of him and his immediate family into that tremendous structure, so the invisible parousia

5. (a) The "days of Noah" for building the ark are also shown to be limited by what fact? (b) The comparison made with the "days of Noah" proves what about the meaning of parousia?

runs for a period of time and comes to a climax in a global "great tribulation."

⁶ In Noah's days the earth was filled with violence and was being ruined. (Genesis 6:11, 12) That, of course, was bad, wrong! But Jesus did not refer to that in showing the resemblance between the days of Noah and the days of his parousia or "presence." Jesus said: "They were eating, they were drinking, men were marrying, women were being given in marriage, until that day when Noah entered into the ark, and the flood arrived and destroyed them all." (Luke 17:27) Such things mentioned were right and proper in themselves. Well, then, what was the wrong thing on the part of the people? It was that they became absorbed in those common, everyday things, and evidenced no faith in Noah's message from God and did not take seriously Noah's backing up his message as absolutely true by building the ark in demonstration of his faith. (Hebrews 11:7) That this was the wrong thing on the part of the people, Jesus said: "And they took no note until the flood came and swept them all away."—Matthew 24:39.

⁷ The people destroyed in the global deluge were condemned for their unrighteous lack of faith. They were ungodly. Consequently, God "did not hold back from punishing an ancient world, but kept Noah, a preacher of righteousness, safe with seven others when he brought a deluge upon a world of ungodly people." (2 Peter 2:5) Jesus' prophecy, "So the presence of the Son of man will be," prompts us to examine the doings and attitude of the people today during his parousia, his unseen "presence." Does Jehovah God find the same absence of faith upon them? The same absorbing concern for the ordinary, everyday procedures of life, eating, drinking, marrying and being given in marriage, with indifference toward what a small group, comparable to Noah and seven family

---

6. (a) In what way, as Jesus said, would the days of Noah resemble the time of his parousia? (b) What, then, was wrong on the part of the people?
7. (a) For what were the people who were destroyed in the Flood condemned, and due to what? (b) How has the same feature on the part of the people been demonstrated since 1914?

members, are saying and doing? Well, for nearly sixty years now, since the beginning of Christ's parousia in 1914 C.E., Jehovah's "chosen ones" and, latterly, a "great crowd" of other sheeplike persons have been proclaiming world wide God's established kingdom and the oncoming "great tribulation," but the people in general have shown no serious concern.

⁸ In Noah's time, during the final week before the deluge, the specimens of the animals and birds that were to be preserved were brought into the ark. On the last day of that crucial week, on the seventeenth day of the second month (Noah's calendar) of the year 2370 B.C.E., Noah and his seven family members themselves entered the ark. "After that Jehovah shut the door behind him." (Genesis 7:1-16) This action shut Noah and his family in for salvation, but the preoccupied people out for destruction. Jesus makes this a warning example for all his disciples who are living in these days of his parousia or "presence." Far be it from us, therefore, to imitate this world of ungodly people in their selfish inattentiveness and faithless indifference! Failure to take note and to act according to the fulfillment of Jesus' prophecy could signify nothing but destruction for us with the unbelieving world. The destructive "great tribulation" will catch the unwary at an unannounced, not now known day and hour.

SELECTED FOR LIFE OR FOR DESTRUCTION

⁹ At that time the salvation will be selective and the destruction will be selective, even with regard to close associates in secular affairs, like farming in a field or grinding grain at home. Said Jesus: "Then two men will be in the field: one will be taken along and the other be abandoned; two women will be grinding at the hand mill: one will be taken along and the other be abandoned." (Matthew 24:40, 41) Weeks

8. (a) On what day of the final week did Noah and his family enter the ark to stay, and what then fixed matters? (b) Against what failure on our part today is this a warning?
9. (a) How did Jesus show that the salvation would be selective and the destruction would be selective? (b) In what way is it important to be sharp-sighted like the eagles?

before this prophecy, when Jesus made a similar statement, his listeners asked him: "Where, Lord?" He answered: "Where the body is, there also the eagles will be gathered together." (Luke 17:34-37) So the ones "taken along" for salvation will be the spiritually sharp-sighted ones, like eagles, who gather to the spiritual feast that Jehovah provides within his place of safety. The ones abandoned to destruction will be those who do not keep spiritually aware of the fulfillment of Jesus' prophecy and who indifferently pursue their selfish way of life. These, seeking to preserve their human souls by worldly means, will lose their souls in the sudden "great tribulation."

¹⁰ We dare not be like the worldly people, even those of Christendom, who resemble the self-absorbed people of Noah's days. In our interest Jesus emphasized the lesson of his illustration, saying: "Keep on the watch, therefore, because you do not know on what day your Lord is coming [Greek: er'khe·tai]." (Matthew 24:42) If we believe in the Lord's parousia since 1914 C.E., there is all the more reason for us to keep awake and on guard lest we be overtaken by the "great tribulation" wrongly occupied.

¹¹ The Lord Jesus did not inform his disciples of the exact day and hour of the particular month of the certain year when he is coming (Greek: er'khe·tai) as Jehovah's executional officer at the "great tribulation such as has not occurred since the world's beginning." He is not letting any of his disciples know of the precise time, so that they can be careless and occupy themselves with worldly pursuits until almost the last minute, and then immediately before the known precise time take on a form of godliness and busy themselves in God's commanded service. Not so! But the failure to advise us of the precise date enforces upon us the need to stay continually on the alert. Our being overtaken by the "great tribulation" as by a

10. How did Jesus here emphasize that we should not be like the worldly people, self-absorbed?
11, 12. (a) Why did Jesus not tell his disciples the precise time of his coming as Jehovah's executional officer to the "great tribulation"? (b) Our being overtaken by the "great tribulation" as by a thief at night will mean what for us, as shown by Jesus' illustration?

thief will mean an eternal loss if we are not active in God's pure worship. Hence, Jesus said:

¹² "But know one thing, that if the householder had known in what watch [of the night] the thief was coming, he would have kept awake and not allowed his house to be broken into. On this account you too prove yourselves ready, because at an hour that you do not think to be it, the Son of man is coming [Greek: *er'khe·tai*]."—Matthew 24:43, 44.

¹³ What is the purpose of this leaving of his disciples uncertain as to the precise time of the Lord's coming to execute the vengeance of Jehovah or to mete out justice upon this system of things, religious and political and social? It is to require all who claim to be Christ's disciples to prove whether they are genuine everyday Christians all the time, continually occupied in preaching the good news of God's Messianic kingdom and constantly exerting themselves in making "disciples of people of all the nations," or are merely opportunists. That is, do they wait until they see that there is no longer any time to delay but now at last they must get busy as if they had always been wholly taken up with God's approved work? Since it is "at an hour that you do not think to be it" that "the Son of man is coming," it behooves us to be awake and active at *all* hours in the worship and service that our Lord approves.

"THE FAITHFUL AND DISCREET SLAVE"

¹⁴ Here the Lord Jesus has got onto the subject of watchfulness and preparedness as required of his disciples. So he now raises a question that challenges each one of his disciples regarding his personal devotion to Jehovah's Messiah and personal use of prudence, foresight and insight in service to the Messiah. Each disciple could determine for himself what kind of slave he wanted to be as he heard the Master ask the

13. (a) What is the purpose of leaving the disciples uncertain as to the precise time when the Lord comes to execute Jehovah's vengeance? (b) So what does this behoove us to do about it?
14. What question did Jesus here raise, leaving his listeners to determine what they cared to be?

question: "Who really is the faithful and discreet slave whom his master appointed over his domestics, to give them their food at the proper time?"—Matthew 24:45.

[15] Knowing, as he did, from the inspired prophecies of his Father's Word that there would be rebellious apostates from the true Christian faith and service, Jesus quite properly raised this searching question that affects each disciple of his. But, by the form of his question, was he speaking about a particular man, an individual disciple of his? Or was he speaking with reference to a class of disciples? *The Critical and Exegetical Hand-Book to the Gospel of Matthew*, by H. A. W. Meyer, Th.D., (1884) makes a suggestion. On page 429, it says regarding the expression "who therefore" (*AV*): "Considering the necessity for preparedness thus indicated. The inference itself is presented in the form of an allegory, the *doûlos* [slave] representing the disciples whom the Lord has appointed to be the guides of His church, in which they are required to show themselves *faithful* (1 Cor. iv. 1 f.) and *prudent*, . . . " This limiting the "slave" to the twelve apostles, however, might allow for the doctrine of an *apostolic succession* or an episcopal succession, a succession of bishops (overseers) by the religious process of ordination.

[16] However, when we view the "faithful and discreet slave" as being the *whole* body of disciples (including spiritual overseers), it eliminates such a thing as "episcopal succession" that history shows has worked such harm and oppression in Christendom. The way in which the disciple Mark words Jesus' discussion of this matter indicates that the *entire* body of disciples is involved. Mark 13:34-36 says: "It is like a man traveling abroad that left his house and gave the authority to his slaves, to each one his work, and commanded the doorkeeper to keep on the watch. Therefore keep

15. (a) Why did Jesus raise the question regarding a slave that would be faithful? (b) What question arises as to the identity of the slave, and what does Meyer's *Hand-Book* on Matthew have to say about this? 16. As to whether the "slave" class includes the *whole* body of disciples, not just overseers, what does Mark 13:34-36 say?

on the watch, for you do not know when the master of the house is coming [Greek: *er'khe·tai*], whether late in the day or at midnight or at cockcrowing or early in the morning; in order that when he arrives suddenly, he does not find you sleeping."

¹⁷ It might sound somewhat harsh that Jesus should liken his disciples to "slaves." But there was a proper basis for this classification for them, for we read, in 1 Corinthians 6:20 and 7:23: "You were bought with a price. By all means, glorify God in the body of you people." "You were bought with a price; stop becoming slaves of men." Besides those words of the apostle Paul, the apostle Peter wrote to the Christians: "You know that it was not with corruptible things, with silver or gold, that you were delivered from your fruitless form of conduct received by tradition from your forefathers. But it was with precious blood, like that of an unblemished and spotless lamb, even Christ's." (1 Peter 1:18, 19) In accord with this, this disciple of Christ opened up his second letter with this introduction: "Simon Peter, a slave and apostle of Jesus Christ." Also, Paul did not feel embarrassed when introducing himself as "Paul and Timothy, slaves of Christ Jesus." (Philippians 1:1) And a fleshly half brother of the Lord introduced his letter with the words: "Jude, a slave of Jesus Christ, but a brother of James." (Jude 1) Slavehood on such a basis makes Christian faithfulness all the more obligatory.

¹⁸ No objection to Christian slavedom was raised by Christ's disciples on account of any mistreatment as in the objection made regarding the mistreatment of the nation of Israel: "Is Israel a servant, or a slave born in the household? Why is it that he has come to be for plunder?" (Jeremiah 2:14) The ancient nation of Israel came to be "for plunder" by the Gentiles because the Israelites failed to act as faithful servants of the Most High God, Jehovah. Because of Jehovah's redemption of them from ancient Egypt, the whole

17. Why was it not harsh on Jesus' part to liken his disciples to "slaves," but what did their slavehood make obligatory?
18. Why was ancient Israel a nation of servants to Jehovah, and how did he liken all those servants to a single person?

people of Israel was a nation of servants of Jehovah. When telling Pharaoh of Egypt concerning the special claim that Jehovah had upon the nation of Israel, He likened this chosen nation to a single person, saying: "Israel is my son, my firstborn. And I say to you: Send my son away that he may serve me."—Exodus 4:22, 23.

[19] More than seven centuries later, Jehovah speaks to the whole nation of Israel as if it were a single individual servant of His, saying: "But you, O Israel, are my servant, you, O Jacob, whom I have chosen, the seed of Abraham my friend; you, whom I have taken hold of from the extremities of the earth, and you, whom I have called even from the remote parts of it. And so I said to you, 'You are my servant; I have chosen you, and I have not rejected you.')" (Isaiah 41:8, 9) To make clear that this composite "servant" is made up of many individuals, the Creator says to the nation of Israel: "'You are my witnesses,' is the utterance of Jehovah, 'even my servant whom I have chosen.' . . . And now listen, O Jacob my servant, and you, O Israel, whom I have chosen. This is what Jehovah has said, . . . 'Have I not from that time on caused you individually to hear and told it out? And you are my witnesses.'"—Isaiah 43:10; 44:1-8; also 42:19; 44:21; 48:20; 49:3; Jeremiah 30:10.

[20] At the Festival of Pentecost of the year 33 C.E., fifty days from the resurrection of Jesus Christ from the dead, the circumcised nation of natural Israel was cast off by Jehovah God. But about the years 50-52 the Christian apostle Paul wrote to his Christian brothers in the Roman province of Galatia and said: "Neither is circumcision anything nor is uncircumcision, but a new creation is something. And all those who will walk orderly by this rule of conduct, upon them be peace and mercy, even upon the Israel of God." (Galatians 6:15, 16) The true Christian congregation was the organization that walked orderly by

19. How did Jehovah speak through Isaiah to the nation of Israel as a single individual slave of His?
20. When was natural Israel rejected, and who became a spiritual Israel, and why do the words of Isaiah 43:10 apply to it?

that rule regarding a "new creation," and now, since natural Israel's being rejected, the congregation of Christ's followers was "the Israel of God." It was a spiritual Israel. As a united congregation it was the "servant" of Jehovah God and his Christ. To it in a spiritual way Isaiah 43:10 could be directed: " 'You are my witnesses,' is the utterance of Jehovah, 'even my servant.' "

21 Although raising the question about the "faithful and discreet slave," Jesus was in no doubt about who this "slave" was. Jesus doubtless had in mind that "servant" of Jehovah God, that "Israel of God." There would be no mistake in fixing upon that composite "servant." With the price of his own blood he had bought that Israel of God as his slave, and in the illustration given in his prophecy he could refer to it as a composite "slave," one that would prove "faithful and discreet." Since Jesus spoke of this "slave" in his prophecy concerning the "sign of [his] presence and of the conclusion of the system of things," did that composite "faithful and discreet slave" first come into existence during his "presence" or parousia from 1914 onward?

22 No; for Jesus' illustration portrays the lord of the "slave" as going away, as a "man traveling abroad that left his house and gave the authority to his slaves." (Mark 13:34) So the "faithful and discreet slave" is one "whom his master appointed over his domestics, to give them their food at the proper time." (Matthew 24:45) It was more than nineteen hundred years ago, at his ascension to heaven, that the "master" of the composite "slave" went away, leaving the "slave" with instructions to feed the "domestics." (Matthew 28:16-20) The "domestics" were not the family of the master but were his "domestic servants" (H. A. W. Meyer) or his "household staff." (New English Bible) They were slaves, just the same as

---

21. (a) Though Jesus raised the question about him, did Jesus know who that composite "slave" was? (b) What question do we ask about when that "slave" class began?
22. (a) Why could the "faithful and discreet slave" class not have come into existence first during Christ's parousia? (b) Who were the "domestics" whom the "slave" had to feed?

the "faithful and discreet slave" charged with feeding them. Thus they were all a body of slaves, and were all subject to the same "master." All were obligated to be "faithful and discreet."

[23] Jesus' illustration began fulfillment at his departure in the year 33 C.E., and the composite "slave" has been existing since then, namely, "the Israel of God," the spirit-begotten, anointed congregation of Christ the membership of which will finally reach 144,000. (Revelation 7:4-8; 14:1-3) The historical records show that at the beginning of the invisible parousia of the "master" at the end of the Gentile Times in 1914 there was still a remnant of this "slave" class on earth. Consequently, the composite "slave" has lived to see the "sign" of the Master's parousia or "presence."

"GIVE THEM THEIR FOOD AT THE PROPER TIME"

[24] In this parable the "slave" was not given silver "talents" with which to do business. So here we are not talking about spiritual "talents." The appointed "slave" was specially made responsible for giving his fellow "domestics" their food at the proper time. They needed food regularly, the same as the appointed "slave" did, in order to be strengthened for their work in the master's house. If the master's number of domestics was large, the appointed "slave" would not be going to all of them individually and serving each one his meals directly. More sensibly, the "slave" would see to it that the food was made available and that it was served to all the "domestics" or "household staff." Some of the "domestics" would aid in the serving of the meals to their fellow domestics. It is not odd, then, that the domestics should be helping in the feeding of one another.

[25] No sooner did the spiritual "food" become avail-

23. (a) So when did the existence of that composite "slave" begin? (b) What shows that such "slave" lived to see the "sign" of his master's parousia?
24. What was that "slave" appointed to do, and why might "domestics" be used in having it done?
25. At what "proper time" did the "slave" class begin to serve the "food," to whom, and with what result that day?

able "at the proper time" on the festival day of
Pentecost of 33 C.E., than the appointed "slave" class
proved itself "faithful and discreet" by passing out
the "food" under the inspiration of God's outpoured
spirit. The congregation of about 120 disciples began
talking among themselves about the "magnificent
things of God." But that small original congregation
did not keep those "things" to themselves. Thousands
of spiritually hungry ones, who professed to be servants of Jehovah God, gathered to listen to these
"things." The apostle Peter took the lead in feeding
those spiritually hungry Jews and proselytes who were
at Jerusalem for the celebrating of the now out-of-date
festival of Pentecost. At heart they wanted to become
"domestics" of the Messianic "master," and they
needed to be fed to become such. At this "proper
time" it was that the "faithful and discreet slave" class
fed them. As a result, about three thousand of them
became believers, got baptized and received the gift
of the holy spirit. Now they were indeed "domestics"
of the Master, but still needed more food.—Acts 2:1-42.

²⁶ Less than three and a half years later the feeding
efforts of the "faithful and discreet slave" class were
extended to other prospective "domestics." These were
to be from "people of all the nations," non-Jews,
Gentiles. The apostle Peter was used to take the lead
in this and was sent under divine guidance to the city
of Caesarea on the eastern Mediterranean seacoast to
convert the Italian centurion Cornelius and the interested ones whom he had gathered into his house.
(Acts 10:1 to 11:18) Thus the door was flung open
wide for Gentiles to become "domestics" of the Messianic Master, Jesus Christ. The "faithful and discreet
slave" class had to go to these prospective "domestics"
with the spiritual food and feed them, that they might
become spiritual Israelites, members of the Israel of
God. After these became spiritual "domestics," they
also had to join in the feeding work. This was in

26, 27. (a) When the feeding program was widened out, who was used to
do the feeding of the prospective "domestics"? (b) This was in harmony with what command of the Master before his going away?

obedience to the Master's command not long before his departure:

27 "Go therefore and make disciples of people of all the nations, baptizing them in the name of the Father and of the Son and of the holy spirit, teaching them to observe all the things I have commanded you. And, look! I am with you all the days until the conclusion of the system of things."—Matthew 28:19, 20.

28 To give lasting aid in the spiritual feeding work, apostles and disciples of Jesus Christ were inspired by God's spirit to write the twenty-seven authentic books of the Christian Greek Scriptures, from the Gospel of Matthew to Revelation. This luscious portion of the spiritual food served to the Christian "domestics" by the "faithful and discreet slave" class of the first century remains available to Christian "domestics" of this twentieth century. This has made for a complete Holy Bible, of sixty-six inspired books, thirty-nine in Hebrew and Aramaic and twenty-seven in first-century common Greek. The whole Bible is needed, not just the inspired Christian Greek Scriptures. When the "faithful and discreet slave" class started out in the first century, it had only the inspired Hebrew-Aramaic Scriptures as spiritual food in writing on which to feed. What the Christian "domestics" then fed on at the start, we need to feed on still today. The original congregation at Jerusalem spoke and read Hebrew. We today need translations of the Hebrew Scriptures.

29 As to just how the "faithful and discreet slave" class existed and served down through the centuries after the death of the apostles of the Master Jesus Christ, we do not have a distinct historical picture. Apparently one generation of the "slave" class fed the next succeeding generation thereof. (2 Timothy 2:2) But in the latter half of the nineteenth century there were God-fearing persons who loved the spiritual food of the Holy Bible and who desired to feed on it, not

---

28. (a) What lasting portion of spiritual food, still available today, was provided in the first century C.E.? (b) Do we today need the spiritual food that the "slave" class fed on at its start?
29. (a) After the first century C.E., how did the feeding work by the "slave" class continue? (b) In the latter half of the nineteenth century, how did a feeding work get under way?

merely entertain themselves by reading it as sacred
literature. Bible study classes apart from the Sunday
Schools and churches of Christendom were formed
and progressed in the understanding of the funda-
mental truths of the Sacred Scriptures. The sincere
unselfish ones among these Bible students were eager
to share these vital portions of spiritual food with
others. They had the faithful spirit of the "slave" appointed to give the "domestics" the needed spiritual
"food at the proper time." They were "discreet" in
discerning that it was then the right and proper time
and what were the best means for serving the food.
They endeavored to serve it.

[30] A "ransom for all" was one of those basic doctrines
of the Bible, and a great danger began to loom up
that this vital dish on the spiritual table of God-fearing
persons would be taken away by the devotees of
higher criticism and the evolution theory. At what
can now be appreciated as "the proper time" there
appeared an uncompromising champion of Christ's
"ransom for all." It was in the form of a brand-new
magazine for Bible lovers, *Zion's Watch Tower and
Herald of Christ's Presence,* its first issue being that
of July, 1879, with an initial edition of 6,000 copies.
Its editor and publisher was a member of the Pittsburgh, Pennsylvania, Bible study group, namely,
Charles Taze Russell. This studious Christian took note
of Jesus' illustration of the "faithful and wise servant"
(Matthew 24:45, *Authorized Version*) and published
his understanding of it in the *Watch Tower* issue of
November, 1881, page 5. In the fourth- and fifth-last
paragraphs of the article "In the Vineyard," he said:

> We believe that every member of this body of Christ is
> engaged in the blessed work, either directly or indirectly,
> of giving meat in due season to the household of faith.
> "Who then is that *faithful* and *wise servant* whom his
> Lord hath made ruler over his household," to give them
> meat in due season? Is it not that "little flock" of conse-
> crated servants who are *faithfully* carrying out their con-

---

30. (a) What danger then existed with regard to the doctrine of a
"ransom for all," but what champion thereof was raised up at the
"proper time"? (b) What did the editor of the *Watch Tower* publish
about the "faithful and wise servant" back in 1881?

secration vows—the body of Christ—and is not the whole body individually and collectively, giving the meat in due season to the household of faith—the great company of believers?

Blessed is that servant (the whole body of Christ) whom his Lord when he has come (Gr. *elthon*) shall find so doing. "Verily, I say unto you, that he shall make him ruler over all his goods." "He shall inherit all things."

[31] From this it is clearly seen that the editor and publisher of *Zion's Watch Tower* disavowed any claim to being individually, in his person, that "faithful and wise servant." He never did claim to be such.[*] However, he did continue to edit the *Watch Tower* magazine down to the day of his death on October 31, 1916. He organized Zion's Watch Tower Tract Society in the year 1881 and got it incorporated under State of Pennsylvania law in December, 1884. He also authored and published the six volumes of *Studies in the Scriptures* during the years 1886-1904, as well as published many booklets on Bible themes and engineered the world-famous Photo-Drama of Creation, which began to be shown in January of 1914 and was thereafter displayed around the earth. He delivered innumerable public lectures all around the globe. His death occurred during his last public lecture tour across the United States of America. It cannot be successfully disputed that, till his death in 1916, he lovingly served as a part of the "faithful and discreet slave" class in giving to the Master's domestics "their food at the proper time."

[32] Since the "slave" of Jesus' illustration is not just one Christian man but is the anointed congregation of Christ's disciples, the "faithful and discreet slave" class continued to serve on after the death of C. T. Russell. However, the sense of appreciation and indebtedness toward Russell moved many of his associates to view him as the fulfillment of the "faithful

---

[*] See the book *The Battle of Armageddon,* published in 1897, page 613, under the heading "Dispensing of Food to the Household.—Matt. 24:45-51; Luke 12:42-46."

31. (a) What must be said as to whether C. T. Russell claimed to be the "faithful and wise servant"? (b) What record proves that he served as a faithful part of that "servant" class?
32. After Russell's death, how did a sectarian trend toward him develop, but when was this halted, and how?

and discreet slave." This view was prominently featured in the book published in July of 1917 by People's Pulpit Association of Brooklyn, New York. This book was called "The Finished Mystery" and furnished a commentary of the Bible books of Revelation and Ezekiel and The Song of Solomon. On its Publishers page the book was called the "Posthumous Work of Pastor Russell." Such a book and religious attitude tended to establish a religious sect centered around a man. Such a drift toward sectarianism was halted, however, by the publication early in 1927 of the articles "The Son and Servant" and "Servant—Good and Evil," in *The Watch Tower* under date of February 1 and 15, 1927. These articles showed that the "servant" of Matthew 24:45 was a composite one.—Isaiah 43:10-12.

[33] Later in the year 1927 any remaining stocks of the six volumes of *Studies in the Scriptures* by Russell and of *The Finished Mystery* were disposed of among the public. But did this leave the Lord's "domestics" or "household staff" without spiritual "food at the proper time"? Not by any means! Why not, we shall shortly see.

THE "HAPPY" SLAVE

[34] Did Jesus, in Matthew 24:45, raise the question regarding the "slave" that was appointed over his master's "domestics" to feed them and how this "slave" would prove his faithfulness and discreetness? In the very next verse (Matthew 24:46) Jesus also answers that question, saying: "Happy is that slave if his master on arriving [Greek: *elthòn*] finds him doing so." He proved his faithfulness to his master and his prudence by continuing to do what his master appointed him to do until his return, namely, "to give [the domestics] their food at the proper time." This was to result in great happiness for the "slave" at his master's return.

---

33. Did disposal of remaining stocks of Russell's books and of *The Finished Mystery* leave Christ's "domestics" with no "food"?
34. Who raised the question regarding the "faithful and discreet slave," and who answered it, and how?

35 Nineteen centuries ago, when the "faithful and discreet slave" class was first formed, it survived the turbulent period of time prophetically described by Jesus in Matthew 24:4-22, Mark 13:5-20 and Luke 21:8-24. More than twenty-five years after the destruction of Jerusalem by the Romans in 70 C.E., the apostle John wrote the Revelation and the Gospel and the three letters of John, all of these being written for the benefit of the "faithful and discreet slave" class and for the feeding of the "domestics" of the heavenly Master. In the year 1914 C.E. the remnant of the "faithful and discreet slave" class entered into the time of the complete or final fulfillment of Jesus' prophecy on the "sign of [his] presence and of the conclusion of the system of things." The events that Jesus foretold to characterize the typical time period from 33 C.E. to 70 C.E. began occurring also in 1914 C.E. The question now arose as to whether the "faithful and discreet slave" class would survive the hard things that were due to occur to correspond with what befell the "slave" class between 33 and 70 C.E.

36 The end of the Gentile Times about October 4/5 of 1914 found World War I already in progress for more than two months. This was something new, not only for the world of mankind, but also for the Master's "slave" class. World War I far exceeded in violence and destructiveness the foretold "wars and reports of wars" and the rise of nation against nation and of kingdom against kingdom such as marked the years after Jesus' ascension to heaven in 33 C.E. (Matthew 24:6, 7) World War conditions and restrictions made it very difficult for the "faithful and discreet slave" class to continue on giving to the "domestics" of the heavenly Master "their food at the proper time." The situation worsened for them until finally many of the domestics were in prison or military encampments

---

35. (a) Back in the first century, what turbulent period foretold in Jesus' prophecy did the "slave" class survive, and what did John write at the end of the century? (b) Correspondingly, when the Gentile Times ended in 1914, what question arose about the "slave" class?
36. During World War I, how difficult did it become for the "slave" class to feed the "domestics," but what about the *Watch Tower* magazine?

and officials of the Watch Tower Bible and Tract Society and members of the editorial staff of *The Watch Tower* were imprisoned in the Atlanta Federal Penitentiary, under heavy sentences, in the summer of 1918 C.E. In spite of this *The Watch Tower and Herald of Christ's Presence* continued to be published, not from Brooklyn but from its original location, Pittsburgh, Pennsylvania.

[37] That was the distressing situation that existed when World War I ended on November 11, 1918. Easy international communications between the Watch Tower Society headquarters and its foreign branches had been broken up or impeded. Bible literature was either under official government ban or withdrawn from circulation among the people. Printers' plates that had been used in the publishing of Bible tracts had somehow been destroyed or lost. What, now, were the prospects ahead of the Master's "slave" class? What was this "slave" class resolved to do in the then opening postwar period?

TIME OF INSPECTION BY THE SLAVE'S MASTER

[38] Without a question of doubt, it was a real time for inspection of the Master's "slave" class. All the facts of the case argue that the Master came for the work of inspection at the time. Such a thing was to be expected according to the prophecy of Malachi 3:1-5. Of course, the sectarian churches of Christendom had made a wartime record for themselves, an open record that had a heavy bearing on their claim to be disciples and slaves of Jesus Christ. Could they, by even their latest record down till 1919, prove that they themselves were the composite "faithful and discreet slave" class of the heavenly Lord and Master, Jesus Christ? He as Judge would indicate what his findings were by the way he thereafter dealt with the hundreds of religious sects of Christendom. Appropriately, now, our attention

37. What was the distressing situation of the "slave" class at the end of World War I, and what question arose about it?
38. Appropriate to the time of inspection then due, what questions arose respecting the religious sects of Christendom and regarding Christians internationally hated?

focuses upon those sincere, Bible-studying Christians who, during World War I, were persecuted for their obedience to Christ and who became "objects of hatred by all the nations" on account of Christ's name. Since they also came under divine inspection, what did the Master show to be his decision on them?

39 According to Jesus' illustration, how did the master who appointed the slave return to his house? Was it in great rage in order to destroy the house? Or was it to enjoy his homecoming and to see how things had been going on during his absence? His return to his house was a peaceful one. He did not come to engage in the "war of the great day of God the Almighty" at Har–Magedon. (Revelation 16:13-16) Rather, he wanted to make sure that his domestic affairs were in the right condition. Had his appointed slave done as he was assigned to do, namely, give to the "domestics" their "food at the proper time"? The master needed to make an inspection.

40 The serving of food, the right sort of food, at the proper time was the issue. It had to be according to this that a decision must be rendered by the returned master. Well, then, what about that body of Christians internationally hated and persecuted? (Matthew 24:9) Down to 1919 C.E. they had endeavored to give "food at the proper time" to the "household of faith" or the "domestics" of the heavenly Master. They did this despite interference by persecutors and the warring nations. Not only was the regularity in serving the spiritual food a problem, but the quality of the food itself was to be considered. In this respect the body of hated, persecuted Christians, who always sought to be faithful slaves of Jesus Christ, met the test. During the years of the world conflict they had not joined Christendom or pagandom in preaching the war propaganda submitted by the political governments. They persisted in preaching the Bible message for the time

39. According to Jesus' parable, in what frame of mind did the master return home, and with what purpose in mind?
40. Since the serving of food regularly, and the right kind of food, was the issue on which to base a decision, what did the returned Master find concerning the persecuted, hated Christians?

and in advocating a Christian adherence to Bible principles for everybody.

41 What, then, did the heavenly Master decide regarding these obedient slaves of his? He was not influenced by their unpopular, persecuted position in the war-mad world, for he had foretold such a hard experience for them during his invisible parousia or "presence." Did he find that body of Christian slaves disregarding the unpopularity of the world and seeking to be pleasing to their Master by doing what he had appointed to be done during his absence? He must have found them so, according to the way the inspection, begun in 1919, has affected his decision since. His actions, his dealings with his Christian slaves, speak louder than words.

42 Let us reflect a moment on the case of Jesus' apostles. Three and a half years after being baptized in the Jordan River, Jesus Christ was betrayed in the garden of Gethsemane. He quoted from the prophecy of Zechariah 13:7 and foretold what would happen to his apostles, saying: "All of you will be stumbled in connection with me on this night, for it is written, 'I will strike the shepherd, and the sheep of the flock will be scattered about.' But after I have been raised up, I will go ahead of you into Galilee.'" (Matthew 26:31, 32) Jesus' application of Zechariah's prophecy to his apostles proved true on that same night of Nisan 14, 33 C.E., for the account in Matthew 26:56 tells what occurred after Jesus' betrayal: "Then all the disciples abandoned him and fled." His "sheep" were indeed scattered.

43 In parallel fashion, three and a half years after the close of the Gentile Times and Christ's enthronement in the heavens in 1914 C.E., there came the annual celebration of the Lord's Supper on Tuesday, March 26, 1918. The scattering of the heavenly Shepherd's "sheep" was then nearing its climax, and *The*

41. When inspecting such Christians, by what was the Master not influenced, and how has his decision expressed itself since?
42, 43. (a) On the night of being betrayed, Jesus applied what prophecy to his apostles, and how was it fulfilled? (b) Three and a half years after Jesus' enthronement in 1914, how was the same prophecy of Zechariah 13:7 being fulfilled?

Watch Tower, under date of March 1, 1918, in its first paragraph of the leading article "In Memory of Our King," said: "Whether the coming Memorial will be the last on earth, we do not, of course, know; but we do know that we are one year nearer the full consummation of our hopes. If it please the Lord to have us celebrate this Memorial other years, then we shall do so gladly." The outlook blackened as prominent ones of the Watch Tower Society who had to do with the feeding of the heavenly Shepherd's "sheep" were arrested, unfairly tried and sentenced to many years in Federal Penitentiary. It was not then appreciated that Zechariah 13:7 was being fulfilled.

[44] However, there was a bright side to this prophecy. It not only foretold the striking of the shepherd and the scattering of the sheep but also added Jehovah's promise: "And I shall certainly turn my hand back upon those who are insignificant." That meant a turning back of Jehovah's hand upon the scattered sheep with favor. And so Jesus, after quoting from the prophecy about the scattering of the sheep, reassured his apostles by adding: "But after I have been raised up, I will go ahead of you into Galilee." (Matthew 26:32) This meant that, after his resurrection from the dead, he would regather them. This actually took place, and concerning this we read: "The eleven disciples went into Galilee to the mountain where Jesus had arranged for them, and when they saw him they did obeisance, but some doubted. And Jesus approached and spoke to them, saying: 'All authority has been given me in heaven and on the earth. Go therefore and make disciples of people of all the nations, baptizing them in the name of the Father and of the Son and of the holy spirit, teaching them to observe all the things I have commanded you.'"—Matthew 28:16-20.

[45] Similarly, in the year 1919, Jehovah did "turn [his] hand back upon those who are insignificant."

---

44. (a) What did the bright side of Zechariah's prophecy say and mean? (b) How was this part of the prophecy fulfilled upon Jesus' apostles?
45. How was this same prophecy fulfilled upon the faithful "slave" class in 1919, and how was this "slave" made "happy"?

(Zechariah 13:7) Jehovah's Shepherd-King, Jesus Christ, did begin regathering the scattered "sheep." Like the slave's master in the illustration, the Lord Jesus did return to his house and inspect the situation within it. He did find there a "faithful and discreet slave" class that was striving, in spite of world conditions, to do as commanded, give the Lord's "domestics" at the proper time their spiritual food, food taken from the inspired Word of God. So the Lord showed his favor by regathering them into a well-organized body of "domestics" in his house. The eight-day general convention held at Cedar Point, Ohio, on September 1-8, 1919, was a notification to all the world that the invisibly present Lord Jesus Christ was regathering his faithful "sheep." It indicated to the world who it was that the returned Lord Jesus had found to be his "faithful and discreet slave" class. This made the "slave" class happy. It meant their being retained in the service of their heavenly Master.

46 The Lord Jesus explained why the state of the "faithful and discreet slave" was a happy one, for Jesus said: "Happy is that slave if his master on arriving [Greek: *elthòn*] finds him doing so. Truly I say to you, He will appoint him over all his belongings." —Matthew 24:46, 47; Luke 12:42-44.

APPOINTED OVER ALL THE MASTER'S BELONGINGS

47 The Lord Jesus pronounced the "faithful and discreet slave" happy because of what awaited him as a reward for his doing as his master appointed him to do. He gets a promotion, with larger responsibilities toward the master to whom he is so faithful. This is so, doubtless, because his master has also been clothed with larger responsibilities. Certainly the master does not leave his house and go on a journey as a mere touring sightseer or for his health. He had a more serious objective in mind, one that would enhance his position and increase his power and authority. And when we

46. Jesus explained that the faithful "slave" was "happy" in view of what reward?
47. The promotion of the faithful "slave" lays what upon him, and how does this agree with the new capacity of his master?

consider that Jesus was making an illustration here that applied to his departing to heaven to receive a kingdom after a long wait at his Father's right hand, we know that this increase in the master's responsibilities is implied in the illustration. The master is to be understood as returning home in a new and larger capacity. (Hebrews 10:12, 13) Hence "all his belongings" take on a larger value. So the promoted "slave" shares honors with his lord.

[48] In the fulfillment of the prophetic illustration, the "master," the Lord Jesus Christ, did obtain a heavenly kingdom when the "appointed times of the nations" ended in 1914 C.E. So his invisible parousia or "presence" began in that year with him as crowned reigning King on the heavenly throne. When he returned to his "household staff" in 1919 to make an inspection of all his "domestics," he did so in a royal capacity such as he had not possessed when he was down here on earth in the first century. This put the "faithful and discreet slave" class in the service of a personage who had greater rank, authority and power than the one whom they had been serving hitherto. This made service to him much more important now. It was a higher honor now to be in his service. And for one to receive a promotion from him and thereby be entrusted with heavier responsibilities was a reward indeed!

[49] In the illustration, before the master departs, he gives a limited responsibility to the one who is expected to be a "faithful and discreet slave." He appoints this slave over only his domestics or household staff with the obligation to give them their due food at the proper time. Consequently, when, at his return, the master appoints the approved slave "over all his belongings," it signifies larger obligations for the promoted slave. Now he can demonstrate his faithfulness and discreetness in a larger way, for he has supervision over more things. He becomes a prized slave.

48. Why was the service committed to the "slave" class by their returned Master more important and honorable than the former service?
49. The returned master's appointing of the "slave" to be "over all his belongings" signified what for the slave, with what opportunity for him?

⁵⁰ In the fulfillment of the illustration, "all his belongings" over which the master appoints the worthy slave do not picture all his belongings up in heaven. The glorified Master, Jesus Christ, to whom "all authority" in heaven and on the earth has been given, is not incapable of taking care of all his "belongings" up in the invisible heavens where his holy angels are in his service. "All his belongings" over which the "faithful and discreet slave" class is appointed must refer to all the spiritual things that belong to him on earth in connection with his established heavenly kingdom. It does not mean any part in the political governments of this world as if the King Jesus Christ were now running and controlling all these man-made political institutions. Those institutions are doomed to destruction. "All his belongings" therefore mean the performing of a role on earth in the fulfillment of the prophecies that apply since the establishment of the Kingdom in the heavens in 1914 C.E.

⁵¹ On inspecting the remnant of his anointed disciples in the year 1919 C.E., the reigning King Jesus Christ did find the appointed "slave" faithful and discreet in the feeding of his "domestics." Accordingly, he appointed this "slave" class over all his belongings. Their enlarged responsible position now was that of serving in fulfillment of the now due Kingdom prophecies. All through the centuries the "faithful and discreet slave" class has been made up of those who are "ambassadors substituting for Christ," which ambassadors make an entreaty to people to become reconciled to God through Christ. (2 Corinthians 5:19, 20) Since their appointment in 1919, however, they are ambassadors of the inaugurated Messianic kingdom, with a Kingdom message that has taken on new meaning and force. (Matthew 24:14; Mark 13:10) Theirs is the privilege and responsibility to lend themselves as instruments for the carrying out of the Kingdom prophecies that have their finalizing fulfillment since 1914

50. "All his belongings" refer to those where, and what are they?
51. How is the ambassadorship of the faithful "slave" class larger now than formerly, and what privilege and responsibility toward prophecy do they now have?

C.E. What an honor it is for them to be used in the working out of what the book of Revelation foretells with all its marvelous symbolisms and its glorious news about the thousand-year reign of Christ!

[52] All these are privileges, responsibilities, dignities and honors that have been reserved for the remnant of the "faithful and discreet slave" class and that are bestowed upon them by their heavenly Master, the reigning King Jesus Christ. No wonder they can be pronounced "happy"! Their being charged with these precious things denotes an elevation of them indeed. It resembles the picture presented in Revelation 11:11, 12 concerning the "two witnesses" killed by the enemy, whose dead bodies lay exposed in the broad way of the Sodom-like "great city" for three and a half days: "And after the three and a half days spirit of life from God entered into them, and they stood upon their feet, and great fear fell upon those beholding them. And they heard a loud voice out of heaven say to them: 'Come on up here.' And they went up into heaven in the cloud, and their enemies beheld them."

[53] Their being charged with such elevated privileges and responsibilities has meant more work for those making up the composite "faithful and discreet slave." It has called for more time and attention on their part, also for the use of larger facilities for getting the work done in order that the Bible prophecies concerning this Kingdom work on earth fail not. They have also had to work over a larger field, all parts of the inhabited earth. (Revelation 14:6, 7; 10:11) Of course, the feeding program toward the Lord's "domestics" has had to continue on. And with what a spiritual table of Scriptural food they have been fed! The disposing of any remaining stocks of the *Studies in the Scriptures* by C. T. Russell and of *The Finished Mystery* in the year 1927 produced no shortage of spiritual food for these "domestics." New and up-to-date bound books

---

52. How was this an elevation of position for the "slave" class, and how was this pictured in the book of Revelation?
53. (a) Why were the privileges and responsibilities of the "slave" class now greater? (b) How did the feeding of the "domestics" continue on despite the disposal of earlier publications?

and booklets and tracts have continued to be published since the book *The Harp of God* in 1921. Yes, in October of 1919 a companion to *The Watch Tower* was published in the form of the magazine *The Golden Age* (now entitled "Awake!").

[54] Added to the privileges and responsibilities of the rewarded "faithful and discreet slave" class was their working for the realization of the beautiful vision seen by the apostle John under inspiration and described by him in Revelation 7:9-17. Yes, since the year 1935 the "slave" class has seen that vision come to reality. Their blessed eyes see the numerically unlimited "great crowd" from everywhere over the earth praising and worshiping Jehovah God at his spiritual temple and crediting salvation to Him and to his Lamb, Jesus Christ. It has meant a great responsibility for the "faithful and discreet slave" class of spiritual Israelites to take care of this continually increasing "great crowd," but they realize that these sheeplike ones "out of all nations and tribes and peoples and tongues" are a precious part of "all his belongings" on the earth and so they are happy to take care of the spiritual needs of these "other sheep." In turn, this "great crowd" is assisting the "faithful and discreet slave" in taking care of all the Lord's earthly "belongings."

"IF THAT EVIL SLAVE"

[55] The Lord Jesus Christ will continue to have a "faithful and discreet slave" class down to the end of its happy service on earth. However, each spirit-begotten, anointed member of that "slave" class today must watch his conduct that he does not prove himself unfit to continue in that highly favored class. By failure to maintain his personal faithfulness and discreetness he would become like a man who turns out

54. To the "slave" class there has been added the privilege of working for the realization of what picture in Revelation, and how has this resulted in larger responsibility and yet with assistance?
55, 56. Why does each member of the "slave" class need to maintain his faithfulness and discreetness, in the light of what warning of Jesus?

to be an "evil slave." Jesus warned of this danger when he continued on with his illustration to say:

⁵⁶ "But if [ever] that evil slave should say in his heart, 'My master is delaying,' and should start to beat his fellow slaves and should eat and drink with the confirmed drunkards [literally, the (ones) getting drunk], the master of that slave will come [Greek: héxei] on a day that he does not expect and in an hour that he does not know, and will punish him with the greatest severity [literally, he will cut asunder him] and will assign him his part with the hypocrites. There is where his weeping and the gnashing of his teeth will be."—Matthew 24:48-51; Luke 12:45, 46; INT.

⁵⁷ When we take a close look at what Jesus here says, we notice that he does not here say that the departing "master" does appoint an "evil slave," to begin with; nor does he say that the "faithful and discreet slave" turns out bad, becomes "evil." He merely raises the question and says, "If ever" (as in Luke 12:45 and Interlinear reading in Matthew 24:48) the slave that was appointed over the domestics were to say, after his becoming "evil" at heart, that his master will yet be a long time in returning and were to start acting improperly, this is the way that his master would deal with him on returning. It would be far opposite from the slave's being put over all his master's belongings. So Jesus' suggestion here is, Suppose that the appointed slave would turn out bad and act unfaithfully and imprudently, what would happen to him when his master suddenly returned? It would be just as Jesus described. Jesus does not speak of the original appointed slave's turning out bad as a certainty or as very likely.

⁵⁸ Some modern translations of Jesus' words bring out that thought more clearly, by a bit of paraphrase. An American Translation says: "But if he is a bad slave and says to himself, 'My master is going to stay

---

57. (a) Does Jesus here say that the master does appoint an "evil slave" at the start, or that the appointed slave turns out bad? (b) By the way in which Jesus introduces the matter, what was Jesus showing?
58. (a) How do other modern translations render the passage by means of paraphrase? (b) If the "slave" class appointed by Jesus went bad, how would this outcome leave Jesus?

a long time,' and begins to beat the other slaves, and eats and drinks with the drunkards." (Matthew 24:48, 49) *The New English Bible* reads similarly. *The New American Bible* says: "But if the servant is worthless and tells himself," etc. *The New Testament in Modern Speech,* by R. F. Weymouth, says: "But, if the man, being a bad servant, should say in his heart," etc. The coming of an "evil slave" into existence is not definitely predicted by Jesus. He merely describes how an unfaithful and indiscreet slave would think, speak and act, and the punishment that he would receive from his master on his sudden returning. If the "slave" appointed by the Lord Jesus turned out bad, it would leave him without a "slave" to reward for his integrity. Jesus does not appoint two slave classes.

⁵⁹ Jesus, before his departure nineteen centuries ago, took care not to appoint a bad, evil, worthless "slave" over his "domestics." The record in the Christian Greek Scriptures proves that the appointed "slave" class did not turn out bad, and the prophecies thereof show that the "slave" class was not expected to turn out bad and would not do so. In his tried and proved apostles he laid the foundation for the building up of a body of faithful slaves. Revelation 7:3-8 foretells that a full 144,000 spiritual Israelites would be sealed as "the slaves of our God." Revelation 12:17 foretells that, after the dragon Satan the Devil is ousted from heaven, he would war upon the remnant of the "seed" of God's "woman," who "observe the commandments of God and have the work of bearing witness to Jesus." And Revelation 14:1-4 foretells that the entire number of 144,000 "that keep following the Lamb no matter where he goes" stand with him upon the Mount Zion. They "have been bought from the earth." "These were bought from among mankind as firstfruits to God and to the Lamb."

⁶⁰ If there is a class of spirit-begotten, anointed Christians who act according to the description of

59. (a) For what kind of "slave" class did Jesus lay the foundation? (b) Did the prophecies indicate that the "slave" class was meant to turn out bad or would do so, or otherwise?
60. (a) Were individuals who act like "that evil slave" appointed as such by the Master? (b) What do all such individuals form in general?

"that evil slave," it is not the Lord Jesus who appointed them and put them in charge of his domestics or "household staff." Individuals who were once members of the "faithful and discreet slave" class may break away for selfish reasons such as personal ambitions, power over others and self-indulgence. These self-seekers may form themselves into groups in pursuit of their goals. However, they would form one general class, separate and distinct from the "faithful and discreet" slave class.

[61] It is reasonable to believe that the Lord Jesus would not use an illustration without having some cases, or a general case, with which to furnish an example of what he meant, as far as conduct and the outcome thereof is concerned. This would illustrate, not that Jesus appointed "that evil slave" class or type of Christians, but that it really happens to unfaithful, unreliable, untrustworthy, indiscreet Christians during his invisible parousia or presence just as he described.

[62] There were instances of this in the ranks of the International Bible Students Association right after the death in 1916 C.E. of the editor of *The Watch Tower* and founder of the Watch Tower Bible and Tract Society. There were attempts on the part of some individuals to seize power and control contrary to the provisions of the Society's Charter. There were disagreements as to who made up the Lord's approved organization. The power-seeking ones and those dissatisfied with sincere efforts to conduct matters according to the legal Charter and Bible principles were frustrated. They indulged in considerable 'beating of their fellow slaves' in a verbal way in print and by word of mouth and in judicial court. They put themselves on the side of the "confirmed drunkards" of this world, spiritually speaking, especially during those days of World War I. All of this put the stability of the organization, which was then under increasing

---

61. What is it reasonable to say as to whether there would be cases that could be used to illustrate what Jesus said about the "evil slave"?
62. What instances of this were there, especially during World War I days, and how did this affect the "faithful and discreet slave" class?

religious persecution, to a great test. It brought a great trial upon the "faithful and discreet slave" class.

[63] Jesus' illustration gave the assurance that during his parousia or presence he would not permit any disloyal ones with the traits of "that evil slave" to break up his "household of faith" or to dominate it and turn it from its appointment to give his "domestics" their spiritual "food at the proper time." At his time of inspection he punished with the greatest severity such an evilly disposed class. Or, according to the literal meaning of the Greek verb used in Matthew 24:51: "He will cut him in two." (Marginal footnote) He "cut asunder" that class of misbehaving ones from the "faithful and discreet slave" class. This manifested itself in what appeared their strike for independence and withdrawing themselves and forming their own religious groups with a headship according to their liking. The outcome of their course of action is there for anyone who cares to investigate to do so.

[64] Such a class that was "cut asunder" displayed the characteristics and suffered the consequences of "that evil slave" described by Jesus and could, at least in a limited way, be called the "evil slave" class. In his illustration Jesus said that the master "will assign him his part with the hypocrites." (Matthew 24:51) In the corresponding illustration in which the "slave" is called a "steward," Jesus says: "He will . . . assign him a part with the unfaithful ones." (Luke 12:46) During his parousia or presence the Lord Jesus definitely does not care to have any professed Christians who take on the traits of "that evil slave" or "steward" within his "household staff" or "domestics." The Christianity of such ones turns out to be hypocritical and they belong with the religious hypocrites of Christendom. They prove themselves unfaithful, not faithful, reliable, trustworthy in what the Lord appointed them to do.

---

63. (a) What assurance did Jesus give that such an "evil slave" group would not break up his house of "domestics"? (b) How did this foretold action take place?
64. With whom does the master assign those like "that evil slave" to have their portion, but with whom did he not want them to be?

They belong with the unfaithful professed Christians of Christendom.

[65] Among the hypocrites and unfaithful ones, those who display the trait of an "evil slave" find no real spiritual pleasure, and they must share the experiences of those hypocrites and unfaithful religionists. "There is where [their] weeping and the gnashing of [their] teeth will be." (Matthew 24:51) This will not be because of repentance on their part. It is not a "sadness in a godly way" such as "makes for repentance to salvation that is not to be regretted." (2 Corinthians 7:10) Their expressions are those of vexation and of bitter disappointment. They may still carry on in a religious way, but they miss the joy and blessing of carrying out the approved slave's appointment "over all [the master's] belongings."

WARNING AGAINST OUR BEING SNARED

[66] In his prophecy on the "sign of [his] presence and of the conclusion of the system of things," Jesus gave more warning than just this illustration of how an "evil slave" will fare. He spoke words to his apostles directly warning all his disciples against adopting the course of such an "evil slave." According to Luke's account of the close of Jesus' remarkable prophecy, Jesus said: "But pay attention to yourselves that your hearts never become weighed down with overeating and heavy drinking and anxieties of life, and suddenly that day be instantly upon you as a snare. For it will come in upon all those dwelling upon the face of all the earth. Keep awake, then, all the time making supplication that you may succeed in escaping all these things that are destined to occur, and in standing before the Son of man."—Luke 21:34-36.

[67] It is highly important now for individuals to heed those words, now that the "faithful and discreet slave"

---

65. The weeping and gnashing of teeth on the part of those like "that evil slave" is because of what?
66. According to Luke's account, what warning did Jesus give to his disciples in closing his prophecy on the "sign"?
67. Now that they have been put over all the "belongings" of their returned Master, why is it highly important for those of the faithful "slave" class to heed his warning?

of the invisibly present Lord Jesus has been appointed
"over all his belongings." The day when the unparalleled "great tribulation" breaks upon antitypical unfaithful Jerusalem, Christendom, is very near. As a
snare that is instantaneous in action that day will be
released upon those dwelling upon the face of all the
earth, and all the unwary ones will be caught during
their overeating and heavy drinking and anxiousness
over the selfish things of life. The snarelike "day" will
bring their destruction. The members of the "faithful
and discreet slave" class do not desire to share with
those selfish heedless ones along with those like "that
evil slave."

[68] There is no reason for us to be uncertain with
regard to the period of time in which we are living.
Because we have done according to Jesus' illustration
of the "fig tree and all the other trees," we know
where we are and what is near. The "faithful and discreet slave" illustration is at the culmination of its
fulfillment. Not just the presence of that "faithful and
discreet slave" class, but the appointment of that
class over all the Lord's belongings and its taking care
of all those belongings—these things are an outstanding
feature of the "sign" proving that we are living in
the parousia, the invisible presence of the enthroned
King Jesus Christ, and at the same time living in the
"conclusion of the system of things." (Matthew 24:3)
The day of the destruction of this "system of things,"
Christendom and all, is near to being released like a
snare. This fact is the thing to which to "keep awake."
"All the time" it is urgent for us to be "making supplication that [we] may succeed in escaping all these
things that are destined to occur, and in standing
before the Son of man."—Luke 21:36.

---

68. (a) What more than just the presence of the "faithful and discreet
slave" is proof of our living where the "sign" indicates that we are?
(b) For what personal success should our supplications therefore be?

CHAPTER 18

Bringing the "Man of Lawlessness" to Nothing

NEVER before has there been such a demand by so many people for peace between the nations. Apparently it is because we are living in the "nuclear age," with already five leading nations possessing the nuclear bomb and many more nations destined to become possessors of the nuclear bomb shortly as the secret of it becomes more widely known and made use of. Nuclear bombs now menace mankind not only from missile sites on dry land but also from missile-launching submarines lurking at strategic places under the waters of the seas.

[2] It is no cause for amazement, then, to behold political rulers making what appear to be honest efforts to prevent the first nuclear war. Faced with a real nuclear holocaust, world rulers incline to become more considerate in their attitudes toward one another. Compromising peace-oriented measures are taken by hitherto intransigent foes of one another. More and more it is being felt that everything must be done to guarantee the peace of the future. Hope rises of "peace for a generation." The 1973 Conference on European Security and Cooperation of thirty-four nations evidences international feeling on the matter. The aim is to curb international lawlessness!

[3] The current of world events appears to be flowing toward the situation when men in control of affairs will jubilantly cry out in a self-congratulating way, "Peace and security!" When that stage of affairs is

---

1. Why, never before now, has there been a demand of so many people for peace between nations?
2. What unusual maneuverings for international peace do we therefore witness today?
3. (a) The current of world affairs seems to be nearing the state where what self-congratulatory cry will be raised? (b) Whose day will then be at hand, and why will it be a surprise to those crying out?

reached, under the benign approving smile of the United Nations, does it mean the start of a "generation of peace for mankind"? Bible prophecy has a word to say on the matter. It has much to say on the times and seasons for things to occur, because the Bible's Author, man's Creator, is a Timekeeper. He will have His day! The seeming success of international politics in at last establishing "peace and security" will not postpone His day. His day is not set by men. Their very arranging of an international accord on the basis of which they feel justified in crying out, "Peace and security!" will be the foretold sign that His day is ready to dawn. What it brings will surprise mankind. Their surprise will be because they have not believed what he predicted in his Word and what he has had proclaimed by his witnesses.

⁴ Centuries before now there were searchers of His inspired Word of prophecy who were looking for the coming of His day. Nineteen hundred years ago the apostle Paul wrote to the newly established Christian congregation in Thessalonica, Macedonia, and said to those Bible researchers: "Now as for the times and the seasons, brothers, you need nothing to be written to you. For you yourselves know quite well that Jehovah's day* is coming exactly as a thief in the night. Whenever it is that they are saying: 'Peace and security!' then sudden destruction is to be instantly upon them just as the pang of distress upon a pregnant woman; and they will by no means escape. But you, brothers, you are not in darkness, so that that day should overtake you as it would thieves, for you are all sons of light and sons of day. We belong neither to night nor to darkness. So, then, let us not sleep on as the rest do, but let us stay awake and keep our senses."—1 Thessalonians 5:1-6.

---

* Seven distinct Hebrew translations of First Thessalonians read "Jehovah's day" here, whereas fourth- and fifth-century Greek manuscripts and the Latin *Vulgate* read: "day of Lord."

4. What did Paul write to the Thessalonian Christians about the time of crying out, "Peace and security!"?

[5] The apostle Paul wrote that first letter to the congregation in Thessalonica, Macedonia, about the year 50 C.E. That was about midway in the time period from 33 C.E. to 70 C.E., the period that Jesus Christ in his prophecy on the Mount of Olives said would be marked by "wars and reports of wars," for, during that period, "nation will rise against nation and kingdom against kingdom." Anything but a peaceful time. (Matthew 24:4-7) And yet, during the year that followed Paul's writing of his first letter, there came to be Christians in Thessalonica who yielded to the impression that "the day of Jehovah is here." And yet there is no evidence that during that time, 50/51 C.E., men of affairs were saying, "Peace and security!" the saying that, as Paul had written in his letter, was immediately to precede the coming of "sudden destruction" on the peacemakers of the world. The Thessalonian Christians were going through a time of tribulation because of persecution from religious opposers, and they inclined toward wanting to be gathered at once to heaven to be with the Lord Jesus Christ and away from trouble.

[6] Consequently, about the year 51 C.E., the apostle Paul deemed it advisable to write the Thessalonian Christians another letter in order to restore their spiritual equilibrium. He expressed pleasure at their endurance and faith under persecution and tribulation and said: "This is a proof of the righteous judgment of God, leading to your being counted worthy of the kingdom of God, for which you are indeed suffering." He did not assure them that they would shortly be relieved of the troublemakers, but pointed forward to the "revelation of the Lord Jesus from heaven with his powerful angels." Realizing that they had to go on demonstrating their Christian faith under difficult circumstances, he said:

[7] "To that very end indeed we always pray for

---

5. (a) Paul wrote his first letter to the Thessalonian Christians about midway during a period for which Jesus predicted what? (b) Yet some of them thought that what was near, and they inclined to wanting what?
6, 7. Because they needed to demonstrate faith under further tribulation, what did Paul write to those Thessalonians?

you, that our God may count you worthy of his calling and perform completely all he pleases of goodness and the work of faith with power; in order that the name of our Lord Jesus may be glorified in you, and you in union with him, in accord with the undeserved kindness of our God and of the Lord Jesus Christ." —2 Thessalonians 1:5-12.

[8] The destruction of earthly Jerusalem (in 70 C.E.) was approaching, within that generation, and the apostle Paul did not wish the Thessalonian Christians to be disappointed in their unfounded expectations before or immediately after that Jewish national calamity. Seeing the need to readjust their thinking, he now proceeded to write: "However, brothers, respecting the presence [Greek: $pa\cdot rou\cdot si'a$] of our Lord Jesus Christ and our being gathered together to him, we request of you not to be quickly shaken from your reason nor to be excited either through an inspired expression or through a verbal message or through a letter as though from us, to the effect that the day of Jehovah is here."—2 Thessalonians 2:1, 2.

[9] Along with his fellow missionaries Silvanus (Silas) and Timothy, the apostle Paul had founded that congregation at Thessalonica, and in his first letter after he was obliged to leave the congregation he wrote to them about what he calls the "presence of our Lord Jesus Christ and our being gathered together to him." In 1 Thessalonians 4:14-18 he wrote: "For if our faith is that Jesus died and rose again, so, too, those who have fallen asleep in death through Jesus God will bring with him. For this is what we tell you by Jehovah's word, that we the living who survive to the presence of the Lord shall in no way precede those who have fallen asleep in death; because the Lord himself will descend from heaven with a commanding call, with an archangel's voice and with God's trumpet, and those who are dead in union with Christ will rise first. Afterward we the living who

---

8. That their expectations might not be disappointed in connection with Jerusalem's coming destruction, Paul requested them not to get excited over what idea?
9. In his first letter, what did Paul tell the Thessalonians about Christ's presence and about Christians being gathered to him?

are surviving will, together with them, be caught away in clouds to meet the Lord in the air; and thus we shall always be with the Lord. Consequently keep comforting one another with these words."

[10] Besides such information through Paul, the Gospel of Matthew was circulating by that time, it having been written about the year 41 C.E., in Hebrew as well as in the common Greek of the first century C.E. So it is possible that the congregation in Thessalonica had had called to their attention what the apostle Matthew had recorded of Jesus' prophecy on the Mount of Olives. Matthew's account tells that, after Jesus had foretold the destruction of Jerusalem (in 70 C.E.), he went on to say:

[11] "Immediately after the tribulation of those days the sun will be darkened, and the moon will not give its light, and the stars will fall from heaven, and the powers of the heavens will be shaken. And then the sign of the Son of man will appear in heaven, and then all the tribes of the earth will beat themselves in lamentation, and they will see the Son of man coming on the clouds of heaven with power and great glory. And he will send forth his angels with a great trumpet sound, and they will gather his chosen ones together from the four winds, from one extremity of the heavens to their other extremity."—Matthew 24:29-31.

[12] Now the apostle Paul knew that right after the destruction of Jerusalem within that generation the gathering of God's chosen ones by the angels under the glorified Son of man would not occur, resulting in a gathering of the Christians in Thessalonica together to the Lord Jesus Christ. He knew that, before the arrival of the destructive "day of Jehovah," more had to occur than the destruction of Jerusalem by the Romans and the deceptive cry of "Peace and security!" on the part of political rulers. This additional preliminary thing the apostle Paul reminded

---

10, 11. From the apostle Matthew's account of Christ's life, what feature of his prophecy might have been called to their attention?
12. (a) Did Paul expect the gathering of the Christians to the heavenly Christ immediately after Jerusalem's destruction? (b) What did Paul remind them must come first before the destructive day of Jehovah?

the Thessalonian Christians of, in these words: "Let no one seduce you in any manner, because it will not come unless the apostasy comes first and the man of lawlessness gets revealed, the son of destruction." —2 Thessalonians 2:3.

¹³ Ah, yes! First there must come an apostasy. What did the apostle Paul mean by "apostasy"? Did he mean a mere careless falling away, a dropping off indifferently of Christ's disciples as respects the Christian faith and practice? No! The word means something far stronger. The apostle Paul knew that. Why, he himself was accused of being guilty of apostasy, but that accusation was made by the unbelieving circumcised Jews. That is why, on his last visit to Jerusalem, Paul was given counsel by the governing body of the Christian congregation for a stated reason, namely: "You behold, brother, how many thousands of believers there are among the Jews; and they are all zealous for the Law. But they have heard it rumored about you that you have been teaching all the Jews among the nations an apostasy from Moses, telling them neither to circumcise their children nor to walk in the solemn customs. What, then, is to be done about it? In any case they are going to hear you have arrived [Greek: *e·le'ly·thas*]. Therefore do this which we tell you." (Acts 21:18-23) For Paul to turn his back on Moses meant apostasy, in Jewish minds.

¹⁴ According to the Greek word used, "apostasy" means, literally, "a standing off from," "a departing," "a withdrawing." For instance, we read, in Luke 8:13: "In the time of testing they desert." (*NE*) Also, in 1 Timothy 4:1: "In after times some will desert from the faith." (*NE; Je*) "Certain people will rebel against the faith." (*Mo*) Also, Hebrews 3:12: "See to it, brothers, that no one among you has the wicked, faithless heart of a deserter from the living God." (*NE*) "Brothers, take care lest there be a wicked,

13. (a) What did Paul not mean by the word "apostasy"? (b) How did Paul know what the word meant by himself having been accused of apostasy?
14. What does the original Greek word literally mean, in itself, and what meanings has it taken on?

unbelieving heart in any of you, moving you to be apostates from the living God." (*Mo*) "A wicked, unbelieving heart, that turns away from the ever-living God." (*AT; Je*) So, to the ancient Greeks, their word from which our "apostasy" is derived meant a "defection" or "revolt," as well as "departure; disappearance." This is why some modern translations convey the thought of "rebellion" at 2 Thessalonians 2:3.

¹⁵ For example, the Roman Catholic *Jerusalem Bible* there reads: "It cannot happen until the Great Revolt has taken place and the Rebel, the Lost One, has appeared." *An American Translation* reads: "For that is not until the rebellion takes place and the embodiment of disobedience makes his appearance—he who is doomed to destruction." The *Revised Standard Version* reads: "For that day will not come, unless the rebellion comes first, and the man of lawlessness is revealed, the son of perdition." *Moffatt* renders it: "It will not come till the Rebellion takes place first of all, with the revealing of the Lawless One, the doomed One." And *The New English Bible* reads: "That day cannot come before the final rebellion against God, when wickedness will be revealed in human form, the man doomed to perdition." From these various renderings of 2 Thessalonians 2:3 we can see that a strong view is taken of the word "apostasy."

AGAINST WHOM?

¹⁶ Against whom, then, is this apostasy, this revolt, this rebellion, this defection? The further description of this rebellious development makes it plain that it is against Jehovah God, whose Day this apostasy is to precede. This apostasy is to result in the revealing of "the man of lawlessness, the son of destruction." A literal man? No, for one single man could not have

---

15. How do modern translations show that a strong view is taken of the word "apostasy"?
16. (a) How do we know from what it is that the apostasy or desertion takes place? (b) What indicates whether this "man of lawlessness" is a single man, and whether this "man" is just an antichrist?

lived over the long period of time that is embraced within the fulfillment of this prophecy. Quite in line with this explanation is the rendering of *An American Translation* that uses the expression "the embodiment of disobedience, . . . who is doomed to destruction." We note that this one is not called "The Antichrist." True, he turns out to be an antichrist. Just as the apostle John, writing about the year 98 C.E., says concerning his own day: "Even now there have come to be many antichrists; . . . Who is the liar if it is not the one that denies that Jesus is the Christ? This is the antichrist, the one that denies the Father and the Son." (1 John 2:18, 22) Not only is the Son of God denied, but also God the Father is denied.

[17] So, then, it is more proper to call the "man of lawlessness" an anti-God. This anti-God is lawless toward God, and, being against God the Father, he is also against the Son of God, Jesus Christ. Before ever he appears, the "man of lawlessness" is termed the "son of destruction." That figurative expression means that he is an heir of destruction, he is condemned to destruction, "doomed to destruction." The "man of lawlessness" deserves destruction; he cannot escape it. This deserved destruction will come to this one on the "day of Jehovah." This anti-God is revealed before that day.

[18] This "man of lawlessness" who is destined for destruction is connected up with the foretold "apostasy," the revolt, the rebellion against God. This fact makes it certain that the "man of lawlessness" was originally associated with God, in peaceful relations with God. At the time that the apostle Paul wrote his letter to the Thessalonian Christians, it was not the natural, circumcised Jews who were at peace with God and in harmonious relationship with Him. It was the Jews that roused up a mob in Thessalonica and obliged the apostle Paul to flee from that city, and,

17. What is meant by calling this anti-God the "son of destruction," and when does the destruction come?
18. (a) Since the lawless one is connected with the "apostasy," what does this indicate as to that one's relationship with God? (b) Were the natural Jews of Paul's day in peaceful relationship with God, from which to apostatize?

later also, from Beroea. (Acts 17:5-15) In his first letter to the Thessalonians, Paul wrote: "They [the congregations in Judea] also are suffering at the hands of the Jews, who killed even the Lord Jesus and the prophets and persecuted us. Furthermore, they are not pleasing God, but are against the interests of all men, as they try to hinder us from speaking to people of the nations that these might be saved, with the result that they always fill up the measure of their sins. But his wrath has at length come upon them." —1 Thessalonians 2:14-16.

[19] Where else, then, could the apostasy be expected to start from but in the Christian congregation? It was to the Christians, as represented by the congregation at Thessalonica, that the apostle wrote: "Paul and Silvanus and Timothy to the congregation of the Thessalonians in union with God our Father and the Lord Jesus Christ: May you have undeserved kindness and peace from God the Father and the Lord Jesus Christ." (2 Thessalonians 1:1, 2) These Christians could apostatize from God, could revolt and rebel against God, because they were in union with Him and with his Messiah Jesus and were receiving undeserved kindness and peace from God their heavenly Father and through his Son Jesus Christ. Who, therefore, are such rebels from the Christian congregation?

[20] The apostle Paul himself warned that the apostasy, the religious revolt or rebellion, would come from the midst of the congregation that now belonged to God, inasmuch as He had rejected the Jewish nation as his chosen people. God's congregation was composed now of spiritual Israelites, spiritual Jews, and was no longer the nation of natural, circumcised Jews. Some years after Paul wrote his second letter to the Thessalonians, Paul found himself at the city of Miletus, Asia Minor, on his last trip to Jerusalem. At Miletus he addressed himself to the presbytery or "body of

19. From whom, then, could the apostasy be expected to start, and why from them?
20, 21. (a) Why was it that the apostasy would start, not from within the Jewish nation, but from within the Christian congregation? (b) With what words did Paul warn the presbytery of Ephesus about the coming apostasy?

elders" of the nearby congregation of Ephesus. Pointing ahead to the apostasy, Paul said to those elders or overseers:

²¹ "Pay attention to yourselves and to all the flock, among which the holy spirit has appointed you overseers, to shepherd the congregation of God, which he purchased with the blood of his own Son. I know that after my going away oppressive wolves will enter in among you and will not treat the flock with tenderness, and from among you yourselves men will rise and speak twisted things to draw away the disciples after themselves."—Acts 20:28-30.

²² Like the apostle Paul, his fellow apostle Peter was also aware of the coming apostasy. In his second and last letter, written about the year 64 C.E., Peter addressed himself "to those who have obtained a faith, held in equal privilege with ours, by the righteousness of our God and the Savior Jesus Christ."

²³ In the course of his letter to these, Peter went on to say: "Prophecy was at no time brought by man's will, but men spoke from God as they were borne along by holy spirit. However, there also came to be false prophets among the people, as there will also be false teachers among you. These very ones will quietly bring in destructive sects and will disown even the owner that bought them, bringing speedy destruction upon themselves. Furthermore, many will follow their acts of loose conduct, and on account of these the way of the truth will be spoken of abusively. Also, with covetousness they will exploit you with counterfeit words. But as for them, the judgment from of old is not moving slowly, and the destruction of them is not slumbering." (2 Peter 1:1, 21 through 2:3) This helps us to identify that lawless "son of destruction."

²⁴ In the light of what the apostles Paul and Peter say about the apostasy, who really is "the man of lawlessness . . . the son of destruction"? To "elders,"

<hr/>

22, 23. (a) In which of his letters, and to whom, did Peter also warn against the coming apostasy? (b) How did Peter, by what he there said, help us to identify the lawless "son of destruction"?
24, 25. In view of what Paul and Peter said above, what questions do we ask toward identifying what the "man of lawlessness" is?

the "overseers" who represented the congregation of Ephesus, the apostle Paul said that men would rise and "speak twisted things," in the religious field. This narrows the matter down to the religious leaders of the Christian congregation, those ordained or appointed to "shepherd the congregation of God." Who, then, are the religious leaders who professed to be of God's congregation and who were like "oppressive wolves"? Who were the professedly Christian leaders who did not "treat the flock with tenderness"? Who were the leading religious men who rose and spoke "twisted things" in order to "draw away the disciples" in the congregation "after themselves"? Who are the men that, like the false prophets among the people of ancient Israel, have proved to be "false teachers" among the spiritual Israelites?

25 Yes, who are the religious leaders that have brought in "destructive sects" among those who think themselves to be God's congregation? Who are those sectarian leaders who, by their religious teachings and their practices really have disowned the heavenly "owner that bought them"? What religious leaders have shown themselves guilty of "loose conduct" in their relations with the secular, worldly authorities? What religious leaders have set the bad example for imitation by their flocks so that the "way of the truth" came to be "spoken of abusively"? What religious leaders have coveted the things that the people of their congregation had and then have exploited them "with counterfeit words"?

IDENTIFYING THE "MAN OF LAWLESSNESS"

26 The identifying finger of human history over the past sixteen hundred years points to the religious clergy of Christendom. Is anyone unclear as to what is meant by the "clergy" of Christendom? If so, then let *The Encyclopedia Americana* (1929 edition), Volume 7, page 90, make it clear for the individual, in the following words:

26. To whom does the identifying finger point, and how does *The Encyclopedia Americana* describe the one identified?

CLERGY (Latin *clericus*, from Greek *kléros*, a lot), in the Christian Church, that portion of the faithful which is set apart for the ministry of religion. The separation from the laity became more marked through the multiplication of offices and titles, privileges, rights, peculiar dress and habits. In the Roman Catholic Church there are eight grades or distinctions of clergy, namely, that of the simple cleric, those of the four minor orders and those of the three sacred orders of subdeacon, deacon and priest. . . . The last three are regarded as being of divine institution. The simple cleric is one who has received the ecclesiastical tonsure; by that rite he is made a clerk or cleric, and as such is entitled to certain rights, privileges and immunities and assumes certain obligations not incumbent on the laity. In Protestant churches the distinction between clergy and laity is much less wide.

²⁷ Did Jesus Christ, the Head of the Christian congregation, give instructions for his disciples to be divided up into clergy and laity? Nowhere in the four Gospels of Matthew, Mark, Luke and John or in the book of Acts of Apostles or in the book of Revelation are there instructions to split up his disciples into two general classes. His instructions are to the direct contrary. In the temple at Jerusalem, to his disciples and to the crowds of Jews, Jesus said: "But you, do not you be called Rabbi, for one is your teacher, whereas all you are brothers. Moreover, do not call anyone your father on earth, for one is your Father, the heavenly One. Neither be called 'leaders,' for your Leader is one, the Christ. But the greatest one among you must be your minister." (Matthew 23:8-11) In the Revelation given to him through Jesus Christ, the apostle John refers to *all* the disciples of Christ as being priests, saying: "He made us to be a kingdom, priests to his God and Father. . . . " "You made them to be a kingdom and priests to our God, and they are to rule as kings over the earth."—Revelation 1:6; 5:10.

²⁸ Likewise, the apostle Peter writes the Christians that they are all priests, saying: "Be you also as living

---

27. (a) What words of Jesus are against dividing the congregation up into clergy and laity? (b) How did John, in the Revelation, classify all members of the congregation?
28. How did Peter's first letter also classify all those of the congregation alike?

stones built up, a spiritual house, a holy priesthood, to offer up spiritual sacrifices, acceptable to God by Jesus Christ. But you are a chosen generation, a kingly priesthood, a holy nation, a purchased people: that you may declare his virtues, who hath called you out of darkness into his marvellous light."—1 Peter 2:5, 9, Roman Catholic *Douay Version*.

²⁹ The English word "clergy" does occur once in the Douay Version of the Bible, in Peter's first letter, as follows: "The ancients therefore that are among you, I beseech who am myself also an ancient and a witness of the sufferings of Christ, as also a partaker of that glory which is to be revealed in time to come: Feed the flock of God which is among you, taking care of it, not by constraint but willingly, according to God: not for filthy lucre's sake but voluntarily: Neither as lording it over the clergy but being made a pattern of the flock from the heart." (1 Peter 5:1-3, *Dy*) But even in this translation of the Bible the whole flock of God's spiritual sheep are called the "clergy," and the "ancients," like the apostle Peter, are told not to lord it over this "clergy." However, not satisfied with that *Douay Version* rendering of the Greek word *kle'ros* (in the plural number) in 1 Peter 5:3, the modern Roman Catholic translations of the Bible render the Greek word differently in English. For example:

³⁰ "Neither be a dictator over any group that is put in your charge, but be an example that the whole flock can follow." (*The Jerusalem Bible*) "Be examples to the flock, not lording it over those assigned to you." (*The New American Bible*) "Nor yet as lording it over your charges, but becoming an example to the flock."—*The New Testament in the Westminster Version of the Sacred Scriptures*.

³¹ Since the inspired apostles of Jesus Christ apply

29, 30. (a) In 1 Peter 5:1-3, how does the Douay Version Bible apply the word "clergy"? (b) How do modern Catholic translations render the Greek word here involved?
31. In view of what Jesus said, in Matthew 23:10-12, 14, 33, why do we ask about the motive of men in distinguishing themselves as "the clergy" separate from "the laity"?

the terms "priesthood" and "clergy" (*Douay Version*) to the whole flock of God and do not confine those terms to the "ancients" or "elders" like the apostle Peter, it is not impertinent here to ask: Who are these religious leaders of Christendom who entitle themselves as "priests" and who call themselves "the clergy" as separate and distinct from what they call "the laity," a term that does not occur in the inspired Holy Scriptures? What is the motivation of these religious leaders in thus distinguishing themselves? What are they trying to make of themselves? We remember that Jesus Christ, when denouncing the Jewish scribes and Pharisees as "hypocrites" and "serpents, generation of vipers," said: "Neither be ye called masters: for one is your master, Christ. He that is the greatest among you shall be your servant. And whosoever shall exalt himself shall be humbled: and he that shall humble himself shall be exalted." —Matthew 23:10-12, 14, 33, *Douay Version*.

[32] When, in fact, did the religious leaders of Christendom begin to call themselves the clergy and to reserve for themselves the title of "priest"? Following the heading: "2. Distinction of Clergy and Laity," M'Clintock and Strong's *Cyclopædia,* Volume II, page 386, says of the "antithesis" or contrast between clergy and laity:

> The Jewish antithesis of clergy and laity was at first unknown among Christians; and it was "only as men fell back from the evangelical to the Jewish point of view" that the idea of the general Christian priesthood of all believers gave place, more or less completely, to that of the special priesthood or clergy. . . . So Tertullian, even (*De Baptismo,* c. 17, before he became a Montanist): "The laity have also the right to administer the sacraments and to teach in the community. The Word of God and the sacraments were by the grace of God communicated to all, and may therefore be communicated by all Christians as instruments of the divine grace. But the question here relates not barely to what is permitted in general, but also to what is expedient under existing circumstances. We may here use the

words of St. Paul, 'All things are lawful for men, but all things are not expedient.' If we look at the order necessary to be maintained in the Church, the laity are therefore to exercise their priestly right of administering the sacraments only when the time and circumstances require it." From the time of Cyprian . . . the father of the hierarchical system, the distinction of clergy and laity became prominent, and very soon was universally admitted. Indeed, from the third century onward, the term *clērus* (*kle'ros, ordo*) was almost exclusively applied to the ministry to distinguish it from the laity. As the Roman hierarchy was developed, the clergy came to be not merely a distinct order (which might consist with all the apostolical regulations and doctrines), but also to be recognised as the only priesthood, and the essential means of communication between man and God.

[33] According to *The Encyclopedia Americana,* Volume 8, page 368, the above-mentioned Thascius Caecilius Cyprian was born about 200 C.E. and died at Carthage, Africa, September 14, 258. "Shortly after being baptized (246) he was ordained priest and then was elected by the Christians of Carthage to be their bishop (248). . . . He did much to relieve and strengthen his episcopate. Under him seven councils were held, the last in 256." Although this African bishop was considered as one of the Church "fathers" and sainted by the Roman Catholic Church, the fact remains that he was a clergyman, one of the clergy that came into existence after the death of the apostles of Jesus Christ and their immediate associates.

[34] It is this so-called "Christian" clergy that demonstrated itself to be "the man of lawlessness . . . the son of destruction," in connection with the "apostasy," the "revolt" or "rebellion." It is evident that by the use of this expression the Holy Bible means a composite "man," who exists over a long period of time and whose makeup or personnel changes as time goes on. Thus the membership of this "man of lawlessness" today differs from that of the third century.

33. Who was this Cyprian, and what office did he hold in the congregation during the third century?
34. By the expression "the man of lawlessness," what kind of individual does the Bible mean, and why so?

PRETENSIONS TO GODSHIP

35 Since the "apostasy" or "rebellion" of this clerical "man of lawlessness" is against Jehovah God, it is no cause for surprise that this composite "man" should aspire to Godship, try to make a god of himself. The first rebel against Jehovah God, namely, Satan the Devil, made a god of himself, so that the apostle Paul calls him the "god of this system of things." (2 Corinthians 4:4) Under Satan the Devil the pagan king of ancient Babylon tried to make himself appear equal to Jehovah God whose temple was at Jerusalem. According to Isaiah 14:14, the king of ancient Babylon said in his heart: "I shall go up above the high places of the clouds; I shall make myself resemble the Most High." He thought he had achieved his ambition when he destroyed Jerusalem and the temple of Jehovah God in the year 607 B.C.E. However, the destruction of Jerusalem and its temple by that Babylonian aspirant to equality with Jehovah God is something minor when it is compared with all the destruction of things connected with Jehovah God as caused by this clerical "man of lawlessness."

36 Being a lawless rebel in things religious, he has acted as if he were not responsible to the Most High and Almighty God, Jehovah, as if he were above the law of the one living and true God. The apostle Paul does not go to any extreme when he says prophetically of this composite "man of lawlessness" this astonishing thing: "He is set in opposition and lifts himself up over everyone who is called 'god' or an object of reverence, so that he sits down in the temple of The God, publicly showing himself to be a god. Do you not remember that, while I was yet with you, I used to tell you these things?"—2 Thessalonians 2:4, 5.

37 Of course, in confirming how the clerical "man of lawlessness" has fulfilled this prophecy, a person might point to how a member of the so-called "Christian"

35. Why is it no cause for surprise that the "man of lawlessness" should aspire to Godship? To what extent?
36. How does that composite "man" act as if not responsible to Jehovah, and what did Paul use to tell the Thessalonians about that "man"?
37. In confirming how Paul's prophecy has been fulfilled, to what prominent religious personage might one point, and why?

clergy has spoken and acted or to the claims of god-ship that have been made for him. For instance, a person might point to the pope of the Roman Catholic Church, and quote what is said concerning this papal bishop of Rome in Ferraris' ecclesiastical dictionary,* namely:

> The pope is of such dignity and highness that he is not simply a man but, as it were, God, and the Vicar of God. . . . Hence the pope is crowned with a triple crown, as king of heaven, of earth and of hell. . . . Nay, the pope's excellence and power are not only about heavenly, terrestrial and infernal things, but he is also above angels, and is their superior . . . So that if it were possible that angels could err from the faith, or entertain sentiments contrary thereto, they could be judged and excommunicated by the pope. . . . He is of such great dignity and power that he occupies one and the same tribunal with Christ . . . So that whatsoever the pope does seems to proceed from the mouth of God. . . . The pope is, as it were, God on earth, the only prince of the faithful of Christ, the greatest king of all kings, possessing the plenitude of power; to whom the government of the earthly and heavenly kingdom is entrusted. . . . The pope is of so great authority and power that he can modify, declare or interpret the divine law. . . . The pope can sometimes counteract the divine law by limiting, explaining," etc.

[38] However, it is not to be forgotten that the "man of lawlessness" is not a single individual religious leader like the pope of Rome or the Greek Orthodox patriarch of Athens, the Greek Orthodox patriarch of Constantinople (Istanbul) or other religious patriarch. The foretold "lawless" one is a composite "man," the whole religious clergy of the professed "Christian" church. Of course, what one prominent member of this clerical "man" does attaches blame to all the other members of the clergy class for their agreeing with what is done or not protesting against it or for acquiescing in it and remaining with the clergy organization.

---

* *Prompta bibliotheca canonica, juridicao-moralis, theologica partim ascetica, polemica, rubricistica, historica,* prepared at Bologna, Emilia-Romagna region, in Italy, in 1746 by Lucio Ferraris, Vol. VI, pp. 31-35; according to copy at Columbia University, New York city.

38. However, in pointing to an individual clergyman, what should be remembered, and so how has this prophecy concerning the "man of lawlessness" really been fulfilled?

They all share a community responsibility and culpability for what a member of the clergy class does in a representative way as when speaking or acting for the whole group. It is what the clergy class as a whole does or joins in doing through the centuries of time that fulfills the prophecy concerning the "man of lawlessness."

³⁹ The "man of lawlessness" class has proved itself to be "set in opposition" by making itself the "friend" of the world, according to the rule stated by the inspired disciple James in his letter: ("The friendship of this world is the enemy of God. Whosoever therefore will be a friend of this world becometh an enemy of God." (James 4:4, *Douay*) He opposes Jehovah God when he opposes and tries to nullify the inspired written Word of God and even tries to take or keep away the Bible from the church-supporting members. He opposes Jehovah God when he opposes and persecutes those disciples of Christ who are worshiping Jehovah God with spirit and truth through Jesus Christ. (John 4:24) He opposes the one living and true God by taking away the worship and adoration that belong to this God and attracting such worship and adoration to a glorified clergy class.

⁴⁰ The "man of lawlessness" class wants to be the only god on the earthly scene, in fact, the god of earthly gods. This has been demonstrated during the relations that the religious Church of Christendom has had with the political State. In this marriage of Church and State, the clergy has always endeavored to be the party on top, to do the dictating. From the time of Constantine there has been this marriage of Church and State. This has really been a marriage of convenience, for what the clergy can get out of it in the way of authority, prestige, protection and immunities, support and other selfish benefits. Concerning "Church and State," *The Encyclopedia Americana*, Volume 6, pages 657, 658, says:

39. How has the "man of lawlessness" class proved itself to be "set in opposition" to Jehovah?
40. How has the "man of lawlessness" class endeavored to be the only earthly god on the scene, as in the matter of Church and State?

Between these two institutions, in modern times, there has rarely, if ever, existed perfect harmony. This struggle, so long protracted, bids fair, unless some astonishing upheaval occurs, to last for all time. It has been a bitter one. It has involved large interests and brought to the forefront momentous discussions. It has fomented uprisings of all kinds and originated a literature of vituperation without parallel outside of political strife. It has been, not seldom, mere political contention. . . . Under Constantine the Church entered the arena of universal activity as a collaborator in the task of civilizing the peoples. Acknowledged as the spiritual ruler, it gradually acquired a local habitation and a name as a temporal potentate. It became a world power. This success was the beginning of all the many disasters of the Church. . . . From Constantine to Charlemagne the civil power, while giving legal recognition to the Church, interfered in its government. From Charlemagne to a period approaching that of the Reformation, Church and state were closely united and there was a generally acknowledged subordination of the civil to the spiritual authority.

[41] It is a fact of history that the emperors of the pagan Roman Empire were ranked as gods, and incense was offered to them as gods or divinities. From the time of Emperor Constantine the Great in the fourth century, the bishops of the "apostasy" became wedded to the State and they sought to gain the ascendancy above the deified Roman emperor. Emperor Constantine endeavored to create a fusion religion between paganism and Christianity, and decreed the religion of the apostate bishops to be the State religion. Down to the day of his death in 337 C.E., he bore the pagan title of Pontifex Maximus, the head of religious matters; and it was as Pontifex Maximus that the as yet unbaptized Constantine called the Nicaean Council of 325 C.E. for the settling of the religious disputings of the church bishops. At the time he decided in favor of the pagan doctrine of the Trinity (One God in Three Persons) as taught by the majority of the church bishops.

41. (a) What religious rank did the Roman emperors hold, above which the "man of lawlessness" needed to set itself up? (b) What religious office did the Roman emperor hold, and how was this used respecting the apostate church?

[42] In the year 379* there came *the* opportunity for the papal bishop of Rome. This was when Emperor Gratian, professing to be Christian, gave up the pagan title and office of Pontifex Maximus. Without qualms of conscience, Pope Damasus picked it up for all the religious power, authority, influence and control it would give him over all the population, the larger part of which was still pagan and recognized the pagan title. This elevated the papal bishop of Rome above the Roman emperor in religious matters. Down to this day the pope of the Roman Catholic Church has continued to claim and use that pagan title. As represented in the pope, the most prominent member of the clergy class, the "man of lawlessness" was lifting himself up "over everyone who is called 'god' or an object of reverence." Everybody knows that the priests and preachers of Christendom like to be addressed and titled as "Reverend," "Most Reverend" and "Most Right Reverend." They command and demand the reverence of their parishioners or church members.

[43] The "temple of The God" in which the "man of lawlessness" sits down, "showing himself to be a god," is what professes to be the Church of God. To the true Christians of the first century the apostle Paul wrote: "Do you not know that you people are God's temple, and that the spirit of God dwells in you? If anyone destroys the temple of God, God will destroy him; for the temple of God is holy, which temple you people are." (1 Corinthians 3:16, 17; also 2 Corinthians 6:16) It was from this spiritual "temple" class that the founders of the "apostasy" first broke away. They refuse to recognize the original true "temple" class, and the apostate congregation that these apostates establish they call "the temple of God." It is in this apostate "temple" that they sit down and maintain

* *New Catholic Encyclopedia*, Vol. 6, page 706, under "Gratian."

42. At the first opportunity, how and through whom did the "man of lawlessness" lift itself up "over everyone called a 'god' or an object of reverence"?
43. In what temple is it that the "man of lawlessness" class seats itself as "a god," and whom does it compel to recognize its power?

their seat as a "clergy" distinct from those whom they call "the laity." There the clergy class of Christendom shows itself to be "a god." It forces the politicians, businessmen and military officers to recognize its power. The power and support of the clergy class is invariably sought by the political governments in time of war.

THE FIRST-CENTURY "RESTRAINT"

[44] Now after so long a time the "man of lawlessness" has stood revealed for centuries. But this was not the case in the first century, in the days of the genuine apostles of Jesus Christ. It was then yet to be revealed. So the apostle Paul wrote to the Thessalonian Christians in his letter of about 51 C.E.: "And so now you know the thing that acts as a restraint, with a view to his being revealed in his own due time." (2 Thessalonians 2:6) Those first-century Christians knew what the "restraint" was, for Paul made it known to them, in fact, demonstrated it to them. Well, what was the thing that was acting as a "restraint" back there? It was the body of genuine apostles of Jesus Christ, including the apostle Paul. Unitedly they resisted the development and formation of the "man of lawlessness . . . the son of destruction." As an illustration of this, here is what the apostle John, writing about the year 98 C.E., said in his third and last letter to the Christians:

[45] "I wrote something to the congregation, but Diotrephes, who likes to have the first place among them, does not receive anything from us with respect. That is why, if I come, I will call to remembrance his works which he goes on doing, chattering about us with wicked words. Also, not being content with these things, neither does he himself receive the brothers with respect, and those who are wanting to receive them he tries to hinder and to throw out of the congregation." (3 John 9, 10) That Diotrephes was indeed

44, 45. (a) What acted as a "restraint" on the development and formation of the "man of lawlessness" in the first century? (b) How did the apostle John illustrate such a restraining influence, as described in his third letter?

showing traits of the "man of lawlessness." The apostle John made an effort to put him under check, under due "restraint." Other apostles acted likewise in similar cases.

[46] Even back there, less than twenty years after the founding of the Christian "temple" class on the day of Pentecost of 33 C.E., the apostle Paul was aware that there were evidences of a tendency to form the "man of lawlessness . . . the son of destruction." That was why he continued on to say to the congregation at Thessalonica: "True, the mystery of this lawlessness is already at work; but only till he who is right now acting as a restraint gets to be out of the way." —2 Thessalonians 2:7.

[47] There was a mystery or religious secret about the identity of this coming "man of lawlessness." To this day there are expounders of the Bible in Christendom who argue that this "man" is an individual male person, whom they designate as The Antichrist. But quite fittingly *An American Translation* renders the designation of this mysterious figure as "the embodiment of disobedience." (2 Thessalonians 2:3) This agrees with the fact that the "man of lawlessness" turns out to be a composite man, a clergy class that is lawless toward Jehovah God and that endures over centuries of time. With good basis the apostle Paul could say that the "mystery of this lawlessness" was already at work in his day. It had not yet taken definite form to be designated under the symbol of a man. But there was an operation that was going on in the Christian congregation that would eventually work out in producing this definitely established and identifiable class. But in Paul's day "mystery" was still connected with the coming of the "lawless one."

[48] Proving that the "mystery of this lawlessness" was already at work within the Christian congregation,

46. How did Paul indicate to the Thessalonians that there was even then a tendency toward forming the "man of lawlessness" class?
47. Why did Paul speak of what was already at work as the "mystery of this lawlessness"?
48. As evidence that the "mystery of this lawlessness" was already at work, what did it become necessary for Paul to write to the Corinthian Christians?

the apostle Paul found it necessary, just a few years after the foregoing discussion of the matter, to write to the congregation in Corinth, Greece: ("Now what I am doing I will still do, that I may cut off the pretext from those who are wanting a pretext for being found equal to us in the office of which they boast. For such men are false apostles, deceitful workers, transforming themselves into apostles of Christ. And no wonder, for Satan himself keeps transforming himself into an angel of light. It is therefore nothing great if his ministers also keep transforming themselves into ministers of righteousness. But their end shall be according to their works.)—2 Corinthians 11:12-15.

⁴⁹ This religious operation for the producing of false leaders, "false apostles," persisted even down into the last decade of the first century C.E. In proof of this, the aged apostle John received the Revelation about the year 96 C.E., and in it he was instructed by the glorified Jesus Christ to write to the "body of elders" of the congregation in Ephesus, Asia Minor. In telling what Jesus in the vision instructed him to do, John says: "To the angel of the congregation in Ephesus write: These are the things that he says who holds the seven stars in his right hand, he who walks in the midst of the seven golden lampstands, 'I know your deeds, and your labor and endurance, and that you cannot bear bad men, and that you put those to the test who say they are apostles, but they are not, and you found them liars. . . . Nevertheless, I hold this against you, that you have left the love you had at first.'" —Revelation 2:1-4; 1 Timothy 4:14, footnote.

⁵⁰ Before finishing his earthly life course, the aged apostle John wrote three letters to the Christians. In evidence of there being an operation of the "mystery of this lawlessness" even in the days of Christ's apostles, John wrote in his first letter: "Young children, it is

49. How was it pointed out through John that the operation of the "mystery of this lawlessness" was still going on in the last decade of the first century?
50. As proving that even in the days of the apostles the "mystery of this lawlessness" was at work, what did John write about antichrists in his first letter?

the last hour, and, just as you have heard that antichrist is coming, even now there have come to be many antichrists; from which fact we gain the knowledge that it is the last hour. They went out from us, but they were not of our sort; for if they had been of our sort, they would have remained with us. But they went out that it might be shown up that not all are of our sort. And you have an anointing from the holy one; all of you have knowledge. Beloved ones, do not believe every inspired expression, but test the inspired expressions to see whether they originate with God, because many false prophets have gone forth into the world." (1 John 2:18-20; 4:1; written about 98 C.E.) By not having the Son of God any longer as the Messiah or Christ, those antichrists did not have God the Father either.—1 John 2:22-24.

[51] From such apostolic writings exposing bad conditions that were coming to the surface here and there in the congregations, we can identify whom the apostle Paul means by the expression "he who is right now acting as a restraint." (2 Thessalonians 2:7) He means, not some individual male member of the entire congregation of God on earth, not any individual apostle like himself, but the entire body of the true apostles of Jesus Christ in that first century. That body of apostles, like a composite person, was then, "right now," as Paul times it, standing in the way of the organizing of a corporate "man of lawlessness" within the entire Christian congregation and in control of it. Consequently, that which was "right now acting as a restraint" was taken "out of the way" of the developing "mystery of this lawlessness" when the last one of Christ's true apostles was taken away in death. This may have been the apostle John, who died near the end of the first century C.E.

[52] That composite "man of lawlessness" was called "the son of destruction." This was another way of saying that this lawless one was condemned by Je-

---

51. What is meant by the expression "he who is right now acting as a restraint," and when was this taken "out of the way"?
52. By means of whom will the destruction of "the son of destruction" be brought about, at what time?

hovah God to destruction. In the carrying out of His sentence of destruction upon the lawless one, Jehovah God uses his glorified Son Jesus Christ. So, in telling what is to happen after the apostolic "restraint" gets to be out of the way by death of all the apostles, Paul says: "Then, indeed, the lawless one will be revealed, whom the Lord Jesus will do away with by the spirit of his mouth and bring to nothing by the manifestation of his presence."—2 Thessalonians 2:8, *NW; NA*.

[53] The Lord Jesus does not do away with the "man of lawlessness" immediately after its being revealed in full, identifiable form, seated in the "temple of The God" and "publicly showing himself to be a god." The apostle Paul locates the time for the bringing of the "man of lawlessness" to nothing as being during the "presence" or parousia of the Lord Jesus. That means now, in our generation, for the royal "presence" or parousia of the Lord Jesus began at the end of the Gentile Times in the year 1914 C.E. We behold the "sign" in proof of this, and we know that we are in the "conclusion of the system of things." (Matthew 24:3 through 25:46) Ours, then, is the time for persons of this generation to witness the doing away with the "man of lawlessness" by means of the "spirit" of the Lord Jesus' mouth and the bringing of that "lawless one" to nothing by means of the manifestation of the Lord Jesus' presence, his parousia! This destructive work will be a "manifestation" proving that the Lord Jesus is invisibly present, that his parousia is a reality. The "spirit," the motivating force, from his mouth will be for the destruction of the entire "man of lawlessness."

EVIDENCE OF THE LAWLESS ONE'S "PRESENCE"

[54] At this point of the discussion the apostle Paul turns from the mention of the "presence" of the Lord Jesus to a consideration of the "presence" or parousia

---

53. (a) Why, then, is ours the time or the generation for the doing away with the "man of lawlessness"? (b) On the other hand, the bringing of this "man" to nothing will be a proof of what fact?
54. (a) When does the presence of the "lawless one" begin in comparison with the presence of the Lord Jesus? (b) By what is the parousia of the "lawless one" to be marked?

of the "man of lawlessness." The presence or parousia of this lawless one precedes or begins before the "presence" of the Lord Jesus in Kingdom power. Note how Paul presents the evidence of the presence of the lawless one. He writes: "But the lawless one's presence [Greek: pa·rou·si′a] is according to the operation of Satan with every powerful work and lying signs and portents and with every unrighteous deception for those who are perishing."—2 Thessalonians 2:9, 10a.

[55] Here the Roman Catholic *Jerusalem Bible* reads: "But when the Rebel comes, Satan will set to work: there will be all kinds of miracles and a deceptive show of signs and portents, and everything evil that can deceive those who are bound for destruction." (2 Thessalonians 2:9, 10; see also *The New American Bible; The New English Bible;* Murdock's *The Syriac New Testament*.) In the opening of verse 9 the Greek text literally reads: "Of whom is the presence." However, just because the words "lawless one" do not occur in this verse 9, it does not mean that the word "presence" or parousia applies to the "presence" (parousia) of the Lord Jesus just mentioned in the preceding verse (8). Rather, the reference is to the "presence" of the other one who is under discussion, namely, the lawless one. That is why *An American Translation* opens up verse 9 by saying: "The other's appearance, by the contrivance of Satan." The *Westminster Version* of "The New Testament" reads similarly: "But that other's coming is through Satan's working." So the Greek relative pronoun "of whom" in verse 9 lines up with "whom" in verse 8, which applies to the lawless one. The connection would be like this: "The lawless one will be revealed, whom the Lord Jesus will do away with . . . of whom is the presence."

[56] The official "presence" or parousia of the anti-God, "the man of lawlessness," since after the death of Christ's apostles and down till now can be attributed to no one but to Satan the Devil. Because this com-

---

55. How do we know that the parousia spoken of in 2 Thessalonians 2:9 refers to that of the "lawless one" rather than that of Jesus?
56. The official "presence" of the "man of lawlessness" can be attributed only to whom, and why?

posite "man of lawlessness" seated himself in the "temple of The God," it cannot be argued that this "lawless one" originated with God, Jehovah. The long "presence" of this "embodiment of disobedience" has had all the earmarks of being due to or according to an "operation of Satan." The name Satan means "Resister," and he is the instigator of all resistance to Jehovah God in heaven and on earth, including the resistance of the "lawless one" to the Most High God. It certainly was not of Jehovah God that the fomenters of the "apostasy" or rebellion raised themselves to the rank of "clergy" and thereby distinguished themselves from the other members of the congregation whom they called "the laity." This was a trick of Satan the Devil to try to turn *all* the congregation of Christ's disciples against Jehovah God.

⁵⁷ To get the so-called "Christian" clergy to power and to keep them there, the operation and activity of Satan had to be "with every powerful work [miracles, *Je*] and lying signs and portents and with every unrighteous deception." The purpose of all this lying, deceptive evidence of supernatural backing for the "clergy" is to get the members of the congregation to believe that the clergy represent the true God and have his appointment, his approval and his backing and are his earthly agents. They are given the appearance of being the ones exclusively set apart and appointed to the ministry of God's Word, with special powers, privileges, rights, immunities, rank and titles not shared by the inferior "laity."

⁵⁸ Hence, those powerful works or miracles, those signs and portents and unrighteous deceptions are for a purpose that is selfish and not for the glory and exaltation of Jehovah God. These manifestations of Satan's operation and activity were produced after the death of Christ's apostles. Those apostles did indeed work miracles, signs and portents, because they had

57. To get the clergy to the position of power and to keep the clergy there, what means were used, and for what purpose such kind of means?
58. Why would the powerful works, signs, portents, and so forth, by the clergy be, not due to connections with the apostles, but by the operation of Satan?

God's spirit through Christ. Those apostles had the power and authority to impart to baptized believers the spirit with its various gifts of the spirit for the doing of miraculous things, such as speaking with foreign languages, prophecies, interpretations, healings, and so forth. At the death of Christ's apostles, the imparting of the spirit accompanied by such miraculous gifts ceased. Likewise, when those who had been thus gifted through the apostles died, not later than in the second century C.E., those miraculous gifts ceased to exist, and no longer were such things an evidence to prove who are true servants of God and who make up the true Christian congregation. (Acts 8:14-18; 1 Corinthians 13:8) Hence, the seeming display of such "gifts" after that would be, not of God, but of Satan.

[59] So, then, let the clergy-ridden churches of Christendom point to all the powerful works, miracles, signs and portents that they want to in behalf of their clergy down through the centuries. Let them point to the grandiose position of the clergy in this world, the high esteem and reverence that have been paid to the clergy, their grand, eye-dazzling regalia, their high-sounding titles, their magnificent church buildings and cathedrals, their impressive church rituals, their transubstantiation of bread and wine in the "Mass," their superior education, their standing and influence with the political State and the military, yet all those things and the effects of those things upon the so-called "laity" prove that the self-exalting clergy of Christendom did not originate with God and are not his ministers. Satan, who transforms himself into an "angel of light," moves his earthly ministers of religion to "keep transforming themselves into ministers of righteousness." (2 Corinthians 11:14, 15) True Christian ministers of Jehovah God prove themselves to be his appointed, approved ministers, not by such external things, but by God's written Word of truth.

59. (a) Do the impressive things that are pointed to in behalf of the clergy prove these to be God's ministers? (b) To what do the true ministers refer for proof of divine appointment?

[60] Highly impressive were the numerical proportions that the clerical "man of lawlessness" class reached world wide. In the year 1971 C.E., when Christendom reached its all-time peak of 985,363,400 members, the number of religious clergymen had risen into the hundreds of thousands. For the Roman Catholic Church alone the published figures showed 419,611 clergymen for 566,771,600 church members world wide in that year of 1971.

[61] Who are the ones whose credulity is played upon by such outwardly impressive things? Who are the ones favorably impressed and deceived by such unscriptural "powerful work and lying signs and portents"? For whom are such things designed by the slyly operating Satan? The apostle Paul says that the "operation of Satan" during the presence of the clerical "lawless one" is "with every unrighteous deception for those who are perishing, as a retribution because they did not accept the love of the truth that they might be saved. So that is why God lets an operation of error go to them, that they may get to believing the lie, in order that they all may be judged because they did not believe the truth but took pleasure in unrighteousness."—2 Thessalonians 2:10-12.

[62] God does not directly send an "operation of error" to these deceived ones. He lets it go to them, in order to prove what it is that they want and also because this is really what they want. This is what the apostle Paul pointed out to his fellow missionary Timothy in a final letter to him. Paul explained why he wanted Timothy to preach God's Word urgently in all seasons in the Christian congregation. Paul said: "For there will be a period of time when they will not put up with the healthful teaching, but, in accord with their own desires, they will accumulate teachers for themselves to have their ears tickled; and they will turn their

60. To what extent were the numerical proportions of the clerical "man of lawlessness" class world wide highly impressive?
61. For whom did Paul say that those deceptive things were designed by the slyly operating Satan? And why by God's permission?
62. Does God directly send an "operation of error" to the deceived ones, and what does He determine by means of this "operation of error"?

ears away from the truth, whereas they will be turned aside to false stories." (2 Timothy 4:2-4) By means of the inspired Word of God a person can protect himself against an "operation of error" during the presence of the "lawless one." But by letting Satan carry on an "operation of error" and by thus letting this operation go to the professed Christians, Jehovah God puts them to the proof as to whether they "accept the love of the truth" or love the lie.

[63] More than ever before during the remaining time of the "presence" of the clerical "man of lawlessness" and during the presence or parousia of the Lord Jesus, an "operation of error" has gone to the people by God's permission. The approaching execution of adverse judgment against those who do not "accept the love of the truth" and who take "pleasure in unrighteousness" makes the world situation a very serious one for all the people. Bible students with spiritual discernment have, since the year 1914 C.E., long seen the "sign" of Christ's invisible presence or parousia, and they appreciate that the time will suddenly be upon us for the "manifestation of his presence" against the clerical "man of lawlessness . . . the son of destruction." (2 Thessalonians 2:8) What, therefore, do we desire—to suffer destruction with the "lawless one" or to experience salvation with lovers of the truth?

THE DOING AWAY WITH THE "MAN OF LAWLESSNESS"

[64] The clerical "man of lawlessness" class has for centuries taught pagan doctrines that originate with ancient Babylon and has put such pagan doctrines and traditions of men above the inspired Holy Bible. Christendom's clergy has opposed and persecuted lovers of Bible truth who have preached that truth to others and who live in harmony with it. The clergymen have made themselves friendly with the world and committed spiritual fornication (immorality) with

---

63. The approaching of what makes the world situation very serious for all mankind, and what choice must we now make?
64. How has the "man of lawlessness" class made itself a part of Babylon the Great?

the political rulers and men of Big Business, and they have served as the handmaid of war makers and military elements. They have thereby made themselves a powerful part of Babylon the Great, which symbolizes the world empire of false religion. Yes, the "man of lawlessness" class is a part, the most reprehensible part, of Babylon the Great, the religious "great harlot," with whom the "kings of the earth committed fornication, whereas those who inhabit the earth were made drunk with the wine of her fornication."—Revelation 17:1, 2.

[65] As being included in religious Babylon the Great, the clerical "man of lawlessness" class rides the symbolic "scarlet-colored wild beast that was full of blasphemous names and that had seven heads and ten horns." That symbolic wild beast is the present-day man-made world organization for international peace and security, the United Nations. This is the symbolic "eighth king," the Eighth World Power, of Bible prophecy. (Revelation 17:1-11) It suits the "man of lawlessness" class, the clergy of Christendom, to speak favorably and commendably of any man-made international organization for world peace and security, even to assigning to that unchristian organization a Messianic role. The wish of the "man of lawlessness" clergy is that such international organization may save the world from a third global conflict, a nuclear war.

[66] The ride on the back of that symbolic "scarlet-colored wild beast" will not be for much longer now. As goes the religious harlot Babylon the Great, so too goes the "man of lawlessness" clergy. As surely as the Revelation vision foretells it, the ten governmental "horns" of the symbolic wild beast will turn upon the filthy rider, Babylon the Great, in hatred. Yes, the seven heads that direct the body movements of the wild beast will hate this international fornicatrix. They will move the body into action against her.

What will body, heads and horns do to her? "These will hate the harlot and will make her devastated and naked, and will eat up her fleshy parts and will completely burn her with fire." (Revelation 17:16) In her being devastated and stripped naked, in her being devoured and burned completely with fire, the "man of lawlessness" clergy gets devastated, denuded, devoured and burned to ashes.

⁶⁷ That will signify "great tribulation" for the "man of lawlessness" clergy, for the clergy are the dominant part of the modern-day antitypical unfaithful Jerusalem, Christendom. Earthly Jerusalem's destruction by the Romans in 70 C.E. was a type of the destruction coming upon Christendom and her religious rulers, the professed "Christian" clergy. Ancient Jerusalem's tribulation at the time that she still had her temple and officiating priesthood was "great" indeed. But what of the tribulation that is soon to smite Christendom and her "man of lawlessness" clergy? It will be the worst tribulation ever to smite the race of mankind. In it that clerical "son of destruction" will be brought to nothing in utter destruction.—Matthew 24:15-22; Mark 13:14-20.

⁶⁸ Can we imagine what that will mean? Those who still have an awe-inducing reverence for the ordained clergy of Christendom cannot imagine these sanctimonious "men of the cloth" violently destroyed with Babylon the Great, for it seems sacrilegious even to think of such a thing. Such persons shrink from daring to imagine the church buildings, in which the clergy sat and seemed to be deserving of reverence like a religious god, reduced to ruins. To them such a thing seems like a profanation of what is holy, consecrated. But that was the way in which the devout, yet unchristianized Jews of the first century viewed any prediction of the destruction of the city of Jerusalem and its holy temple. Nevertheless, what Jesus Christ foretold in his prophecy while seated on

67. Why will this signify for the "man of lawlessness" clergy a "tribulation" that is indeed "great"?
68. From what foretold historical example can we imagine what this will mean for religious Christendom?

the Mount of Olives came true, in all its horrible reality.—Matthew 24:1, 2.

[69] To the devoted adherents of Christendom, the bringing of the clerical "man of lawlessness" class to nothing will be astounding, shocking their religious susceptibilities. It will mark the death of a god, for the "man of lawlessness" class is one that "sits down in the temple of The God, publicly showing himself to be a god." (2 Thessalonians 2:4) Jesus Christ himself agreed with the inspired Hebrew Scriptures that there are men on earth who are ranked as "gods," mighty ones. To prove this point, according to John 10:34-36, he quoted from the eighty-second psalm, which says:

"God is stationing himself in the assembly of the Divine One; in the middle of the gods he judges: 'How long will you keep on judging with injustice and showing partiality to the wicked themselves? . . . Be judges for the lowly one and the fatherless boy. To the afflicted one and the one of little means do justice. Provide escape for the lowly one and the poor one; out of the hand of the wicked ones deliver them.'

"They [these judicial gods] have not known, and they do not understand; in darkness they keep walking about; all the foundations of the earth are made to totter.

" 'I myself have said, "You are gods, and all of you are sons of the Most High. Surely you will die just as men do; and like any one of the princes you will fall! " ' "

The clerical "man of lawlessness" class is no immortal god, but will die like an ordinary man, like the traitorous Judas Iscariot who also was called "the son of destruction." (John 17:12) In spite of lifting itself up "over everyone who is called 'god' or an object of reverence," that princely "man of lawlessness" will prove to be like any one of the unfaithful human princes and will fall, put to death by Jehovah's Messiah.—Psalm 82:1-7.

[70] In view of these things, we need to ask ourselves some personal questions now, without postponement: Am I still under the "unrighteous deception" that Sa-

---

69. (a) To religionists, destruction of the "man of lawlessness" class will be astounding because of its being reverenced as what? (b) Like whom will that class fall and die, being put to death by whom?
70. In view of those things, what questions do we need to ask ourselves because of what Paul wrote about the "operation of error"?

tan has created in connection with Christendom's "man of lawlessness" class? Have I been affected by the "operation of error" that God has let go to those who are perishing, and so am I still believing the lie? Have I refused to "accept the love of the truth," and therefore do I prefer the lie and take pleasure in the unrighteousness committed by Christendom's clergy?

[71] No benefit comes from being dishonest with oneself, self-deceiving, in answering these questions. By being unfair with oneself one walks deliberately into destruction, for, as the apostle Paul said: the "unrighteous deception" is designed "for those who are perishing." What reasonable person cares to perish when God's adverse judgment is executed against the deceived ones? Such execution is now close at hand for those who persist in believing the lie. We are not mistaken about this, inasmuch as the "man of lawlessness . . . the son of destruction" has been revealed and exposed. We are also far along into the parousia or "presence" of the Lord Jesus. The foretold "apostasy" has come to its climax. These are the things that had to precede the coming of the destructive "day of Jehovah." That day means the fulfilling of the doom upon the "man of lawlessness" as expressed in his title, "the son of destruction."

[72] This is no mere "scare" story. It is God's own Word that now sounds the solemn warning amplified by the sounding board of the conditions and events in Christendom! Is it not high time, then, for every lover of God's law to dissociate himself from that revealed "man of lawlessness"? Our doing so means avoiding destruction with him in the world's approaching "great tribulation."—Revelation 7:14, 15.

---

71. Our now being dishonest with ourselves in this connection will mean what for us, and on what "day" evidently now close at hand?
72. Dissociating ourselves now from that "man of lawlessness" will mean avoidance of what for ourselves?

CHAPTER 19

Preserved for God's Kingdom of a Thousand Years

THE KINGDOM of God by his Messiah for a thousand years has approached! The basis for announcing this good news is solid, firmly established in inspired Scripture and in world events since 1914 C.E. The millennial kingdom's approach means that the political governments of imperfect, dying human rulers are approaching their end. "In the days of those kings," said the inspired prophet Daniel to King Nebuchadnezzar of Babylon, "the God of heaven will set up a kingdom that will never be brought to ruin. And the kingdom itself will not be passed on to any other people. It will crush and put an end to all these kingdoms, and it itself will stand to times indefinite."—Daniel 2:44.

[2] The crushing of those man-made worldly kingdoms will be the climax of the "great tribulation" that the Messiah Jesus foretold in his prophecy when he answered the question: "When will these things be, and what will be the sign of your presence and of the conclusion of the system of things?" (Matthew 24:3) Since the inaugurating of his kingdom for a thousand years must be preceded by the crushing of all the present kingdoms and republics of men, Jesus was not exaggerating matters when he called that approaching tribulation a great one, a "great tribulation such as has not occurred since the world's beginning until now, no, nor will occur again." The greatness of that tribulation would be such that human survival of it, the preserving of the human race alive

---

1. The approach of God's millennial Messianic kingdom means what for human political governments?
2. (a) Such crushing of the worldly kingdoms will be the climax of what occurrence? (b) Despite the problem then, what will be "saved" on earth?

398

through it, would be a problem. "In fact, unless those days were cut short, no flesh would be saved; but on account of the chosen ones those days will be cut short." (Matthew 24:21, 22) Not just the "chosen ones" would be saved; other "flesh" would also.

[3] Ah, yes! The human race will be preserved on earth despite the approaching unparalleled "great tribulation," just as it was preserved through the global deluge of Noah's day. (Matthew 24:37-39) The remnant of "chosen ones" will witness this preservation of "flesh" on earth before they leave the earthly scene for the heavenly kingdom for which they were called and chosen in union with Jesus Christ. (Revelation 17:14; 20:4-6) No member of that clerical "man of lawlessness" class will be preserved; nor will those with whom they used to associate in politics, militarism and commercialism be preserved. The faithful remnant of "chosen ones" and the "great crowd" of sheeplike persons who take their stand uncompromisingly on the side of God's kingdom by his Messiah will be preserved clear through the destruction of religious Babylon the Great and the "war of the great day of God the Almighty" at Har-Magedon. (Revelation 7: 9-17; 16:13-16; 17:1-16; Matthew 25:31-46) Not by human means, but only by God's power will they be preserved.

[4] Such preservation is plainly brought to our attention in the inspired words of Psalm 116, from which the apostle Paul himself makes a quotation in 2 Corinthians 4:13. The writer of that psalm could have been speaking representatively for his whole nation, because not just he himself but also his people, Jehovah's chosen people, were threatened with death, with an extermination. In the near future, all those who hold unbreakably to Jehovah's kingdom by Jesus Christ will be threatened with death at the hands of

---

3. (a) Before they do what, will the remnant witness this preservation of "flesh" alive on earth? (b) By what means will those surviving the "great tribulation" be preserved?
4, 5. (a) Such preservation is called to our attention in what psalm, and for how many does the psalmist express himself? (b) After their preservation, the "chosen ones" and the "great crowd" will be moved, like the psalmist, to voice what toward their Preserver?

the religious and political foes of God's Messianic kingdom. Not fighting back with carnal weapons but relying solely on Almighty God and his Messiah to protect, these staunch loyal defenders and upholders of God's kingdom will have to ascribe their preservation to Almighty God. Will they love Him for this? For His answering their cry for salvation in the time of worldwide danger to life, their hearts will move them to express their affection for their divine Savior as did the psalmist for a like reason:

[5] "I do love, because Jehovah hears my voice, my entreaties. For he has inclined his ear to me, and throughout my days I shall call. The ropes of death encircled me and the distressing circumstances of Sheol themselves found me. Distress and grief I kept finding. But upon the name of Jehovah I proceeded to call: 'Ah, Jehovah, do provide my soul with escape!' Jehovah is gracious and righteous; and our God is One showing mercy. Jehovah is guarding the inexperienced ones. I was impoverished, and he proceeded to save even me."—Psalm 116:1-6.

[6] The psalmist did not want to die. And yet death seemed a sure thing for him. It was already as if death had its ropes tied fast and unbreakable around him, preventing all moves for escape. It was as if he were already in Sheol (the common grave of mankind), feeling the distressing circumstances of being squeezed in by the narrow walls of a burial pit. He was grieved and distressed at having his life cut short. He was inexperienced in the ways of the world and could not appeal to human aid. He felt impoverished of all earthly help. But wait! His case was not hopeless. There was the God whom he and his nation worshiped. This One could guard him from death and Sheol. He is gracious, he is righteous, he shows mercy, he can provide escape, he can save. His is the name upon which to call for salvation. In appreciation of such a God as this, the endangered psalmist lifted his voice to Him. He entreated him. And, O joy!

6. (a) Facing seemingly certain death, how did the psalmist feel, according to his descriptions? (b) With what expression did he burst out, and why?

Jehovah did incline his ear. He did hear the desperate voice, the soulful entreaties. He did save. He did save —"even me," exclaimed the humble psalmist. How could the psalmist refrain from bursting out with the exclamation, "I do love." Just that!

⁷ When finally in our generation the uproar of the foretold "war of the great day of God the Almighty" dies down and peaceful quiet settles down at the battle-field of Har–Magedon, the surviving remnant of "chosen ones" and the "great crowd" of fellow survivors will look back and appreciate just what a salvation God the Almighty has wrought in their behalf. It was a near-death experience for them. Whose name could they call upon with assurance of being heard when there seemed to be no other eventuality but violent death—except the name of Jehovah? Not in vain did they do so. For this was not the time for him to let them fall in death, to let them descend into the narrow confines of Sheol. Let the threatening enemies go down into destruction, indeed—but not His worshipers who called upon his name in spite of the taunts and jeers of the enemy. Miraculous divine escape was provided! The ones inexperienced in the wicked ways of the world, the ones who, like Jesus, were not part of this world, were guarded. The gracious, righteous, merciful Jehovah did save them! How could these saved ones but look to Jehovah and say: "I do love"?

WALKING "IN THE LANDS OF THOSE LIVING"

⁸ Feeling now a tremendous sense of relief, the once deeply disturbed psalmist could say: "Return to your resting-place, O my soul, for Jehovah himself has acted appropriately toward you. For you have rescued my soul from death, my eye from tears, my foot from stumbling. I will walk before Jehovah in the lands of those living. I had faith, for I proceeded to speak. I myself was very much afflicted. I, for my part, said,

7. Why will Jehovah answer the call of the "chosen ones" and the "great crowd" as they face near death, and why will they cry out, "I do love!"?

8. He having been rescued from the death of his soul, what was the psalmist determined to do as respects his walking?

when I became panicky: 'Every man is a liar.'" —Psalm 116:7-11.

⁹ Having experienced deliverance from the death of his soul and finding himself walking among those living on earth, the psalmist could relax and bid his soul, his own self, to return to its resting-place. There was no more need for him to shed tears of frustration. His feet had not stumbled and precipitated him into death. Once indeed he had been panicky, for he had come to the realization that all human help was of no avail: every man proved to be a liar who said that he could help the apparently doomed psalmist or who did try to rescue him. Mankind seemed a delusion to him. But though he had lost faith in the power of mankind to save him from the menacing death, he still held onto his faith in his God. So he spoke in faith, in expression of his faith. If no one else could help him, his God could. In voicing his faith, he spoke of deliverance by means of God. Such kind of speech did not prove to be false, futile. He was kept from stumbling in a death-dealing fall. So now he determined to "walk before Jehovah in the lands of those living."

¹⁰ Faith in *God* is never in vain! The apostle Paul knew that. Whereas he realized that his strenuous missionary efforts were working for the life of those who heard his message but were also working for his earlier death, he still had faith in the sustaining power of God. He spoke of living on, not just here on earth, but also by a resurrection from the dead during the "presence" or parousia of Christ. Paul remembered Psalm 116 and wrote to the congregation in Corinth, Greece: "Consequently death is at work in us, but life in you. Now because we have the same spirit of faith as that of which it is written: 'I exercised faith, therefore I spoke,' we too exercise faith and therefore we speak, knowing that he who raised

9. (a) What did the psalmist mean by saying that every man was a liar? (b) Because of what did he then speak, and was his speech to no avail?
10. According to 2 Corinthians 4:12-14, why did Paul remember and quote from Psalm 116, in demonstration of what quality?

Jesus up will raise us up also together with Jesus and will present us [in whom death is right now at work] together with you [in whom life is presently at work]."—2 Corinthians 4:12-14; Psalm 116:10.

[11] Faith in God, even in the face of seemingly inescapable death, will be a vital necessity for the remnant of "chosen ones" and the "great crowd" of their loyal companions in the very near future. Certainly these will need to exercise faith when the combined irreligious secular powers make a final assault upon them after the clerical "man of lawlessness" has been done away with and all the rest of religious Babylon the Great has been consumed as with fire. There will then be no human aid to which to appeal, so that it could be said: 'Every man is a liar.' Yes, all human assistance proves unavailable, fails, and would be a delusion. But, in order to strengthen faith in Almighty God, they can think of the apostle Paul, who, before speaking of his own faith, said: 'We are pressed in every way, but not cramped beyond movement; we are perplexed, but not absolutely with no way out; we are persecuted, but not left in the lurch; we are thrown down, but not destroyed. Always we endure everywhere in our body the death-dealing treatment given to Jesus, that the life of Jesus may also be made manifest in our body.'—2 Corinthians 4:8-10.

[12] Under similar circumstances during the final part of the "great tribulation," the "chosen ones" and the "great crowd" can imitate Paul and "have the same spirit of faith as that of which it is written: 'I exercised faith, therefore I spoke.'" They too can exercise faith and therefore speak with unabandoned faith in God, in spite of acknowledging that things look very black for them. (2 Corinthians 4:13) Soon after the final assault upon their existence as made by the

---

11. (a) As respects the "chosen ones" and the "great crowd," when will it be that they too can say, "Every man is a liar"? (b) Why will it then be fitting to think upon the words of Paul in 2 Corinthians 4:8-10?
12. In the final part of the "great tribulation," how will they imitate Paul when quoting from Psalm 116, and what will they, like the psalmist, say to themselves thereafter?

earthly agents of Satan the Devil, there will come the occasion when the "chosen ones" and the "great crowd" will be able to say: "Return to your resting-place, O my soul, for Jehovah himself has acted appropriately toward you."—Psalm 116:7.

[13] "Acted appropriately"—in what way? In a way that was appropriate for Jehovah to act toward his faithful worshipers in their dire distress. In the "war of the great day of God the Almighty" he acts in full harmony with his precious promises recorded in his Holy Word for the benefit and security of his obedient servants. "Jehovah is guarding all those loving him, but all the wicked ones he will annihilate." (Psalm 145:20) In the desperate situation of the "chosen ones" and the "great crowd," he acts in the way appropriate to their faith, obedience, loyalty and devotion to Him. He "becomes the rewarder of those earnestly seeking him." (Hebrews 11:6) So he rescues their souls from the death that the earthly enemies would like to inflict upon them. He rescues them from any cause for shedding tears. He rescues them from any stumbling that the enemies would like to cause, resulting in a fall into death. Could anything be more appropriate for Jehovah to do than this, for the vindication of his Word and name and the complete foiling of the vicious enemies? No!

[14] For the remnant of God's "chosen ones" and the "great crowd," this signifies emerging alive in the flesh from the "great tribulation" in which the entire present "system of things" will be wiped out. Before them will stretch all the lands of the cleansed earth. Not only has the earth been cleansed of all the evildoers by the "great tribulation," but now there is a cleansing of the invisible spirit realm in the immediate neighborhood of the earth. How? In that the "dragon . . . the original serpent, the one called Devil and Satan," and

13. During the "war of the great day of God the Almighty," how does Jehovah 'act appropriately' toward his worshipers, as in contrast with their earthly enemies?
14. (a) Into what kind of earth will Jehovah's preserved ones emerge, but where else will there also be a cleansing, and how? (b) So as not to miss the purpose of their deliverance, what will Jehovah's preserved ones determine to do?

all his demon angels are seized, chained, and hurled into an "abyss" from which it is impossible for them to deceive and mislead the nations on earth during the thousand-year reign of Jehovah's Messiah and all the 144,000 "chosen" ones. What a unique occasion that will be to manifest appreciation! Jehovah's worshipers had been threatened with lying slain among the dead, but, look! here they are alive! So now they can show determination not to miss the purpose of their being spared from death. Having been rescued just as the psalmist was, they can say, like him: "I will walk before Jehovah in the lands of those living." (Psalm 116:9) This they now can do with freedom from disturbance, with rest for their souls.

TAKING UP THE "CUP OF GRAND SALVATION"

¹⁵ Thus when the glorious thousand years of Messiah's reign over all the earth are ready to begin, a "grand salvation" will indeed have been wrought by God for all his loyal ones on earth. Just think of it! For these loyal ones there has come a good riddance of all the wicked ones on earth and in the invisible realm about the earth. There can now follow a preservation of such loyal ones all during the thousand years of God's Messianic kingdom, the loyal ones of the "great crowd" being the ones that will forever keep living upon the cleansed earth. In appreciation of this the preserved loyal ones should feel moved to say what the psalmist said: "What shall I repay to Jehovah for all his benefits to me? The cup of grand salvation I shall take up, and on the name of Jehovah I shall call. My vows I shall pay to Jehovah, yes, in front of all his people."—Psalm 116:12-14.

¹⁶ A cup contains a portion of drink for one to imbibe or even to pour out as a drink offering to Jehovah God. It is He who has offered to his loyal ones on earth the "cup of grand salvation." How? By pre-

15. Thus, when Christ's millennial reign begins, what salvation will have been wrought on the earth, and what "cup" will God's loyal ones take up?
16. (a) Who offers to the loyal ones the "cup of grand salvation," and how? (b) How do they drink that "cup," and upon what do they call?

serving them through the "great tribulation." The portion for them to drink is the "grand salvation." All his acts of salvation Jehovah has wrought for them through the heavenly Messiah. The loyal ones do not refuse this gift of "grand salvation" that extends their life on earth into the blessed thousand years of earth-wide rule by the Messiah. Gratefully they will drink it, enjoying life "in the lands of those living." But as they do so, they will call upon the name of Jehovah. Using his name, they will call upon Him through his Messiah to bless and guide them in all their efforts henceforth to use their lives on earth in full harmony with his will. They will openly, publicly, name Him as their God.

17 Have they any dues to pay Him? That is, during the time that their souls were in danger and death seemed imminent, did they make any vows, any solemn promises to Jehovah God through Jesus Christ? If they did so in their desire for divine deliverance, then such "vows" they will dutifully and lovingly pay to Jehovah who acted in harmony with their vows and preserved them for uninterrupted life on earth. At Jehovah's spiritual temple they will do so, inasmuch as their doing what they vowed to do will be "in front of all his people."

18 Even those of the remnant of God's "chosen ones" will do so, for whatever time these spirit-begotten ones are retained on earth before they pass off the earthly stage of activity and are gloriously united with all the others of the 144,000 joint heirs of Christ in his heavenly throne.—Ecclesiastes 5:2-6.*

---

* Christ's thousand-year reign will go ahead in spite of there being yet a remnant of Kingdom heirs on the earth. After a temporary post-tribulation work on earth, they will be taken into the heavenly kingdom to share with him in his reign up there, this reign being, in the case of Jesus Christ himself, a full thousand years long. Thus this remnant does not fail to have some share in Christ's thousand-year-long reign in heaven.

---

17. What will be done about any "vows" that Jehovah's loyal ones may have made during the time of danger to their lives?
18. For how long will the preserved remnant of "chosen ones" do this on earth?

"THE DEATH OF HIS LOYAL ONES"
—HOW PRECIOUS!

[19] Placing a high value on what affects the feelings of his God, the rescued psalmist could exclaim: "Precious in the eyes of Jehovah is the death of his loyal ones. Ah, now, O Jehovah, for I am your servant. I am your servant, the son of your slave girl. You have loosened my bands." (Psalm 116:15, 16) The psalmist exclaimed, "Ah, now, O Jehovah," in a beseeching, entreating way. This supplicating attitude was what he did have during the period of his being endangered with death. At that time he appealed to God that those bands with which he appeared to be tied to death might be loosened and he be freed from death. He pleaded with God for this favor on the basis that he was Jehovah's servant, yes, Jehovah's servant of a second generation, for he was a son of Jehovah's "slave girl." As it were, the psalmist reminded Jehovah of His responsibility for his servants, to preserve them alive. And now, after his confrontation with death, the psalmist could speak of Jehovah as having lovingly carried out His responsibility.

[20] The psalmist classed himself as being one of Jehovah's "loyal ones," when he let his deep appreciation move him to say: "Precious in the eyes of Jehovah is the death of his loyal ones." The psalmist did not thus classify himself presumptuously, for Jehovah showed that he considered the psalmist to be loyal because Jehovah spared him from death. Instead of letting the psalmist suffer death and thereafter have a Levitical priest preach a funeral sermon and say over him, "Precious in the eyes of Jehovah is the death of his loyal ones," Jehovah considered the death of the psalmist too costly to let it occur. So he rescued the psalmist's "soul from death." Consequently, the psalmist could now appreciate how costly the death of a loyal one would be to Jehovah. As it were, the

19. In order to be untied from the bands of death, the psalmist appealed to God on the basis of what relationship? And why rightly so?
20. (a) With what kind of persons did the psalmist classify himself, and why not presumptuously so? (b) How costly did the psalmist appraise the death of one of Jehovah's "loyal ones" to be to him?

death of the loyal servant was too high a price for Jehovah to pay. Too much is involved for Jehovah by letting death occur.

²¹ After the lives of the "chosen ones" and the "great crowd" have been spared clear through the "great tribulation," they too will be moved with the correct appreciation of values to exclaim: "Precious in the eyes of Jehovah is the death of his loyal ones." (Psalm 116:15) They will appreciate that Jehovah has considered it too costly to allow their death to occur during the "great tribulation" at the hands of their enemies, religious and secular. For Him to let these enemies triumph over them and wipe them from the face of the earth would be a blot upon his universal sovereignty, his rulership over heaven and earth. He is the Creator of the earth and he created it for those loyal to him. If he cannot preserve his loyal ones on earth even under the heaviest, most dastardly attack by anti-God enemies, it would be as if his enemies were more powerful than he is and they had the right to say who shall live permanently on the earth. The wiping out of his loyal ones by his enemies during the "great tribulation" would impugn his rulership of the earth, in fact, his whole universal sovereignty. So he cannot let their death, forced by the enemies, occur!

²² What is more, if Jehovah were to let his earthly enemies defiantly destroy the remnant of His "chosen ones" and the "great crowd" during the "great tribulation," not only would the enemies have momentarily triumphed and the onlooking Satan and his demon angels feel great glee, but what else? The forced "death" of all Jehovah's loyal ones from the earth would leave the earth without those worshiping Him as the only living and true God. It would leave the courtyards of his great spiritual temple, which are at

21. (a) After the "great tribulation," what will the loyal ones in a correct appreciation of values be moved to say because of their preservation? (b) How has their death been too costly to permit as respects His sovereignty?
22. Why is the forced "death of his loyal ones" too costly for Jehovah to allow when His worship and the founding of the "new earth" are considered?

the earth, without those who offer up to Him the sacrifices of praise, thanksgiving and sacred service. Also, the basis for the "new earth" under "new heavens" would have been removed, before the thousand years of Jehovah's Messiah Jesus were timed to begin! Could the Most High and Almighty God Jehovah let such a highly important thing take place by the forced "death of his loyal ones"? No! Their death under such circumstances in which a universal issue was involved would be "precious," costly, for Jehovah. Out of respect for Himself, it is too costly to allow.

²³ The coming "great tribulation" is the time for Almighty God Jehovah to vindicate his universal sovereignty and to sanctify his worthy name and to force all his foes to know that He is the Jehovah of the divinely inspired written Word, the Holy Bible. In full favor and support of this he will do as he has solemnly promised in his unchangeable Word, namely, rescue the souls of his loyal ones on earth from death during the "great tribulation," when the universal issue will be finally settled for all time to come! As in the case of the patient Job, whose life Jehovah preserved because of Job's unbroken integrity, Jehovah will prove once again that he can put loyal men on earth who under the severest test by Satan the Devil will hold fast their loving integrity to Jehovah.

²⁴ Certainly Jehovah will recognize the remnant of His "chosen ones" and the "great crowd" as his servants in view of their choice of Him as their God and in view of His purchase of them through the sin-atoning blood of his High Priest, Jesus the Messiah. At the crucial time Jehovah will hear their earnest appeal to him and will loosen the "bands" of violent death that the foes of Jehovah and his Messianic kingdom try to fasten upon them. What a lasting reason this will be for them never to forget their servanthood to their heavenly Owner and Supreme Master, Jehovah!

---

23. The "great tribulation" is the time for what with regard to Jehovah's sovereignty and name and the taking care of the universal issue, and in what way?
24. For what reasons will Jehovah recognize these "loyal ones" as his servants, and what "bands" will he loosen for them at the critical time?

HALLELUJAH!

25 For all such divine undeserved kindness, thanksgiving is due indeed to the Great Preserver and Rescuer from death. The psalmist was overwhelmed with a feeling of gratitude, so that he concluded his beautiful psalm, saying: "To you I shall offer the sacrifice of thanksgiving, and on the name of Jehovah I shall call. My vows I shall pay to Jehovah, yes, in front of all his people, in the courtyards of the house of Jehovah, in the midst of you, O Jerusalem. Praise Jah, you people!"—Psalm 116:17-19.

26 The psalmist, whoever he was, was a worshiper of the God whose name he was inspired to use fifteen times in the name's full form in his psalm, finally bursting out with the closing exclamation, in Hebrew, "Hallelujah!" or, "Praise Jah, you people!" The psalmist worshiped Him at His temple in the holy city of Jerusalem, it not mattering whether that temple was the one built by King Solomon or the one built afterward by Governor Zerubbabel after Israel's exile in Babylon. The unnamed psalmist desired to do more than offer merely a private expression of thanksgiving to his divine Rescuer. He desired to offer thanksgiving publicly by means of a sacrifice on God's altar in the temple courtyard, calling on Jehovah's name in the hearing of all His people there. Possibly he was the first one to recite this psalm of his own composition, thus furnishing a part of what became the Hallel ("Praise") for the Jews on special occasions. (Psalms 113-118, 136) How could his grateful self hold back from exhorting all the worshipers in the temple courtyards to "praise Jah" by concluding his psalm with "Hallelujah"?

27 The psalmist is not alone in offering a sacrifice of thanksgiving to Jehovah for a rescue from death.

25. With what words did the psalmist conclude Psalm 116, in a sense of debt to Jehovah?
26. (a) How did the composer of Psalm 116 not leave unknown the God whom he worshiped? (b) How did this psalmist desire to express his thanksgiving to his God and to exhort the people to offer praise?
27. (a) In view of what earlier thankful sacrificers was the composer of Psalm 116 not alone in offering sacrifices of thanksgiving for a rescue from death? (b) How will the survivors of the end of this system of things act true to that pattern?

Many centuries earlier there were the Flood survivors, Noah and his family. Although they had no temple courtyard in which to worship, what was the first thing that they did after emerging from the ark up there on Mount Ararat? On a newly built altar they offered a grand sacrifice of thanksgiving to Jehovah for having preserved them through the global deluge. (Genesis 8:18-22) What a fine pattern for imitation was thus set by those eight human souls whom Almighty God kept from being destroyed with the "ancient world" of that time. True to that prophetic pattern, after the approaching spectacular end of the present violent system of things thanksgiving to Jehovah will be offered up like sacrifices by the surviving remnant of His "chosen ones" and by their companions, the "great crowd," because Jehovah has preserved them by His miraculous saving power.—Psalm 116:17.

²⁸ In the earthly courtyards of Jehovah's spiritual temple these survivors of mankind's greatest tribulation of human history will offer their sacrifices of thanksgiving as they enter the blessed thousand years of Christ's reign. In an ecstasy of joy and jubilation they will make the whole earth resound with their irrepressible cry, "Hallelujah!" What a pleasurable sense of being alive there will be then, especially after one has been snatched from the jaws of death! With a mutual love, like that between David and his loyal friend Jonathan, the remnant of Jehovah's "chosen ones" and the loyal "great crowd" will peacefully take up work together under the "new heavens" of God's Messianic kingdom. (2 Peter 3:13) Side by side they will continue to work together on the cleansed earth until God's due time for calling the remnant of His spirit-begotten "chosen ones" to their thrones with the King Jesus Christ in the "heavenly Jerusalem." How the departure of this spiritual remnant will be brought about is not now known from the Scriptures. But the "chosen ones" know that they must be faith-

---

28. (a) Where will the survivors of the end of this system offer their sacrifices, and with what cry will they make earth resound? (b) How long will the spiritual "chosen ones" and the "great crowd" work together on the cleansed earth?

Gain Further Benefit from Your Bible Study

The Watch Tower Society publishes many aids to help you gain added benefit from your Bible study.

New World Translation of the Holy Scriptures

LARGE-PRINT EDITION: Excellent maps, illuminating footnotes, a helpful appendix. Hard black cover, 1,376 pages; size: 7 1/2" x 9 1/2" x 1 1/2". English only $5.00

REGULAR EDITION: Bound in green vinyl; 1,472 pages; size: 7 1/4" x 4 7/8" x 1 1/8". Available in English, Spanish, Portuguese, Italian, Dutch and German $1.00

DELUXE EDITION: Same as regular, but with a black flexible cover and gold-edged pages. English only $3.00

THE KINGDOM INTERLINEAR TRANSLATION OF THE GREEK SCRIPTURES: A volume to help you discern the flavor and literal meaning of the Christian Greek Scriptures. Has a word-for-word English translation under the Greek Bible text. In the right-hand column appears the "New World Translation of the Holy Scriptures," Matthew through Revelation. 1,184 pages $2.00

Other Aids

COMPREHENSIVE CONCORDANCE OF THE NEW WORLD TRANSLATION OF THE HOLY SCRIPTURES: 1,280 pages $5.00

THE EMPHATIC DIAGLOTT: Greek text of the Christian Scriptures with English interlinear and a modern English translation by Benjamin Wilson. 924 pages $2.00

THE BIBLE IN LIVING ENGLISH: A translation by the late Steven T. Byington. Large print, marginal notes $6.00

AMERICAN STANDARD VERSION: This is the Watchtower edition of the "American Standard Version" of 1901 .... $1.00

AUTHORIZED (KING JAMES) VERSION: The Bible text is that of the "King James Version," unchanged, with marginal references $1.00

AID TO BIBLE UNDERSTANDING: A new Bible dictionary that gives you excellent help in acquiring understanding of the Holy Scriptures. Covers Bible subjects from A to Z. 1,700 pages $7.00

To order, see addresses on the last page.

A Wealth of Wisdom in Pocket Size

A number of pocket-size books have been published by the Watch Tower Society. Dealing with a variety of topics, they provide a wealth of divine wisdom. All these books are hardbound, with 192 pages, and are only 25c each.

TRUE PEACE AND SECURITY—FROM WHAT SOURCE?: In frank terms this book discusses the problems facing mankind and which must be solved to bring true peace and security. Bible standards that lead to a successful, secure life are considered. This book analyzes problems and clearly identifies the source from which true peace and security will come in our generation.

THE TRUTH THAT LEADS TO ETERNAL LIFE: For many persons, understanding the Bible has been a great problem. They have wanted something easy to read, something that presents Bible teachings simply and clearly. Now this is available in "The Truth That Leads to Eternal Life." This book may be obtained in over eighty languages. The English edition will be sent unless you specify otherwise.

LISTENING TO THE GREAT TEACHER: One of today's great problems is how to rear children in the right way. They need to learn and apply the high moral standards found in the Holy Scriptures. This book helps parents to teach their children the Bible. It is designed to be read by parents and children together. Illustrated; large print; easily understood.

IS THE BIBLE REALLY THE WORD OF GOD?: Because of living in a materialistic, faithless world, many persons today need help if they are to accept the Bible as God's inspired Word. Convincing evidence is required to aid them. Now, in this one book, you will find an array of convincing facts, real evidence showing that the Bible is truly God's Word.

DID MAN GET HERE BY EVOLUTION OR BY CREATION?: Today the teaching of evolution saturates school textbooks and other publications. Now you can help school-age youths and other persons to evaluate the evidence. The facts can be examined and the reader can see for himself which is most reasonable—a popular theory or the Bible's account of man's origin and his future. Illustrated.

To order, see addresses on the last page.

CHIEF OFFICE AND OFFICIAL ADDRESS OF

Watch Tower Bible and Tract Society of Pennsylvania
Watchtower Bible and Tract Society of New York, Inc.
International Bible Students Association

124 Columbia Heights, Brooklyn, New York 11201, U.S.A.

ADDRESSES OF BRANCH OFFICES:

ALASKA 99507: 2552 East 48th Ave., Anchorage. ARGENTINA: Gorriti 5647-49, Buenos Aires 14. AUSTRALIA: 11 Beresford Road, Strathfield, N.S.W. 2135. AUSTRIA: Gallgasse 44, A-1130 Vienna. BAHAMAS: Box N-1247, Nassau, N.P. BARBADOS, W.I.: Fontabelle Rd., Bridgetown. BELGIUM: rue d'Argile 60, B-1950 Kraainem. BOLIVIA: Casilla No. 1440, La Paz. BRAZIL: Rua Guaíra, 216, Bosque da Saúde, 04142 São Paulo, SP. BRITISH HONDURAS: Box 257, Belize. BURMA: P.O. Box 62, Rangoon. CANADA: 150 Bridgeland Ave., Toronto, Ontario M6A 1Z5. CENTRAL AFRICAN REPUBLIC: B.P. 662, Bangui. CHILE: Clorinda Wilshaw 501, Nuñoa, Casilla 261-V, Correo 21, Santiago. COLOMBIA: Apartado Aéreo 2587, Barranquilla. CONGO REPUBLIC: B.P. 2.114, Brazzaville. COSTA RICA: Apartado 10043, San José. CUBA: Avenida 15 Núm. 4608, Almendares, Marianao, Havana. CYPRUS: P.O. Box 1590, Nicosia. DAHOMEY: B.P. 874, Cotonou. DENMARK: Kongevejen 207, 2830 Virum. DOMINICAN REPUBLIC: Avenida Francia 33, Santo Domingo. ECUADOR: Casilla 4512, Guayaquil. EL SALVADOR: Apartado 401, San Salvador. ENGLAND: Watch Tower House, The Ridgeway, London NW7 1RN. FIJI: Box 23, Suva. FINLAND: Kuismatie 58, Postbox 68, SF-01301 Tikkurila. FRANCE: 81 rue du Point-du-Jour, 92100 Boulogne-Billancourt. GERMANY (WESTERN): Postfach 13025, 62 Wiesbaden-Dotzheim. GHANA: Box 760, Accra. GREECE: No. 4 Kartali St., Athens 611. GUADELOUPE: B.P. 239, 97153 Pointe-à-Pitre. GUATEMALA: 11 Avenida 5-67, Guatemala 1. GUYANA: 50 Brickdam, Georgetown 16. HAITI: Post Box 185, Port-au-Prince. HAWAII 96814: 1228 Pensacola St., Honolulu. HONDURAS: Apartado 147, Tegucigalpa. HONG KONG: 312 Prince Edward Rd., Second Floor, Kowloon. ICELAND: P.O. Box 251, Reykjavik. INDIA: South Avenue, Santa Cruz, Bombay 400054. INDONESIA: Jl Batuceper 47, Jakarta, DKI. IRELAND: 86 Lindsay Rd., Glasnevin, Dublin 9. ISRAEL: P.O. Box 44520, Haifa 31 040. ITALY: Via della Bufalotta 1281, 00138 Rome. IVORY COAST: B.P. 10250 Koumassi, Abidjan. JAMAICA, W.I.: 41 Trafalgar Rd., Kingston 10. JAPAN: 5-5-8 Mita Minato-Ku, Tokyo, 108. KENYA: Box 47788, Nairobi. KOREA: Box 7 Sodaemun P.O., Seoul, 120. LEEWARD ISLANDS, W.I.: Box 119, St. Johns, Antigua. LIBERIA: P.O. Box 171, Monrovia. LUXEMBOURG: 15, rue de l'Egalite, Luxembourg-Bonnevoie, G.D. MALAYSIA: 20 Scotland Close, Penang. MAURITIUS: 106A Prince of Wales St., Rose Hill. MEXICO: Apartado Postal 42-048, Mexico 4, D.F. NETHERLANDS: Voorburgstraat 250 Amsterdam 1017. NETHERLANDS ANTILLES: Oosterbeekstraat 11, Willemstad, Curaçao. NEWFOUNDLAND, CANADA: 239 Pennywell Rd., St. John's. NEW ZEALAND: 621 New North Rd., Auckland 3. NICARAGUA: Apartado 183, Managua, D.N. NIGERIA: P.O. Box 194, Yaba, Lagos State. NORWAY: Inkognitogaten 28 B., Oslo 2. OKINAWA: Higashi P.O. Box 2004, 91 Asato, Naha City. PAKISTAN: 8-E Habibullah Rd., Lahore 3. PANAMA: Apartado 1386, Panama 1. PAPUA: Box 113, Port Moresby. PARAGUAY: Casilla de Correo 482, Asunción. PERU: Gervasio Santillana 370, Miraflores, Lima. PHILIPPINE REPUBLIC: 186 Roosevelt Ave., San Francisco del Monte, Quezon City D-503. PUERTO RICO 00927: Calle Onix 23, Urb. Bucaré, Río Piedras. RHODESIA: P.O. Box 1462, Salisbury. SENEGAL: B.P. 3107, Dakar. SIERRA LEONE: Box 136, Freetown. SOUTH AFRICA: Private Bag 2, P.O. Elandsfontein, Transvaal. SPAIN: Calle Pardo 65, Barcelona 16. SRI LANKA, REP. OF: 62 Layard's Road, Colombo 5. SURINAM: Wicherstraat 8-10, Box 49, Paramaribo. SWEDEN: Box 8, S-175 21 Järfälla 1. SWITZERLAND: Ulmenweg 45, P.O. Box 477, CH-3601 Thun. TAIWAN (REPUBLIC OF CHINA): 5 Lane 99, Yun-Ho St., Taipei, Taiwan 106. THAILAND: 69/1 Soi 2, Sukhumwit Rd., Bangkok 11. TOGO REPUBLIC: B.P. 1237, Lomé. TRINIDAD, W.I.: 2 La Seiva Road, Maraval, Port of Spain. UNITED STATES OF AMERICA: 117 Adams St., Brooklyn, N.Y. 11201. URUGUAY: Francisco Bauzá 3372, Montevideo. VENEZUELA: Avda. Honduras, Qta. Luz, Urb. Las Acacias, Caracas 104. ZAÏRE, REP. OF: B.P. 634, Limete, Kinshasa. ZAMBIA: Box 1598, Kitwe.